2008 EDITION

NATIONAL SAFETY COUNCIL

INJURY FACTS®

The National Safety Council, chartered by an act of Congress, is a nongovernmental, not-for-profit, public service organization with a mission to educate and influence people to prevent accidental injury and death.

Injury Facts®, the Council's annual statistical report on unintentional injuries and their characteristics and costs, was prepared by:

Research and Statistical Services Group
Mei-Li Lin, Executive Director
Alan F. Hoskin, Manager, Statistics Department
Kevin T. Fearn, Sr. Statistical Associate
Kathleen T. Porretta, Production Manager
Sergey Sinelnikov, Research Associate

Questions or comments about the content of *Injury Facts*® should be directed to the Research and Statistics Department, National Safety Council, 1121 Spring Lake Drive, Itasca, IL 60143, or telephone 630-775-2322, or fax 630-285-0242, or E-mail rssdept@nsc.org.

For price and ordering information, visit www.nsc.org or write Customer Relations, National Safety Council, 1121 Spring Lake Drive, Itasca, IL 60143, or telephone 800-621-7619, or fax 630-285-0797.

Acknowledgments
The information presented in *Injury Facts*® was made possible by the cooperation of many organizations and individuals, including state vital and health statistics authorities, state traffic authorities, state workers' compensation authorities, trade associations, Bureau of the Census, Bureau of Labor Statistics, Consumer Product Safety Commission, Federal Highway Administration, Federal Railroad Administration, International Labour Office, National Center for Health Statistics, National Fire Protection Association, National Highway Traffic Safety Administration, National Transportation Safety Board, National Weather Service, Mine Safety and Health Administration, and the World Health Organization. Specific contributions are acknowledged in footnotes and source notes throughout the book.

Visit the National Safety Council's website:

http://www.nsc.org

Suggested citation: National Safety Council. (2008). *Injury Facts*®, *2008 Edition*. Itasca, IL: Author.

Library of Congress Catalog Card Number: 99-74142

Printed in U.S.A.   ISBN 978-0-87912-278-2   NSC Press Product No. 02309-0000

Unintentional-injury deaths were up 2% in 2006 compared to the revised 2005 total. Unintentional-injury deaths were estimated to total 120,000 in 2006 and 118,000 in 2005.

The resident population of the United States was 299,398,000 in 2006, an increase of 1% from 2005. The death rate in 2006 was 40.1 per 100,000 population—up 1% from 2005 and 18% greater than the lowest rate on record, which was 34.0 in 1992.

The graph on page *v* shows the overall trends in the number of unintentional-injury deaths, the population, and the death rate per 100,000 population. A more complete summary of the situation in 2006 and recent trends is given on page 2.

Changes in the 2008 Edition

Once again, some important improvements have been made to *Injury Facts*. A whole new chapter has been added on intentional injuries—homicide, assault, suicide, and self-harm—in support of the Council's Safe Communities America initiative (www.safecommunitiesamerica.com). Safe Communities America addresses all injury risks faced by community members, including both intentional and unintentional injuries. The new chapter includes basic data on deaths and nonfatal injuries associated with violence.

Look for *new* data on …

• Work injuries by part of body

• Sports-related traumatic brain injuries

• Poisoning trends

• Smoke alarms and automatic sprinklers

• Fall injuries among older people

• Injury risks by age group

• And more

and *updated* or *expanded* data on …

• General mortality

• Occupational injury and illness incidence rates by industry

• Occupational injury and illness profile data by industry sector

• Workers' compensation claims and costs

• Disasters

• Comparing safety of transportation modes

• Traffic safety issues—alcohol, occupant protection, speeding, distracted driving, and others

• Sports and recreation injuries

• Consumer product-related injuries

• Accidental deaths by state

• And more

There are several products related to the book. One is the *Injury Facts Challenge*—an interactive, intranet-based, weekly quiz derived from the content of *Injury Facts*. The *Challenge* helps to build or maintain a safety culture within an organization by providing safety facts and tips and stimulating discussion of safety among employees. The other products, *Injury Facts Talks*, are a series of Microsoft® PowerPoint® presentations loaded with data from *Injury Facts* that may be used as the basis for presentations to build safety awareness among various audiences, both at work and in the community. For more information on these products, visit the Council's web site (www.nsc.org), call Customer Service at 800-621-7619, or contact your local council.

Your comments and suggestions to improve *Injury Facts* are welcome. Information on how to contact us is given on page *ii*.

UNINTENTIONAL-INJURY DEATHS, DEATH RATES, AND POPULATION, UNITED STATES, 1903–2006

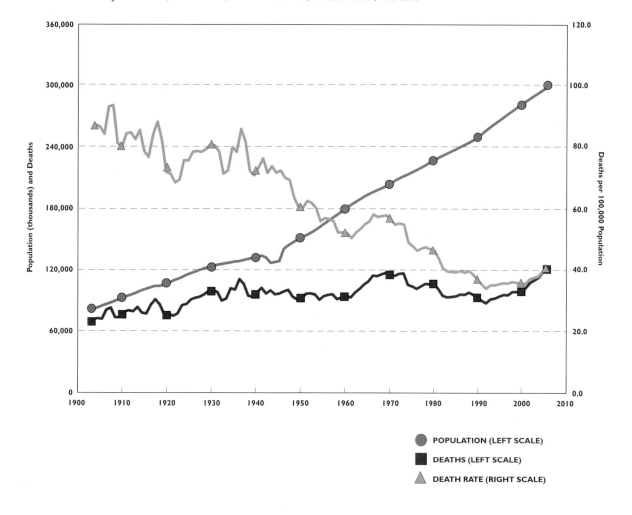

- ● POPULATION (LEFT SCALE)
- ■ DEATHS (LEFT SCALE)
- ▲ DEATH RATE (RIGHT SCALE)

NATIONAL SAFETY COUNCIL

INJURY FACTS®

ALL UNINTENTIONAL INJURIES, 2006

Unintentional-injury deaths were up 2% in 2006 compared to the revised 2005 estimate. Unintentional-injury deaths were estimated to total 120,000 in 2006 and 118,000 in 2005. The 2006 estimate is 7% greater than the 2004 final count of 112,012. **The 2006 estimate is 38% greater than the 1992 total of 86,777 (the lowest annual total since 1924) and 3% greater the previous highest total of 116,385 deaths in 1969.**

The death rate in 2006 was 40.1 per 100,000 population—18% greater than the lowest rate on record, which was 34.0 in 1992. The 2006 death rate was up 1% from the 2005 revised rate.

Comparing 2006 to 2005, motor-vehicle deaths decreased while home and public deaths increased. Work deaths were virtually unchanged. The population death rate in the motor-vehicle class declined and the rates increased in the home and public classes.

The motor-vehicle death total was down 2% in 2006. The motor-vehicle death rate per 100,000,000 vehicle-miles was 1.49 in 2006, down 2% from the revised 2005 rate (1.52) and from the revised 2004 rate which was also 1.52.

According to the latest final data (2004), unintentional injuries continued to be the fifth leading cause of death, exceeded only by heart disease, cancer, stroke, and chronic lower respiratory diseases. Preliminary death certificate data for 2005 indicate that unintentional injuries will remain in fifth place.

Nonfatal injuries also affect millions of Americans. In 2005, 33.2 million people—about 1 out of 9—sought medical attention for an injury and 2.8 million people were hospitalized for injuries. About 28.4 million were treated in hospital emergency departments and about 5.4 million visits to hospital outpatient departments were for unintentional injuries. About 40.9 million visits to physicians' offices were for unintentional injuries.

The economic impact of these fatal and nonfatal unintentional injuries amounted to $652.1 billion in 2006. This is equivalent to about $2,200 per capita, or about $5,700 per household. These are costs that every individual and household pays whether directly out of pocket, through higher prices for goods and services, or through higher taxes.

Between 1912 and 2006, unintentional-injury deaths per 100,000 population were reduced 49% (after adjusting for the classification change in 1948) from 82.4 to 40.1. The reduction in the overall rate during a period when the nation's population tripled has resulted in 5,200,000 fewer people being killed due to unintentional injuries than there would have been if the rate had not been reduced.

ALL UNINTENTIONAL INJURIES, 2006

Class	Deaths	Change from 2005	Deaths per 100,000 Persons	Disabling Injuries[a]
All Classes[b]	**120,000**	**+2%**	**40.1**	**26,200,000**
Motor-vehicle	44,700	–2%	14.9	2,400,000
Public nonwork	*42,457*			*2,300,000*
Work	*2,043*			*2,300,000*
Home	*200*			*([c])*
Work	4,988	0%	1.7	3,700,000
Nonmotor-vehicle	*2,945*			*3,600,000*
Motor-vehicle	*2,043*			*100,000*
Home	42,600	+5%	14.2	10,200,000
Nonmotor-vehicle	*42,400*			*10,200,000*
Motor-vehicle	*200*			*([c])*
Public	30,000	+2%	10.0	10,000,000

Source: National Safety Council estimates (rounded) based on data from the National Center for Health Statistics, state departments of health, and state traffic authorities, except for the work figures which are from the Bureau of Labor Statistics, Census of Fatal Occupational Injuries (CFOI). The National Safety Council adopted the CFOI count for work-related unintentional injuries beginning with 1992. See the Glossary for definitions and the Technical Appendix for estimating procedures. Beginning with 1999 data, deaths are classified according to the 10th revision of the International Classification of Diseases. Caution should be used in comparing data classified under the two systems.
[a]Disabling beyond the day of injury. Disabling injuries are not reported on a national basis, so the totals shown are approximations based on ratios of disabling injuries to deaths developed by the National Safety Council. The totals are the best estimates for the current year. They should not, however, be compared with totals shown in previous editions of this book to indicate year-to-year changes or trends. See the Glossary for definitions and the Technical Appendix for estimating procedures.
[b]Deaths and injuries above for the four separate classes add to more than the All Classes figures due to rounding and because some deaths and injuries are included in more than one class. For example, 2,043 work deaths involved motor vehicles and are in both the work and motor-vehicle totals and 200 motor-vehicle deaths occurred on home premises and are in both home and motor-vehicle. The total of such duplication amounted to about 2,243 deaths and 100,000 injuries in 2006.
[c]Less than 10,000.

UNINTENTIONAL-INJURY DEATHS BY CLASS, UNITED STATES, 2006

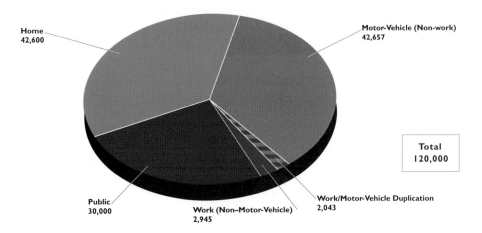

Home
42,600

Motor-Vehicle (Non-work)
42,657

Total
120,000

Work/Motor-Vehicle Duplication
2,043

Public
30,000

Work (Non–Motor-Vehicle)
2,945

UNINTENTIONAL DISABLING INJURIES BY CLASS, UNITED STATES, 2006

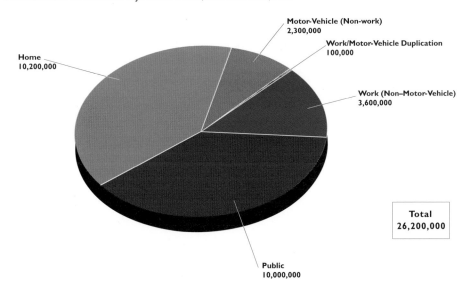

Motor-Vehicle (Non-work)
2,300,000

Work/Motor-Vehicle Duplication
100,000

Home
10,200,000

Work (Non–Motor-Vehicle)
3,600,000

Total
26,200,000

Public
10,000,000

COSTS OF UNINTENTIONAL INJURIES BY CLASS, 2006

The total cost of unintentional injuries in 2006, $652.1 billion, includes estimates of economic costs of fatal and nonfatal unintentional injuries together with employers' uninsured costs, vehicle damage costs, and fire losses. Wage and productivity losses, medical expenses, administrative expenses, and employers' uninsured costs are included in all four classes of injuries. Cost components unique to each class are identified below.

Motor-vehicle crash costs include property damage from motor-vehicle accidents. Work costs include the value of property damage in on-the-job motor-vehicle accidents and fires. Home and public costs include estimated fire losses, but do not include other property damage costs.

Besides the estimated $652.1 billion in economic losses from unintentional injuries in 2006, lost quality of life from those injuries is valued at an additional $3,080.1 billion, making the comprehensive cost $3,732.2 billion in 2006.

Several cost benchmarks were updated for the 2005–2006 edition making 2004 and later costs not comparable to previous years. The method for estimating the number of medically attended injuries by class was revised to use the latest National Health Interview Survey data. Estimated property damage costs in motor-vehicle crashes were rebenchmarked using National Highway Traffic Safety Administration data. The value of a statistical life also was updated, which affects only the comprehensive cost mentioned in the paragraph above.

CERTAIN COSTS OF UNINTENTIONAL INJURIES BY CLASS, 2006 ($ BILLIONS)

Cost	Total[a]	Motor-Vehicle	Work	Home	Public Nonmotor-Vehicle
Total	$652.1	$258.6	$164.7	$150.1	$101.8
Wage and productivity losses	329.8	89.7	78.5	97.7	68.3
Medical expenses	116.3	33.4	30.1	32.8	21.8
Administrative expenses[b]	134.5	91.5	42.4	7.9	7.5
Motor-vehicle damage	41.7	41.7	1.7	(c)	(c)
Employers' uninsured costs	18.5	2.3	9.4	4.5	2.7
Fire loss	11.3	(c)	2.6	7.2	1.5

Source: National Safety Council estimates. See the Technical Appendix. Cost estimating procedures were revised extensively for the 1993 edition of Accident Facts.® In general, cost estimates are not comparable from year to year. As additional data or new benchmarks become available, they are used from that point forward. Previously estimated figures are not revised.
[a]Duplication between work and motor-vehicle, which amounted to $23.1 billion, was eliminated from the total.
[b]Home and public insurance administration costs may include costs of administering medical treatment claims for some motor-vehicle injuries filed through health insurance plans.
[c]Not included; see comments above.

COSTS OF UNINTENTIONAL INJURIES BY CLASS, 2006

TOTAL COST $652.1 BILLION

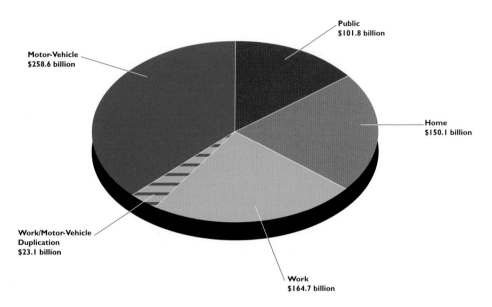

Public
$101.8 billion

Motor-Vehicle
$258.6 billion

Home
$150.1 billion

Work/Motor-Vehicle
Duplication
$23.1 billion

Work
$164.7 billion

COSTS OF UNINTENTIONAL INJURIES BY COMPONENT

Wage and Productivity Losses
A person's contribution to the wealth of the nation usually is measured in terms of wages and household production. The total of wages and fringe benefits together with an estimate of the replacement-cost value of household services provides an estimate of this lost productivity. Also included is travel delay for motor-vehicle accidents.

Medical Expenses
Doctor fees, hospital charges, the cost of medicines, future medical costs, and ambulance, helicopter, and other emergency medical services are included.

Administrative Expenses
Include the administrative cost of public and private insurance, and police and legal costs. Private insurance administrative costs are the difference between premiums paid to insurance companies and claims paid out by them. It is their cost of doing business and is a part of the cost total. Claims paid by insurance companies are not identified separately, as every claim is compensation for losses such as wages, medical expenses, property damage, etc.

Motor-Vehicle Damage
Includes the value of damage to vehicles from motor-vehicle crashes. The cost of normal wear and tear to vehicles is not included.

Employers' Uninsured Costs
This is an estimate of the uninsured costs incurred by employers, representing the dollar value of time lost by uninjured workers. It includes time spent investigating and reporting injuries, giving first aid, hiring and training of replacement workers, and the extra cost of overtime for uninjured workers.

Fire Loss
Includes losses from both structure fires and nonstructure fires such as vehicles, outside storage, crops, and timber.

Work–Motor-Vehicle Duplication
The cost of motor-vehicle crashes that involve persons in the course of their work is included in both classes but the duplication is eliminated from the total. The duplication in 2006 amounted to $23.1 billion and was made up of $4.4 billion in wage and productivity losses, $1.8 billion in medical expenses, $14.8 billion in administrative expenses, $1.7 billion in vehicle damage, and $0.4 billion in employers' uninsured costs.

COSTS OF UNINTENTIONAL INJURIES BY COMPONENT, 2006

TOTAL COST $652.1 BILLION

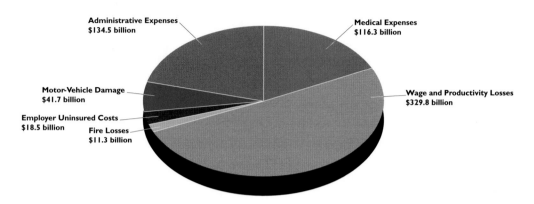

Administrative Expenses
$134.5 billion

Medical Expenses
$116.3 billion

Motor-Vehicle Damage
$41.7 billion

Wage and Productivity Losses
$329.8 billion

Employer Uninsured Costs
$18.5 billion

Fire Losses
$11.3 billion

COST EQUIVALENTS

The costs of unintentional injuries are immense—billions of dollars. Since figures this large can be difficult to comprehend, it is sometimes useful to reduce the numbers to a more understandable scale by relating them to quantities encountered in daily life. The table below shows how the costs of unintentional injuries compare to common quantities such as taxes, corporate profits, or stock dividends.

COST EQUIVALENTS, 2006

The Cost of ...	Is Equivalent to ...
...All Injuries ($652.1 billion)	...62 cents of every dollar paid in federal personal income taxes, **or** ...52 cents of every dollar spent on food in the U.S.
...Motor-Vehicle Crashes ($258.6 billion)	...purchasing 400 gallons of gasoline for each registered vehicle in the U.S., **or** ...more than $1,300 per licensed driver.
...Work Injuries ($164.7 billion)	...24 cents of every dollar of corporate dividends to stockholders, **or** ...9 cents of every dollar of pre-tax corporate profits, **or** ...exceeds the combined profits reported by the 11 largest Fortune 500 companies.
...Home Injuries ($150.1 billion)	...a $90,700 rebate on each new single-family home built, **or** ...41 cents of every dollar of property taxes paid.
...Public Injuries ($101.8 billion)	...a $11.1 million grant to each public library in the U.S., **or** ...a $96,800 bonus for each police officer and firefighter.

Source: National Safety Council estimates.

DEATHS DUE TO UNINTENTIONAL INJURIES, 2006

TYPE OF EVENT AND AGE OF VICTIM

All Unintentional Injuries

The term "unintentional" covers most deaths from injury and poisoning. Excluded are homicides (including legal intervention), suicides, deaths for which none of these categories can be determined, and war deaths.

	Total	Change from 2005	Death Rate[a]
Deaths	120,000	+2%	40.1

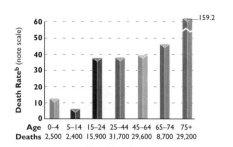

Motor-Vehicle Accidents

Includes deaths involving mechanically or electrically powered highway-transport vehicles in motion (except those on rails), both on and off the highway or street.

	Total	Change from 2005	Death Rate[a]
Deaths	44,700	−2%	14.9

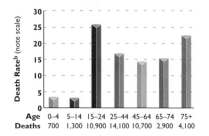

Poisoning

Includes deaths from drugs, medicines, other solid and liquid substances, and gases and vapors. Excludes poisonings from spoiled foods, salmonella, etc., which are classified as disease deaths.

	Total	Change from 2005	Death Rate[a]
Deaths	25,300	+9%	8.5

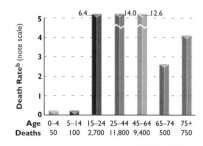

Falls

Includes deaths from falls from one level to another or on the same level. Excludes falls in or from transport vehicles, or while boarding or alighting from them.

	Total	Change from 2005	Death Rate[a]
Deaths	21,200	+2%	7.1

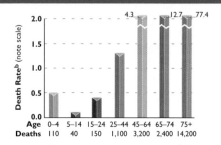

Choking

Includes deaths from unintentional ingestion or inhalation of food or other objects resulting in the obstruction of respiratory passages.

	Total	Change from 2005	Death Rate[a]
Deaths	4,100	−16%	1.4

See footnotes on page 9.

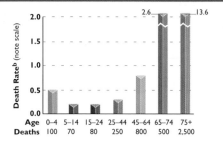

Drowning

Includes nontransport-related drownings such as those resulting from swimming, playing in the water, or falling in. Excludes drownings in floods and other cataclysms, which are classified to the cataclysm, and boating-related drownings.

	Total	Change from 2005	Death Rate[a]
Deaths	3,800	+6%	1.3

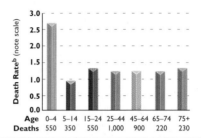

Age	0–4	5–14	15–24	25–44	45–64	65–74	75+
Deaths	550	350	550	1,000	900	220	230

Fires, flames, and smoke

Includes deaths from exposure to fires, flames, and smoke, and from injuries in fires—such as falls and struck by falling objects. Excludes burns from hot objects or liquids.

	Total	Change from 2005	Death Rate[a]
Deaths	2,800	+4%	0.9

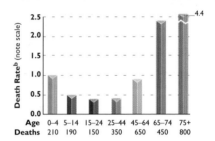

Age	0–4	5–14	15–24	25–44	45–64	65–74	75+
Deaths	210	190	150	350	650	450	800

Mechanical Suffocation

Includes deaths from hanging and strangulation, and suffocation in enclosed or confined spaces, cave-ins, or by bed clothes, plastic bags, or similar materials.

	Total	Change from 2005	Death Rate[a]
Deaths	1,100	−15%	0.4

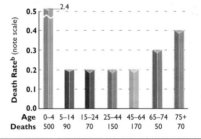

Age	0–4	5–14	15–24	25–44	45–64	65–74	75+
Deaths	500	90	70	150	170	50	70

Natural Heat or Cold

Includes deaths resulting from exposure to excessive natural heat and cold (e.g., extreme weather conditions).

	Total	Change from 2005	Death Rate[a]
Deaths	800	0%	0.3

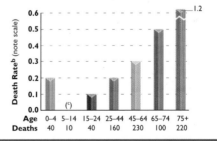

Age	0–4	5–14	15–24	25–44	45–64	65–74	75+
Deaths	40	10	40	160	230	100	220

All Other Types

Most important types included are: firearms, struck by or against object, machinery, electric current, and air, water, and rail transport.

	Total	Change from 2005	Death Rate[a]
Deaths	16,200	+7%	5.4

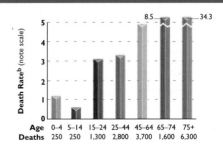

Age	0–4	5–14	15–24	25–44	45–64	65–74	75+
Deaths	250	250	1,300	2,800	3,700	1,600	6,300

Note: Category descriptions have changed due to adoption of ICD-10. See Technical Appendix for comparability.
[a]*Deaths per 100,000 population.*
[b]*Deaths per 100,000 population in each age group.*
[c]*Death rate less than 0.05.*

LEADING CAUSES OF DEATH

Unintentional injuries are the fifth leading cause of death overall and first among persons in age groups from 1 to 44. By single years of age, unintentional injuries are the leading cause from 1 to 41.

Causes are ranked for both sexes combined. Some leading causes for males and females separately may not

be shown. Beginning with 1999 data, deaths are classified according to the 10th revision of the International Classification of Diseases. See the Technical Appendix for comparability.

DEATHS AND DEATH RATES BY AGE AND SEX, 2004

Cause	Number of Deaths			Death Rates[a]		
	Total	Male	Female	Total	Male	Female
All Ages[b]						
All Causes	**2,397,615**	**1,181,668**	**1,215,947**	**816.5**	**817.9**	**815.1**
Heart disease	652,486	321,973	330,513	222.2	222.9	221.6
Cancer (malignant neoplasms)	553,888	286,830	267,058	188.6	198.5	179.0
Stroke (cerebrovascular disease)	150,074	58,800	91,274	51.1	40.7	61.2
Chronic lower respiratory diseases	121,987	58,646	63,341	41.5	40.6	42.5
Unintentional injuries	**112,012**	**72,050**	**39,962**	**38.1**	**49.9**	**26.8**
Motor-vehicle	44,933	30,837	14,096	15.3	21.3	9.4
Poisoning	20,950	13,934	7,016	7.1	9.6	4.7
Falls	18,807	9,856	8,951	6.4	6.8	6.0
Choking[c]	4,470	2,264	2,206	1.5	1.6	1.5
Drowning	3,308	2,594	714	1.1	1.8	0.5
All other unintentional injuries	19,544	12,565	6,979	6.7	8.7	4.7
Diabetes mellitus	73,138	35,267	37,871	24.9	24.4	25.4
Alzheimer's disease	65,965	18,974	46,991	22.5	13.1	31.5
Influenza and pneumonia	59,664	26,861	32,803	20.3	18.6	22.0
Nephritis and nephrosis	42,480	20,370	22,110	14.5	14.1	14.8
Septicemia	33,373	15,011	18,362	11.4	10.4	12.3
Under 1 Year						
All Causes	**27,936**	**15,718**	**12,218**	**682.8**	**751.0**	**611.4**
Congenital anomalies	5,622	2,898	2,724	137.4	138.5	136.3
Short gestation, low birth weight, n.e.c.	4,642	2,639	2,003	113.5	126.1	100.2
Sudden infant death syndrome	2,246	1,328	918	54.9	63.5	45.9
Maternal complications of pregnancy	1,715	962	753	41.9	46.0	37.7
Unintentional injuries	**1,052**	**604**	**448**	**25.7**	**28.9**	**22.4**
Mechanical suffocation	667	370	297	16.3	17.7	14.9
Motor-vehicle	143	80	63	3.5	3.8	3.2
Drowning	62	38	24	1.5	1.8	1.2
Choking[c]	58	47	11	1.4	2.2	0.6
Fires and flames	26	14	12	0.6	0.7	0.6
All other unintentional injuries	96	55	41	2.3	2.6	2.1
Complications of placenta, cord, membranes	1,042	555	487	25.5	26.5	24.4
Respiratory distress	875	501	374	21.4	23.9	18.7
Bacterial sepsis	827	473	354	20.2	22.6	17.7
Neonatal hemorrhage	616	381	235	15.1	18.2	11.8
Diseases of the circulatory system	593	325	268	14.5	15.5	13.4
1 to 4 Years						
All Causes	**4,785**	**2,649**	**2,136**	**29.9**	**32.4**	**27.4**
Unintentional injuries	**1,641**	**964**	**677**	**10.3**	**11.8**	**8.7**
Motor-vehicle	635	344	291	4.0	4.2	3.7
Drowning	430	265	165	2.7	3.2	2.1
Fires and flames	223	120	103	1.4	1.5	1.3
Choking[c]	70	45	25	0.4	0.6	0.3
Mechanical suffocation	55	36	19	0.3	0.4	0.2
All other unintentional injuries	228	154	74	1.4	1.9	0.9
Congenital anomalies	569	318	251	3.6	3.9	3.2
Cancer (malignant neoplasms)	399	212	187	2.5	2.6	2.4
Homicide	377	204	173	2.4	2.5	2.2
Heart disease	187	94	93	1.2	1.2	1.2
Influenza and pneumonia	119	47	72	0.7	0.6	0.9
Septicemia	84	41	43	0.5	0.5	0.6
Certain conditions originating in the perinatal period	61	38	23	0.4	0.5	0.3
Benign neoplasms	53	28	25	0.3	0.3	0.3
Chronic lower respiratory diseases	48	30	18	0.3	0.4	0.2

See source and footnotes on page 12.

DEATHS AND DEATH RATES BY AGE AND SEX, 2004, Cont.

Cause	Number of Deaths			Death Rates[a]		
	Total	Male	Female	Total	Male	Female
5 to 14 Years						
All Causes	**6,834**	**3,999**	**2,835**	**16.8**	**19.2**	**14.2**
Unintentional injuries	**2,666**	**1,661**	**1,005**	**6.5**	**8.0**	**5.1**
Motor-vehicle	1,653	975	678	4.1	4.7	3.4
Drowning	269	194	75	0.7	0.9	0.4
Fires and flames	255	152	103	0.6	0.7	0.5
Mechanical suffocation	82	71	11	0.2	0.3	0.1
Poisoning	55	30	25	0.1	0.1	0.1
All other unintentional injuries	352	239	113	0.9	1.1	0.6
Cancer (malignant neoplasms)	1,019	572	447	2.5	2.7	2.2
Congenital anomalies	389	211	178	1.0	1.0	0.9
Homicide	329	200	129	0.8	1.0	0.6
Suicide	285	187	98	0.7	0.9	0.5
Heart disease	245	122	123	0.6	0.6	0.6
Chronic lower respiratory diseases	120	75	45	0.3	0.4	0.2
Benign neoplasms	84	46	38	0.2	0.2	0.2
Influenza and pneumonia	82	47	35	0.2	0.2	0.2
Stroke (cerebrovascular disease)	77	40	37	0.2	0.2	0.2
15 to 24 Years						
All Causes	**33,421**	**24,587**	**8,834**	**80.2**	**114.8**	**43.6**
Unintentional injuries	**15,449**	**11,423**	**4,026**	**37.1**	**53.3**	**19.9**
Motor-vehicle	10,987	7,814	3,173	26.4	36.5	15.7
Poisoning	2,259	1,765	494	5.4	8.2	2.4
Drowning	574	522	52	1.4	2.4	0.3
Falls	241	206	35	0.6	1.0	0.2
Fires and flames	186	107	79	0.4	0.5	0.4
All other unintentional injuries	1,202	1,009	193	2.9	4.7	1.0
Homicide	5,085	4,380	705	12.2	20.4	3.5
Suicide	4,316	3,596	720	10.4	16.8	3.6
Cancer	1,709	1,027	682	4.1	4.8	3.4
Heart disease	1,038	691	347	2.5	3.2	1.7
Congenital anomalies	483	282	201	1.2	1.3	1.0
Stroke (cerebrovascular disease)	211	116	95	0.5	0.5	0.5
Human immunodeficiency virus infection	191	107	84	0.5	0.5	0.4
Influenza and pneumonia	185	118	67	0.4	0.6	0.3
Chronic lower respiratory diseases	179	110	69	0.4	0.5	0.3
25 to 34 Years						
All Causes	**40,868**	**28,359**	**12,509**	**102.2**	**139.7**	**63.5**
Unintentional injuries	**13,032**	**9,871**	**3,161**	**32.6**	**48.6**	**16.0**
Motor-vehicle	7,036	5,245	1,791	17.6	25.8	9.1
Poisoning	3,641	2,673	968	9.1	13.2	4.9
Drowning	385	332	53	1.0	1.6	0.3
Falls	320	274	46	0.8	1.3	0.2
Fires and flames	240	165	75	0.6	0.8	0.4
All other unintentional injuries	1,410	1,182	228	3.5	5.8	1.2
Suicide	5,074	4,142	932	12.7	20.4	4.7
Homicide	4,495	3,764	731	11.2	18.5	3.7
Cancer	3,633	1,750	1,883	9.1	8.6	9.6
Heart disease	3,163	2,143	1,020	7.9	10.6	5.2
Human immunodeficiency virus infection	1,468	917	551	3.7	4.5	2.8
Diabetes mellitus	599	340	259	1.5	1.7	1.3
Stroke (cerebrovascular disease)	567	284	283	1.4	1.4	1.4
Congenital anomalies	420	235	185	1.0	1.2	0.9
Septicemia	328	165	163	0.8	0.8	0.8
35 to 44 Years						
All Causes	**85,362**	**53,677**	**31,685**	**193.6**	**243.8**	**143.5**
Unintentional injuries	**16,471**	**11,671**	**4,800**	**37.4**	**53.0**	**21.7**
Motor-vehicle	6,663	4,826	1,837	15.1	21.9	8.3
Poisoning	6,444	4,176	2,268	14.6	19.0	10.3
Falls	659	526	133	1.5	2.4	0.6
Drowning	435	367	68	1.0	1.7	0.3
Fires and flames	313	209	104	0.7	0.9	0.5
All other unintentional injuries	1,957	1,567	390	4.4	7.1	1.8
Cancer	14,723	6,408	8,315	33.4	29.1	37.7
Heart disease	12,925	9,011	3,914	29.3	40.9	17.7
Suicide	6,638	5,067	1,571	15.1	23.0	7.1
Human immunodeficiency virus infection	4,826	3,466	1,360	10.9	15.7	6.2
Homicide	2,984	2,224	760	6.8	10.1	3.4
Chronic liver disease and cirrhosis	2,799	1,916	883	6.3	8.7	4.0
Stroke (cerebrovascular disease)	2,361	1,240	1,121	5.4	5.6	5.1
Diabetes mellitus	2,026	1,258	768	4.6	5.7	3.5
Influenza and pneumonia	891	494	397	2.0	2.2	1.8

See source and footnotes on page 12.

LEADING CAUSES OF DEATH (CONT.)

DEATHS AND DEATH RATES BY AGE AND SEX, 2004, Cont.

Cause	Number of Deaths			Death Rates[a]		
	Total	Male	Female	Total	Male	Female
45 to 54 Years						
All Causes	**177,697**	**111,163**	**66,534**	**427.0**	**543.6**	**314.3**
Cancer	49,520	25,432	24,088	119.0	124.4	113.8
Heart disease	37,556	27,050	10,506	90.2	132.3	49.6
Unintentional injuries	**16,942**	**11,988**	**4,954**	**40.7**	**58.6**	**23.4**
Motor-vehicle	6,276	4,486	1,790	15.1	21.9	8.5
Poisoning	6,033	3,910	2,123	14.5	19.1	10.0
Falls	1,184	912	272	2.8	4.5	1.3
Fires and flames	490	329	161	1.2	1.6	0.8
Drowning	444	358	86	1.1	1.8	0.4
All other unintentional injuries	2,515	1,993	522	6.0	9.7	2.5
Chronic liver disease and cirrhosis	7,496	5,382	2,114	18.0	26.3	10.0
Suicide	6,906	5,078	1,828	16.6	24.8	8.6
Stroke (cerebrovascular disease)	6,181	3,409	2,772	14.9	16.7	13.1
Diabetes mellitus	5,567	3,376	2,191	13.4	16.5	10.3
Human immunodeficiency virus infection	4,422	3,327	1,095	10.6	16.3	5.2
Chronic lower respiratory diseases	3,511	1,806	1,705	8.4	8.8	8.1
Septicemia	2,251	1,207	1,044	5.4	5.9	4.9
55 to 64 Years						
All Causes	**264,697**	**158,032**	**106,665**	**910.4**	**1,129.1**	**707.3**
Cancer	96,956	52,738	44,218	333.5	376.8	293.2
Heart disease	63,613	43,788	19,825	218.8	312.8	131.5
Chronic lower respiratory diseases	11,754	6,029	5,725	40.4	43.1	38.0
Diabetes mellitus	10,780	6,153	4,627	37.1	44.0	30.7
Stroke (cerebrovascular disease)	9,966	5,523	4,443	34.3	39.5	29.5
Unintentional injuries	**9,651**	**6,562**	**3,089**	**33.2**	**46.9**	**20.5**
Motor-vehicle	4,093	2,770	1,323	14.1	19.8	8.8
Poisoning	1,577	929	648	5.4	6.6	4.3
Falls	1,393	987	406	4.8	7.1	2.7
Fires and flames	412	251	161	1.4	1.8	1.1
Choking[c]	386	228	158	1.3	1.6	1.0
All other unintentional injuries	1,790	1,397	393	6.2	10.0	2.6
Chronic liver disease and cirrhosis	6,569	4,587	1,982	22.6	32.8	13.1
Suicide	4,011	3,088	923	13.8	22.1	6.1
Nephritis and nephrosis	3,963	2,120	1,843	13.6	15.1	12.2
Septicemia	3,745	1,934	1,811	12.9	13.8	12.0
65 to 74 Years						
All Causes	**399,666**	**222,891**	**176,775**	**2,162.7**	**2,642.1**	**1,760.1**
Cancer	139,417	76,487	62,930	754.4	906.6	626.6
Heart disease	99,999	61,000	38,999	541.1	723.1	388.3
Chronic lower respiratory diseases	28,390	14,503	13,887	153.6	171.9	138.3
Stroke (cerebrovascular disease)	19,901	10,207	9,694	107.7	121.0	96.5
Diabetes mellitus	16,093	8,430	7,663	87.1	99.9	76.3
Unintentional injuries	**8,116**	**4,992**	**3,124**	**43.9**	**59.2**	**31.1**
Motor-vehicle	2,974	1,799	1,175	16.1	21.3	11.7
Falls	2,255	1,394	861	12.2	16.5	8.6
Choking[c]	538	300	238	2.9	3.6	2.4
Poisoning	421	222	199	2.3	2.6	2.0
Fires and flames	349	210	139	1.9	2.5	1.4
All other unintentional injuries	1,579	1,067	512	8.5	12.6	5.1
Nephritis and nephrosis	7,119	3,677	3,442	38.5	43.6	34.3
Influenza and pneumonia	6,382	3,605	2,777	34.5	42.7	27.6
Septicemia	5,983	3,017	2,966	32.4	35.8	29.5
Chronic liver disease and cirrhosis	5,119	3,122	1,997	27.7	37.0	19.9
75 Years and Older[b]						
All Causes	**1,356,349**	**560,593**	**795,756**	**7,607.4**	**8,340.3**	**7,163.9**
Heart disease	433,339	177,846	255,493	2,430.5	2,645.9	2,300.1
Cancer	246,438	122,167	124,271	1,382.2	1,817.6	1,118.8
Stroke (cerebrovascular disease)	110,642	37,887	72,755	620.6	563.7	655.0
Chronic lower respiratory diseases	76,808	35,487	41,321	430.8	528.0	372.0
Alzheimer's disease	61,672	17,120	44,552	345.9	254.7	401.1
Influenza and pneumonia	46,378	19,225	27,153	260.1	286.0	244.4
Diabetes mellitus	37,866	15,605	22,261	212.4	232.2	200.4
Nephritis and nephrosis	27,988	12,620	15,368	157.0	187.8	138.4
Unintentional injuries	**26,992**	**12,314**	**14,678**	**151.4**	**183.2**	**132.1**
Falls	12,648	5,491	7,157	70.9	81.7	64.4
Motor-vehicle	4,473	2,498	1,975	25.1	37.2	17.8
Choking[c]	2,724	1,241	1,483	15.3	18.5	13.4
Fires and flames	735	345	390	4.1	5.1	3.5
Poisoning	489	211	278	2.7	3.1	2.5
All other unintentional injuries	5,923	2,528	3,395	33.2	37.6	30.6
Septicemia	19,664	7,945	11,719	110.3	118.2	105.5

Source: National Safety Council analysis of National Center for Health Statistics mortality data and Bureau of the Census population data.
[a] *Deaths per 100,000 population in each age group.*
[b] *Includes 346 deaths where the age is unknown.*
[c] *Inhalation or ingestion of food or other objects.*

ALL UNINTENTIONAL INJURIES

LEADING CAUSES OF NONFATAL UNINTENTIONAL INJURIES

Falls are the leading cause of nonfatal unintentional injuries that are treated in hospital emergency departments (ED) according to data from the All Injury Program, a cooperative program involving the National Center for Injury Prevention and Control, CDC, and the Consumer Product Safety Commission. Nearly eight million people were treated in an ED for fall-related injuries in 2005. Falls were the leading cause of nonfatal injuries for all age groups except 15–24 years old for which struck by or against an object or person was the leading cause. Struck by or against, overexertion, and motor-vehicle crashes involving vehicle occupants were also leading causes for most age groups.

LEADING CAUSES OF NONFATAL UNINTENTIONAL INJURIES TREATED IN HOSPITAL EMERGENCY DEPARTMENTS BY AGE GROUP, UNITED STATES, 2005

Rank	All Ages	Age Group									
		<1	1–4	5–9	10–14	15–24	25–34	35–44	45–54	55–64	65+
1	Falls 7,938,467	Falls 118,292	Falls 862,993	Falls 644,546	Falls 622,613	Struck by/against 984,523	Falls 758,333	Falls 811,860	Falls 811,179	Falls 617,660	Falls 1,800,763
2	Struck by/against 4,336,688	Struck by/against 31,293	Struck by/against 365,619	Struck by/against 389,048	Struck by/against 556,822	Falls 889,721	Overexertion 668,119	Overexertion 646,712	Overexertion 436,517	Struck by/against 212,455	Struck by/against 205,467
3	Overexertion 3,284,022	Other bite/sting[a] 13,996	Other bite/sting[a] 138,508	Cut/pierce 115,980	Overexertion 276,544	Motor-vehicle occupant 869,708	Struck by/against 639,864	Struck by/against 548,619	Struck by/against 402,932	Overexertion 192,284	Motor-vehicle occupant 177,7515
4	Motor-vehicle occupant 2,857,722	Fire/burn 12,003	Foreign body 118,101	Pedalcyclist 100,203	Cut/pierce 145,247	Overexertion 747,081	Motor-vehicle occupant 596,872	Motor-vehicle occupant 464,692	Motor-vehicle occupant 350,923	Motor-vehicle occupant 191,931	Overexertion 167,942
5	Cut/Pierce 2,236,861	Foreign body 9,440	Cut/pierce 87,920	Other bite/sting[a] 89,351	Pedalcyclist 126,468	Cut/pierce 510,873	Cut/pierce 439,800	Cut/pierce 381,872	Cut/pierce 278,090	Cut/pierce 155,344	Cut/pierce 114,491
6	Other bite/sting[a] 1,096,234	Other specified[b] 7,213	Overexertion 74,345	Overexertion 67,774	Unknown/ unspecified 119,074	Other bite/sting[a] 198,757	Other bite/sting[a] 175,120	Other specified[b] 179,024	Other specified[b] 142,483	Other bite/sting[a] 71,459	Other bite/sting[a] 70,903
7	Other specified[b] 880,543	Cut/Pierce 6,993	Fire/burn 59,267	Motor-vehicle occupant 67,740	Motor-vehicle occupant 92,902	Other specified[b] 191,715	Other specified[b] 154,178	Other bite/sting[a] 151,367	Other bite/sting[a] 124,531	Other specified[b] 62,578	Poisoning 59,033
8	Unknown/ unspecified 678,967	Inhalation/ Suffocation 6,611	Other specified[b] 59,059	Foreign body 55,405	Other bite/sting[a] 62,219	Unknown/ unspecified 175,432	Other transport[c] 101,938	Poisoning 131,126	Poisoning 99,999	Poisoning 49,445	Other transport[c] 47,748
9	Poisoning 617,617	Overexertion 6,588	Unknown/ unspecified 49,152	Dog bite 46,439	Other transport[c] 59,209	Other transport[c] 136,789	Poisoning 95,595	Other transport[c] 90,675	Other transport[c] 69,155	Other transport[c] 34,057	Unknown/ unspecified 42,548
10	Unknown/ transport[c] 612,558	Motor-vehicle occupant 6,547	Poisoning 39,940	Unknown/ unspecified 44,627	Dog bite 36,873	Poisoning 115,998	Foreign body 92,588	Foreign body 79,891	Foreign body 55,622	Foreign body 30,946	Other specified[b] 38,668
All Causes											
Number	27,156,734	2,229,165		1,732,477	2,234,592	5,328,433	4,115,120	3,838,660	3,055,124	1,762,139	2,860,753[d]
Per 1,000 population	91.6	109.8		88.7	107.1	126.6	102.5	87.5	71.9	58.0	77.8[d]

Source: NEISS All Injury Program, Office of Statistics and Programming, National Center for Injury Prevention and Control, CDC, and Consumer Product Safety Commission.
[a] Other than dog bite.
[b] Includes electric current, explosions, fireworks, radiation, animal scratch, etc. Excludes all causes listed in the table and bb/pellet gunshot, drowning and near drowning, firearm gunshot, suffocation, machinery, natural and environmental conditions, pedestrians, and motorcyclists.
[c] Includes occupant of any transport vehicle other than a motor vehicle or motor cycle (e.g., airplane, rail car, boat, ATV, animal rider).
[d] Includes 3,387 cases with age unknown.

LEADING CAUSES OF UNINTENTIONAL-INJURY DEATH BY AGE, 2004

UNINTENTIONAL-INJURY DEATHS BY AGE AND EVENT, UNITED STATES, 2004

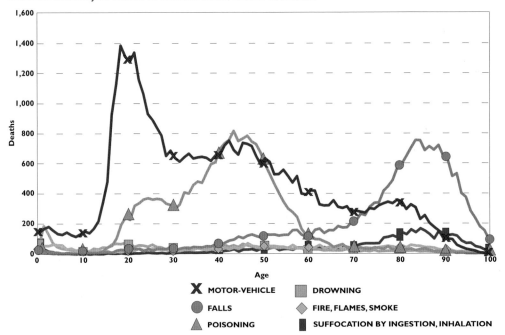

X MOTOR-VEHICLE	▨ DROWNING
● FALLS	◆ FIRE, FLAMES, SMOKE
▲ POISONING	■ SUFFOCATION BY INGESTION, INHALATION

Motor-vehicle crashes, poisonings, falls, choking (suffocation by inhalation or ingestion of food or other object), drownings, fires and flames, and mechanical suffocation were the seven leading causes of unintentional-injury death in the United States in 2004. The graph above depicts the number of deaths attributed to the top six causes by single years of age through age 99.

In 2004, motor-vehicle crashes were the leading cause of unintentional-injury death for all ages combined and the leading cause of unintentional-injury deaths for each single year of age from 2 to 39, and again for each single year of age from 50 to 72. Furthermore, for those aged 2 through 34, motor-vehicle crashes caused more deaths than any other injury type or illness, combining to account for 24% of the total for that age range.

The distribution of 2004 motor-vehicle fatalities shows a sharp increase during adolescence, rising from 478 for 15-year-olds to 1,384 for 18-year-olds. The greatest number of motor-vehicle fatalities occurred to persons aged 18 in 2004.

The second leading cause of unintentional-injury death overall in 2004 was poisoning. Poisoning fatalities reached a high of 816 for 43-year-olds and **poisoning was the leading cause of unintentional-injury death for those aged 40–49**. Poisonings were the second leading cause of unintentional-injury death for those

aged 15, for each year of age from 17 to 39, and again for each year from 50 to 60. Falls were the third leading cause of unintentional-injury death in the United States in 2004. **Falls were the leading cause of unintentional-injury death of persons aged 73 and older** and second leading cause from ages 61 through 72 for each year of age; deaths resulting from falls peaked at 751 for individuals age 83.

Choking[a] was the fourth leading cause of unintentional-injury death in 2004. Choking deaths peaked at age 84 with 169 deaths. It was the second leading cause of unintentional-injury death for each year of age 88 and over. The fifth leading cause of unintentional-injury death was drowning, which peaked at 184 for 1-year-olds and was the leading cause for that age. Drownings were the second leading cause of injury death for children ages 2–3, 6, 8, 10, 12–14, and 16.[b]

Fires, flames, and smoke were the sixth leading cause of unintentional-injury death in 2004. Fatalities due to fires, flames, and smoke were the second leading cause of death for children aged 4–9[b] and for those aged 11. Mechanical suffocation was the seventh leading cause overall and the leading cause for infants under 1 year old, with 667 deaths.

Source: National Safety Council tabulations of National Center for Health Statistics data. See the Technical Appendix for ICD-10 codes for the leading causes and comparability with prior years.
[a] Inhalation or ingestion of food or other objects.
[b] Drowning and fires, flames, and smoke were tied as the second leading cause for those aged 6 and 8.

UNINTENTIONAL-INJURY DEATH RATES BY AGE, 2004

UNINTENTIONAL-INJURY DEATHS PER 100,000 POPULATION BY AGE AND EVENT, UNITED STATES, 2004

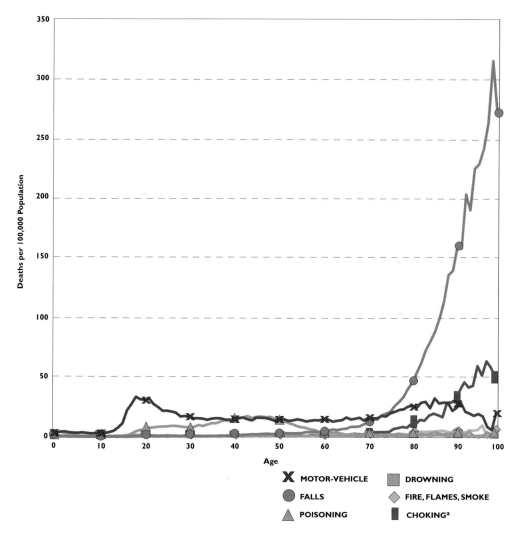

On the basis of deaths per 100,000 population at each age, motor-vehicle death rates in 2004 rose to an initial peak of 33.6 for persons 18 years of age. This rate declined to an average of about 15.0 for those aged 30 to 72, then increased to another peak at 32.7 for those 85 years of age.

While motor-vehicle crashes are a significant problem for all ages, deaths resulting from falls for certain older ages have even higher death rates. Beginning at about age 70, the death rate from falls increases dramatically. At age 73, the falls death rate surpasses that for motor-vehicle, with the death rate continuing to rise with increasing age.

The poisoning death rate remains low until about age 15 where it starts to increase up to its peak rate of 17.6 at 43 years of age and then falls again.

Death rates due to choking on inhaled or ingested food or other objects are quite low for most ages. Rates are slightly elevated for infants and toddlers and rise rapidly beginning at about age 70. The death rates for drownings show peaks at very young ages, in the late teens, and again at some very old ages.

The graph above depicts death rates per 100,000 population for the six leading causes of unintentional-injury deaths in 2004 for single years of age through age 99.

Source: National Safety Council tabulations of National Center for Health Statistics data. See the Technical Appendix for ICD-10 codes for the leading causes and comparability with prior years.
[a] *Inhalation or ingestion of food or other objects.*

UNINTENTIONAL-INJURY DEATHS BY SEX AND AGE, 2004

UNINTENTIONAL-INJURY DEATHS BY SEX AND AGE, UNITED STATES, 2004

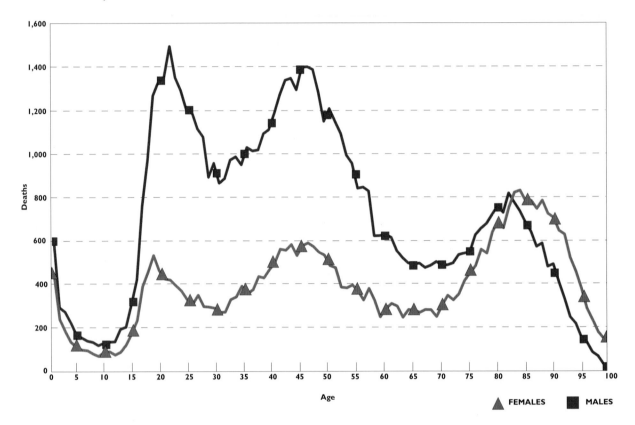

Males incur more deaths due to unintentional injuries than females at all ages from birth to age 82. The difference between the unintentional-injury death totals ranges from 41 at age 9 to 1,070 at age 21. The excess number of deaths for males compared to females is most evident from the late teenage years to the late forties where the gap begins to narrow. Beginning at age 83, deaths of females exceed those of males by as little as 47 deaths to as much as 294 at age 92.

Unintentional-injury deaths are at their lowest level for both sexes from about age 4 to about age 13. For males the highest number of deaths (1,491) occurs at age 21,

with high totals—including another peak of 1,396 deaths for those aged 46—occurring from the late teens until the late forties or early fifties. For females, however, the highest totals occur among the elderly from about age 79 and older. The greatest number of female deaths (830) occurs at age 84.

The graph above shows the number of unintentional-injury deaths in 2004 for each sex by single years of age from under 1 year old to age 99. It is based on death certificate data from the National Center for Health Statistics.

UNINTENTIONAL-INJURY DEATH RATES BY SEX AND AGE, 2004

UNINTENTIONAL-INJURY DEATHS PER 100,000 POPULATION BY SEX AND AGE, UNITED STATES, 2004

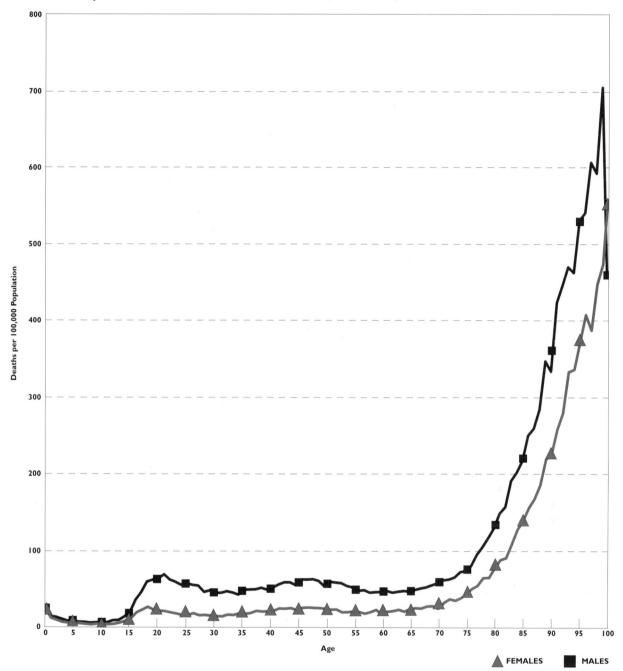

Until the very end of the lifespan, males have greater unintentional-injury death rates for each year of age compared to females. The graph above shows the unintentional-injury death rates for males and females by single year of age from under 1 year old to age 99. It is based on National Center for Health Statistics mortality data and U.S. Census Bureau population data.

Death rates for both sexes are lowest from birth until the mid-teenage years where rates rise rapidly. Rates then remain fairly constant until the late sixties where they again rise steadily with increasing age. For comparison, the overall unintentional-injury death rate for all ages and both sexes was 38.1.

MORTALITY BY SELECTED EXTERNAL CAUSES, UNITED STATES, 2002–2004

Type of Accident or Manner of Injury	2004[a]	2003	2002
All External Causes of Mortality, V01–Y89[b]	**167,184**	**166,857**	**164,112**
Deaths Due to Unintentional (Accidental) Injuries, V01–X59, Y85–Y86	**112,012**	**109,277**	**106,742**
Transport Accidents, V01–V99, Y85	**47,385**	**48,071**	**48,366**
Motor-vehicle accidents, V02–V04, V09.0, V09.2, V12–V14, V19.0–V19.2, V19.4– V19.6, V20–V79, V80.3–V80.5, V81.0–V81.1, V82.0–V82.1, V83–V86, V87.0–V87.8, V88.0–V88.8, V89.0, V89.2	44,933	44,757	45,380
Pedestrian, V01–V09	5,976	5,991	6,091
Pedalcyclist, V10–V19	843	762	767
Motorcycle rider, V20–V29	4,018	3,676	3,215
Occupant of three-wheeled motor vehicle, V30–V39	13	13	21
Car occupant, V40–V49	15,282	15,797	16,337
Occupant of pick-up truck or van, V50–V59	3,908	4,163	4,286
Occupant of heavy transport vehicle, V60–V69	439	442	456
Bus occupant, V70–V79	40	36	43
Animal rider or occupant of animal-drawn vehicle, V80	91	101	118
Occupant of railway train or railway vehicle, V81	27	24	28
Occupant of streetcar, V82	1	2	4
Other and unspecified land transport accidents, V83–V89	15,494	15,107	15,100
Occupant of special industrial vehicle, V83	*12*	*12*	*15*
Occupant of special agricultural vehicle, V84	*105*	*175*	*149*
Occupant of special construction vehicle, V85	*27*	*20*	*32*
Occupant of all-terrain or other off-road motor vehicle, V86	*951*	*906*	*776*
Other and unspecified person, V87–V89	*14,399*	*13,994*	*14,128*
Water transport accidents, V90–V94	574	573	617
Drowning, V90, V92	*421*	*412*	*413*
Other and unspecified injuries, V91, V93–V94	*153*	*161*	*204*
Air and space transport accidents, V95–V97	679	742	653
Other and unspecified transport accidents and sequelae, V98–V99, Y85	668	642	630
Other specified transport accidents, V98	*0*	*2*	*2*
Unspecified transport accident, V99	*0*	*0*	*1*
Nontransport Unintentional (Accidental) Injuries, W00–X59, Y86	**63,959**	**61,206**	**58,376**
Falls, W00–W19	18,807	17,229	16,257
Fall on same level from slipping, tripping, and stumbling, W01	*584*	*597*	*646*
Other fall on same level, W00, W02–W03, W18	*4,458*	*3,896*	*3,610*
Fall involving bed, chair, other furniture, W06–W08	*774*	*838*	*785*
Fall on and from stairs and steps, W10	*1,638*	*1,588*	*1,598*
Fall on and from ladder or scaffolding, W11–W12	*392*	*417*	*406*
Fall from out of or through building or structure, W13	*587*	*600*	*557*
Other fall from one level to another, W09, W14–W17	*724*	*701*	*766*
Other and unspecified fall, W04–W05, W19	*9,650*	*8,592*	*7,889*
Exposure to inanimate mechanical forces, W20–W49	2,759	2,658	2,727
Struck by or striking against object, W20–W22	*833*	*809*	*864*
Caught between objects, W23	*134*	*136*	*115*
Contact with machinery, W24, W30–W31	*795*	*640*	*652*
Contact with sharp objects, W25–W29	*106*	*99*	*105*
Firearms discharge, W32–W34	*649*	*730*	*762*
Explosion and rupture of pressurized devices, W35–W38	*28*	*30*	*27*
Fireworks discharge, W39	*2*	*11*	*5*
Explosion of other materials, W40	*148*	*147*	*137*
Foreign body entering through skin or natural orifice, W44–W45	*32*	*22*	*23*
Other and unspecified inanimate mechanical forces, W41–W43, W49	*32*	*34*	*37*
Exposure to animate mechanical forces, W50–W64	139	171	144
Struck by or against another person, W50–W52	*13*	*39*	*26*
Bitten or struck by dog, W54	*27*	*32*	*18*
Bitten or struck by other mammals, W53, W55	*77*	*78*	*75*
Bitten or stung by nonvenomous insect and other arthropods, W57	*5*	*12*	*13*
Bitten or crushed by other reptiles, W59	*0*	*0*	*0*
Other and unspecified animate mechanical forces, W56, W58, W60, W64	*17*	*10*	*12*
Accidental drowning and submersion, W65–W74	3,308	3,306	3,447
Drowning and submersion while in or falling into bath-tub, W65–W66	*402*	*332*	*352*
Drowning and submersion while in or falling into swimming-pool, W67–W68	*625*	*515*	*636*
Drowning and submersion while in or falling into natural water, W69–W70	*1,333*	*1,225*	*1,325*
Other and unspecified drowning and submersion, W73–W74	*948*	*1,234*	*1,134*
Other accidental threats to breathing, W75–W84	5,891	5,579	5,517
Accidental suffocation and strangulation in bed, W75	*596*	*497*	*509*
Other accidental hanging and strangulation, W76	*252*	*277*	*297*
Threat to breathing due to cave-in, falling earth and other substances, W77	*48*	*46*	*57*
Inhalation of gastric contents, W78	*377*	*393*	*369*
Inhalation and ingestion of food causing obstruction of respiratory tract, W79	*878*	*875*	*819*
Inhalation and ingestion of other objects causing obstruction of respiratory tract, W80	*3,215*	*3,004*	*2,940*
Confined to or trapped in a low-oxygen environment, W81	*16*	*16*	*19*
Other and unspecified threats to breathing, W83–W84	*509*	*471*	*507*

See source and footnotes on page 19.

MORTALITY BY SELECTED EXTERNAL CAUSES, UNITED STATES, 2002–2004, Cont.

Type of Accident or Manner of Injury	2004[a]	2003	2002
Exposure to electric current, radiation, temperature, and pressure, W85–W99	405	396	454
Electric transmission lines, W85	94	96	109
Other and unspecified electric current, W86–W87	288	280	322
Radiation, W88–W91	0	0	0
Excessive heat or cold of man-made origin, W92–W93	14	10	10
High and low air pressure and changes in air pressure, W94	9	10	13
Other and unspecified man-made environmental factors, W99	0	0	0
Exposure to smoke, fire and flames, X00–X09	3,229	3,369	3,159
Uncontrolled fire in building or structure, X00	2,635	2,761	2,533
Uncontrolled fire not in building or structure, X01	37	57	53
Controlled fire in building or structure, X02	28	35	35
Controlled fire not in building or structure, X03	48	39	30
Ignition of highly flammable material, X04	55	55	71
Ignition or melting of nightwear, X05	7	3	13
Ignition or melting of other clothing and apparel, X06	119	104	104
Other and unspecified smoke fire and flames, X08–X09	300	315	320
Contact with heat and hot substances, X10–X19	93	88	102
Contact with hot tap-water, X11	30	26	40
Other and unspecified heat and hot substances, X10, X12–X19	63	62	62
Contact with venomous animals and plants, X20–X29	81	94	76
Contact with venomous snakes and lizards, X20	6	2	3
Contact with venomous spiders, X21	14	8	10
Contact with hornets, wasps and bees, X23	52	66	54
Contact with other and unspecified venomous animal or plant, X22, X24–X29	9	18	9
Exposure to forces of nature, X30–X39	1,102	1,140	1,219
Exposure to excessive natural heat, X30	226	273	350
Exposure to excessive natural cold, X31	676	620	646
Lightning, X33	46	47	66
Earthquake and other earth movements, X34–X36	30	32	31
Cataclysmic storm, X37	63	75	63
Flood, X38	22	26	9
Exposure to other and unspecified forces of nature, X32, X39	39	67	54
Accidental poisoning by and exposure to noxious substances, X40–X49	20,950	19,457	17,550
Nonopioid analgesics, antipyretics, and antirheumatics, X40	212	210	222
Antiepileptic, sedative-hypnotic, antiparkinsonism, and psychotropic drugs n.e.c., X41	1,300	1,205	1,024
Narcotics and psychodysleptics [hallucinogens] n.e.c., X42	9,798	9,231	8,264
Other and unspecified drugs, medicaments, and biologicals, X43–X44	8,528	7,648	6,884
Alcohol, X45	358	373	355
Gases and vapors, X46–X47	629	690	691
Other and unspecified chemicals and noxious substances, X48–X49	125	100	110
Overexertion, travel and privation, X50–X57	39	48	128
Accidental exposure to other and unspecified factors and sequelae, X58–X59, Y86	7,156	7,671	7,596
Intentional self-harm, X60–X84, Y87.0, *U03	**32,439**	**31,484**	**31,655**
Intentional self-poisoning, X60–X69	5,800	5,462	5,486
Intentional self-harm by hanging, strangulation, and suffocation, X70	7,336	6,635	6,462
Intentional self-harm by firearm, X72–X74	16,750	16,907	17,108
Other and unspecified means and sequelae, X71, X75–X84, Y87.0	2,553	2,480	2,599
Terrorism, *U03	0	0	0
Assault, X85–Y09, Y87.1, *U01	**17,357**	**17,732**	**17,638**
Assault by firearm, X93–X95	11,624	11,920	11,829
Assault by sharp object, X99	2,079	2,049	2,074
Other and unspecified means and sequelae, X85–X92, X96–X98, Y00–Y09, Y87.1	3,654	3,763	3,734
Terrorism, *U01	0	0	1
Event of undetermined intent, Y10–Y34, Y87.2, Y89.9	**4,976**	**5,072**	**4,830**
Poisoning, Y10–Y19	3,455	3,700	3,336
Hanging, strangulation, and suffocation, Y20	152	108	133
Drowning and submersion, Y21	223	215	259
Firearm discharge, Y22–Y24	235	232	243
Exposure to smoke, fire, and flames, Y26	83	100	99
Falling, jumping, or pushed from a high place, Y30	71	77	103
Other and unspecified means and sequelae, Y25, Y27–Y29, Y31–Y34, Y87.2, Y89.9	757	640	657
Legal intervention, Y35, Y89.0	**372**	**423**	**384**
Legal intervention involving firearm discharge, Y35.0	311	347	300
Legal execution, Y35.5	52	60	67
Other and unspecified means and sequelae, Y35.1–Y35.4, Y35.6–Y35.7, Y89.0	9	16	17
Operations of war and sequelae, Y36, Y89.1	**28**	**14**	**20**
Complications of medical and surgical care and sequelae, Y40–Y84, Y88.0–Y88.3	**2,883**	**2,855**	**2,843**

Source: National Center for Health Statistics. Deaths are classified on the basis of the Tenth Revision of "The International Classification of Diseases" (ICD-10), which became effective in 1999.
Note: "n.e.c." means not elsewhere classified.
[a] Latest official figures.
[b] Numbers following titles refer to external cause of injury and poisoning classifications in ICD-10.

DEATHS BY AGE, SEX, AND TYPE

UNINTENTIONAL-INJURY DEATHS BY AGE, SEX, AND TYPE, UNITED STATES, 2004[a]

Age & Sex	Total[b]	Motor-vehicle	Poisoning	Falls	Choking[c]	Fires/Flames	Drowning[d]	Mechanical Suffocation	Natural Heat/Cold	All Types Males	All Types Females
Total	112,012	44,933	20,950	18,807	4,470	3,229	3,308	1,421	902	72,050	39,962
0–4	2,693	778	31	70	128	249	492	722	36	1,568	1,125
5–14	2,666	1,653	55	37	31	255	269	82	6	1,661	1,005
15–24	15,449	10,987	2,259	241	68	186	574	85	40	11,423	4,026
25–44	29,503	13,699	10,085	979	260	553	820	235	159	21,542	7,961
45–64	26,593	10,369	7,610	2,577	721	902	715	190	279	18,550	8,043
65–74	8,116	2,974	421	2,255	538	349	188	42	99	4,992	3,124
75+	26,992	4,473	489	12,648	2,724	735	250	65	283	12,314	14,678
Males	72,050	30,837	13,934	9,856	2,264	1,902	2,594	956	617		
Females	39,962	14,096	7,016	8,951	2,206	1,327	714	465	285		

Source: National Safety Council analysis of National Center for Health Statistics mortality data.
[a]Latest official figures.
[b]Includes types not shown separately.
[c]Inhalation or ingestion of food or other object obstructing breathing.
[d]Excludes transport drownings.

Of the 112,012 unintentional-injury deaths in 2004, men accounted for 64% of all deaths. Women had the greatest share of deaths in the 75 and over age group (54% women). By type of accident, men accounted for 78% of all drowning deaths, but only 51% of deaths due to choking (inhalation or ingestion of food or other object obstructing breathing) and 52% of fatal falls.

UNITENTIONAL-INJURY DEATH RATES BY TYPE AND SEX, UNITED STATES, 2004[a]

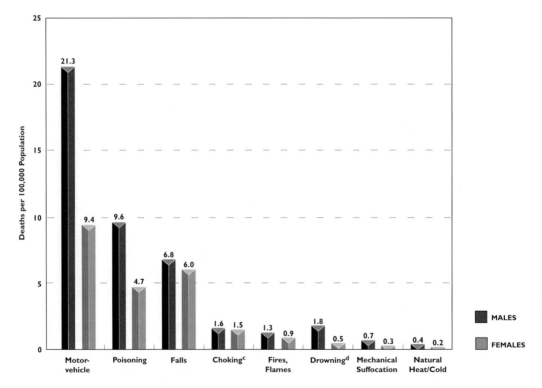

See footnotes in table above.

UNINTENTIONAL-INJURY DEATHS BY MONTH AND TYPE, UNITED STATES, 2004[a]

Month	All Types	Motor-vehicle	Poisoning	Falls	Choking[b]	Fires/Flames	Drowning[c]	Mechanical Suffocation	Natural Heat/Cold	Struck By/Against	All Other Types
Total	112,012	44,933	20,950	18,807	4,470	3,229	3,308	1,421	902	833	13,159
January	9,540	3,410	1,861	1,695	427	486	137	132	216	63	1,113
February	8,466	3,128	1,720	1,523	394	351	124	89	130	52	955
March	8,981	3,422	1,758	1,595	424	335	205	132	56	67	987
April	8,769	3,567	1,688	1,476	354	260	243	118	31	74	958
May	9,555	3,952	1,788	1,512	349	204	407	126	31	64	1,122
June	9,546	3,960	1,728	1,498	327	187	482	119	46	64	1,135
July	10,105	4,132	1,799	1,494	369	188	597	137	83	70	1,236
August	9,900	4,212	1,735	1,553	356	183	394	106	53	70	1,238
September	9,215	3,733	1,644	1,553	366	176	292	115	33	95	1,208
October	9,582	3,991	1,765	1,660	372	220	179	119	35	77	1,164
November	8,687	3,640	1,627	1,517	345	248	115	107	41	68	979
December	9,666	3,786	1,837	1,731	387	391	133	121	147	69	1,064
Average	9,334	3,744	1,746	1,567	373	269	276	118	75	69	1,097

Source: National Safety Council tabulations of National Center for Health Statistics mortality data.
[a]*Latest official figures.*
[b]*Inhalation or ingestion of food or other object obstructing breathing.*
[c]*Excludes water transport drownings.*

UNINTENTIONAL-INJURY DEATHS BY MONTH AND TYPE, UNITED STATES, 2004[a]

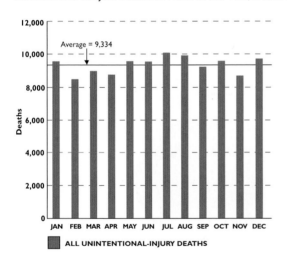

ALL UNINTENTIONAL-INJURY DEATHS

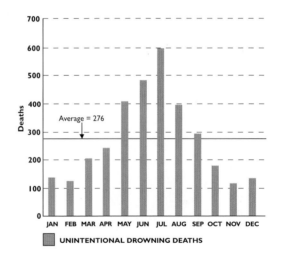

UNINTENTIONAL DROWNING DEATHS

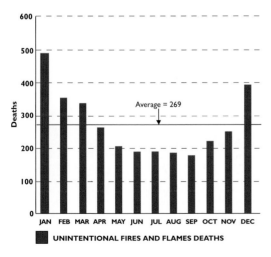

UNINTENTIONAL FIRES AND FLAMES DEATHS

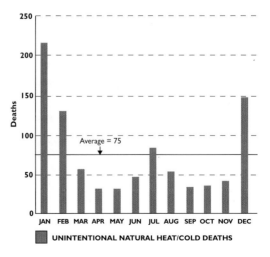

UNINTENTIONAL NATURAL HEAT/COLD DEATHS

See page 107 for motor-vehicle deaths by month.

THE NATIONAL HEALTH INTERVIEW SURVEY, 2005

The National Health Interview Survey, conducted by the National Center for Health Statistics, is a continuous, personal-interview sampling of households to obtain information about the health status of household members, including injuries experienced during the 5 weeks prior to the interview. Responsible family members residing in the household supplied the information found in the survey. In 2005, interviews were completed for 98,649 persons living in 38,509 households throughout the United States. See page 23 for definitions.

NUMBER OF LEADING EXTERNAL CAUSES OF INJURY AND POISONING EPISODES BY AGE, UNITED STATES, 2005

	Population[a] (000)	External Cause of Injury and Poisoning (number in thousands)						
		Fall	Transportation[b]	Overexertion	Struck by or Against Person or Object	Cutting-Piercing Instruments	Poisoning[b]	Other Injury Causes[b]
All Ages	**295,316**	**11,798**	**3,832**	**4,479**	**4,188**	**2,274**	**536**	**6,094**
Under 12 years	48,018	2,289	650[c]	([d])	694	228[c]	([d])	718
12–17 years	25,514	996	362[c]	570	892	([d])	([d])	1,346
18–44 years	112,217	2,531	1,655	2,097	1,710	999	([d])	2,134
45–64 years	72,780	2,926	865	1,391	557	739	206[c]	1,216
65–74 years	18,650	1,035	235[c]	200[c]	163[c]	285[c]	0	376[c]
75 years and over	18,137	2,021	([d])	([d])	171[c]	0	([d])	305[c]

[a]Civilian noninstitutionalized population.
[b]"Transportation" includes motor vehicle, bicycle, motorcycle, pedestrian, train, boat, or airplane. "Poisoning" does not include food poisoning or allergic reaction. "Other Injury Causes" includes fire/burn/scald related, animal or insect bites, machinery, and unknown causes.
[c]Figure does not meet standard of reliability or precision and should be used with caution.
[d]Estimate is not shown because it does not meet standard of reliability or precision.

LEADING EXTERNAL CAUSES OF INJURY AND POISONING EPISODES BY SEX, UNITED STATES, 2005

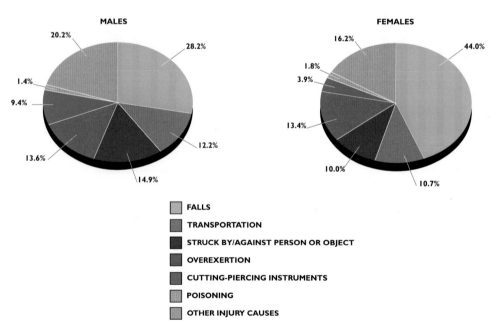

MALES

20.2% 28.2% 1.4% 9.4% 13.6% 14.9% 12.2%

FEMALES

16.2% 44.0% 1.8% 3.9% 13.4% 10.0% 10.7%

- FALLS
- TRANSPORTATION
- STRUCK BY/AGAINST PERSON OR OBJECT
- OVEREXERTION
- CUTTING-PIERCING INSTRUMENTS
- POISONING
- OTHER INJURY CAUSES

Source: Adams, P.F, Dey, A.N. & Vickerie, J.L. (2007, January). Summary health statistics for the U.S. population: National Health Interview Survey, 2005. Vital and Health Statistics, Series 10 (No. 233). Hyattsville, MD: National Center for Health Statistics.

In 2005, an estimated 33.2 million medically consulted injury and poisoning episodes were recorded, of which 53.5% were among males and 46.5% among females. The overall injury rate was 114 episodes per 1,000 population with men (125 per 1,000 men) experiencing higher rates than women (102 per 1,000 women). Most injuries occurred in or around the home (46.4%) followed by injuries at recreational and sport facilities (14.2%) and injuries on streets, highways and parking lots (13.3%).

For the 17.8 million injuries reported by men, the single most common place of injury occurrence was inside the home (21.7%) with injuries outside the home contributing an additional 18.3%. Injuries in public areas, such as schools, hospitals, streets, recreational facilities, industrial and trade areas, and public buildings, together accounted for 52.1% of the total.

Similar to men, about half of injuries among women occurred either in or outside the home environment. However, over twice as many women got injured inside than outside the home. Streets, parking lots and highways were the third most common location for injuries among women, accounting for 14.7%. The proportion of injuries at recreational and sport facilities was much lower among women (10.6%) than men (17.3%).

The 2005 NHIS injury definitions are listed below for comparability with prior years and other injury figures published in *Injury Facts®*.

NUMBER AND PERCENT OF INJURY EPISODES BY PLACE OF OCCURRENCE AND SEX, UNITED STATES, 2005

Place of Occurrence of Injury Episode	Both Sexes		Male		Female	
	Number of Episodes (000)	Percent	Number of Episodes (000)	Percent	Number of Episodes (000)	Percent
Total episodes[a]	**33,202**	**100%**	**17,750**	**100%**	**15,451**	**100%**
Home (inside)	9,641	29.0	3,858	21.7	5,783	37.4
Home (outside)	5,774	17.4	3,240	18.3	2,533	16.4
School/child care center/preschool	2,410	7.3	1,683	9.5	728	4.7
Hospital/residential institution	629	1.9	187[b]	1.1	442[b]	2.9
Street/highway/parking lot	4,410	13.3	2,145	12.1	2,265	14.7
Sport facility/recreation area/lake/river/pool	4,720	14.2	3,079	17.3	1,641	10.6
Industrial/construction/farm/mine/quarry	1,345	4.1	1,095	6.2	250[b]	1.6
Trade/service area	1,434	4.3	695	3.9	739	4.8
Other public building	518	1.6	359[b]	2.0	([c])	—
Other (unspecified)	2,134	6.4	1,371	7.7	763	4.9

Source: Adams, P.F, Dey, A.N. & Vickerie, J.L. (2007, January). Summary health statistics for the U.S. population: National Health Interview Survey, 2005. Vital and Health Statistics, Series 10 (No. 233). Hyattsville, MD: National Center for Health Statistics.
[a] Numbers and percents may not sum to respective totals due to rounding and unknowns.
[b] Figure does not meet standard of reliability or precision and should be used with caution.
[c] Estimate is not shown because it does not meet standard of reliability or precision.

Injury definitions

National Health Interview Survey definitions. The 2005 National Health Interview Survey (NHIS) figures include medically consulted injury and poisoning episodes (e.g., call to a poison control center; use of an emergency vehicle or emergency room; visit to a doctor's office or other health clinic; phone call to a doctor, nurse, or other health care professional) that reportedly occurred during the three months prior to the date of the interview and resulted in one or more conditions. Beginning in 2004, injury and poisoning estimates were calculated using only those episodes that occurred five weeks or less before the interview date. This reflects a change from 1997–2003, when the NHIS data contained injury and poisoning episodes that were reported to occur within four months of the interview, and estimates were calculated using a three-month recall period. Also, an imputation procedure was performed for injury and poisoning episodes to assign a date of occurrence if it was not reported. Therefore, figures for 2004 and subsequent years are not comparable to estimates from prior years.

In the 2005 NHIS Injury and Poisoning file, an injury episode refers to the traumatic event in which the person was injured one or more times from an external cause (e.g., a fall, a motor vehicle traffic accident). An injury condition is the acute condition or the physical harm caused by the traumatic event. Likewise, a poisoning episode refers to the event resulting from ingestion of or contact with harmful substances, as well as overdoses or wrong use of any drug or medication, while a poisoning condition is the acute condition or the physical harm caused by the event. Each episode must have at least one injury condition or poisoning classified according to the nature-of-injury codes 800–909.2, 909.4, 909.9, 910–994.9, 995.5–995.59, and 995.80–995.85 in the Ninth Revision of the International Classification of Diseases (ICD-9-CM). Poisoning episodes exclude food poisoning, sun poisoning, or poison ivy rashes.

National Safety Council definition of injury. A disabling injury is defined as one that results in death, some degree of permanent impairment, or renders the injured person unable to effectively perform their regular duties or activities for a full day beyond the day of the injury. This definition applies to all unintentional injuries. All injury totals labeled "disabling injuries" in *Injury Facts®* are based on this definition. Some rates in the Work section are based on OSHA definitions of recordable cases (see Glossary).

THE NATIONAL HEALTH INTERVIEW SURVEY, 2005 (CONT.)

Of the 33,202 injuries for which professional medical care was sought in 2005, over 40% were related to leisure or sports activities. Leisure and sports injuries accounted for 65% of all injury episodes among children under the age of 12 and about 80% of injury episodes among teenagers between the ages of 12 and 17 years.

The rate of injuries occurring during leisure activities was slightly higher for men (29.9 cases per 1,000 population) than for women (27.7 per 1,000 pop.). The rate of sports injuries among men (25.0 per 1,000 pop.) was more than twice the injury rate among women (12.2 per 1,000 pop.). The charts on this page illustrate these gender differences in terms of percentages and rates.

NUMBER OF INJURY EPISODES BY AGE AND ACTIVITY AT TIME OF INJURY, UNITED STATES, 2005

| | Total[a] | Activity at Time of Injury[b] (number in thousands) | | | | | | |
		Leisure Activities	Sports	Working Around House or Yard	Working at Paid Job	Driving[c]	Attending School	Other[d]
All Ages	**33,202**	**8,374**	**5,397**	**4,996**	**4,101**	**2,803**	**754**	**6,474**
Under 12 years	4,851	2,321	852	(e)	0	(e)	369[f]	871
12–17 years	4,238	783	2,641	(e)	(e)	224[f]	290[f]	254[f]
18–44 years	11,220	2,413	1,390	1,566	2,404	1,364	(e)	1,935
45–64 years	7,899	1,383	455	1,707	1,577	736	0	1,921
65–74 years	2,295	641	(e)	788	(e)	(e)	0	640
75 years and over	2,699	832	0	845	(e)	0	(e)	852

[a]Numbers and percents may not sum to respective totals due to rounding and unknowns.
[b]Activity at time of injury and poisoning episodes is based on the question, "What was [person] doing when the injury/poisoning happened?" Respondents could indicate up to two activities.
[c]Driving includes both drivers and passengers.
[d]"Other" includes unpaid work such as housework, shopping, volunteer work, sleeping, resting, eating, drinking, cooking, hands-on care from another person, and other unspecified activities.
[e]Estimate is not shown because it does not meet standard of reliability or precision.
[f]Figure does not meet standard of reliability or precision and should be used with caution.

PERCENT AND RATES OF INJURY EPISODES BY SEX AND ACTIVITY AT TIME OF INJURY, UNITED STATES, 2005

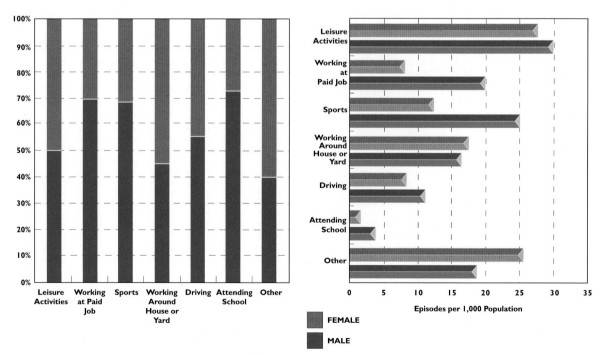

Source: Adams, P.F., Dey, A.N. & Vickerie, J.L. (2007, January). Summary health statistics for the U.S. population: National Health Interview Survey, 2005. Vital and Health Statistics, Series 10 (No. 233). Hyattsville, MD: National Center for Health Statistics.

There is a wealth of research demonstrating the role of socioeconomic status (SES) in the etiology of heart disease, lung disease, stroke, cancer, hypertension, and diabetes. In general, persons with the highest levels of income and education are healthier than those with median income and education, who, in turn, tend to be in better health than the poor and less educated[a].

Lower SES is known to contribute to increased rates of fatal injuries among children and adults. Although research provides some evidence of links between SES and nonfatal injuries, the results at present are inconsistent and depend in part on the study design, population, and context.

The National Health Interview Survey provides an opportunity to look at the occurrence of unintentional injuries in the U.S. population as a function of socioeconomic position using two SES measures—family income and education[b].

Although NHIS data indicate that all people are affected by injuries regardless of income or educational attainment, college graduates had the lowest medically consulted injury rate in 2005 followed by persons who had not graduated from high school. Persons with an incomplete college degree had the highest injury rate. The relationship between injury rates and family income followed a U-shaped curve with peaks among the very poor (less than $20,000) as well as persons with annual family incomes of at least $75,000.

[a]Banks, J., Marmot, M., Oldfield, Z., Smith, J.P. (2006). Disease and disadvantage in the United States and in England. Journal of American Medical Association, 295 (17); 2037–2045.
[b]Education data is shown for persons aged 25 years and older.

PERCENTAGES AND RATES OF MEDICALLY CONSULTED INJURIES BY LEVEL OF EDUCATION, UNITIED STATES, 2005

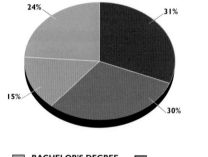

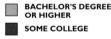

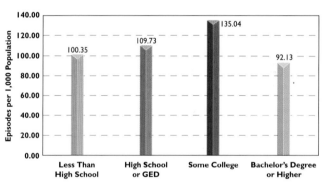

PERCENTAGES AND RATES OF MEDICALLY CONSULTED INJURIES BY FAMILY INCOME, UNITED STATES, 2005

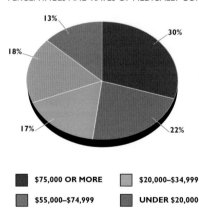

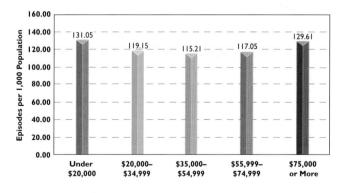

INJURY-RELATED HOSPITAL EMERGENCY DEPARTMENT VISITS, 2005
About 41.9 million visits to hospital emergency departments in 2005 were due to injuries.

About 36% of all hospital emergency department visits in the United States were injury related, according to information from the 2005 National Hospital Ambulatory Medical Care Survey conducted for the National Center for Health Statistics. There were approximately 115.3 million visits made to emergency departments, of which about 41.9 million were injury related. This resulted in an annual rate of about 39.6 emergency department visits per 100 persons, of which about 14.4 visits per 100 persons were injury related.

Males had a higher rate of injury-related visits than females. For males, about 15.8 visits per 100 males were recorded; for females the rate was 13.0 per 100 females. Those aged 15 to 24 had the highest rate of injury-related visits for males, while those aged 75 and over had the highest rate for females.

Falls and motor-vehicle accidents were the leading causes of injury-related emergency department visits,

accounting for 21% and 10% of the total, respectively. In total, about 8.7 million visits to emergency departments were made in 2005 due to accidental falls, and about 4.6 million were made due to motor-vehicle accidents. The next leading types were struck against or struck accidentally by objects or persons with 3.3 million visits (8% of the total), and accidents caused by cutting or piercing instruments, which accounted for about 2.5 million visits (6% of the total).

Black or African American persons had higher rates of injury-related visits to emergency departments than did whites for every age group. The difference varied from a high of 8.9 injuries per 100 population in the 25- to 44-year-old age group to a low of 0.6 injuries per 100 population for those in the 75-years-and-over age group.

NUMBER AND PERCENT DISTRIBUTION OF EMERGENCY DEPARTMENT VISITS BY CAUSE OF INJURY, UNITED STATES, 2005

Cause of Injury and E-code[a]	Number of Visits (000)	Percent
All Injury-Related Visits	**41,937**	**100.0%**
Unintentional Injuries, E800–E869, E880–E929	**28,375**	**67.7**
Accidental Falls, E880.0–E886.9, E888	8,728	20.8
Total Motor-Vehicle Accidents, E810–E825 (.0–.5, .7–.9)	4,583	10.9
Motor-vehicle traffic, E810–E819	*4,241*	*10.1*
Motor-vehicle, nontraffic, E820–E825(.0–.5, .7–.9)	*342*	*0.8*
Striking Against or Struck Accidentally by Objects or Persons, E916–E917	3,327	7.9
Accidents Caused by Cutting or Piercing Instruments, E920	2,522	6.0
Accidents Due to Natural and Environmental Factors, E900–E909, E928.0–E928.2	2,033	4.8
Overexertion and Strenuous Movements, E927	1,821	4.3
Accidental Poisoning by Drugs, Medicinal Substances, Biologicals, Other Solid and Liquid Substances, Gases and Vapors, E850–E869	913	2.2
Foreign Body, E914–E915	912	2.2
Accidents Caused by Fire and Flames, Hot Substances or Object, Caustic or Corrosive Material, and Steam, E890–E899, E924	593	1.4
Caught Accidentally In or Between Objects, E918	433	1.0
Pedalcycle, Nontraffic and Other, E800–E807(.3), E820–E825(.6), E826.1, E826.9	405	1.0
Machinery, E919	278	0.7
Other Transportation, E800–E807(.0–.2, .8–.9), E826(.0, .2–.8), E827–E829, E831, E833–E845	127	0.3

Cause of Injury and E-code[a]	Number of Visits (000)	Percent
Suffocation, E911–E913	(b)	(b)
Other Mechanism,[c] E830, E832, E846–E848, E910, E921–E923, E925–E926, E928.3, E928.8, E929.0–E929.5	1,552	3.7
Mechanism Unspecified, E887, E928.9, E929.8, E929.9	(b)	(b)
Intentional Injuries, E950–E959, E960–E969, E970–E978, E990–E999	**2,198**	**5.2**
Assault, E960–E969	1,774	4.2
Unarmed Fight or Brawl and Striking by Blunt or Thrown Object, E960.0, E968.2	1,134	2.7
Assault by Cutting and Piercing Instrument, E966	138	0.3
Assault by Other and Unspecified Mechanism,[d] E960.1, E961–E964, E965.0–E965.9, E967–E968.1, E968.3–E969	473	1.1
Self-inflicted Injury, E950–E959	420	1.0
Poisoning by Solid or Liquid Substances, Gases or Vapors, E950–E952	284	0.7
Other and Unspecified Mechanism,[e] E954–E959	136	0.3
Injuries of Undetermined Intent, E980–E989	**269**	**0.6**
Adverse Effects of Medical Treatment, E870–E879, E930–E949	**1,837**	**4.4**
Medical and Surgical Complications, E870–E879	1,082	2.6
Adverse Drug Effects, E930–E949	755	1.8
Alcohol and/or Drug Abuse[f]	**1,799**	**4.3**
Other and Unknown[g]	**7,460**	**17.8**

Source: Nawar, E.W., Niska, R. W., & Jianmin, X. (2007). National Hospital Ambulatory Medical Care Survey: 2005 Emergency Department Summary (Advance Data, Number 386, June 29, 2007). Hyattsville, MD: National Center for Health Statistics.

Note: Sum of parts may not add to total due to rounding.

[a] Based on the International Classification of Diseases, 9th Revision, Clinical Modification (ICD-9-CM).
[b] Figure did not meet standard of reliability or precision.
[c] Includes drowning, firearms, and other mechanism.
[d] Includes assault by firearms and explosives, and other mechanism.
[e] Includes injury by cutting and piercing instrument, and other and unspecified mechanism.
[f] Alcohol and drug abuse are not contained in the "Supplementary Classification of External Causes of Injury and Poisoning," but are frequently recorded as a cause of injury or poisoning.
[g] Includes illegible and blank E-codes.

INJURY-RELATED HOSPITAL EMERGENCY DEPARTMENT VISITS, 2005 (CONT.)

RATE[a] OF INJURY-RELATED VISITS TO EMERGENCY DEPARTMENTS BY PATIENT AGE AND SEX, 2005

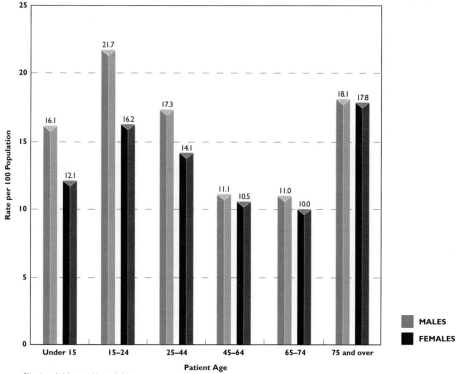

[a]Number of visits per 100 populations.

RATE[a] OF INJURY-RELATED VISITS TO EMERGENCY DEPARTMENTS BY PATIENT AGE AND RACE, 2005

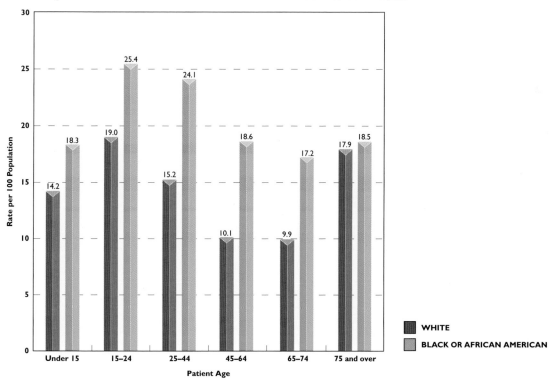

[a]Number of visits per 100 populations.

PRINCIPAL CLASSES BY STATE

The states listed below participate in the Injury Mortality Tabulations reporting system. Reports from these states are used to make current year estimates. See the Technical Appendix for more information.

The estimated Total number of unintentional-injury deaths for All Classes increased 2% in 2006 from the revised 2005 estimate. The number of unintentional-injury deaths in the Motor-Vehicle class was down 2%, while the number in the Work class remained

unchanged. The Home and Public Nonmotor-vehicle classes showed increases of 5% and 2%, respectively. The population death rate for the Motor-Vehicle class decreased 3% and the rate for the Work class remained unchanged. The rate for the Home class rose 4%, while the rates for the Total and Public Nonmotor-Vehicle classes each showed increases of 1% from 2005 to 2006.

PRINCIPAL CLASSES OF UNINTENTIONAL-INJURY DEATHS BY STATE, 2006

State	Total[a]		Motor-Vehicle[b]		Work[c]		Home		Public Nonmotor-Vehicle	
	Deaths	Rate[d]	Deaths	Rate[d]	Deaths	Rate[d]	Deaths	Rate[d]	Deaths	Rate[d]
Total U.S.	120,000	40.1	44,700	14.9	4,988	1.7	42,600	14.2	30,000	10.0
Florida	8,419	47.3	3,525	19.8	237	1.3	2,596	14.6	1,938	10.9
Idaho	708	49.5	293	20.5	39	2.7	216	15.1	169	11.8
Kansas	1,118	40.7	478	17.4	65	2.4	332	12.1	284	10.3
Missouri	3,129	53.9	1,218	21.0	108	1.9	1,118	19.3	720	12.4
Ohio	4,675	40.8	1,281	11.2	—	—	—	—	—	—
South Dakota	478	61.6	199	25.6	28	3.6	—	—	—	—
Virginia	2,370	31.3	810	10.7	67	0.9	759	10.0	324	4.3

Source: Provisional reports of vital statistics registrars; deaths are by place of occurrence. U.S. totals are National Safety Council estimates.
[a] The all-class total may not equal the sum of the separate class totals because Motor-Vehicle and other transportation deaths occurring to persons in the course of their employment are included in the Work death totals as well as the Motor-Vehicle and Public Nonmotor-Vehicle totals and also because unclassified deaths are included in the total.
[b] Differences between the figures given above and those on pages 170 and 171 are due in most cases to the inclusion of nontraffic deaths in this table.
[c] Work death totals may be too low where incomplete information on death certificates results in the deaths being included in the Public class. The Work totals may include some cases that are not compensable. For compensable cases only, see page 53.
[d] Deaths per 100,000 population.

RACE AND HISPANIC ORIGIN

The rank of unintentional-injuries as a cause of death varies with race and Hispanic origin. While ranking fifth overall (following heart disease, cancer, stroke, and chronic lower respiratory diseases), unintentional injuries rank third for Hispanics after heart disease and cancer.

By race, unintentional injuries rank fifth for whites and blacks, and fourth (after cancer, heart disease, and stroke) for Asians, Pacific Islanders, American Indians, and Alaskan Natives.

UNINTENTIONAL-INJURY DEATH RATES BY RACE, HISPANIC ORIGIN, AND SEX, UNITED STATES, 2004

| | | | | Hispanic Origin | | | | | |
| | Total | | | Non-Hispanic | | | Hispanic | | |
Race and Sex	Rank	Number	Rate	Rank	Number	Rate	Rank	Number	Rate
All Races	5	112,012	38.5	5	101,235	40.3	3	10,408	26.1
Males	3	72,050	50.4	3	63,982	52.3	3	7,796	37.8
Females	6	39,962	27.0	6	37,253	29.0	5	2,612	13.5
White	5	95,890	40.9	5	85,466	43.3	3	10,145	(b)
Males	3	61,267	52.9	3	53,465	55.3	3	7,597	(b)
Females	6	34,623	29.2	6	32,001	31.8	5	2,548	(b)
Black	5	12,670	34.2	5	12,446	35.0	3	154	(b)
Males	3	8,603	48.7	3	8,430	49.8	3	120	(b)
Females	6	4,067	20.9	6	4,016	21.5	5	34	(b)
Not White or Black[a]	4	3,452	17.7	4	3,323	18.5	3	109	(b)
Males	3	2,180	22.8	3	2,087	23.8	3	79	(b)
Females	4	1,272	12.8	4	1,236	13.4	4	30	(b)

Source: National Safety Council analysis of National Center for Health Statistics mortality data and Census Bureau population data.
Note: Rates are deaths per 100,000 population in each race/sex/Hispanic origin group. Total column includes 369 deaths for which Hispanic origin was not determined.
[a]Includes American Indian, Alaskan Native, Asian, Native Hawaiian and Pacific Islander.
[b]Race is not well reported for persons of Hispanic origin. Population death rates are unreliable.

LEADING CAUSES OF UNINTENTIONAL-INJURY DEATH BY RACE, HISPANIC ORIGIN, AND SEX, UNITED STATES, 2004

| | All Races | | | White | | | Black | | | Not White or Black[a] | | |
Cause of Death	Both	Male	Female	Both	Male	Female	Both	Male	Female	Both	Male	Female
Total	112,012	72,050	39,962	95,890	61,267	34,623	12,670	8,603	4,067	3,452	2,180	1,272
Motor Vehicle	44,933	30,837	14,096	37,618	25,816	11,802	5,513	3,910	1,603	1,802	1,111	691
Poisoning	20,950	13,934	7,016	18,042	12,022	6,020	2,498	1,638	860	410	274	136
Fall	18,807	9,856	8,951	17,383	8,988	8,395	999	628	371	425	240	185
Suffocation by inhalation or ingestion	4,470	2,264	2,206	3,867	1,955	1,912	517	262	255	86	47	39
Drowning	3,308	2,594	714	2,565	2,004	561	533	426	107	210	164	46
Fires, flames, smoke	3,229	1,902	1,327	2,334	1,375	959	799	475	324	96	52	44
Population (thousands)	290,850	143,058	147,792	234,241	115,843	118,398	37,082	17,663	19,419	19,527	9,552	9,975

| | Non-Hispanic | | | Hispanic | | | Unknown | | |
Cause of Death	Both	Male	Female	Both	Male	Female	Both	Male	Female
Total	101,235	63,982	37,253	10,408	7,796	2,612	369	272	97
Motor Vehicle	39,059	26,427	12,632	5,739	4,318	1,421	135	92	43
Poisoning	19,153	12,541	6,612	1,716	1,327	389	81	66	15
Fall	17,780	9,170	8,610	978	653	325	49	33	16
Suffocation by inhalation or ingestion	4,253	2,136	2,117	205	122	83	12	6	6
Drowning	2,856	2,220	636	427	355	72	25	19	6
Fires, flames, smoke	3,038	1,785	1,253	179	107	72	12	10	2
Population (thousands)	250,915	122,442	128,473	39,935	20,616	19,319	—	—	—

Source: National Safety Council analysis of National Center for Health Statistics mortality data.
Note: Dashes (—) indicate not applicable.
[a]Includes American Indian, Alaskan Native, Asian, Native Hawaiian and Pacific Islander.

Disasters are front page news even though the lives lost in the United States are relatively few when compared to the day-to-day life losses from unintentional injuries (see "While You Speak!" page 31). Listed below are the United States disasters, of which the National Safety Council is aware, that occurred in 2006 and took 5 or more lives.

In addition to the disasters listed in the table, there were 15 residential fires that claimed five or six lives each. There were also 46 motor-vehicle traffic crashes in 2006 that resulted in five or six deaths each.

DISASTER DEATHS, UNITED STATES, 2006

Type and Location	No. of Deaths	Date of Disaster
Major Disasters (25 or more deaths)		
Heat waves, U.S.	150	July 16–25
Commuter plane crash, Kentucky	49	August 27
Other Disasters (5–24 deaths)		
Tornadoes, Ark., Ind., Ill., Iowa., Ky., Ohio, Miss., and Tenn.	23	April 2
Storms and flooding, Northeast	16	June 22–28
Storms, Northwest	14	December 14–15
Storms and tornadoes, Midwest and South	13	October 22
Mine explosion, West Virginia	12	January 2
Tornadoes and storms, Tennessee	12	April 7–8
Storms and tornadoes, La., Ala., Miss., N.C., Md., Pa., and N.Y.	12	November 14–16
Blizzards, Colo., Kan., Neb., and Okla.	12	December 29
Residential fire, Nevada	12	October
Wildfire, Texas	12	March
Fire in group home, Missouri	11	November 29
Tornadoes, Southern Plains and Midwest	10	March 10–13
Storms and flooding, Kentucky	10	September 22
Motor-vehicle traffic crash, Arizona	10	August 7
Residential fire, Tennessee	9	March
Dam collapse, Hawaii	7	March 14
Residential fire, Oklahoma	7	July
Motor-vehicle traffic crash, Arizona	7	May 1
Motor-vehicle traffic crash, Florida	7	January 25
Tugboat, barge, and gas pipeline fire, Louisiana	6	October
Mine fire, Kentucky	5	May
Aircraft crash, Georgia	5	July
Wildfire, California	5	October

Source: National Climatic Data Center, infoplease.com, National Fire Protection Association, and National Highway Traffic Safety Administration.
Note: Some death totals are estimates and may differ among sources.

While you make a 10-minute safety speech, 2 persons will be killed and about 498 will suffer a disabling injury. Costs will amount to $12,400,000. On the average, there are 14 unintentional-injury deaths and about 2,990 disabling injuries every hour during the year.

Deaths and disabling injuries by class occurred in the nation at the following rates in 2006:

DEATHS AND DISABLING INJURIES BY CLASS, 2006

| Class | Severity | One Every— | Number per ... | | | 2004 Total |
			Hour	Day	Week	
All	**Deaths**	4 minutes	14	329	2,310	120,000
	Injuries	1 second	2,990	71,800	503,800	26,200,000
Motor-Vehicle	Deaths	12 minutes	5	122	860	44,700
	Injuries	13 seconds	270	6,600	46,200	2,400,000
Work	Deaths	105 minutes	1	14	100	4,988
	Injuries	9 seconds	420	10,100	71,200	3,700,000
Workers Off-the-Job	Deaths	10 minutes	6	146	1,020	53,200
	Injuries	3 seconds	1,070	25,800	180,800	9,400,000
Home	Deaths	12 minutes	5	117	820	42,600
	Injuries	3 seconds	1,160	27,900	196,200	10,200,000
Public Nonmotor-Vehicle	Deaths	18 minutes	3	82	580	30,000
	Injuries	3 seconds	1,140	27,400	192,300	10,000,000

Source: National Safety Council estimates.

DEATHS EVERY HOUR ...

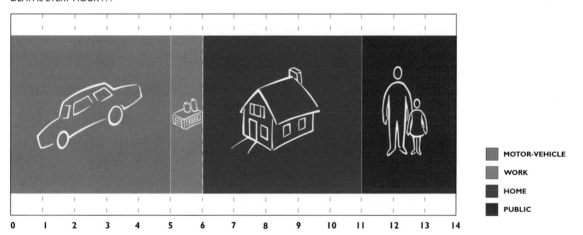

MOTOR-VEHICLE
WORK
HOME
PUBLIC

0 1 2 3 4 5 6 7 8 9 10 11 12 13 14

AN UNINTENTIONAL-INJURY DEATH EVERY FOUR MINUTES ...

Four Minutes

CHILDREN AND YOUTHS

Motor-vehicle crashes are the leading cause of injury deaths among children.

Unintentional injuries are a major public health concern affecting children and adolescents in the United States. They are the underlying cause of death in one out of five childhood mortality cases for persons aged 1–19 years, and 15 to 19 year olds account for more than half of the total.

Fatal injuries in the first year of life numbered 1,052 in 2004, or approximately 26 deaths per 100,000 population. Mechanical suffocation constituted the majority (63%) of all injury-related mortality cases for infants. Motor-vehicle crashes were the second leading cause of injury mortality. In addition, over 200 infant deaths that year were attributed to homicide (for more information on intentional injuries, see pages 150–155).

In the second year of life, the risk of fatal injury is reduced by half. In 2004, 535 fatal injury cases, or 13 deaths per 100,000 population, were recorded among one-year-old children. Unintentional drowning was the leading cause of injury death in this age group.

In the following three-year period (ages 2–4), the injury mortality rate drops even lower, averaging about 9 deaths per 100,000 population in 2004. Motor-vehicle

crashes were the number one cause of injury mortality followed by drowning and fires/burns/flames.

From the age of 5 to the late tween years (ages 12–14), the injury mortality rate shows a U-shaped pattern, reaching its lowest level at around the age of 8. Motor-vehicle crashes, unintentional drowning, and incidents related to fire, burns, and smoke were the leading causes of injury mortality for children aged 5–14 years in 2004.

Teenagers (15–19 years) make up 27% of the U.S. population between the ages of 1 and 19 and 60% of all injury mortality cases in that age group. Most importantly, three out of four teenage injury deaths are attributed to motor-vehicle crashes. Of the 6,800 injury deaths among teens in 2004, more than 5,200 occurred in crashes. That same year, the injury mortality rate for 18 to 19 year olds exceeded 43 deaths per 100,000 population.

For all children and adolescents under 19 years old, the injury mortality rate by age can be described as a J-shaped relationship, peaking during infancy and again in the late teenage years.

UNINTENTIONAL-INJURY DEATHS BY EVENT, AGE 0–19, UNITED STATES, 2004

| Age | Population (000) | Unintentional-Injury Deaths | | | | | | | | | | |
		Total	Rates[a]	Motor-vehicle	Falls	Poisoning	Drowning	Fires/ Flames	Choking[b]	Mechanical Suffocation	Firearms	All Other
<1 year	4,091	1,052	25.7	143	23	13	62	26	58	667	1	59
1–19 years	**77,481**	**11,132**	**14.4**	**7,512**	**171**	**716**	**1,003**	**544**	**131**	**175**	**142**	**738**
1 year	4,035	535	13.3	167	20	7	184	52	33	31	0	41
2 years	3,998	459	11.5	180	11	6	131	52	19	12	3	45
3 years	4,051	362	8.9	155	8	2	71	61	15	7	4	39
4 years	3,895	285	7.3	133	8	3	44	58	3	5	7	24
5 years	3,852	256	6.6	127	1	0	34	56	7	2	5	24
6 years	3,864	239	6.2	143	5	1	29	29	4	9	1	18
7 years	3,891	218	5.6	125	3	1	24	35	2	5	3	20
8 years	3,976	192	4.8	114	2	2	21	21	1	3	3	25
9 years	4,041	221	5.5	131	0	4	23	27	5	7	1	23
10 years	4,076	229	5.6	149	5	2	18	14	5	9	3	24
11 years	4,160	215	5.2	138	3	11	15	19	0	8	6	15
12 years	4,231	285	6.7	169	6	5	34	19	3	19	8	22
13 years	4,299	328	7.6	217	4	8	29	24	2	10	10	24
14 years	4,376	483	11.0	340	8	21	42	11	2	10	8	41
15 years	4,212	657	15.6	478	10	44	40	18	8	11	10	38
16 years	4,145	1,151	27.8	926	7	56	61	6	5	8	18	64
17 years	4,101	1,426	34.8	1,126	21	105	67	13	5	1	14	74
18 years	4,124	1,798	43.6	1,384	26	194	64	10	8	7	16	89
19 years	4,154	1,793	43.2	1,310	23	244	72	19	4	11	22	88
0–4 years	**20,070**	**2,693**	**13.4**	**778**	**70**	**31**	**492**	**249**	**128**	**722**	**15**	**208**
5–9 years	**19,624**	**1,126**	**5.7**	**640**	**11**	**8**	**131**	**168**	**19**	**26**	**13**	**110**
10–14 years	**21,142**	**1,540**	**7.3**	**1,013**	**26**	**47**	**138**	**87**	**12**	**56**	**35**	**126**
15–19 years	**20,736**	**6,825**	**32.9**	**5,224**	**87**	**643**	**304**	**66**	**30**	**38**	**80**	**353**

Source: National Safety Council tabulations of National Center for Health Statistics mortality data.
Note: Data does not include "age unknown" cases, which totaled 88 in 2004.
[a] Deaths per 100,000 population in each age group.
[b] Suffocation by inhalation or ingestion of food or other object.

ADULTS

Injury mortality rate increases with age.

Unintentional injuries cause significant mortality among adults in the United States. In 2004 alone, injuries were responsible for nearly 100,000 deaths among Americans age 20 and older.

The leading causes of injury mortality include falls, motor-vehicle crashes, poisoning, drowning, fires and burns, choking, and others. Motor-vehicle crashes (38.1%), poisoning (19.3%), and falls (17.5%), the three leading causes of injury mortality, combined to account for three-fourths of all fatal injuries sustained by adults over the age of 20 in 2004.

Age plays an important role in the occurrence of injuries. Motor-vehicle crashes, without a doubt, are the leading cause of injury mortality until about the age of 40, when the incidence of poisoning cases reaches its peak. Starting at around the age of 70, fall-related injuries become the leading cause of death in part as a consequence of driving cessation among older adults.

The highest fall mortality rates occur among adults age 75 and older, who are particularly prone to falls and fall-related injuries because of a high prevalence of

chronic illness and age-related physiologic changes that may adversely affect injury severity and, furthermore, increase the risk of complications and re-injury following an injury episode. Clinical studies demonstrate that after a serious trauma, elderly patients have higher in-hospital and long-term mortality than their younger counterparts even when other factors (e.g., injury severity, number of injuries, presence of other medical conditions, complications) are taken into consideration. At the same time, injury severity, number of injuries, and complications each independently correlates with increased injury mortality among the elderly.[a]

The increase in the incidence of fatal falls appears to be the driving force behind a surge in the overall injury mortality rate in later life. As the table below illustrates, the number of injury-related deaths per 100,000 population in 2004 increased from 50 for 70–74 year olds to 347 for 90-94 year olds—a seven-fold increase.

[a] Jacoby, S.F., Ackerson, T.H., & Richmond, T.S. (2006). Outcome from serious injury in older adults. Journal of Nursing Scholarship, 38 (2), 133–140.

UNINTENTIONAL-INJURY DEATHS BY EVENT, AGES 20 AND OLDER, UNITED STATES, 2004

Age	Population (000)	Unintentional-Injury Deaths											
		Total	Rates[a]	Motor-vehicle	Falls	Poisoning	Drowning	Fires/ Flames	Choking[b]	Mechanical Suffocation	Natural Heat/Cold	Firearms	All Other
20–24	20,957	8,624	41.2	5,763	154	1,616	270	120	38	47	23	92	501
25–29	19,539	6,771	34.7	3,849	151	1,747	220	131	37	37	21	58	520
30–34	20,467	6,261	30.6	3,187	169	1,894	165	109	51	55	23	42	566
35–39	21,047	7,319	34.8	3,190	241	2,694	198	142	59	67	51	44	633
40–44	23,050	9,152	39.7	3,473	418	3,750	237	171	113	76	64	53	797
45–49	22,121	9,426	42.6	3,422	567	3,696	240	252	152	71	85	41	900
50–54	19,498	7,516	38.5	2,854	617	2,337	204	238	183	62	75	65	881
55–59	16,487	5,408	32.8	2,293	669	1,111	152	205	187	32	70	25	664
60–64	12,589	4,243	33.7	1,800	724	466	119	207	199	25	49	10	644
65–69	9,960	3,819	38.3	1,547	885	240	105	183	207	24	48	20	560
70–74	8,520	4,297	50.4	1,427	1,370	181	83	166	331	18	51	20	650
75–79	7,422	5,900	79.5	1,683	2,246	175	76	214	523	20	69	15	879
80–84	5,559	7,557	135.9	1,497	3,436	140	82	245	748	17	63	13	1,316
85–89	3,077	6,780	220.3	887	3,447	107	51	163	672	20	61	5	1,367
90–94	1,344	4,666	347.2	319	2,433	49	23	81	529	4	57	3	1,168
95–99	367	1,709	465.7	57	934	9	3	22	211	2	11	0	460
100 and older	60	292	486.7	4	148	0	1	7	41	2	2	0	87
20 and older	212,064	99,740	47.0	37,252	18,609	20,212	2,229	2,656	4,281	579	823	506	12,593
25 and older	191,107	91,116	47.7	31,489	18,455	18,596	1,959	2,536	4,243	532	800	414	12,092
35 and older	151,101	78,084	51.7	24,453	18,135	14,955	1,574	2,296	4,155	440	756	314	11,006
45 and older	107,004	61,613	57.6	17,790	17,476	8,511	1,139	1,983	3,983	297	641	217	9,576
55 and older	65,385	44,671	68.3	11,514	16,292	2,478	695	1,493	3,648	164	481	111	7,795
65 and older	36,309	35,020	96.4	7,421	14,899	901	424	1,081	3,262	107	362	76	6,487
75 and older	17,829	26,904	150.9	4,447	12,644	480	236	732	2,724	65	263	36	5,277

Source: National Safety Council tabulations of National Center for Health Statistics mortality data.
Note: Data does not include "age unknown" cases, which totaled 88 in 2004.
[a] Deaths per 100,000 population in each age group.
[b] Suffocation by inhalation or ingestion of food or other object.

TRENDS IN UNINTENTIONAL-INJURY DEATH RATES

Age-adjusted rates, which eliminate the effect of shifts in the age distribution of the population, have decreased 57% from 1912 to 2006—from 100.4 to 39.8. The adjusted rates, which are shown in the graph on the opposite page, are standardized to the year 2000 standard U.S. population. The break in the lines at 1948 shows the estimated effect of changes in the International Classification of Diseases (ICD). The break in the lines at 1992 resulted from the adoption of the Bureau of Labor Statistics Census of Fatal Occupational Injuries for work-related deaths. Another change in the ICD in 1999 also affects the trends. See the Technical Appendix for comparability.

The table below shows the change in the age distribution of the population since 1910.

The age-adjusted death rate for all unintentional-injuries increased and decreased significantly several times during the period from 1910 to 1940. Since 1940, there were some setbacks, such as in the early 1960s, but the overall trend through the early 1990s was positive. The age-adjusted death rates for unintentional-injury deaths in the work and home classes declined fairly steadily since they became available in the late 1920s, although the home class rates have increased since the early 1990s. The rates in the public class declined for three decades, rose in the 1960s, and then continued declining until leveling in the 1990s and rising in recent years. The age-adjusted motor-vehicle death rate rose steadily from 1910 to the late 1930s as the automobile became more widely used. A sharp drop in use occurred during World War II and a sharp rise in rates occurred in the 1960s, with death rates reflecting economic cycles and a long-term downward trend since then.

UNITED STATES POPULATION, SELECTED YEARS

Year	All Ages	0–14	15–24	25–44	45–64	65 & Older
Number (in thousands)						
1910	91,973[a]	29,499	18,121	26,810	13,424	3,950
2000[b]	274,634	58,964	38,077	81,892	60,991	34,710
2006	299,398	60,755	42,435	84,083	74,865	37,260
Percent						
1910	100.0%	32.1%	19.7%	29.2%	14.6%	4.3%
2000[b]	100.0%	21.5%	13.9%	29.8%	22.2%	12.6%
2006	100.0%	20.3%	14.2%	28.1%	25.0%	12.4%

Source: For 1910: U.S. Bureau of the Census. (1960). Historical Statistics of the United States, Colonial Times to 1957. Series A 71-85. Washington, DC: U.S. Government Printing Office. For 2000: Anderson, R.N., & Rosenberg, H.M. (1998). Age standardization of death rates: Implementation of the year 2000 standard. National Vital Statistics Reports, 47(3), 13. For 2006: U.S. Census Bureau, Monthly Postcensal Resident Population, by Single Year of Age, Sex, Race, and Hispanic Origin. Retrieved June 28, 2007 from: www.census.gov/popest/national/asrh/2006_nat_res.html.
[a] Includes 169,000 persons with age unknown.
[b] This is the population used for standardization (age-adjustment) and differs slightly from the actual 2000 population, which totaled 275,306,000.

AGE-ADJUSTED DEATH RATES BY CLASS OF INJURY, UNITED STATES, 1910–2006

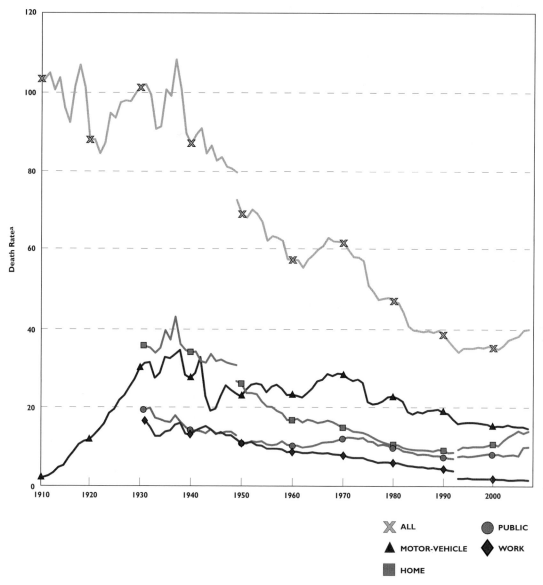

X ALL		● PUBLIC
▲ MOTOR-VEHICLE		◆ WORK
■ HOME		

ᵃDeaths per 100,000 population, adjusted to 2000 standard population. The break at 1948 shows the estimated effect of classification changes.
The break at 1992 is due to the adoption of the Bureau of Labor Statistics' Census of Fatal Occupational Injuries for work-related deaths.

PRINCIPAL CLASSES OF UNINTENTIONAL-INJURY DEATHS

PRINCIPAL CLASSES OF UNINTENTIONAL-INJURY DEATHS, UNITED STATES, 1903–2006

Year	Total[a] Deaths	Total[a] Rate[b]	Motor-Vehicle Deaths	Motor-Vehicle Rate[b]	Work Deaths	Work Rate[b]	Home Deaths	Home Rate[b]	Public Nonmotor-Vehicle Deaths	Public Nonmotor-Vehicle Rate[b]
1903	70,600	87.2	(c)	—	(c)	—	(c)	—	(c)	—
1904	71,500	86.6	(c)	—	(c)	—	(c)	—	(c)	—
1905	70,900	84.2	(c)	—	(c)	—	(c)	—	(c)	—
1906	80,000	93.2	400	0.5	(c)	—	(c)	—	(c)	—
1907	81,900	93.6	700	0.8	(c)	—	(c)	—	(c)	—
1908	72,300	81.2	800	0.9	(c)	—	(c)	—	(c)	—
1909	72,700	80.1	1,300	1.4	(c)	—	(c)	—	(c)	—
1910	77,900	84.4	1,900	2.0	(c)	—	(c)	—	(c)	—
1911	79,300	84.7	2,300	2.5	(c)	—	(c)	—	(c)	—
1912	78,400	82.5	3,100	3.3	(c)	—	(c)	—	(c)	—
1913	82,500	85.5	4,200	4.4	(c)	—	(c)	—	(c)	—
1914	77,000	78.6	4,700	4.8	(c)	—	(c)	—	(c)	—
1915	76,200	76.7	6,600	6.6	(c)	—	(c)	—	(c)	—
1916	84,800	84.1	8,200	8.1	(c)	—	(c)	—	(c)	—
1917	90,100	88.2	10,200	10.0	(c)	—	(c)	—	(c)	—
1918	85,100	82.1	10,700	10.3	(c)	—	(c)	—	(c)	—
1919	75,500	71.9	11,200	10.7	(c)	—	(c)	—	(c)	—
1920	75,900	71.2	12,500	11.7	(c)	—	(c)	—	(c)	—
1921	74,000	68.4	13,900	12.9	(c)	—	(c)	—	(c)	—
1922	76,300	69.4	15,300	13.9	(c)	—	(c)	—	(c)	—
1923	84,400	75.7	18,400	16.5	(c)	—	(c)	—	(c)	—
1924	85,600	75.6	19,400	17.1	(c)	—	(c)	—	(c)	—
1925	90,000	78.4	21,900	19.1	(c)	—	(c)	—	(c)	—
1926	91,700	78.7	23,400	20.1	(c)	—	(c)	—	(c)	—
1927	92,700	78.4	25,800	21.8	(c)	—	(c)	—	(c)	—
1928	95,000	79.3	28,000	23.4	19,000	15.8	30,000	24.9	21,000	17.4
1929	98,200	80.8	31,200	25.7	20,000	16.4	30,000	24.6	20,000	16.4
1930	99,100	80.5	32,900	26.7	19,000	15.4	30,000	24.4	20,000	16.3
1931	97,300	78.5	33,700	27.2	17,500	14.1	29,000	23.4	20,000	16.1
1932	89,000	71.3	29,500	23.6	15,000	12.0	29,000	23.2	18,000	14.4
1933	90,932	72.4	31,363	25.0	14,500	11.6	29,500	23.6	18,500	14.7
1934	100,977	79.9	36,101	28.6	16,000	12.7	34,000	26.9	18,000	14.2
1935	99,773	78.4	36,369	28.6	16,500	13.0	32,000	25.2	18,000	14.2
1936	110,052	85.9	38,089	29.7	18,500	14.5	37,000	28.9	19,500	15.2
1937	105,205	81.7	39,643	30.8	19,000	14.8	32,000	24.8	18,000	14.0
1938	93,805	72.3	32,582	25.1	16,000	12.3	31,000	23.9	17,000	13.1
1939	92,623	70.8	32,386	24.7	15,500	11.8	31,000	23.7	16,000	12.2
1940	96,885	73.4	34,501	26.1	17,000	12.9	31,500	23.9	16,500	12.5
1941	101,513	76.3	39,969	30.0	18,000	13.5	30,000	22.5	16,500	12.4
1942	95,889	71.6	28,309	21.1	18,000	13.4	30,500	22.8	16,000	12.0
1943	99,038	73.8	23,823	17.8	17,500	13.0	33,500	25.0	17,000	12.7
1944	95,237	71.7	24,282	18.3	16,000	12.0	32,500	24.5	16,000	12.0
1945	95,918	72.4	28,076	21.2	16,500	12.5	33,500	25.3	16,000	12.1
1946	98,033	70.0	33,411	23.9	16,500	11.8	33,000	23.6	17,500	12.5
1947	99,579	69.4	32,697	22.8	17,000	11.9	34,500	24.1	18,000	12.6
1948 (5th Rev.)[d]	98,001	67.1	32,259	22.1	16,000	11.0	35,000	24.0	17,000	11.6
1948 (6th Rev.)[d]	93,000	63.7	32,259	22.1	16,000	11.0	31,000	21.2	16,000	11.0
1949	90,106	60.6	31,701	21.3	15,000	10.1	31,000	20.9	15,000	10.1
1950	91,249	60.3	34,763	23.0	15,500	10.2	29,000	19.2	15,000	9.9
1951	95,871	62.5	36,996	24.1	16,000	10.4	30,000	19.6	16,000	10.4
1952	96,172	61.8	37,794	24.3	15,000	9.6	30,500	19.6	16,000	10.3
1953	95,032	60.1	37,955	24.0	15,000	9.5	29,000	18.3	16,500	10.4
1954	90,032	55.9	35,586	22.1	14,000	8.7	28,000	17.4	15,500	9.6
1955	93,443	56.9	38,426	23.4	14,200	8.6	28,500	17.3	15,500	9.4
1956	94,780	56.6	39,628	23.7	14,300	8.5	28,000	16.7	16,000	9.6
1957	95,307	55.9	38,702	22.7	14,200	8.3	28,000	16.4	17,500	10.3
1958	90,604	52.3	36,981	21.3	13,300	7.7	26,500	15.3	16,500	9.5
1959	92,080	52.2	37,910	21.5	13,800	7.8	27,000	15.3	16,500	9.3
1960	93,806	52.1	38,137	21.2	13,800	7.7	28,000	15.6	17,000	9.4
1961	92,249	50.4	38,091	20.8	13,500	7.4	27,000	14.8	16,500	9.0
1962	97,139	52.3	40,804	22.0	13,700	7.4	28,500	15.3	17,000	9.2
1963	100,669	53.4	43,564	23.1	14,200	7.5	28,500	15.1	17,500	9.3
1964	105,000	54.9	47,700	25.0	14,200	7.4	28,000	14.6	18,500	9.7
1965	108,004	55.8	49,163	25.4	14,100	7.3	28,500	14.7	19,500	10.1
1966	113,563	58.1	53,041	27.1	14,500	7.4	29,500	15.1	20,000	10.2
1967	113,169	57.3	52,924	26.8	14,200	7.2	29,000	14.7	20,500	10.4
1968	114,864	57.6	54,862	27.5	14,300	7.2	28,000	14.0	21,500	10.8
1969	116,385	57.8	55,791	27.7	14,300	7.1	27,500	13.7	22,500	11.2
1970	114,638	56.2	54,633	26.8	13,800	6.8	27,000	13.2	23,500	11.5
1971	113,439	54.8	54,381	26.3	13,700	6.6	26,500	12.8	23,500	11.4
1972	115,448	55.2	56,278	26.9	14,000	6.7	26,500	12.7	23,500	11.2
1973	115,821	54.8	55,511	26.3	14,300	6.8	26,500	12.5	24,500	11.6

See source and footnotes on page 37.

PRINCIPAL CLASSES OF UNINTENTIONAL-INJURY DEATHS, UNITED STATES, 1903–2006, Cont.

Year	Total[a] Deaths	Rate[b]	Motor-Vehicle Deaths	Rate[b]	Work Deaths	Rate[b]	Home Deaths	Rate[b]	Public Nonmotor-Vehicle Deaths	Rate[b]
1974	104,622	49.0	46,402	21.8	13,500	6.3	26,000	12.2	23,000	10.8
1975	103,030	47.8	45,853	21.3	13,000	6.0	25,000	11.6	23,000	10.6
1976	100,761	46.3	47,038	21.6	12,500	5.7	24,000	11.0	21,500	10.0
1977	103,202	47.0	49,510	22.5	12,900	5.9	23,200	10.6	22,200	10.1
1978	105,561	47.5	52,411	23.6	13,100	5.9	22,800	10.3	22,000	9.9
1979	105,312	46.9	53,524	23.8	13,000	5.8	22,500	10.0	21,000	9.4
1980	105,718	46.5	53,172	23.4	13,200	5.8	22,800	10.0	21,300	9.4
1981	100,704	43.9	51,385	22.4	12,500	5.4	21,700	9.5	19,800	8.6
1982	94,082	40.6	45,779	19.8	11,900	5.1	21,200	9.2	19,500	8.4
1983	92,488	39.6	44,452	19.0	11,700	5.0	21,200	9.1	19,400	8.3
1984	92,911	39.4	46,263	19.6	11,500	4.9	21,200	9.0	18,300	7.8
1985	93,457	39.3	45,901	19.3	11,500	4.8	21,600	9.1	18,800	7.9
1986	95,277	39.7	47,865	19.9	11,100	4.6	21,700	9.0	18,700	7.8
1987	95,020	39.2	48,290	19.9	11,300	4.7	21,400	8.8	18,400	7.6
1988	97,100	39.7	49,078	20.1	11,000	4.5	22,700	9.3	18,400	7.5
1989	95,028	38.5	47,575	19.3	10,900	4.4	22,500	9.1	18,200	7.4
1990	91,983	36.9	46,814	18.8	10,100	4.0	21,500	8.6	17,400	7.0
1991	89,347	35.4	43,536	17.3	9,800	3.9	22,100	8.8	17,600	7.0
1992	86,777	34.0	40,982	16.1	4,968[e]	1.9[e]	24,000[e]	9.4[e]	19,000[e]	7.4[e]
1993	90,523	35.1	41,893	16.3	5,035	2.0	26,100	10.1	19,700	7.6
1994	91,437	35.1	42,524	16.3	5,338	2.1	26,300	10.1	19,600	7.5
1995	93,320	35.5	43,363	16.5	5,018	1.9	27,200	10.3	20,100	7.6
1996	94,948	35.8	43,649	16.5	5,058	1.9	27,500	10.4	21,000	7.9
1997	95,644	35.7	43,458	16.2	5,162	1.9	27,700	10.3	21,700	8.1
1998	97,835	36.2	43,501	16.1	5,120	1.9	29,000	10.7	22,600	8.4
1999[f]	97,860	35.9	42,401	15.5	5,185	1.9	30,500	11.2	22,200	8.1
2000	97,900	35.6	43,354	15.7	5,022	1.8	29,200	10.6	22,700	8.2
2001	101,537	35.6	43,788	15.4	5,042	1.8	33,200	11.6	21,800	7.6
2002	106,742	37.1	45,380	15.8	4,726	1.6	36,400	12.6	22,500	7.8
2003	109,277	37.6	44,757	15.4	4,725	1.6	38,800	13.3	23,200	8.0
2004[g]	112,012	38.1	44,933	15.3	5,000	1.7	41,700	14.2	22,700	7.7
2005[g]	118,000	39.8	45,500	15.3	4,986	1.7	40,600	13.7	29,400	9.9
2006[h]	120,000	40.1	44,700	14.9	4,988	1.7	42,600	14.2	30,000	10.0
Changes										
1996 to 2006	+26%	+12%	+2%	−10%	−1%	−11%	+55%	+37%	+43%	+27%
2005 to 2006	+2%	+1%	−2%	−3%	0%	0%	+5%	+4%	+2%	+1%

Source: Total and motor-vehicle deaths, 1903–1932 based on National Center for Health Statistics death registration states; 1933-1948 (5th Rev.), 1949–1963, 1965–2004 are NCHS totals for the U.S. Work deaths for 1992–2006 are from the Bureau of Labor Statistics, Census of Fatal Occupational Injuries. All other figures are National Safety Council estimates.
[a] *Duplications between Motor-Vehicle, Work, and Home are eliminated in the Total column.*
[b] *Rates are deaths per 100,000 population.*
[c] *Data insufficient to estimate yearly totals.*
[d] *In 1948 a revision was made in the International Classification of Diseases. The first figures for 1948 are comparable with those for earlier years, the second with those for later years.*
[e] *Adoption of the Census of Fatal Occupational Injuries figure for the Work class necessitated adjustments to the Home and Public classes. See the Technical Appendix for details.*
[f] *In 1999 a revision was made in the International Classification of Diseases. See the Technical Appendix for comparability with earlier years.*
[g] *Revised.*
[h] *Preliminary.*

UNINTENTIONAL-INJURY DEATHS BY AGE

UNINTENTIONAL-INJURY DEATHS BY AGE, UNITED STATES, 1903–2006

Year	All Ages	Under 5 Years	5–14 Years	15–24 Years	25–44 Years	45–64 Years	65–74 Years	75 Years & Over[a]
1903	70,600	9,400	8,200	10,300	20,100	12,600	10,000	
1904	71,500	9,700	9,000	10,500	19,900	12,500	9,900	
1905	70,900	9,800	8,400	10,600	19,600	12,600	9,900	
1906	80,000	10,000	8,400	13,000	24,000	13,600	11,000	
1907	81,900	10,500	8,300	13,400	24,900	14,700	10,100	
1908	72,300	10,100	7,600	11,300	20,500	13,100	9,700	
1909	72,700	9,900	7,400	10,700	21,000	13,300	10,400	
1910	77,900	9,900	7,400	11,900	23,600	14,100	11,000	
1911	79,300	11,000	7,500	11,400	22,400	15,100	11,900	
1912	78,400	10,600	7,900	11,500	22,200	14,700	11,500	
1913	82,500	9,800	7,400	12,200	24,500	16,500	12,100	
1914	77,000	10,600	7,900	11,000	21,400	14,300	11,800	
1915	76,200	10,300	8,200	10,800	20,500	14,300	12,100	
1916	84,800	11,600	9,100	7,700	24,900	17,800	13,700	
1917	90,100	11,600	9,700	11,700	24,400	18,500	14,200	
1918	85,100	10,600	10,100	10,600	21,900	17,700	14,200	
1919	75,500	10,100	10,000	10,200	18,600	13,800	12,800	
1920	75,900	10,200	9,900	10,400	18,100	13,900	13,400	
1921	74,000	9,600	9,500	9,800	18,000	13,900	13,200	
1922	76,300	9,700	9,500	10,000	18,700	14,500	13,900	
1923	84,400	9,900	9,800	11,000	21,500	16,900	15,300	
1924	85,600	10,200	9,900	11,900	20,900	16,800	15,900	
1925	90,000	9,700	10,000	12,400	22,200	18,700	17,000	
1926	91,700	9,500	9,900	12,600	22,700	19,200	17,800	
1927	92,700	9,200	9,900	12,900	22,900	19,700	18,100	
1928	95,000	8,900	9,800	13,100	23,300	20,600	19,300	
1929	98,200	8,600	9,800	14,000	24,300	21,500	20,000	
1930	99,100	8,200	9,100	14,000	24,300	22,200	21,300	
1931	97,300	7,800	8,700	13,500	23,100	22,500	21,700	
1932	89,000	7,100	8,100	12,000	20,500	20,100	21,200	
1933	90,932	6,948	8,195	12,225	21,005	20,819	21,740	
1934	100,977	7,034	8,272	13,274	23,288	24,197	24,912	
1935	99,773	6,971	7,808	13,168	23,411	23,457	24,958	
1936	110,052	7,471	7,866	13,701	24,990	26,535	29,489	
1937	105,205	6,969	7,704	14,302	23,955	24,743	27,532	
1938	93,805	6,646	6,593	12,129	20,464	21,689	26,284	
1939	92,628	6,668	6,378	12,066	20,164	20,842	26,505	
1940	96,885	6,851	6,466	12,763	21,166	21,840	27,799	
1941	101,513	7,052	6,702	14,346	22,983	22,509	27,921	
1942	95,889	7,220	6,340	13,732	21,141	20,764	26,692	
1943	99,038	8,039	6,636	15,278	20,212	20,109	28,764	
1944	95,237	7,912	6,704	14,750	19,115	19,097	27,659	
1945	95,918	7,741	6,836	12,446	19,393	20,097	29,405	
1946	98,033	7,949	6,545	13,366	20,705	20,249	29,219	
1947	99,579	8,219	6,069	13,166	21,155	20,513	30,457	
1948 (5th Rev.)[b]	98,001	8,387	5,859	12,595	20,274	19,809	31,077	
1948 (6th Rev.)[b]	93,000	8,350	5,850	12,600	20,300	19,300	9,800	16,800
1949	90,106	8,469	5,539	11,522	19,432	18,302	9,924	16,918
1950	91,249	8,389	5,519	12,119	20,663	18,665	9,750	16,144
1951	95,871	8,769	5,892	12,366	22,363	19,610	10,218	16,653
1952	96,172	8,871	5,980	12,787	21,950	19,892	10,026	16,667
1953	95,032	8,678	6,136	12,837	21,422	19,479	9,927	16,553
1954	90,032	8,380	5,939	11,801	20,023	18,299	9,652	15,938
1955	93,443	8,099	6,099	12,742	29,911	19,199	9,929	16,464
1956	94,780	8,173	6,319	13,545	20,986	19,207	10,160	16,393
1957	95,307	8,423	6,454	12,973	20,949	19,495	10,076	16,937
1958	90,604	8,789	6,514	12,744	19,658	18,095	9,431	15,373
1959	92,080	8,748	6,511	13,269	19,666	18,937	9,475	15,474
1960	93,806	8,950	6,836	13,457	19,600	19,385	9,689	15,829
1961	92,249	8,622	6,717	13,431	19,273	19,134	9,452	15,620
1962	97,139	8,705	6,751	14,557	19,955	20,335	10,149	16,687
1963	100,669	8,688	6,962	15,889	20,529	21,262	10,194	17,145
1964	100,500	8,670	7,400	17,420	22,080	22,100	10,400	16,930
1965	108,004	8,586	7,391	18,688	22,228	22,900	10,430	17,781
1966	113,563	8,507	7,958	21,030	23,134	24,022	10,706	18,206
1967	113,169	7,825	7,874	21,645	23,255	23,826	10,645	18,099
1968	114,864	7,263	8,369	23,012	23,684	23,896	10,961	17,679
1969	116,385	6,973	8,186	24,668	24,410	24,192	10,643	17,313
1970	114,638	6,594	8,203	24,336	23,979	24,164	10,644	16,718
1971	113,439	6,496	8,143	24,733	23,535	23,240	10,494	16,798
1972	115,448	6,142	8,242	25,762	23,852	23,658	10,446	17,346
1973	115,821	6,037	8,102	26,550	24,750	23,059	10,243	17,080

See source and footnotes on page 39.

UNINTENTIONAL-INJURY DEATHS BY AGE, UNITED STATES, 1903–2006, Cont.

Year	All Ages	Under 5 Years	5–14 Years	15–24 Years	25–44 Years	45–64 Years	65–74 Years	75 Years & Over[a]
1974	104,622	5,335	7,037	24,200	22,547	20,334	9,323	15,846
1975	103,030	4,948	6,818	24,121	22,877	19,643	9,220	15,403
1976	100,761	4,692	6,308	24,316	22,399	19,000	8,823	15,223
1977	103,202	4,470	6,305	25,619	23,460	19,167	9,006	15,175
1978	105,561	4,766	6,118	26,622	25,024	18,774	9,072	15,185
1979	105,312	4,429	5,689	26,574	26,097	18,346	9,013	15,164
1980	105,718	4,479	5,224	26,206	26,722	18,140	8,997	15,950
1981	100,704	4,130	4,866	23,582	26,928	17,339	8,639	15,220
1982	94,082	4,108	4,504	21,306	25,135	15,907	8,224	14,898
1983	92,488	3,999	4,321	19,756	24,996	15,444	8,336	15,636
1984	92,911	3,652	4,198	19,801	25,498	15,273	8,424	16,065
1985	93,457	3,746	4,252	19,161	25,940	15,251	8,583	16,524
1986	95,277	3,843	4,226	19,975	27,201	14,733	8,499	16,800
1987	95,020	3,871	4,198	18,695	27,484	14,807	8,686	17,279
1988	97,100	3,794	4,215	18,507	28,279	15,177	8,971	18,157
1989	95,028	3,770	4,090	16,738	28,429	15,046	8,812	18,143
1990	91,983	3,496	3,650	16,241	27,663	14,607	8,405	17,921
1991	89,347	3,626	3,660	15,278	26,526	13,693	8,137	18,427
1992	86,777	3,286	3,388	13,662	25,808	13,882	8,165	18,586
1993	90,523	3,488	3,466	13,966	27,277	14,434	8,125	19,767
1994	91,437	3,406	3,508	13,898	27,012	15,200	8,279	20,134
1995	93,320	3,067	3,544	13,842	27,660	16,004	8,400	20,803
1996	94,948	2,951	3,433	13,809	27,092	16,717	8,780	22,166
1997	94,644	2,770	3,371	13,367	27,129	17,521	8,578	22,908
1998	97,835	2,689	3,254	13,349	27,172	18,286	8,892	24,193
1999[c]	97,860	2,743	3,091	13,656	27,121	18,924	8,208	24,117
2000	97,900	2,707	2,979	14,113	27,182	19,783	7,698	23,438
2001	101,537	2,690	2,836	14,411	27,784	21,002	7,835	24,979
2002	106,742	2,587	2,718	15,412	29,279	23,020	8,086	25,640
2003	109,277	2,662	2,618	15,272	29,307	25,007	8,081	26,330
2004[d]	112,012	2,693	2,666	15,449	29,503	26,593	8,116	26,992
2005[d]	118,000	2,600	2,500	15,700	31,400	28,500	8,600	28,700
2006[e]	120,000	2,500	2,400	15,900	31,700	29,600	8,700	29,200
Changes								
1996 to 2006	+26%	−15%	−30%	+15%	+17%	+77%	−1%	+32%
2005 to 2006	+2%	−4%	−4%	+1%	+1%	+4%	+1%	+2%

Source: 1903 to 1932 based on National Center for Health Statistics data for registration states; 1933–1948 (5th Rev.), 1949–1963, 1965–2004 are NCHS totals. All other figures are National Safety Council estimates. See Technical Appendix for comparability.
[a] Includes age unknown. In 2004, these deaths numbered 88.
[b] In 1948, a revision was made in the International Classification of Diseases. The first figures for 1948 are comparable with those for earlier years, the second with those for later years.
[c] In 1999, a revision was made in the International Classification of Diseases. See the Technical Appendix for comparability with earlier years.
[d] Revised.
[e] Preliminary.

UNINTENTIONAL-INJURY DEATH RATES BY AGE

UNINTENTIONAL-INJURY DEATH RATES[a] BY AGE, UNITED STATES, 1903–2006

Year	Standardized Rate[b]	All Ages	Under 5 Years	5–14 Years	15–24 Years	25–44 Years	45–64 Years	65–74 Years	75 Years & Over[c]
1903	99.4	87.2	98.7	46.8	65.0	87.4	111.7	299.8	
1904	103.4	86.6	99.1	50.9	64.9	84.6	108.1	290.0	
1905	98.4	84.2	98.6	47.0	64.1	81.4	106.2	282.5	
1906	114.2	93.2	99.1	46.5	77.1	97.3	111.7	306.0	
1907	112.4	93.6	102.7	45.5	78.0	98.8	117.8	274.2	
1908	99.7	81.2	97.5	41.2	64.4	79.5	102.2	256.7	
1909	97.4	80.1	94.2	39.6	59.9	79.6	101.0	268.2	
1910	103.0	84.4	92.8	39.1	65.3	87.3	104.0	276.0	
1911	104.7	84.7	101.9	39.3	62.1	81.4	108.7	292.1	
1912	100.4	82.5	97.1	40.5	62.3	79.2	103.2	275.8	
1913	103.5	85.5	88.4	37.4	65.2	85.6	112.5	281.7	
1914	95.9	78.6	94.3	38.9	58.5	73.2	94.6	268.1	
1915	92.1	76.7	90.8	39.7	57.3	69.0	92.1	268.8	
1916	101.4	84.1	101.4	43.3	40.8	82.5	112.1	297.6	
1917	106.7	88.2	108.4	45.3	62.1	79.8	113.8	301.3	
1918	101.2	82.1	91.0	46.5	58.7	72.2	106.3	294.2	
1919	87.7	71.9	87.2	45.9	55.3	60.1	81.8	262.0	
1920	87.8	71.2	87.4	44.9	55.5	56.9	85.6	289.5	
1921	84.3	68.4	80.8	42.4	51.4	55.5	79.4	259.8	
1922	86.9	69.4	80.6	41.5	51.4	57.1	81.4	265.1	
1923	94.5	75.7	82.0	42.4	55.6	64.5	92.6	282.8	
1924	93.3	75.6	82.9	42.4	58.6	61.7	90.2	283.5	
1925	97.2	78.4	78.6	42.3	59.7	64.7	97.8	293.9	
1926	97.7	78.7	77.9	41.4	59.9	65.4	98.2	298.7	
1927	97.5	78.4	75.9	41.0	60.2	65.2	98.0	295.4	
1928	99.6	79.3	74.4	40.4	59.9	65.6	99.9	306.2	
1929	101.2	80.8	73.3	40.0	63.1	67.7	102.1	308.9	
1930	101.8	80.5	71.8	36.9	62.3	67.0	102.9	317.9	
1931	99.2	78.5	69.9	35.2	59.7	63.0	102.1	313.3	
1932	90.5	71.3	65.1	32.8	52.7	55.6	89.3	296.9	
1933	91.1	72.4	65.5	33.4	53.6	56.3	90.8	295.3	
1934	100.5	79.9	68.1	33.9	57.8	61.8	103.3	328.5	
1935	97.9	78.4	68.5	32.2	56.9	61.6	98.0	319.8	
1936	108.1	85.9	74.4	32.9	58.8	65.3	108.6	367.4	
1937	100.7	81.7	69.6	32.7	60.9	62.1	99.3	333.4	
1938	89.4	72.3	65.3	28.5	51.3	52.5	85.4	308.9	
1939	86.7	70.8	62.9	28.2	50.7	51.2	81.0	300.0	
1940	89.1	73.4	64.8	28.8	53.5	53.2	83.4	305.7	
1941	90.7	76.3	65.0	29.7	60.9	57.2	84.8	297.4	
1942	84.3	71.6	63.9	27.9	59.8	52.4	77.1	275.5	
1943	86.3	73.8	66.9	29.0	69.7	50.3	73.6	287.8	
1944	82.5	71.7	63.2	29.1	72.9	48.9	68.9	268.6	
1945	83.4	72.4	59.8	29.5	64.5	50.5	71.6	277.6	
1946	81.0	70.0	60.2	28.1	61.7	48.8	70.9	267.9	
1947	80.5	69.4	57.4	25.8	59.6	49.0	70.6	270.7	
1948 (5th Rev.)[d]	79.5	67.1	56.3	24.6	56.8	46.2	66.8	267.4	
1948 (6th Rev.)[d]	72.5	63.7	56.0	24.5	56.8	46.2	65.1	122.4	464.3
1949	69.0	60.6	54.4	23.0	52.2	43.5	60.6	120.4	450.7
1950	68.1	60.3	51.4	22.6	55.0	45.6	60.5	115.8	414.7
1951	70.1	62.5	50.8	23.6	57.7	49.0	62.7	117.1	413.6
1952	69.0	61.8	51.5	22.5	60.9	47.7	62.7	111.1	399.8
1953	67.0	60.1	49.5	22.1	61.4	46.4	60.5	106.7	383.6
1954	62.2	55.9	46.7	20.5	56.4	43.0	55.9	100.7	354.4
1955	63.4	56.9	43.9	20.7	60.1	44.7	57.7	100.8	350.2
1956	63.0	56.6	43.3	20.2	63.3	44.7	56.7	100.6	335.6
1957	62.2	55.9	43.5	19.9	59.5	44.6	56.6	97.5	333.3
1958	57.5	52.3	44.5	19.6	56.2	42.0	51.7	89.3	292.6
1959	57.4	52.2	43.6	18.9	56.5	42.1	53.2	87.7	284.7
1960	57.3	52.1	44.0	19.1	55.6	42.0	53.6	87.6	281.4
1961	55.4	50.4	42.0	18.1	54.0	41.2	52.1	83.8	267.9
1962	57.5	52.3	42.6	18.0	55.0	42.7	54.6	88.5	277.7
1963	58.6	53.4	42.8	18.2	57.2	44.0	56.3	87.9	277.0
1964	60.0	54.9	43.1	19.1	59.9	47.3	57.6	88.9	263.9
1965	61.9	55.8	43.4	18.7	61.6	47.7	58.8	88.5	268.7
1966	63.0	58.1	44.4	19.9	66.9	49.6	60.7	89.8	267.4
1967	62.1	57.3	42.2	19.4	66.9	49.7	59.2	88.5	257.4
1968	62.0	57.6	40.6	20.5	69.2	50.1	58.5	90.2	244.0
1969	61.8	57.8	40.2	20.0	71.8	51.2	58.4	86.6	232.0
1970	59.8	56.2	38.4	20.1	68.0	49.8	57.6	85.2	219.6
1971	58.1	54.8	37.7	20.1	66.1	48.4	54.7	82.7	213.2
1972	58.0	55.2	35.9	20.6	67.6	47.5	55.2	80.8	214.2
1973	57.1	54.8	35.8	20.6	68.2	48.0	53.3	77.3	206.3

See source and footnotes on page 41.

UNINTENTIONAL-INJURY DEATHS BY AGE, UNITED STATES, 1903–2006, Cont.

Year	Standardized Rate[b]	All Ages	Under 5 Years	5–14 Years	15–24 Years	25–44 Years	45–64 Years	65–74 Years	75 Years & Over[c]
1974	50.9	49.0	32.4	18.2	60.9	42.7	46.7	68.7	186.7
1975	49.3	47.8	30.7	17.8	59.5	42.3	44.9	66.2	175.5
1976	47.3	46.3	30.0	16.7	58.9	40.3	43.2	62.0	168.4
1977	47.6	47.0	28.7	17.0	61.3	40.9	43.4	61.5	164.0
1978	47.8	47.5	30.3	16.9	63.1	42.3	42.4	60.5	159.7
1979	47.0	46.9	27.6	16.1	62.6	42.7	41.3	58.8	154.8
1980	46.5	46.5	27.2	15.0	61.7	42.3	40.8	57.5	158.6
1981	44.0	43.9	24.4	14.2	55.9	41.2	39.0	54.4	147.4
1982	40.6	40.6	23.8	13.2	51.2	37.3	35.8	50.9	140.0
1983	39.6	39.6	22.8	12.7	48.2	36.0	34.7	50.8	142.8
1984	39.4	39.4	20.6	12.4	48.9	35.7	34.3	50.7	142.8
1985	39.2	39.3	21.0	12.6	47.9	35.3	34.2	50.9	143.0
1986	39.4	39.7	21.4	12.6	50.5	36.1	33.0	49.6	141.5
1987	39.0	39.2	21.4	12.4	48.1	35.7	33.0	49.8	141.6
1988	39.5	39.7	20.9	12.3	48.5	36.1	33.4	50.9	145.3
1989	38.4	38.5	20.4	11.8	44.8	35.7	32.8	49.3	141.5
1990	36.8	36.9	18.5	10.4	44.0	34.2	31.6	46.4	136.5
1991	35.3	35.4	18.9	10.2	42.0	32.3	29.3	44.5	136.7
1992	34.0	34.0	16.8	9.3	37.8	31.3	28.7	44.2	134.5
1993	35.0	35.1	17.7	9.4	38.8	33.0	29.1	43.6	139.9
1994	35.0	35.1	17.3	9.4	38.4	32.5	29.9	44.3	139.2
1995	35.0	35.5	15.7	9.3	38.2	33.2	30.6	44.8	140.6
1996	35.3	35.8	15.3	8.9	38.1	32.3	31.1	47.0	145.9
1997	35.1	35.7	14.5	8.7	36.5	32.5	31.6	46.3	146.2
1998	35.5	36.2	14.2	8.3	35.9	32.6	31.9	48.3	151.1
1999[e]	35.2	35.9	14.5	7.8	36.1	32.7	32.0	45.0	147.7
2000	34.8	35.6	14.3	7.5	36.7	33.0	32.3	42.3	140.8
2001	35.7	35.6	13.9	6.9	36.1	32.7	32.6	42.8	146.8
2002	37.1	37.1	13.2	6.6	37.9	34.7	34.6	44.2	148.2
2003	37.6	37.6	13.5	6.4	37.0	34.8	36.4	44.0	149.6
2004[f]	38.1	38.1	13.4	6.5	37.1	35.1	37.6	43.9	151.4
2005[f]	39.6	39.8	12.8	6.2	37.3	37.4	39.1	46.5	158.2
2006[g]	39.8	40.1	12.2	5.9	37.5	37.7	39.5	46.0	159.2

Changes									
1996 to 2006		+12%	−20%	−34%	−2%	+17%	+27%	−2%	+9%
2005 to 2006		+1%	−5%	−5%	+1%	+1%	+1%	−1%	+1%

2006 Population (Millions)									
Total[h]		299.398	20.418	40.337	42.435	84.083	74.865	18.917	18.343
Male		147.512	10.442	20.640	21.845	42.415	36.514	8.670	6.987
Female		151.886	9.976	19.697	20.590	41.668	38.351	10.247	11.357

Source: All figures are National Safety Council estimates. See Technical Appendix for comparability.
[a] *Rates are deaths per 100,000 resident population in each age group.*
[b] *Adjusted to the year 2000 standard population to remove the influence of changes in age distribution between 1903 and 2006.*
[c] *Includes age unknown.*
[d] *In 1948, a revision was made in the International Classification of Diseases. The first figures for 1948 are comparable with those for earlier years, the second with those for later years.*
[e] *In 1999, a revision was made in the International Classification of Diseases. See the Technical Appendix for comparability.*
[f] *Revised.*
[g] *Preliminary.*
[h] *Sum of parts may not equal total due to rounding.*

PRINCIPAL TYPES OF UNINTENTIONAL-INJURY DEATHS

PRINCIPAL TYPES OF UNINTENTIONAL-INJURY DEATHS, UNITED STATES, 1903–1998

Year	Total	Motor-Vehicle	Falls	Drowning[a]	Fires/Burns[b]	Ingest. of Food/Object	Firearms	Poison (Solid, Liquid)	Poison (Gas, Vapor)	All Other
1903	70,600	(c)	(c)	9,200	(c)	(c)	2,500	(c)	(c)	58,900
1904	71,500	(c)	(c)	9,300	(c)	(c)	2,800	(c)	(c)	59,400
1905	70,900	(c)	(c)	9,300	(c)	(c)	2,000	(c)	(c)	59,600
1906	80,000	400	(c)	9,400	(c)	(c)	2,100	(c)	(c)	68,100
1907	81,900	700	(c)	9,000	(c)	(c)	1,700	(c)	(c)	70,500
1908	72,300	800	(c)	9,300	(c)	(c)	1,900	(c)	(c)	60,300
1909	72,700	1,300	(c)	8,500	(c)	(c)	1,600	(c)	(c)	61,300
1910	77,900	1,900	(c)	8,700	(c)	(c)	1,900	(c)	(c)	65,400
1911	79,300	2,300	(c)	9,000	(c)	(c)	2,100	(c)	(c)	65,900
1912	78,400	3,100	(c)	8,600	(c)	(c)	2,100	(c)	(c)	64,600
1913	82,500	4,200	15,100	10,300	8,900	(c)	2,400	3,200	(c)	38,400
1914	77,000	4,700	15,000	8,700	9,100	(c)	2,300	3,300	(c)	33,900
1915	76,200	6,600	15,000	8,600	8,400	(c)	2,100	2,800	(c)	32,700
1916	84,800	8,200	15,200	8,900	9,500	(c)	2,200	2,900	(c)	37,900
1917	90,100	10,200	15,200	7,600	10,800	(c)	2,300	2,800	(c)	41,200
1918	85,100	10,700	13,200	7,000	10,200	(c)	2,500	2,700	(c)	38,800
1919	75,500	11,200	11,900	9,100	9,100	(c)	2,800	3,100	(c)	28,300
1920	75,900	12,500	12,600	6,100	9,300	(c)	2,700	3,300	(c)	29,400
1921	74,000	13,900	12,300	7,800	7,500	(c)	2,800	2,900	(c)	26,800
1922	76,300	15,300	13,200	7,000	8,300	(c)	2,900	2,800	(c)	26,800
1923	84,400	18,400	14,100	6,800	9,100	(c)	2,900	2,800	2,700	27,600
1924	85,600	19,400	14,700	7,400	7,400	(c)	2,900	2,700	2,900	28,200
1925	90,000	21,900	15,500	7,300	8,600	(c)	2,800	2,700	2,800	28,400
1926	91,700	23,400	16,300	7,500	8,800	(c)	2,800	2,600	3,200	27,100
1927	92,700	25,800	16,500	8,100	8,200	(c)	3,000	2,600	2,700	25,800
1928	95,000	28,000	17,000	8,600	8,400	(c)	2,900	2,800	2,800	24,500
1929	98,200	31,200	17,700	7,600	8,200	(c)	3,200	2,600	2,800	24,900
1930	99,100	32,900	18,100	7,500	8,100	(c)	3,200	2,600	2,500	24,200
1931	97,300	33,700	18,100	7,600	7,100	(c)	3,100	2,600	2,100	23,000
1932	89,000	29,500	18,600	7,500	7,100	(c)	3,000	2,200	2,100	19,000
1933	90,932	31,363	18,962	7,158	6,781	(c)	3,014	2,135	1,633	19,886
1934	100,977	36,101	20,725	7,077	7,456	(c)	3,033	2,148	1,643	22,794
1935	99,773	36,369	21,378	6,744	7,253	(c)	2,799	2,163	1,654	21,413
1936	110,052	38,089	23,562	6,659	7,939	(c)	2,817	2,177	1,665	27,144
1937	105,205	39,643	22,544	7,085	7,214	(c)	2,576	2,190	1,675	22,278
1938	93,805	32,582	23,239	6,881	6,491	(c)	2,726	2,077	1,428	18,381
1939	92,623	32,386	23,427	6,413	6,675	(c)	2,618	1,963	1,440	17,701
1940	96,885	34,501	23,356	6,202	7,521	(c)	2,375	1,847	1,583	19,500
1941	101,513	39,969	22,764	6,389	6,922	(c)	2,396	1,731	1,464	19,878
1942	95,889	28,309	22,632	6,696	7,901	(c)	2,678	1,607	1,741	24,325
1943	99,038	23,823	24,701	7,115	8,726	921	2,282	1,745	2,014	27,711
1944	95,237	24,282	22,989	6,511	8,372	896	2,392	1,993	1,860	25,942
1945	95,918	28,076	23,847	6,624	7,949	897	2,385	1,987	2,120	22,033
1946	98,033	33,411	23,109	6,442	7,843	1,076	2,801	1,961	1,821	19,569
1947	99,579	32,697	24,529	6,885	8,033	1,206	2,439	1,865	1,865	14,060
1948 (5th Rev.)[d]	98,001	32,259	24,836	6,428	7,743	1,315	2,191	1,753	2,045	19,611
1948 (6th Rev.)[d]	93,000	32,259	22,000	6,500	6,800	1,299	2,330	1,600	2,020	17,192
1949	90,106	31,701	22,308	6,684	5,982	1,341	2,326	1,634	1,617	16,513
1950	91,249	34,763	20,783	6,131	6,405	1,350	2,174	1,584	1,769	16,290
1951	95,871	36,996	21,376	6,489	6,788	1,456	2,247	1,497	1,627	17,395
1952	96,172	37,794	20,945	6,601	6,922	1,434	2,210	1,440	1,397	17,429
1953	95,032	37,955	20,631	6,770	6,579	1,603	2,277	1,391	1,223	16,603
1954	90,032	35,586	19,771	6,334	6,083	1,627	2,271	1,339	1,223	15,798
1955	93,443	38,426	20,192	6,344	6,352	1,608	2,120	1,431	1,163	15,807
1956	94,780	39,628	20,282	6,263	6,405	1,760	2,202	1,422	1,213	15,605
1957	95,307	38,702	20,545	6,613	6,269	2,043	2,369	1,390	1,143	16,233
1958	90,604	36,981	18,248	6,582e	7,291e	2,191e	2,172	1,429	1,187	14,523
1959	92,080	37,910	18,774	6,434	6,898	2,189	2,258	1,661	1,141	14,815
1960	93,806	38,137	19,023	6,529	7,645	2,397	2,334	1,679	1,253	14,809
1961	92,249	38,091	18,691	6,525	7,102	2,499	2,204	1,804	1,192	14,141
1962	97,139	40,804	19,589	6,439	7,534	1,813	2,092	1,833	1,376	15,659
1963	100,669	43,564	19,335	6,347	8,172	1,949	2,263	2,061	1,489	15,489
1964	105,000	47,700	18,941	6,709	7,379	1,865	2,275	2,100	1,360	16,571
1965	108,004	49,163	19,984	6,799	7,347	1,836	2,344	2,110	1,526	16,895
1966	113,563	53,041	20,066	7,084	8,084	1,831	2,558	2,283	1,648	16,968
1967	113,169	52,924	20,120	7,076	7,423	1,980	2,896	2,506	1,574	16,670
1968	114,864	54,862	18,651	7,372e	7,335	3,100e	2,394e	2,583	1,526	17,041
1969	116,385	55,791	17,827	7,699	7,163	3,712	2,309	2,967	1,549	16,368
1970	114,638	54,633	16,926	7,860	6,718	2,753	2,406	3,679	1,620	18,043
1971	113,439	54,381	16,755	7,396	6,776	2,877	2,360	3,710	1,646	17,538
1972	115,448	56,278	16,744	7,586	6,714	2,830	2,442	3,728	1,690	17,436
1973	115,821	55,511	16,506	8,725	6,503	3,013	2,618	3,683	1,652	17,610

See source and footnotes on page 43.

ALL UNINTENTIONAL INJURIES

PRINCIPAL TYPES OF UNINTENTIONAL-INJURY DEATHS, UNITED STATES, 1903–1998, Cont.

Year	Total	Motor-Vehicle	Falls	Drowning[a]	Fires/Burns[b]	Ingest. of Food/Object	Firearms	Poison (Solid, Liquid)	Poison (Gas, Vapor)	All Other
1974	104,622	46,402	16,339	7,876	6,236	2,991	2,513	4,016	1,518	16,731
1975	103,030	45,853	14,896	8,000	6,071	3,106	2,380	4,694	1,577	16,453
1976	100,761	47,038	14,136	6,827	6,338	3,033	2,059	4,161	1,569	15,600
1977	103,202	49,510	13,773	7,126	6,357	3,037	1,982	3,374	1,596	16,447
1978	105,561	52,411	13,690	7,026	6,163	3,063	1,806	3,035	1,737	16,630
1979	105,312	53,524	13,216	6,872	5,991	3,243	2,004	3,165	1,472	15,825
1980	105,718	53,172	13,294	7,257	5,822	3,249	1,955	3,089	1,242	16,638
1981	100,704	51,385	12,628	6,277	5,697	3,331	1,871	3,243	1,280	14,992
1982	94,082	45,779	12,077	6,351	5,210	3,254	1,756	3,474	1,259	14,922
1983	92,488	44,452	12,024	6,353	5,028	3,387	1,695	3,382	1,251	14,916
1984	92,911	46,263	11,937	5,388	5,010	3,541	1,668	3,808	1,103	14,193
1985	93,457	45,901	12,001	5,316	4,938	3,551	1,649	4,091	1,079	14,931
1986	95,277	47,865	11,444	5,700	4,835	3,692	1,452	4,731	1,009	14,549
1987	95,020	48,290	11,733	5,100	4,710	3,688	1,440	4,415	900	14,744
1988	97,100	49,078	12,096	4,966	4,965	3,805	1,501	5,353	873	14,463
1989	95,028	47,575	12,151	4,015	4,716	3,578	1,489	5,603	921	14,980
1990	91,983	46,814	12,313	4,685	4,175	3,303	1,416	5,055	748	13,474
1991	89,347	43,536	12,662	4,818	4,120	3,240	1,441	5,698	736	13,096
1992	86,777	40,982	12,646	3,542	3,958	3,182	1,409	6,449	633	13,976
1993	90,523	41,893	13,141	3,807	3,900	3,160	1,521	7,877	660	14,564
1994	91,437	42,524	13,450	3,942	3,986	3,065	1,356	8,309	685	14,120
1995	93,320	43,363	13,986	4,350	3,761	3,185	1,225	8,461	611	14,378
1996	94,948	43,649	14,986	3,959	3,741	3,206	1,134	8,872	638	14,763
1997	95,644	43,458	15,447	4,051	3,490	3,275	981	9,587	576	14,779
1998	97,835	43,501	16,274	4,406	3,255	3,515	866	10,255	546	15,217

PRINCIPAL TYPES OF UNINTENTIONAL-INJURY DEATHS, UNITED STATES, 1999–2006

Year	Total	Motor-Vehicle	Falls	Poisoning	Ingest. of Food/Object	Drowning[f]	Fires, Flames, Smoke[b]	Mechanical Suffocation	Firearms	All Other
1999[g]	97,860	42,401	13,162	12,186	3,885	3,529	3,348	1,618	824	16,907
2000	97,900	43,354	13,322	12,757	4,313	3,482	3,377	1,335	776	15,184
2001	101,537	43,788	15,019	14,078	4,185	3,281	3,309	1,370	802	15,705
2002	106,742	45,380	16,257	17,550	4,128	3,447	3,159	1,389	762	13,670
2003	109,277	44,757	17,229	19,457	4,272	3,306	3,369	1,309	730	14,850
2004[h]	112,012	44,933	18,807	20,950	4,470	3,308	3,229	1,421	649	14,245
2005[h]	118,000	45,500	20,800	23,200	4,900	3,600	2,700	1,300	630	15,370
2006[i]	120,000	44,700	21,200	25,300	4,100	3,800	2,800	1,100	680	16,320

Changes										
1996 to 2006	+26%	+2%	(j)	(j)	+28%	(j)	−25%	(j)	−40%	(j)
2005 to 2006	+2%	−2%	+2%	+9%	−16%	+6%	+4%	−15%	+8%	+6%

Source: National Center for Health Statistics and National Safety Council. See Technical Appendix for comparability.
[a] *Includes drowning in water transport accidents.*
[b] *Includes burns by fire, and deaths resulting from conflagration regardless of nature of injury.*
[c] *Comparable data not available.*
[d] *In 1948, a revision was made in the International Classification of Diseases. The first figures for 1948 are comparable with those for earlier years, the second with those for later years.*
[e] *Data are not comparable to previous years shown due to classification changes in 1958 and 1968.*
[f] *Excludes water transport drownings.*
[g] *In 1999, a revision was made in the International Classification of Diseases. See the Technical Appendix for comparability.*
[h] *Revised.*
[i] *Preliminary.*
[j] *Comparison not valid because of change in classifications (see footnote "g").*

UNINTENTIONAL-INJURY DEATH RATES[a] FOR PRINCIPAL TYPES, UNITED STATES, 1903–1998

Year	Total	Motor-Vehicle	Falls	Drowning[b]	Fires/Burns[c]	Ingest. of Food/Object	Firearms	Poison (Solid, Liquid)	Poison (Gas, Vapor)	All Other
1903	87.2	(d)	(d)	11.4	(d)	(d)	3.1	(d)	(d)	72.7
1904	86.6	(d)	(d)	11.3	(d)	(d)	3.4	(d)	(d)	71.9
1905	84.2	(d)	(d)	11.1	(d)	(d)	2.4	(d)	(d)	70.7
1906	93.2	0.5	(d)	11.0	(d)	(d)	2.4	(d)	(d)	79.3
1907	93.6	0.8	(d)	10.4	(d)	(d)	2.0	(d)	(d)	80.4
1908	81.2	0.9	(d)	10.5	(d)	(d)	2.1	(d)	(d)	67.7
1909	80.1	1.4	(d)	9.4	(d)	(d)	1.8	(d)	(d)	67.5
1910	84.4	2.0	(d)	9.4	(d)	(d)	2.1	(d)	(d)	70.9
1911	84.7	2.5	(d)	9.6	(d)	(d)	2.2	(d)	(d)	70.4
1912	82.5	3.3	(d)	9.0	(d)	(d)	2.2	(d)	(d)	68.0
1913	85.5	4.4	15.5	10.6	9.1	(d)	2.5	3.3	(d)	40.1
1914	78.6	4.8	15.1	8.8	9.1	(d)	2.3	3.3	(d)	35.2
1915	76.7	6.6	14.9	8.6	8.4	(d)	2.1	2.8	(d)	33.3
1916	84.1	8.1	14.9	8.7	9.3	(d)	2.2	2.8	(d)	38.1
1917	88.2	10.0	14.7	7.4	10.5	(d)	2.2	2.7	(d)	40.7
1918	82.1	10.3	12.8	6.8	9.9	(d)	2.4	2.6	(d)	37.3
1919	71.9	10.7	11.4	6.9	8.7	(d)	2.7	3.0	(d)	28.5
1920	71.2	11.7	11.8	5.7	8.7	(d)	2.5	3.1	(d)	27.7
1921	68.4	12.9	11.3	7.2	6.9	(d)	2.6	2.7	(d)	24.8
1922	69.4	13.9	12.0	6.4	7.5	(d)	2.6	2.5	(d)	24.5
1923	75.7	16.5	12.6	6.1	8.1	(d)	2.6	2.5	2.4	24.9
1924	75.6	17.1	12.9	6.5	8.4	(d)	2.5	2.4	2.5	23.3
1925	78.4	19.1	13.4	6.3	7.4	(d)	2.4	2.3	2.4	25.1
1926	78.7	20.1	13.9	6.4	7.5	(d)	2.4	2.2	2.7	23.5
1927	78.4	21.8	13.9	6.8	6.9	(d)	2.5	2.2	2.3	22.0
1928	79.3	23.4	14.1	7.1	7.0	(d)	2.4	2.3	2.3	20.7
1929	80.8	25.7	14.5	6.2	6.7	(d)	2.6	2.1	2.3	20.7
1930	80.5	26.7	14.7	6.1	6.6	(d)	2.6	2.1	2.0	19.7
1931	78.5	27.2	14.6	6.1	5.7	(d)	2.5	2.1	1.7	18.6
1932	71.3	23.6	14.9	6.0	5.7	(d)	2.4	1.8	1.7	15.2
1933	72.4	25.0	15.1	5.7	5.4	(d)	2.4	1.7	1.3	15.8
1934	79.9	28.6	16.4	5.6	5.9	(d)	2.4	1.7	1.3	18.0
1935	78.4	28.6	16.8	5.3	5.7	(d)	2.2	1.7	1.3	16.8
1936	85.9	29.7	18.4	5.2	6.2	(d)	2.2	1.7	1.3	21.2
1937	81.7	30.8	17.5	5.5	5.6	(d)	2.0	1.7	1.3	17.3
1938	72.3	25.1	17.9	5.3	5.0	(d)	2.1	1.6	1.1	14.2
1939	70.8	24.7	17.9	4.9	5.1	(d)	2.0	1.5	1.1	13.6
1940	73.4	26.1	17.7	4.7	5.7	(d)	1.8	1.4	1.2	14.8
1941	76.3	30.0	17.1	4.8	5.2	(d)	1.8	1.3	1.1	15.0
1942	71.6	21.1	16.9	5.0	5.9	(d)	2.0	1.2	1.3	18.2
1943	73.8	17.8	18.4	5.3	6.5	0.7	1.7	1.3	1.5	20.6
1944	71.7	18.3	17.3	4.9	6.3	0.7	1.8	1.5	1.4	19.5
1945	72.4	21.2	18.0	5.0	6.0	0.7	1.8	1.5	1.6	16.6
1946	70.0	23.9	16.5	4.6	5.6	0.8	2.0	1.4	1.3	13.9
1947	69.4	22.8	17.1	4.8	5.6	0.8	1.7	1.3	1.3	14.0
1948 (5th Rev.)[e]	67.1	22.1	17.0	4.4	5.3	0.9	1.5	1.2	1.4	13.3
1948 (6th Rev.)[e]	63.7	22.1	15.1	4.5	4.7	0.9	1.6	1.1	1.4	12.3
1949	60.6	21.3	15.0	4.5	4.0	0.9	1.6	1.1	1.1	11.1
1950	60.3	23.0	13.7	4.1	4.2	0.9	1.4	1.1	1.2	10.7
1951	62.5	24.1	13.9	4.2	4.4	1.0	1.5	1.0	1.1	11.3
1952	61.8	24.3	13.5	4.2	4.5	0.9	1.4	0.9	0.9	11.2
1953	60.1	24.0	13.0	4.3	4.2	1.0	1.4	0.9	0.8	10.2
1954	55.9	22.1	12.3	3.9	3.8	1.0	1.4	0.8	0.8	9.8
1955	56.9	23.4	12.3	3.9	3.9	1.0	1.3	0.9	0.7	9.5
1956	56.6	23.7	12.1	3.7	3.8	1.1	1.3	0.8	0.7	9.4
1957	55.9	22.7	12.1	3.9	3.7	1.2	1.4	0.8	0.7	9.4
1958	52.3	21.3	10.5	3.8[f]	4.2[f]	1.3[f]	1.3	0.8	0.7	8.4
1959	52.2	21.5	10.6	3.7	3.9	1.2	1.3	0.9	0.7	8.4
1960	52.1	21.2	10.6	3.6	4.3	1.3	1.3	0.9	0.7	8.2
1961	50.4	20.8	10.2	3.6	3.9	1.4	1.2	1.0	0.7	7.6
1962	52.3	22.0	10.5	3.5	4.1	1.0	1.1	1.0	0.7	8.4
1963	53.4	23.1	10.3	3.4	4.3	1.0	1.2	1.1	0.8	8.2
1964	54.9	25.0	9.9	3.5	3.9	1.0	1.2	1.1	0.7	8.4
1965	55.8	25.4	10.3	3.5	3.8	1.0	1.2	1.1	0.8	8.7
1966	58.1	27.1	10.3	3.6	4.8	0.9	1.3	1.2	0.8	8.1
1967	57.3	26.8	10.2	3.6	3.8	1.0	1.5	1.3	0.8	8.3
1968	57.6	27.5	9.4	3.7[f]	3.7[f]	1.6[f]	1.2[f]	1.3	0.8	8.4
1969	57.8	27.7	8.9	3.8	3.6	1.8	1.2	1.5	0.8	8.5
1970	56.2	26.8	8.3	3.9	3.3	1.4	1.2	1.8	0.8	8.7
1971	54.8	26.3	8.1	3.6	3.3	1.4	1.1	1.8	0.8	8.4
1972	55.2	26.9	8.0	3.6	3.2	1.4	1.2	1.8	0.8	8.3
1973	54.8	26.3	7.8	4.1	3.1	1.4	1.2	1.7	0.8	8.4

See source and footnotes on page 45.

UNINTENTIONAL-INJURY DEATH RATES[a] FOR PRINCIPAL TYPES, UNITED STATES, 1903–1998, Cont.

Year	Total	Motor-Vehicle	Falls	Drowning[b]	Fires/Burns[c]	Ingest. of Food/Object	Firearms	Poison (Solid, Liquid)	Poison (Gas, Vapor)	All Other
1974	49.0	21.8	7.7	3.7	2.9	1.4	1.2	1.8	0.7	7.8
1975	47.8	21.3	6.9	3.7	2.8	1.4	1.1	2.2	0.7	7.7
1976	46.3	21.6	6.5	3.1	2.9	1.4	0.9	1.9	0.7	7.3
1977	47.0	22.5	6.3	3.2	2.9	1.4	0.9	1.5	0.7	7.6
1978	47.5	23.6	6.2	3.2	2.8	1.4	0.8	1.4	0.8	7.3
1979	46.9	23.8	5.9	3.1	2.7	1.4	0.9	1.4	0.7	7.0
1980	46.5	23.4	5.9	3.2	2.6	1.4	0.9	1.4	0.5	7.2
1981	43.9	22.4	5.5	2.7	2.5	1.5	0.8	1.4	0.6	6.5
1982	40.6	19.8	5.2	2.7	2.2	1.4	0.8	1.5	0.5	6.5
1983	39.6	19.0	5.1	2.7	2.2	1.4	0.7	1.4	0.5	6.6
1984	39.4	19.6	5.1	2.3	2.1	1.5	0.7	1.6	0.5	6.0
1985	39.3	19.3	5.0	2.2	2.1	1.5	0.7	1.7	0.5	6.3
1986	39.7	19.9	4.8	2.4	2.0	1.5	0.6	2.0	0.4	6.1
1987	39.2	19.9	4.8	2.1	1.9	1.5	0.6	1.8	0.4	6.2
1988	39.7	20.1	4.9	2.0	2.0	1.6	0.6	2.2	0.4	5.9
1989	38.5	19.3	4.9	1.9	1.9	1.4	0.6	2.3	0.4	5.8
1990	36.9	18.8	4.9	1.9	1.7	1.3	0.6	2.0	0.3	5.4
1991	35.4	17.3	5.0	1.8	1.6	1.3	0.6	2.3	0.3	5.2
1992	34.0	16.1	5.0	1.4	1.6	1.2	0.6	2.5	0.2	5.4
1993	35.1	16.3	5.1	1.5	1.5	1.2	0.6	3.1	0.3	5.5
1994	35.1	16.3	5.2	1.5	1.5	1.2	0.5	3.2	0.3	5.4
1995	35.5	16.5	5.3	1.7	1.4	1.2	0.5	3.2	0.2	5.5
1996	35.8	16.5	5.6	1.5	1.4	1.2	0.4	3.3	0.2	5.7
1997	35.7	16.2	5.8	1.5	1.3	1.2	0.4	3.6	0.2	5.5
1998	36.2	16.1	6.0	1.6	1.2	1.3	0.3	3.8	0.2	5.7

UNINTENTIONAL-INJURY DEATH RATES[a] FOR PRINCIPAL TYPES, UNITED STATES, 1999–2006

Year	Total	Motor-Vehicle	Falls	Poisoning	Ingest. of Food/Object	Drowning[g]	Fires, Flames Smoke[c]	Mechanical Suffocation	Firearms	All Other
1999[h]	35.9	15.5	4.8	4.5	1.4	1.3	1.2	0.6	0.3	6.3
2000	35.6	15.7	4.8	4.6	1.6	1.3	1.2	0.5	0.3	5.5
2001	35.6	15.4	5.3	4.9	1.5	1.2	1.2	0.5	0.3	5.5
2002	37.1	15.8	5.6	6.4	1.4	1.2	1.1	0.5	0.3	4.7
2003	37.6	15.4	5.9	6.7	1.5	1.1	1.2	0.4	0.3	5.1
2004[i]	38.1	15.3	6.4	7.1	1.5	1.1	1.1	0.5	0.2	4.9
2005[i]	39.8	15.3	7.0	7.8	1.7	1.2	0.9	0.4	0.2	5.2
2006[j]	40.1	14.9	7.1	8.5	1.4	1.3	0.9	0.4	0.2	5.5
Changes										
1996 to 2006	+12%	−10%	(k)	(k)	+17%	(k)	−36%	(k)	−50%	(k)
2005 to 2006	+1%	−3%	+1%	+9%	−18%	+8%	0%	0%	0%	+6%

Source: National Safety Council estimates. See Technical Appendix for comparability.
[a] Deaths per 100,000 population.
[b] Includes drowning in water transport accidents.
[c] Includes burns by fire, and deaths resulting from conflagration regardless of nature of injury.
[d] Comparable data not available.
[e] In 1948, a revision was made in the International Classification of Diseases. The first figures for 1948 are comparable with those for earlier years, the second with those for later years.
[f] Data are not comparable to previous years shown due to classification changes in 1958 and 1968.
[g] Excludes water transport drownings.
[h] In 1999, a revision was made in the International Classification of Diseases. See the Technical Appendix for comparability.
[i] Revised.
[j] Preliminary.
[k] Comparison not valid because of change in classifications (see footnote "h").

NATIONAL SAFETY COUNCIL

INJURY FACTS®

WORK, 2006

Between 1912 and 2006, unintentional work deaths per 100,000 population were reduced 92% , from 21 to 1.7. In 1912, an estimated 18,000 to 21,000 workers' lives were lost. In 2005, in a work force nearly quadrupled in size and producing ten times the goods and services, there were only 4,988 accidental work deaths.

In addition to unintentional (accidental) fatal work injuries, 715 homicides and suicides occurred in the workplace in 2006. These intentional injuries are not included in the unintentional-injury data shown here.

The State Data section, which begins on page 158, shows fatal occupational injuries and nonfatal injury and illness incidence rates by state.

Unintentional-Injury Deaths **4,988**
Unintentional-Injury Deaths per 100,000 workers **3.4**
Disabling Unintentional Injuries **3,700,000**
Workers **145,607,000**
Costs .... **$164.7 billion**

UNINTENTIONAL INJURIES AT WORK BY INDUSTRY, UNITED STATES, 2006

Industry Division	Workers[a] (000)	Deaths[a]		Deaths per 100,000 Workers[a]		Disabling Injuries
		2006	Change from 2005	2006	Change from 2005	
All Industries[b]	**145,607**	**4,988**	**0%**	**3.4**	**-2%**	**3,700,000**
Agriculture[c]	2,155	626	−10%	28.7	−9%	80,000
Mining[c]	683	188	+22%	27.5	+11%	20,000
Construction	11,312	1,187	+2%	10.5	−3%	480,000
Manufacturing	16,297	417	+17%	2.6	+16%	450,000
Wholesale trade	4,550	206	+5%	4.5	+5%	120,000
Retail trade	16,673	186	−6%	1.1	−6%	460,000
Transportation & warehousing	5,112	781	−6%	15.3	-8%	270,000
Utilities	844	51	+82%	6.0	+80%	20,000
Information	3,374	59	+5%	1.7	0%	50,000
Financial activities	10,239	80	+21%	0.8	+18%	100,000
Professional & business services	14,475	400	−10%	2.8	−13%	200,000
Educational & health services	19,551	137	+12%	0.7	+8%	530,000
Leisure & hospitality	11,720	128	+12%	1.1	+11%	250,000
Other services[c]	7,053	138	−7%	2.0	−8%	120,000
Government	21,569	396	−2%	1.8	−2%	550,000

Source: Deaths from Bureau of Labor Statistics, Census of Fatal Occupational Injuries. All other figures are National Safety Council estimates based on data from the Bureau of Labor Statistics.
Note: The National Safety Council adopted the Bureau of Labor Statistics' Census of Fatal Occupational Injuries (CFOI), beginning with the 1992 data year, as the authoritative count of work-related deaths. See the Technical Appendix for additional information.
[a] Deaths include persons of all ages. Workers and death rates include persons 16 years and older.
[b] All Industries includes 8 deaths for which industry could not be determined.
[c] Agriculture includes forestry, fishing, and hunting. Mining includes oil and gas extraction. Other services excludes public administration.

OCCUPATIONAL UNINTENTIONAL-INJURY DEATHS AND DEATH RATES BY INDUSTRY, UNITED STATES, 2006

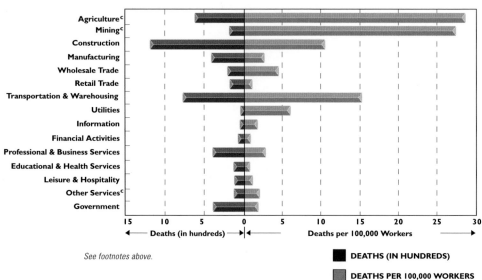

See footnotes above.

■ **DEATHS (IN HUNDREDS)**

▓ **DEATHS PER 100,000 WORKERS**

UNINTENTIONAL WORK-INJURY DEATHS AND DEATH RATES, UNITED STATES, 1992–2006

Year	Deaths	Workers (in thousands)	Death per 100,000 workers
1992	4,965	119,168	4.2
1993	5,034	120,778	4.2
1994	5,338	124,470	4.3
1995	5,015	126,248	4.0
1996	5,069	127,997	4.0
1997	5,160	130,810	3.9
1998	5,117	132,772	3.9
1999	5,184	134,688	3.8
2000	5,022	136,402	3.7
2001	5,042	136,246	3.7
2002	4,726	137,731	3.4
2003	4,725	138,988	3.4
2004[a]	4,995	140,504	3.6
2005[a]	4,984	142,946	3.5
2006[b]	4,988	145,607	3.4

Source: Deaths are from the Bureau of Labor Statistics, Census of Fatal Occupational Injuries. Employment is from the Bureau of Labor Statistics and is based on the Current Population Survey. All other data are National Safety Council estimates.
Note: Deaths include persons of all ages. Workers and death rates include persons 16 years and older. Workers are persons ages 16 and older gainfully employed, including owners, managers, other paid employees, the self-employed, unpaid family workers, and active duty resident military personnel. Because of adoption of the Census of Fatal Occupational Injuries, deaths and rates from 1992 to the present are not comparable to prior years. See the Technical Appendix for additional information.
[a] Revised.
[b] Preliminary.

WORKERS, UNINTENTIONAL-INJURY DEATHS, AND DEATH RATES, UNITED STATES, 1992–2006

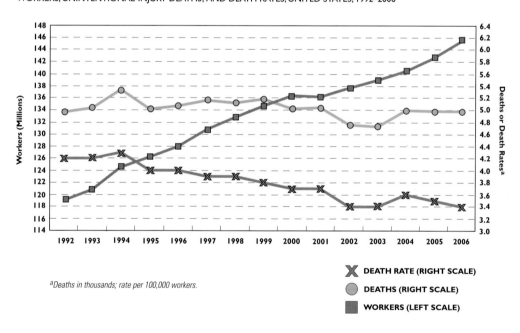

[a]Deaths in thousands; rate per 100,000 workers.

✕ DEATH RATE (RIGHT SCALE)

● DEATHS (RIGHT SCALE)

■ WORKERS (LEFT SCALE)

WORK, 2006 (CONT.)

OCCUPATIONAL-INJURY DEATHS AND DEATH RATES, UNITED STATES, 1992–2002

Year	Total	Homicide & Suicide	Unintentional								
			All Industries[a]	Agri-culture[b]	Mining, Quarrying[c]	Construc-tion	Manufac-turing	Transportation & Public Utilities	Trade[d]	Services[e]	Govern-ment
Deaths											
1992	6,217	1,252	4,965	779	175	889	707	767	415	601	586
1993	6,331	1,297	5,034	842	169	895	698	753	450	631	527
1994	6,632	1,294	5,338	814	177	1,000	734	819	492	676	534
1995	6,275	1,260	5,015	769	155	1,021	640	784	461	608	528
1996	6,202	1,133	5,069	762	151	1,025	660	883	451	615	321
1997	6,238	1,078	5,160	799	156	1,075	678	882	451	593	504
1998	6,055	938	5,117	808	143	1,136	631	830	443	634	465
1999	6,054	870	5,184	776	122	1,168	671	918	425	623	451
2000	5,920	898	5,022	693	153	1,114	624	872	447	643	460
2001	5,915	873[f]	5,042	714	169	1,183	546	844	431	636	507
2002	5,534	808	4,726	758	120	1,092	523	843	381	569	437
Deaths per 100,000 Workers											
1992	5.2	1.0	4.2	23.1	26.4	13.7	3.6	11.5	1.7	1.6	3.0
1993	5.2	1.0	4.2	26.0	25.3	13.3	3.6	11.0	1.8	1.6	2.6
1994	5.3	1.0	4.3	22.8	26.5	14.4	3.7	11.6	1.9	1.7	2.7
1995	4.9	1.0	4.0	21.4	24.8	14.3	3.1	11.0	1.8	1.5	2.7
1996	4.8	0.9	4.0	21.2	26.6	13.7	3.2	12.2	1.7	1.4	1.6
1997	4.8	0.8	3.9	22.5	24.7	13.7	3.3	11.6	1.7	1.3	2.6
1998	4.5	0.7	3.9	22.7	23.1	14.1	3.1	10.8	1.6	1.4	2.4
1999	4.5	0.6	3.8	22.6	21.7	13.8	3.4	11.5	1.5	1.3	2.2
2000	4.3	0.7	3.7	20.1	29.4	12.4	3.1	10.8	1.6	1.4	2.3
2001	4.3	0.6[f]	3.7	22.0	29.9	13.0	2.9	10.4	1.6	1.3	2.5
2002	4.0	0.6	3.4	21.8	23.3	11.9	2.9	10.5	1.4	1.1	2.1

Source: Deaths are from Bureau of Labor Statistics, Census of Fatal Occupational Injuries. Rates are National Safety Council estimates based on Bureau of Labor Statistics employment data. Deaths include persons of all ages. Death rates include persons 16 years and older. Industry divisions based on the Standard Industrial Classification Manual.
[a] Includes deaths with industry unknown.
[b] Agriculture includes forestry, fishing, and agricultural services.
[c] Mining includes oil and gas extraction.
[d] Trade includes wholesale and retail trade.
[e] Services includes finance, insurance, and real estate.
[f] Excludes 2,886 homicides of workers on September 11, 2001.

OCCUPATIONAL-INJURY DEATHS AND DEATH RATES, UNITED STATES, 2003–2006

Year	Total	Homicide & Suicide	Unintentional															
			All Industries[a]	Agriculture, Forestry, Fishing & Hunting	Mining	Construction	Manufacturing	Wholesale Trade	Retail Trade	Transportation & Warehousing	Utilities	Information	Financial Activities	Professional & Business Services	Educational & Health Services	Leisure & Hospitality	Other Services	Government
Deaths																		
2003	5,575	850	4,725	676	141	1,094	379	169	148	735	29	57	82	396	116	142	123	434
2004	5,764	769	4,995	651	151	1,203	421	187	189	779	49	49	68	401	123	144	144	432
2005[b]	5,734	750	4,984	697	154	1,161	357	197	198	831	28	56	66	442	122	114	149	404
2006[c]	5,703	719	4,988	626	188	1,187	417	206	186	781	51	59	80	400	137	128	138	396
Deaths per 100,000 Workers																		
2003	4.0	0.6	3.4	30.0	26.9	11.4	2.3	3.8	0.9	16.0	3.3	1.6	0.9	2.9	0.6	1.3	1.8	2.1
2004	4.1	0.5	3.6	29.7	28.1	11.7	2.6	4.1	1.2	16.7	5.9	1.5	0.7	2.9	0.7	1.3	2.1	2.0
2005[b]	4.0	0.5	3.5	31.7	24.8	10.8	2.2	4.3	1.2	16.7	3.4	1.7	0.7	3.2	0.6	1.0	2.1	1.9
2006[c]	3.9	0.5	3.4	28.7	27.5	10.5	2.6	4.5	1.1	15.3	6.0	1.7	0.8	2.8	0.7	1.1	2.0	1.8

Source: Deaths are from Bureau of Labor Statistics, Census of Fatal Occupational Injuries. Rates are National Safety Council estimates based on Bureau of Labor Statistics employment data. Deaths include persons of all ages. Death rates include persons 16 years and older. Industry divisions based on the North American Industry Classification System.
[a] Includes deaths with industry unknown.
[b] Revised.
[c] Preliminary.

WORK INJURY COSTS

The true cost to the nation, to employers, and to individuals of work-related deaths and injuries is much greater than the cost of workers' compensation insurance alone. The figures presented below show the National Safety Council's estimates of the total economic costs of occupational deaths and injuries. Cost estimating procedures were revised for the 1993 edition of *Accident Facts®* and additional revisions were made for the 2005–2006 edition. For this reason, **costs should not be compared to prior years.**

TOTAL COST IN 2006 . . . . **$164.7 billion**

Includes wage and productivity losses of $78.5 billion, medical costs of $30.1 billion, and administrative expenses of $42.4 billion. Includes employers' uninsured costs of $9.4 billion such as the money value of time lost by workers other than those with disabling injuries, who are directly or indirectly involved in injuries, and the cost of time required to investigate injuries, write up injury reports, etc. Also includes damage to motor vehicles in work injuries of $1.7 billion and fire losses of $2.6 billion.

Cost per Worker **$1,100**
This figure indicates the value of goods or services each worker must produce to offset the cost of work injuries. It is *not* the average cost of a work injury.

Cost per Death **$1,240,000**
Cost per Disabling Injury **$39,000**

These figures include estimates of wage losses, medical expenses, administrative expenses, and employer costs, and exclude property damage costs except to motor-vehicles.

TIME LOST BECAUSE OF WORK INJURIES

DAYS LOST

TOTAL TIME LOST IN 2006 . . . . **120,000,000**
Due to Injuries in 2006 . . . . **80,000,000**
Includes primarily the actual time lost during the year from disabling injuries, except that it does not include time lost on the day of the injury or time required for further medical treatment or check-up following the injured person's return to work.

Fatalities are included at an average loss of 150 days per case, and permanent impairments are included at actual days lost plus an allowance for lost efficiency resulting from the impairment.

Not included is time lost by persons with nondisabling injuries or other persons directly or indirectly involved in the incidents.

DAYS LOST

Due to Injuries in Prior Years **40,000,000**
This is an indicator of the productive time lost in 2006 due to permanently disabling injuries that occurred in prior years.

DAYS LOST

TIME LOSS IN FUTURE YEARS
FROM 2006 INJURIES **65,000,000**
Includes time lost in future years due to on-the-job deaths and permanently disabling injuries that occurred in 2006.

WORKER DEATHS AND INJURIES
ON AND OFF THE JOB

Nine out of 10 deaths and more than two thirds of the disabling injuries suffered by workers in 2006 occurred off the job. The ratios of off-the-job deaths and injuries to on-the-job were 10.7 to 1 and 2.2 to 1, respectively.

Production time lost due to off-the-job injuries totaled about 225,000,000 days in 2006, compared with 80,000,000 days lost by workers injured on the job.

Production time lost in future years due to off-the-job injuries in 2006 will total an estimated 515,000,000 days, nearly eight times the 65,000,000 days lost in future years from 2006's on-the-job injuries.

Off-the-job injuries to workers cost the nation at least $240.3 billion in 2006 compared to $164.7 billion for on-the-job injuries.

WORKERS' ON- AND OFF-THE-JOB INJURIES, UNITED STATES, 2006

	Deaths		Disabling Injuries	
Place	Number	Rate[a]	Number	Rate[a]
On- and off-the-job	**58,188**	**0.014**	**13,100,000**	**3.1**
On-the-job	4,988	0.003	3,700,000	2.4
Off-the-job	53,200	0.019	9,400,000	3.4
Motor-vehicle	*24,000*	*0.082*	*1,300,000*	*4.5*
Public nonmotor-vehicle	*11,000*	*0.024*	*3,700,000*	*8.2*
Home	*18,200*	*0.009*	*4,400,000*	*2.2*

Source: National Safety Council estimates. Procedures for allocating time spent on and off the job were revised for the 1990 edition. Rate basis changed to 200,000 hours for the 1998 edition. Death and injury rates are not comparable to rate estimates prior to the 1998 edition.
[a] Per 200,000 hours exposure by place.

WORKERS' ON- AND OFF-THE-JOB INJURIES, 2006

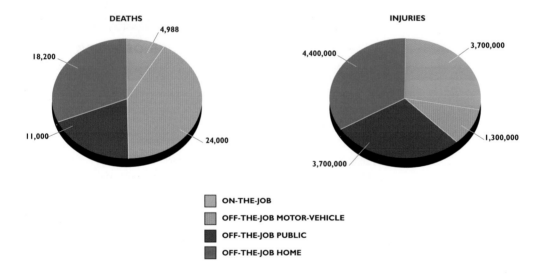

DEATHS

4,988

18,200

11,000

24,000

INJURIES

4,400,000

3,700,000

3,700,000

1,300,000

■ ON-THE-JOB
■ OFF-THE-JOB MOTOR-VEHICLE
■ OFF-THE-JOB PUBLIC
■ OFF-THE-JOB HOME

WORKERS' COMPENSATION CASES

According to the National Academy of Social Insurance, an estimated $55.3 billion, including benefits under deductible provisions, was paid out under workers' compensation in 2005 (the latest year for which data were available), a decrease of about 1.4% from 2004. Of this total, $29.1 billion was for income benefits and $26.2 billion was for medical and hospitalization costs. Private carriers paid about $28.1 billion of the total workers' compensation benefits in 2005. In 2005,

approximately 128.1 million workers were covered by workers' compensation—an increase of 1.8% from the 125.9 million in 2004.

The table below shows the trend in the number of compensated or reported cases in each reporting state. Due to the differences in population, industries, and coverage of compensation laws, comparison among states should not be made.

WORKERS' COMPENSATION CASES, 2004–2006

State	Deaths[a]			Cases[a]			2005 Compensation Paid ($000)
	2006	2005	2004	2006	2005	2004	
Alabama[b]	86	86	66	19,439	18,848	19,201	608,522
Colorado	—	108	111	—	29,282	29,231	896,430
Connecticut	58	66	70	53,582	53,786	56,362	713,275
Hawaii[c]	32	21	32	27,440	28,018	26,321	250,779
Indiana	100	129	100	60,333	67,174	68,576	609,596
Iowa[d]	52	49	52	17,429	18,514	19,219	473,724
Kansas[c]	52	54	59	68,882	65,723	66,336	383,283
Kentucky	29	33	—	33,633	36,986	—	705,802
Louisiana[c]	62	66	61	18,568	13,447	17,618	667,097
Maine[d]	15	12	14	5,168	5,772	6,168	268,936
Maryland	73	71	66	26,143	27,122	28,380	769,563
Michigan	80	—	81	31,944[e]	—	37,022	1,473,598
Minnesota[c]	44	53	59	—	126,042	124,866	945,888
Missouri	110[f]	126	146	134,615	145,475	141,381	1,050,889
Montana	23	22	17	29,596	33,042	31,976	239,498
Nebraska	24	43	48	49,844	52,755	53,597	298,366
Nevada[c]	47	71	55	78,625	82,864	86,653	394,373
New Hampshire	17	24	23	46,349	46,797	47,596	216,968
North Carolina	126	138	157	68,339	64,975	65,881	1,398,001
North Dakota[g]	19	13	18	21,588	19,887	19,184	82,282
Oregon[c,h]	37	31	45	23,373	22,114	22,325	550,878
Pennsylvania[b]	133	122	130	110,657	102,259	93,566	2,677,899
Rhode Island[b]	6	4	2	7,215	6,967	7,224	142,170
Virginia	164	169	135	86,997	97,121	113,045	853,877
Washington	—	—	—	193,699	193,526	192,715	1,864,015
Wisconsin[b]	162	199	143	43,327	45,906	47,264	1,188,459

Source: Deaths and Cases—State workers' compensation authorities for calendar or fiscal year. States not listed did not respond to the survey. Compensation Paid—Sengupta, I., Reno, V., P., & Burton, J. F., Jr., (August, 2007). Workers' compensation: benefits, coverage, and costs, 2005. Washington DC: National Academy of Social Insurance.

Note: Dash (—) indicates data not available.

Definitions:
Reported case—a reported case may or may not be work-related and may not receive compensation.
Compensated case—a case determined to be work-related and for which compensation was paid.

[a]Reported cases involving medical and indemnity benefits, unless otherwise noted.
[b]Reported cases involving indemnity benefits only.
[c]Closed or compensated cases only.
[d]Closed or compensated cases involving indemnity benefits only.
[e]Lost time claims over 7 days.
[f]Preliminary.
[g]Reported and closed or compensated cases.
[h]Includes all accepted disabling claims received and processed.

WORKERS' COMPENSATION CLAIMS COSTS, 2004–2005

Head injuries are the most costly workers' compensation claims.

The data in the graphs on this and the next page are from the National Council on Compensation Insurance's (NCCI) Detailed Claim Information (DCI) file, a stratified random sample of lost-time claims in 41 states. Total incurred costs consist of medical and indemnity payments plus case reserves on open claims, and are calculated as of the second report (18 months after the initial report of injury). Injuries that result in medical payments only, without lost time, are not included. For open claims, costs include all payments as of the second report plus case reserves for future payments. Because the estimates are based on a sample, they can be volatile from year to year due to the influence of a small but variable number of large claims.

The average cost for all claims combined in 2004–2005 was $20,953, up 8% from the 2003–2004 average of $19,382.

Cause of Injury. The most costly lost-time workers' compensation claims by cause of injury, according to the NCCI data, are for those resulting from motor-vehicle crashes. These injuries averaged $46,033 per workers' compensation claim filed in 2004 and 2005. The other cause with above average costs was fall or slip ($23,929).

Nature of Injury. The most costly lost-time workers' compensation claims by the nature of the injury are for those resulting from amputation. These injuries averaged $42,637 per workers' compensation claim filed in 2004 and 2005. The next highest costs were for injuries resulting in fracture ($29,250), and other trauma ($26,649).

Part of Body. The most costly lost-time workers' compensation claims are for those involving the head or central nervous system. These injuries averaged $46,898 per workers' compensation claim filed in 2004 and 2005. The next highest costs were for injuries involving multiple body parts ($37,069), and the neck ($30,208). Injuries to the arm/shoulder; hip, thigh, and pelvis; leg; and lower back also had above average costs.

AVERAGE TOTAL INCURRED COSTS PER CLAIM BY CAUSE OF INJURY, 2004–2005

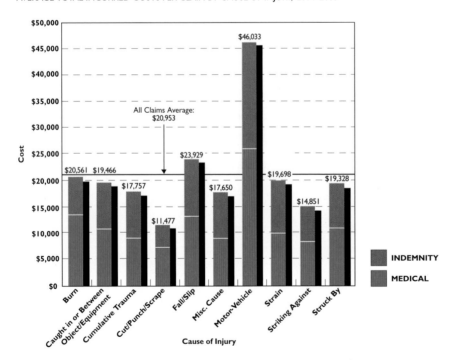

AVERAGE TOTAL INCURRED COSTS PER CLAIM BY NATURE OF INJURY, 2004–2005

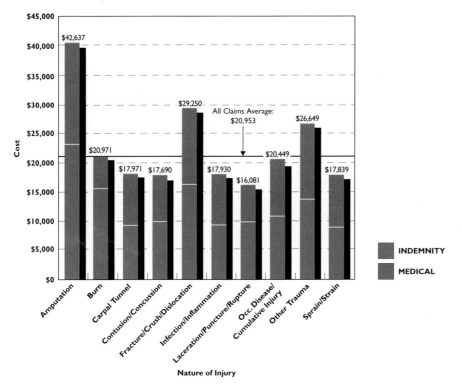

AVERAGE TOTAL INCURRED COSTS PER CLAIM BY PART OF BODY, 2004–2005

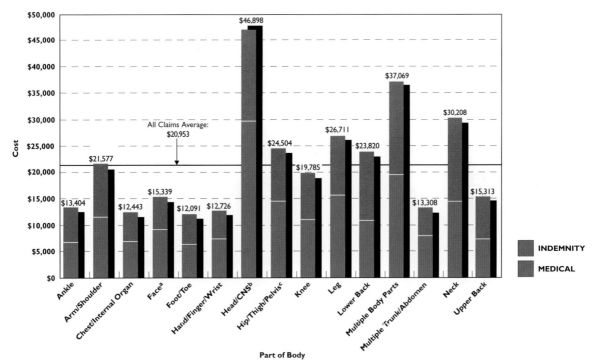

[a]Includes teeth, mouth, and eyes.
[b]Central nervous system.
[c]Includes sacrum and coccyx.
 Please note that these are estimates based on a sample of claims reported to NCCI and can be volatile from year to year due to the influence
 of a small but variable number of large claims.

CAUSES OF WORK-RELATED DEATHS AND INJURIES

Incidents involving motor-vehicles are the leading cause of work-related deaths followed by contacts with objects or equipment and assaults and violent acts. For nonfatal cases with days away from work, contact with objects or equipment is the leading cause followed by overexertion and falls.

WORK-RELATED DEATHS AND INJURIES BY EVENT OR EXPOSURE, UNITED STATES, 2005

Event or Exposure	Deaths[a]
Total, all events or exposures	**5,734**
Contact with object or equipment	1,005
Struck against object	8
Struck by object	607
Caught in objects or equipment	278
Caught in collapsing materials	109
Fall	770
Fall to lower level	664
Fall on same level	84
Bodily reaction and exertion	11
Exposure to harmful substance	501
Contact with electric current	251
Contact with temperature extremes	55
Exposure to caustic or noxious substances	136
Oxygen deficiency	59
Drowning	48
Choking on object or substance	8
Transportation accidents	2,493
Motor-vehicle accidents	2,168
Highway accident	1,437
Nonhighway accident except rail, air, water	340
Pedestrian struck by vehicle, mobile equipment	391
Railway accident	83
Water vehicle accident	88
Aircraft accident	149
Fires, explosions	159
Fires	93
Explosions	65
Assaults and violent acts	792
By person	567
Self-inflicted	180
By animals	42
Other and nonclassifiable	3

Event or Exposure	Cases With Days Away From Work[b]
Total, all events or exposures	**1,234,680**
Contact with object or equipment	338,080
Struck against object	85,500
Struck by object	167,730
Caught in object or equipment	54,600
Caught in collapsing material	360
Fall	255,750
Fall to lower level	79,310
Fall on same level	167,180
Bodily reaction and exertion	489,790
Bodily reaction	133,550
Bending, climbing, crawling, reaching, twisting	51,250
Slips, trips, loss of balance—without fall	36,150
Overexertion	298,130
Overexertion in lifting	159,970
Repetitive motion	43,790
Exposure to harmful substance	51,860
Contact with electric current	2,950
Contact with temperature extremes	18,830
Exposure to caustic or noxious substances	25,910
Transportation accidents	61,170
Highway accident	39,070
Nonhighway accident except rail, air, water	9,500
Pedestrian struck by vehicle, mobile equipment	9,760
Railway accident	280
Water vehicle accident	620
Aircraft accident	520
Fires, explosions	2,600
Fires	1,250
Explosions	1,340
Assaults and violent acts	21,470
By person	14,560
By animals	6,560
Other and nonclassifiable	13,960

Source: Bureau of Labor Statistics.
[a]Includes deaths among all workers.
[b]Includes cases with days away from work among private sector wage and salary workers. Excludes government employees, the self employed, and unpaid family workers.

DEATHS[a] BY EVENT OR EXPOSURE, UNITED STATES, 2005

- 0.2%
- 8.7%
- 13.4%
- 17.5%
- <0.1%
- 13.8%
- 2.8%
- 43.5%

CASES WITH DAYS AWAY FROM WORK[b] BY EVENT OR EXPOSURE, UNITED STATES, 2005

- 4.2%
- 5.0%
- 0.2%
- 1.7%
- 1.1%
- 39.7%
- 27.4%
- 20.7%

- BODILY REACTION AND EXERTION
- FALL
- CONTACT WITH OBJECT OR EQUIPMENT
- OTHER AND NONCLASSIFIABLE
- ASSAULTS AND VIOLENT ACTS
- FIRES, EXPLOSIONS
- TRANSPORTATION ACCIDENTS
- EXPOSURE TO HARMFUL SUBSTANCE

[a]Includes deaths among all workers.
[b]Includes cases with days away from work among private sector wage and salary workers. Excludes government employees, the self employed, and unpaid family workers.

PART OF BODY

According to the Bureau of Labor Statistics, the back was the body part most frequently affected in injuries involving days away from work in 2005, accounting for 22% of the total 1,234,680 injuries in private industry. Multiple-part injuries were the second most common, followed by finger, knee, and head injuries. Overall, the manufacturing, education and health services, and retail trade industry sectors had the highest number of injuries, combining to make up over 46% of the total.

NUMBER OF NONFATAL OCCUPATIONAL INJURIES AND ILLNESSES INVOLVING DAYS AWAY FROM WORK[a] BY PART OF BODY AFFECTED AND INDUSTRY SECTOR, PRIVATE INDUSTRY, UNITED STATES, 2005

Part of Body Affected	Private Sector[b,c,d]	Industry Sector								
		Manufac-turing	Education and Health Services	Retail Trade	Construc-tion	Trans. & Ware-housing	Leisure and Hospitality	Prof. and Business Services	Wholesale Trade	All Other Sectors[b,d]
Total[c]	1,234,680	209,130	186,400	175,880	157,070	117,440	93,900	91,840	80,170	122,850
Head	81,090	16,000	8,750	11,710	12,860	7,680	4,770	5,640	4,520	9,160
Eye	34,740	9,670	2,510	3,810	6,390	2,910	1,620	2,070	1,670	4,090
Neck	18,470	2,250	3,620	2,520	2,370	2,290	640	1,610	1,350	1,820
Trunk	428,500	68,380	78,330	61,710	48,420	46,520	27,300	29,270	31,350	37,220
Shoulder	77,800	15,150	12,000	11,260	7,980	9,960	4,920	5,060	5,430	6,040
Back	270,890	38,590	55,960	38,630	30,190	28,570	17,490	19,040	19,310	23,100
Upper extremities	284,750	68,110	29,060	40,330	37,580	16,880	29,920	19,610	15,940	27,320
Wrist	56,250	12,680	7,950	8,520	5,120	3,670	4,010	4,220	3,260	6,800
Hand, except finger	47,020	10,940	4,150	6,860	7,160	2,120	6,200	3,330	2,160	4,090
Finger	111,090	30,750	7,760	15,680	15,710	4,800	13,260	7,080	6,210	9,850
Lower extremities	271,740	37,760	35,730	40,700	39,200	28,690	19,630	21,640	19,680	28,710
Knee	100,560	13,380	15,390	15,480	12,630	10,420	7,740	7,430	7,540	10,560
Foot, except toe	43,840	7,550	4,290	7,150	7,000	4,580	2,550	3,250	3,210	4,260
Toe	12,880	2,180	1,320	2,660	1,590	1,220	680	1,070	890	1,270
Body systems	17,950	2,510	3,220	1,830	1,650	1,260	1,520	1,900	590	3,470
Multiple parts	120,960	12,910	26,380	15,650	13,690	13,280	8,200	10,450	6,390	14,020

Source: Bureau of Labor Statistics (2007). OSH and CFOI Profiles and Charts, 2005 (CD-ROM).

[a]*Days-away-from-work cases include those that result in days away from work with or without job transfer or restriction.*
[b]*Excludes farms with less than 11 employees.*
[c]*Data may not sum to row and column totals because of rounding and exclusion of nonclassifiable responses.*
[d]*Includes Agriculture, Forestry, Fishing and Hunting; Financial Activities; Information; Mining (including oil and gas extraction); Other Services (except Public Administration); and Utilities. Data for mining do not reflect the changes OSHA made to its recordkeeping requirements effective January 1, 2002; therefore, estimates for these industries are not comparable with estimates for other industries.*

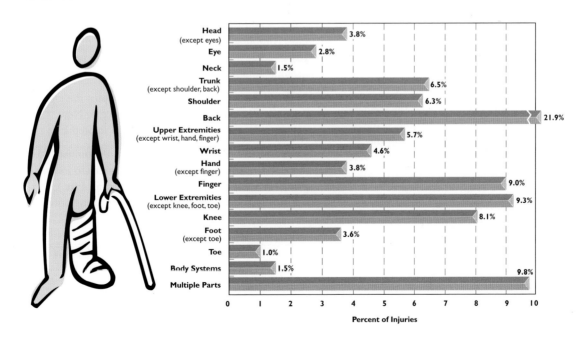

Safety professionals in business and industry often want to compare, or benchmark, the occupational injury and illness incidence rates of their establishments with the national average rates compiled by the U.S. Bureau of Labor Statistics (BLS) through its annual Survey of Occupational Injuries and Illnesses.[a] The incidence rates published on the following pages are for 2006 and were compiled under the revised OSHA record-keeping requirements that became effective in 2002.

Step 1.

The first step in benchmarking is to calculate the incidence rates for the establishment. The basic formula for computing incidence rates is $(N \times 200,000)/EH$, or, the number of cases (N) multiplied by $200,000$ then divided by the number of hours worked (EH) by all employees during the time period, where $200,000$ is the base for 100 full-time workers (working 40 hours per week, 50 weeks per year). Because the BLS rates are based on reports from entire establishments, both the OSHA 300 Log and the number of hours worked should cover the whole establishment being benchmarked. The hours worked and the log also should cover the same time period, (e.g., a month, quarter, or full year). The following rates may be calculated.

Total Cases — the incidence rate of total OSHA-recordable cases per 200,000 hours worked. For this rate, N is the total number of cases on the OSHA 300 Log.

Cases With Days Away From Work or Job Transfer or Restriction — the incidence rate of cases with days away from work, or job transfer, or restriction. N is the count of cases with a check in column H or column I of the OSHA 300 Log.

Cases With Days Away From Work — the incidence rate of cases with days away from work. N is the count of cases with a check in column H of the OSHA 300 Log.

Cases With Job Transfer or Restriction — the incidence rate of cases with job transfer or restriction, but no days away from work. N is the count of cases with a check in column I of the OSHA 300 Log.

Other Recordable Cases — the incidence rate of recordable cases without days away from work or job transfer or restriction. N is the count of cases with a check in column J of the OSHA 300 Log.

In the flow chart on the opposite page, post the number of cases to each box in the top row and the number of employee hours worked in its box. Then use the formula to calculate the rates and write them in the last row of boxes in Step 1.

Step 2.

After computing one or more of the rates, the next step is to determine the North American Industry Classification System (NAICS) code for the establishment.[b] (NAICS replaced the Standard Industrial Classification [SIC] code beginning in 2003.) This code is used to find the appropriate BLS rate for comparison. NAICS codes may be found on the Internet at www.census.gov/naics. The site also contains a crosswalk between NAICS and SIC codes. Otherwise, call a regional BLS office for assistance.

Write the establishment's NAICS code in the box in Step 2 of the flow chart.

Step 3.

Once the NAICS code is known, the national average incidence rates may be found by (a) consulting the table of rates on pages 62–64, (b) visiting the BLS Internet site (www.bls.gov/iif), or (c) by calling a regional BLS office. Note that some tables on the Internet site provide incidence rates by size of establishment and rate quartiles within each NAICS code. These rates may be useful for a more precise comparison. Note that the incidence rates for 2001 and earlier years were compiled under the old OSHA record-keeping requirements in effect at that time. Caution must be used in comparing rates computed for 2002 and later years with earlier years — keeping in mind the differences in record-keeping requirements.

In the flow chart on the opposite page, post the rates from the BLS survey to the boxes in Step 3. Now compare these with the rates calculated in Step 1.

An alternative way of benchmarking is to compare the current incidence rates for an establishment to its own prior historical rates to determine if the rates are improving and if progress is satisfactory (using criteria set by the organization).

[a]Bureau of Labor Statistics. (1997). BLS Handbook of Methods. Washington, DC: U.S. Government Printing Office (or on the Internet at http://www.bls.gov/opub/hom/home.htm).
[b]Executive Office of the President, Office of Management and Budget. (2002). North American Industry Classification System, United States 2002. Springfield, VA: National Technical Information Service.

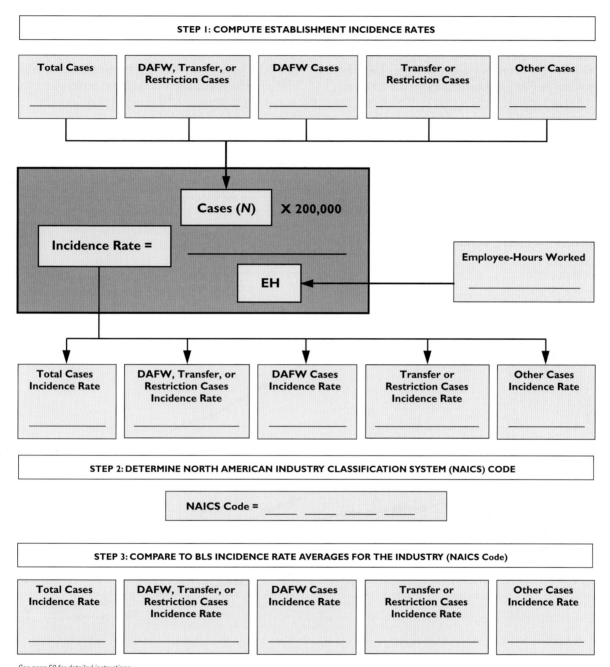

STEP 1: COMPUTE ESTABLISHMENT INCIDENCE RATES

Total Cases	DAFW, Transfer, or Restriction Cases	DAFW Cases	Transfer or Restriction Cases	Other Cases

Cases (*N*)   X 200,000

Incidence Rate =

EH

Employee-Hours Worked

Total Cases Incidence Rate	DAFW, Transfer, or Restriction Cases Incidence Rate	DAFW Cases Incidence Rate	Transfer or Restriction Cases Incidence Rate	Other Cases Incidence Rate

STEP 2: DETERMINE NORTH AMERICAN INDUSTRY CLASSIFICATION SYSTEM (NAICS) CODE

NAICS Code = _____ _____ _____ _____

STEP 3: COMPARE TO BLS INCIDENCE RATE AVERAGES FOR THE INDUSTRY (NAICS Code)

Total Cases Incidence Rate	DAFW, Transfer, or Restriction Cases Incidence Rate	DAFW Cases Incidence Rate	Transfer or Restriction Cases Incidence Rate	Other Cases Incidence Rate

See page 58 for detailed instructions.
DAFW = Days Away From Work

TRENDS IN OCCUPATIONAL INCIDENCE RATES

Incidence rates continue recent downward trend.

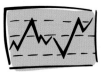

Four of the five occupational injury and illness incidence rates published by the Bureau of Labor Statistics for 2006 decreased from 2005. The incidence rate for total recordable cases was 4.4 per 100 full-time workers in 2006, down 4% from the 2005 rate of 4.6. The incidence rate for total cases with days away from work, job transfer, or restriction was 2.3, a decrease of 4%. The incidence rate for cases with days away from work was 1.3 in 2006, down 7% from 1.4 in 2005. The incidence rate for cases with job transfer or restriction was 1.0 in 2006, unchanged from 2005. The incidence rate for other recordable cases was 2.1, down 5% from the 2005 rate of 2.2.

There have been several changes that affect comparability of incidence rates from year to year. The North American Industry Classification System (NAICS) replaced the Standard Industrial Classification (SIC) system beginning with the 2003 survey of occupational injuries and illnesses. Revisions to the Occupational Safety and Health Administration's (OSHA) occupational injury and illness recordkeeping requirements became effective in 2002. Beginning with 1992, the Bureau of Labor Statistics revised its annual survey to include only nonfatal cases and stopped publishing the incidence rate of lost workdays.

OCCUPATIONAL INJURY AND ILLNESS INCIDENCE RATES, PRIVATE INDUSTRY, UNITED STATES, 1986–2006

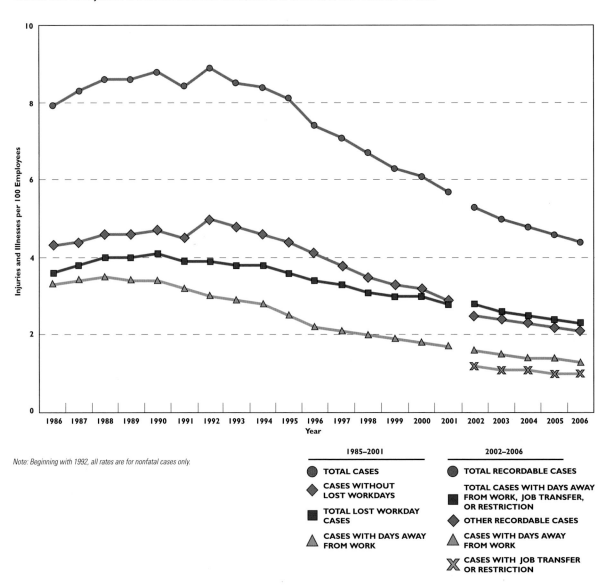

Note: Beginning with 1992, all rates are for nonfatal cases only.

OCCUPATIONAL INJURIES AND ILLNESSES

The tables below and on pages 62–64 present the results of the 2006 Survey of Occupational Injuries and Illnesses conducted by the Bureau of Labor Statistics (BLS), U.S. Department of Labor. The survey collects data on injuries and illnesses (from the OSHA 300 Log) and employee-hours worked from a nationwide sample of about 195,200 establishments representing the private sector of the economy. The survey excludes public employees, private households, the self-employed, and farms with fewer than 11 employees. The incidence rates give the number of cases per 100 full-time workers per year using 200,000 employee-hours as the equivalent. Definitions of the terms are given in the Glossary on page 191.

Beginning with 1992 data, the BLS revised its annual survey to include only nonfatal cases and stopped publishing incidence rates of lost workdays. Beginning with 2003 data, the BLS adopted the North American Industry Classification System for publication of the incidence rates by industry.

BLS ESTIMATES OF NONFATAL OCCUPATIONAL INJURY AND ILLNESS INCIDENCE RATES AND NUMBER OF INJURIES AND ILLNESSES BY INDUSTRY SECTOR, 2006

Industry Sector	Total Recordable Cases	Cases With Days Away From Work, Job Transfer, or Restriction			Other Recordable Cases
		Total	Cases With Days Away From Work	Cases With Job Transfer or Restriction	
Incidence Rate per 100 Full-Time Workers[c]					
Private Sector[d]	**4.4**	**2.3**	**1.3**	**1.0**	**2.1**
Goods Producing[d]	5.9	3.2	1.7	1.6	2.7
Natural Resources and Mining[d]	4.9	2.7	1.7	1.0	2.2
Agriculture, forestry, fishing & hunting[d]	6.0	3.2	1.9	1.2	2.8
Mining	3.5	2.1	1.4	0.7	1.4
Construction	5.9	3.2	2.2	1.0	2.7
Manufacturing	6.0	3.3	1.4	1.9	2.7
Service Providing	3.9	2.0	1.1	0.8	1.9
Trade, Transportation, and Utilities	5.0	2.9	1.6	1.3	2.1
Wholesale trade	4.1	2.5	1.3	1.2	1.6
Retail trade	4.9	2.6	1.4	1.2	2.4
Transportation and warehousing	6.5	4.3	2.7	1.6	2.2
Utilities	4.1	2.2	1.2	1.0	1.9
Information	1.9	1.0	0.7	0.4	0.9
Financial Activities	1.5	0.7	0.5	0.2	0.8
Professional and Business Services	2.1	1.1	0.7	0.4	1.1
Education and Health Services	5.4	2.5	1.4	1.1	3.0
Leisure and Hospitality	4.6	1.8	1.1	0.7	2.8
Other Services	2.9	1.4	0.9	0.5	1.5
Number of Injuries and Illnesses (in thousands)					
Private Sector[d]	**4,085.4**	**2,114.6**	**1,183.5**	**931.1**	**1,970.8**
Goods Producing[d]	1,347.6	738.6	380.4	358.1	609.0
Natural Resources and Mining[d]	75.6	41.5	26.3	15.2	34.1
Agriculture, forestry, fishing & hunting[d]	52.1	27.6	16.9	10.7	24.5
Mining	23.5	14.0	9.4	4.6	9.6
Construction	412.9	223.7	153.2	70.5	189.2
Manufacturing	859.1	473.4	201.0	272.4	385.7
Service Providing	2,737.8	1,376.0	803.1	573.0	1,361.7
Trade, Transportation, and Utilities	1,107.9	637.4	354.5	282.9	470.6
Wholesale trade	232.0	140.6	75.7	64.9	91.4
Retail trade	588.5	308.6	162.8	145.8	279.8
Transportation and warehousing	265.2	176.3	109.8	66.5	88.9
Utilities	22.2	11.8	6.2	5.6	10.4
Information	52.1	28.3	18.6	9.8	23.8
Financial Activities	111.1	50.7	33.3	17.4	60.4
Professional and Business Services	276.7	139.4	89.9	49.5	137.3
Education and Health Services	711.5	324.5	182.2	142.3	387.0
Leisure and Hospitality	389.4	153.3	96.9	56.4	236.1
Other Services	88.9	42.4	27.6	14.7	46.5

Source: Bureau of Labor Statistics.
[a] Industry Sector and 2 and 3 digit NAICS code totals on pages 62–64 include data for industries not shown separately.
[b] North American Industry Classification System, 2002 Edition, for industries shown on pages 62–64.
[c] Incidence Rate = $\dfrac{\text{Number of injuries \& illnesses} \times 200{,}000}{\text{Total hours worked by all employees during period covered}}$

where 200,000 is the base for 100 full-time workers (working 40 hours per week, 50 weeks per year). The "Total Recordable Cases" rate is based on the number of cases with check marks in columns (G), (H), (I), and (J) of the OSHA 300 Log. The "Cases With Days Away From Work, Job Transfer, or Restriction — Total" rate is based on columns (H) and (I). The "Cases With Days Away From Work" rate is based on column (H). The "Cases With Job Transfer or Restriction" rate is based on column (I). The "Other Recordable Cases" rate is based on column (J).
[d] Excludes farms with less than 11 employees.
[e] Data not available.

OCCUPATIONAL INJURIES AND ILLNESSES (CONT.)

BLS ESTIMATES OF NONFATAL OCCUPATIONAL INJURY AND ILLNESS INCIDENCE RATES FOR SELECTED INDUSTRIES, 2006

Industry[a]	NAICS Code[b]	Total Recordable Cases	Incidence Rates[c] Cases With Days Away From Work, Job Transfer, or Restriction			Other Recordable Cases
			Total	Cases With Days Away From Work	Cases With Job Transfer or Restriction	
PRIVATE SECTOR[d]		**4.4**	**2.3**	**1.3**	**1.0**	**2.1**
Goods Producing[d]		**5.9**	**3.2**	**1.7**	**1.6**	**2.7**
Natural Resources and Mining[d]		**4.9**	**2.7**	**1.7**	**1.0**	**2.2**
Agriculture, forestry, fishing and hunting[d]	11	6.0	3.2	1.9	1.2	2.8
Crop production	111	5.8	3.1	1.8	1.4	2.7
Animal production	112	8.1	3.9	2.4	1.5	4.2
Forestry and logging	113	5.3	2.4	2.2	0.2	3.0
Fishing, hunting, and trapping	114	8.4	3.4	3.3	(e)	5.0
Support activities for agriculture and forestry	115	5.1	3.0	1.9	1.1	2.1
Mining	21	3.5	2.1	1.4	0.7	1.4
Oil and gas extraction	211	2.0	0.9	0.5	0.4	1.1
Mining (except oil and gas)	212	3.8	2.5	1.9	0.7	1.3
Coal mining	2121	4.8	3.3	2.9	0.3	1.5
Metal ore mining	2122	3.1	1.9	1.1	0.8	1.1
Nonmetallic mineral mining and quarrying	2123	3.2	2.2	1.3	0.9	1.1
Support activities for mining	213	3.9	2.2	1.4	0.8	1.7
Construction		**5.9**	**3.2**	**2.2**	**1.0**	**2.7**
Construction of buildings	236	5.1	2.6	1.8	0.8	2.5
Residential building construction	2361	5.0	2.5	1.9	0.6	2.5
Nonresidential building construction	2362	5.4	2.7	1.7	1.0	2.6
Heavy and civil engineering construction	237	5.3	3.0	2.0	1.0	2.3
Utility system construction	2371	5.4	3.1	2.2	0.9	2.3
Land subdivision	2372	2.0	0.8	0.5	0.3	1.2
Highway, street, and bridge construction	2373	6.0	3.5	2.3	1.3	2.5
Other heavy and civil engineering construction	2379	5.5	3.0	2.1	0.9	2.5
Specialty trade contractors	238	6.3	3.5	2.4	1.1	2.9
Foundation, structure, and building exterior contractors	2381	7.4	4.5	3.0	1.6	2.8
Building equipment contractors	2382	6.4	3.1	2.2	1.0	3.3
Building finishing contractors	2383	5.9	3.5	2.3	1.2	2.4
Other specialty trade contractors	2389	5.1	2.8	2.1	0.7	2.3
Manufacturing		**6.0**	**3.3**	**1.4**	**1.9**	**2.7**
Food manufacturing	311	7.4	4.8	1.6	3.2	2.6
Animal food manufacturing	3111	6.1	2.9	1.7	1.2	3.2
Grain and oilseed milling	3112	5.3	3.0	1.2	1.8	2.3
Sugar and confectionery product manufacturing	3113	8.1	4.6	1.8	2.8	3.5
Fruit and vegetable preserving and specialty food mfg.	3114	6.4	3.8	1.5	2.3	2.6
Dairy product manufacturing	3115	8.2	5.2	2.4	2.8	3.1
Animal slaughtering and processing	3116	9.1	6.2	1.3	4.9	2.9
Seafood product preparation and packaging	3117	7.5	4.7	2.7	2.0	2.8
Bakeries and tortilla manufacturing	3118	5.9	4.0	1.7	2.3	1.9
Other food manufacturing	3119	5.8	3.6	1.6	2.0	2.2
Beverage and tobacco product manufacturing	312	8.1	5.5	2.3	3.2	2.6
Beverage manufacturing	3121	8.6	6.0	2.4	3.6	2.6
Tobacco manufacturing	3122	3.9	1.8	1.3	0.5	2.0
Textile mills	313	4.4	2.3	0.9	1.5	2.0
Fiber, yarn, and thread mills	3131	4.2	2.4	0.5	1.9	1.7
Fabric mills	3132	4.4	2.2	0.9	1.4	2.2
Textile and fabric finishing and fabric coating mills	3133	4.4	2.5	1.2	1.3	1.9
Textile product mills	314	4.5	2.6	0.9	1.7	1.9
Textile furnishings mills	3141	4.1	2.5	0.7	1.7	1.6
Other textile product mills	3149	5.0	2.7	1.1	1.6	2.4
Apparel manufacturing	315	2.9	1.4	0.7	0.8	1.4
Apparel knitting mills	3151	3.6	1.5	0.5	1.0	2.1
Cut and sew apparel manufacturing	3152	2.6	1.3	0.6	0.7	1.2
Apparel accessories and other apparel manufacturing	3159	4.7	2.4	1.4	1.0	2.3
Leather and allied product manufacturing	316	5.9	3.1	1.2	1.9	2.8
Footwear manufacturing	3162	6.4	3.1	1.1	2.0	3.3
Other leather and allied product manufacturing	3169	3.6	2.1	1.1	1.0	1.5
Wood product manufacturing	321	8.5	4.7	2.3	2.4	3.8
Sawmills and wood preservation	3211	7.2	4.1	2.4	1.7	3.1
Veneer, plywood, and engineered wood product mfg.	3212	7.1	4.1	1.9	2.2	3.0
Other wood product manufacturing	3219	9.6	5.2	2.5	2.7	4.4
Paper manufacturing	322	4.3	2.5	1.2	1.3	1.8
Pulp, paper, and paperboard mills	3221	3.6	1.9	1.2	0.7	1.7
Converted paper product manufacturing	3222	4.7	2.8	1.2	1.5	1.9
Printing and related support activities	323	4.2	2.4	1.2	1.2	1.8
Petroleum and coal products manufacturing	324	2.7	1.4	0.9	0.5	1.3
Chemical manufacturing	325	2.9	1.7	0.8	1.0	1.2
Basic chemical manufacturing	3251	2.1	1.2	0.6	0.6	0.9
Resin, synthetic rubber, and artificial and synthetic fibers and filaments manufacturing	3252	3.0	1.9	0.7	1.1	1.1
Pesticide, fertilizer, and other agricultural chemical mfg.	3253	4.2	2.6	0.7	1.9	1.6
Pharmaceutical and medicine manufacturing	3254	2.4	1.4	0.6	0.8	1.0
Paint, coating, and adhesive manufacturing	3255	3.8	2.3	1.1	1.2	1.4
Soap, cleaning compound, and toilet preparation mfg.	3256	3.4	2.1	0.9	1.2	1.3
Other chemical product and preparation mfg.	3259	3.9	2.3	1.0	1.3	1.6

See source and footnotes on page 61.

BLS ESTIMATES OF NONFATAL OCCUPATIONAL INJURY AND ILLNESS INCIDENCE RATES FOR SELECTED INDUSTRIES, 2006, Cont.

Industry[a]	NAICS Code[b]	Total Recordable Cases	Cases With Days Away From Work, Job Transfer, or Restriction			Other Recordable Cases
			Total	Cases With Days Away From Work	Cases With Job Transfer or Restriction	
Plastics and rubber products manufacturing	326	6.8	3.9	1.6	2.3	2.9
Plastics product manufacturing	3261	6.8	3.8	1.5	2.3	3.0
Rubber product manufacturing	3262	7.1	4.3	1.7	2.6	2.8
Nonmetallic mineral product manufacturing	327	7.1	4.1	2.0	2.2	3.0
Clay product and refractory manufacturing	3271	7.8	4.9	1.3	3.6	2.9
Glass and glass product manufacturing	3272	7.5	3.9	1.5	2.5	3.6
Cement and concrete product manufacturing	3273	7.4	4.4	2.5	2.0	2.9
Lime and gypsum product manufacturing	3274	3.6	1.6	0.7	0.9	1.9
Other nonmetallic mineral product manufacturing	3279	6.1	3.5	1.9	1.6	2.6
Primary metal manufacturing	331	8.6	4.7	2.1	2.6	3.9
Iron and steel mills and ferroalloy manufacturing	3311	5.4	2.9	1.7	1.2	2.6
Steel product manufacturing from purchased steel	3312	8.8	4.7	2.2	2.5	4.0
Alumina and aluminum production and processing	3313	6.3	3.7	1.6	2.1	2.6
Nonferrous metal (except aluminum) production and processing	3314	7.5	4.6	2.1	2.5	2.9
Foundries	3315	11.9	6.2	2.5	3.7	5.7
Fabricated metal product manufacturing	332	7.6	3.8	1.8	2.0	3.8
Forging and stamping	3321	9.3	5.2	2.4	2.9	4.0
Cutlery and handtool manufacturing	3322	6.3	3.0	1.8	1.2	3.3
Architectural and structural metals manufacturing	3323	8.4	4.6	2.2	2.5	3.8
Boiler, tank, and shipping container manufacturing	3324	8.8	3.6	2.0	1.6	5.1
Hardware manufacturing	3325	6.0	3.0	1.2	1.8	2.9
Spring and wire product manufacturing	3326	8.8	4.9	2.3	2.7	3.9
Machine shops; turned product; and screw, nut, and bolt manufacturing	3327	6.7	2.8	1.6	1.2	3.9
Coating, engraving, heat treating, and allied activities	3328	8.1	3.9	1.5	2.3	4.3
Other fabricated metal product manufacturing	3329	6.6	3.3	1.5	1.8	3.3
Machinery manufacturing	333	6.2	3.0	1.4	1.6	3.2
Agriculture, construction, and mining machinery mfg.	3331	7.5	3.7	1.8	1.9	3.8
Industrial machinery manufacturing	3332	6.0	2.8	1.3	1.5	3.1
Commercial and service machinery manufacturing	3333	4.2	2.2	1.1	1.2	2.0
Ventilation, heating, air-conditioning, and commercial refrigeration equipment manufacturing	3334	6.8	3.3	1.3	2.0	3.5
Metalworking machinery manufacturing	3335	6.0	2.5	1.4	1.2	3.5
Engine, turbine, and power transmission equipment manufacturing	3336	5.5	2.7	1.1	1.5	2.8
Other general purpose machinery manufacturing	3339	6.2	3.1	1.4	1.8	3.1
Computer and electronic product manufacturing	334	2.0	1.0	0.5	0.6	1.0
Computer and peripheral equipment manufacturing	3341	1.0	0.5	0.3	0.3	0.4
Communications equipment manufacturing	3342	2.0	1.0	0.5	0.5	0.9
Audio and video equipment manufacturing	3343	3.4	2.1	0.7	1.5	1.2
Semiconductor and other electronic component mfg.	3344	2.2	1.1	0.6	0.5	1.1
Navigational, measuring, electromedical, and control instruments manufacturing	3345	2.1	1.0	0.5	0.6	1.1
Manufacturing and reproducing magnetic and optical media	3346	2.5	1.8	0.6	1.2	0.7
Electrical equipment, appliance, and component mfg.	335	5.1	2.7	1.0	1.6	2.4
Electric lighting equipment manufacturing	3351	5.4	2.5	1.0	1.4	3.0
Household appliance manufacturing	3352	5.3	2.6	0.8	1.7	2.8
Electrical equipment manufacturing	3353	5.1	2.8	1.0	1.7	2.3
Other electrical equipment and component mfg.	3359	4.8	2.7	1.1	1.6	2.1
Transportation equipment manufacturing	336	8.0	4.3	1.6	2.7	3.7
Motor vehicle manufacturing	3361	11.4	6.5	1.8	4.7	4.9
Motor vehicle body and trailer manufacturing	3362	13.2	5.8	2.4	3.4	7.4
Motor vehicle parts manufacturing	3363	7.7	4.3	1.5	2.9	3.4
Aerospace product and parts manufacturing	3364	4.2	2.2	0.9	1.3	2.0
Railroad rolling stock manufacturing	3365	6.1	3.3	1.4	2.0	2.7
Ship and boat building	3366	10.2	5.6	2.8	2.7	4.6
Other transportation equipment manufacturing	3369	7.1	3.3	1.8	1.5	3.8
Furniture and related product manufacturing	337	7.5	4.2	1.8	2.4	3.3
Household and institutional furniture and kitchen cabinet manufacturing	3371	7.5	4.2	1.8	2.4	3.2
Office furniture (including fixtures) manufacturing	3372	7.8	4.1	1.8	2.3	3.8
Other furniture related product manufacturing	3379	6.7	4.3	1.4	2.9	2.4
Miscellaneous manufacturing	339	4.2	2.1	1.0	1.1	2.1
Medical equipment and supplies manufacturing	3391	3.2	1.8	0.7	1.0	1.5
Other miscellaneous manufacturing	3399	5.1	2.4	1.2	1.2	2.7
Service Providing		**3.9**	**2.0**	**1.1**	**0.8**	**1.9**
Trade, Transportation, and Utilities		**5.0**	**2.9**	**1.6**	**1.3**	**2.1**
Wholesale trade	42	4.1	2.5	1.3	1.2	1.6
Merchant wholesalers, durable goods	423	3.9	2.1	1.2	0.9	1.8
Merchant wholesalers, nondurable goods	424	5.4	3.7	1.9	1.8	1.7

See source and footnotes on page 61.

BLS ESTIMATES OF NONFATAL OCCUPATIONAL INJURY AND ILLNESS INCIDENCE RATES FOR SELECTED INDUSTRIES, 2006, Cont.

Industry[a]	NAICS Code[b]	Total Recordable Cases	Incidence Rates[c] Cases With Days Away From Work, Job Transfer, or Restriction — Total	Cases With Days Away From Work	Cases With Job Transfer or Restriction	Other Recordable Cases
Wholesale electronic markets and agents and brokers	425	1.7	1.0	0.5	0.5	0.7
Retail trade	44–45	4.9	2.6	1.4	1.2	2.4
Motor vehicle and parts dealers	441	4.4	1.9	1.3	0.6	2.6
Furniture and home furnishings stores	442	4.7	2.8	1.7	1.1	1.9
Electronics and appliance stores	443	2.8	1.2	0.6	0.6	1.6
Building material & garden equipment and supplies dealers	444	7.4	4.3	2.0	2.3	3.1
Food and beverage stores	445	5.9	3.2	1.7	1.5	2.7
Health and personal care stores	446	2.2	1.0	0.6	0.4	1.2
Gasoline stations	447	3.6	1.5	0.9	0.6	2.0
Clothing and clothing accessories stores	448	2.7	1.1	0.8	0.3	1.6
Sporting goods, hobby, book, and music stores	451	3.0	1.1	0.6	0.4	2.0
General merchandise stores	452	6.7	3.9	1.7	2.2	2.8
Miscellaneous store retailers	453	3.9	2.0	1.2	0.8	1.9
Nonstore retailers	454	4.2	2.6	1.3	1.3	1.6
Transportation and warehousing	48–49	6.5	4.3	2.7	1.6	2.2
Air transportation	481	9.9	7.7	5.4	2.2	2.2
Rail transportation	482	2.3	1.7	1.5	0.2	0.6
Water transportation	483	4.4	2.6	1.9	0.7	1.8
Truck transportation	484	5.8	3.7	2.7	0.9	2.2
Transit and ground passenger transportation	485	5.4	3.0	2.2	0.9	2.3
Pipeline transportation	486	2.2	0.9	0.6	0.3	1.3
Scenic and sightseeing transportation	487	4.3	2.8	2.1	0.6	1.6
Support activities for transportation	488	4.5	2.6	1.8	0.9	1.8
Couriers and messengers	492	10.5	7.2	3.5	3.7	3.3
Warehousing and storage	493	8.0	5.6	2.2	3.4	2.4
Utilities	22	4.1	2.2	1.2	1.0	1.9
Electric power generation, transmission and distribution	2211	3.8	1.9	1.1	0.8	1.9
Natural gas distribution	2212	5.1	2.9	1.3	1.6	2.2
Water, sewage and other systems	2213	5.2	3.1	1.6	1.4	2.1
Information		**1.9**	**1.0**	**0.7**	**0.4**	**0.9**
Publishing industries (except Internet)	511	2.1	1.1	0.6	0.4	1.0
Motion picture and sound recording industries	512	2.0	0.6	0.4	0.2	(e)
Broadcasting (except Internet)	515	1.9	1.0	0.6	0.4	1.0
Telecommunications	517	2.2	1.4	1.0	0.4	0.8
Internet service providers, web search portals, and data processing services	518	0.9	0.4	0.2	0.2	0.4
Other information services	519	2.0	1.0	0.8	0.2	1.0
Financial Activities		**1.5**	**0.7**	**0.5**	**0.2**	**0.8**
Finance and insurance	52	0.9	0.3	0.2	0.1	0.6
Monetary authorities	521	2.7	1.9	1.1	0.8	0.8
Credit intermediation and related activities	522	1.0	0.3	0.2	0.1	0.6
Securities, commodity contracts, and other financial investments and related activities	523	(e)	0.1	0.1	(e)	(e)
Insurance carriers and related activities	524	1.0	0.4	0.3	0.1	0.7
Funds, trusts, and other financial activities	525	1.2	0.7	0.5	0.2	0.5
Real estate and rental and leasing	53	3.3	1.8	1.1	0.7	1.5
Real estate	531	2.9	1.5	1.0	0.5	1.4
Rental and leasing services	532	4.2	2.6	1.5	1.1	1.7
Lessors of nonfinancial intangible assets (except copyrighted works)	533	0.8	0.2	0.1	(e)	0.6
Professional and Business Services		**2.1**	**1.1**	**0.7**	**0.4**	**1.1**
Professional, scientific, and technical services	54	1.2	0.5	0.3	0.2	0.7
Management of companies and enterprises	55	2.1	1.1	0.6	0.5	1.1
Administrative and support and waste management and remediation services	56	3.4	1.9	1.2	0.6	1.5
Administrative and support services	561	3.1	1.7	1.1	0.6	1.5
Waste management and remediation services	562	6.5	3.9	2.5	1.4	2.5
Education and Health Services		**5.4**	**2.5**	**1.4**	**1.1**	**3.0**
Educational services	61	2.3	0.9	0.7	0.3	1.4
Health care and social assistance	62	5.8	2.7	1.5	1.2	3.2
Ambulatory health care services	621	3.1	1.1	0.8	0.3	2.0
Hospitals	622	8.1	3.2	1.8	1.4	4.9
Nursing and residential care facilities	623	8.9	5.4	2.6	2.7	3.6
Social assistance	624	3.9	1.9	1.2	0.8	1.9
Leisure and Hospitality		**4.6**	**1.8**	**1.1**	**0.7**	**2.8**
Arts, entertainment, and recreation	71	5.3	2.5	1.3	1.2	2.8
Accommodation and food services	72	4.5	1.7	1.1	0.6	2.8
Accommodation	721	5.8	3.1	1.5	1.5	2.8
Food services and drinking places	722	4.2	1.4	1.0	0.4	2.8
Other Services, Except Public Administration		**2.9**	**1.4**	**0.9**	**0.5**	**1.5**
Repair and maintenance	811	3.5	1.6	1.2	0.4	1.9
Personal and laundry services	812	2.6	1.5	0.9	0.6	1.1
Religious, grantmaking, civic, professional, and similar organizations	813	2.7	1.0	0.7	0.4	1.6

See source and footnotes on page 61.

OCCUPATIONAL INJURIES AND ILLNESSES (CONT.)

65

BLS ESTIMATES OF NONFATAL OCCUPATIONAL INJURY AND ILLNESS INCIDENCE RATES FOR SELECTED INDUSTRIES, 2006

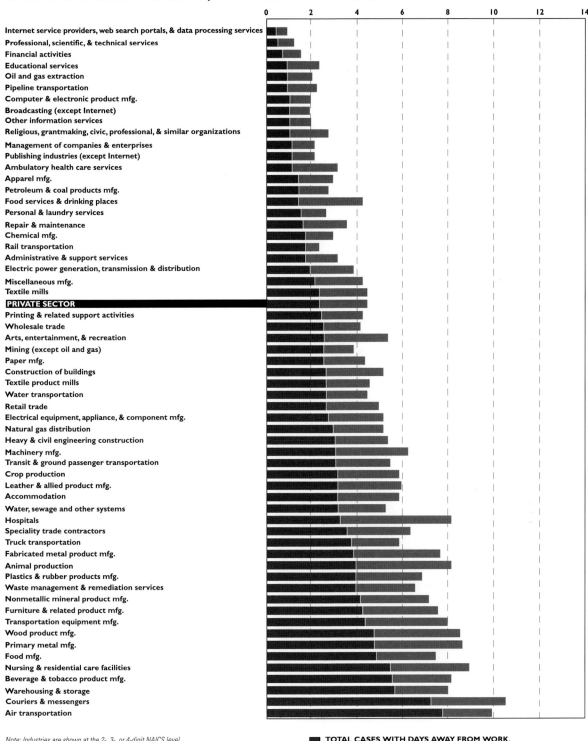

Note: Industries are shown at the 2-, 3-, or 4-digit NAICS level.
Total Cases with Days Away from Work, Job Transfer, or Restriction plus Other Recordable
Cases equals Total Recordable Cases.

■ **TOTAL CASES WITH DAYS AWAY FROM WORK, JOB TRANSFER, OR RESTRICTION**

■ **OTHER RECORDABLE CASES**

OCCUPATIONAL

NATIONAL SAFETY COUNCIL® INJURY FACTS® 2008 EDITION

The tables on pages 67 through 82 present data on the characteristics of injured and ill workers and the injuries and illnesses that affected them. These data indicate how many workers died from on-the-job injuries and how many were affected by nonfatal injuries and illnesses. The data may be used to help set priorities for occupational safety and health programs and for benchmarking.

The fatality information covers only deaths due to injuries and comes from the Bureau of Labor Statistics (BLS) Census of Fatal Occupational Injuries. The data are for the calendar year 2005 and include wage and salary workers, the self-employed, and unpaid family workers in all types of businesses and industries.

The data on nonfatal cases cover both occupational injuries and illnesses and come from the BLS Survey of Occupational Injuries and Illnesses for 2005. The Survey also is used to produce the incidence rates shown on the preceding pages. The estimates on the following pages are the number of cases involving days away from work (with or without days of restricted work activity). The survey does not cover the self-employed or unpaid family workers or federal, state, or local government employees.

Data are presented for the sex, age, occupation, and race or ethnic origin of the worker and for the nature of injury/illness, the part of body affected, the source of injury/illness, and the event or exposure that produced the injury/illness.

The text at the top of each page describes the kind of establishments that are included in the industry sector and gives the total number of workers in the industry in 2005 and the number working in the private sector.

How to Benchmark

Incidence rates, percent distributions, or ranks may be used for benchmarking purposes. The results of the calculations described here may be compared to similar rates, percent distributions, and rankings based on data for a company.

For nonfatal cases incidence rates, multiply the number of cases by 1,000 and then divide by the *private-sector* employment given in the text at the top of the page. This will give the number of cases with days away from work per 1,000 employees per year. For fatality rates, multiply the number of fatalities by 100,000 then divide by the *total* employment given at the top of the page. This will give the number of deaths per 100,000 employees per year.

To compute percent distributions, divide number of cases for each characteristic by the total number of cases found on the first line of the table. Multiply the quotient by 100 and round to one decimal place. Percent distributions may not add to 100.0% because of unclassifiable cases not shown.

Ranks are determined by arranging the characteristics from largest to smallest within each group and then numbering consecutively starting with 1 for the largest.

Industry Sectors

Page 67 shows nonfatal injury/illness data for the private sector of the economy (excluding government entities) and fatal injury data for all industries (including government). Pages 68 through 81 present the data for industry sectors based on the North American Industry Classification System (NAICS). Page 82 presents the fatal injury data for government (the BLS Survey does not cover government entities nationwide so no nonfatal case data are available).

The nonfatal occupational injury and illness data cover only private sector employees and exclude employees in federal, state, and local government entities and the self-employed. The fatal injury data cover all workers in both the private sector and government.

There were 142,946,000 people employed in 2005, of which 110,730,000 worked in the private sector.

NUMBER OF NONFATAL OCCUPATIONAL INJURIES AND ILLNESSES INVOLVING DAYS AWAY FROM WORK[a] AND FATAL OCCUPATIONAL INJURIES BY SELECTED WORKER AND CASE CHARACTERISTICS, UNITED STATES, 2005

Characteristic	Private Industry[b,c] Nonfatal Cases	All Industries Fatalities
Total	**1,234,680**	**5,734**
Sex		
Men	814,250	5,328
Women	415,880	406
Age		
Under 16	90	23
16 to 19	41,530	142
20 to 24	133,760	403
25 to 34	290,500	1,017
35 to 44	311,880	1,243
45 to 54	282,310	1,389
55 to 64	135,290	933
65 and over	27,050	578
Occupation		
Management, business, and financial	28,110	606
Professional and related	83,060	76
Service	247,270	825
Sales and related	80,020	324
Office and administrative support	91,400	110
Farming, fishing, and forestry	15,540	325
Construction and extractive	152,490	1,184
Installation, maintenance, and repair	107,770	397
Production	173,440	272
Transportation and material moving	253,570	1,551
Military occupations	—	48
Race or ethnic origin[d]		
White, non-Hispanic	567,790	3,966
Black, non-Hispanic	101,170	584
Hispanic	163,440	923
Other, multiple, and not reported	402,420	261
Nature of injury, illness		
Sprains, strains	503,530	12
Fractures	95,830	42
Cuts, lacerations, punctures	118,870	625
Bruises, contusions	107,770	5
Heat burns	17,150	129
Chemical burns	6,360	—
Amputations	8,450	19
Carpal tunnel syndrome	16,460	—
Tendonitis	5,720	—
Multiple injuries	50,090	1,950
Soreness, Pain	100,800	—
Back pain	35,650	—
All other	203,660	2,947

Characteristic	Private Industry[b,c] Nonfatal Cases	All Industries Fatalities
Part of body affected		
Head	81,090	1,309
Eye	34,740	—
Neck	18,470	130
Trunk	428,500	1,001
Back	270,890	68
Shoulder	77,800	—
Upper extremities	284,750	19
Finger	111,090	—
Hand, except finger	47,020	—
Wrist	56,250	—
Lower extremities	271,740	61
Knee	100,560	10
Foot, toe	56,730	6
Body systems	17,950	968
Multiple	120,960	2,236
All other	11,220	10
Source of injury, illness		
Chemicals, chemical products	18,440	160
Containers	151,710	81
Furniture, fixtures	46,780	18
Machinery	80,460	458
Parts and materials	128,700	380
Worker motion or position	181,820	5
Floor, ground surfaces	234,430	753
Handtools	56,970	100
Vehicles	109,630	2,599
Health care patient	54,520	—
All other	171,210	1,178
Event or exposure		
Contact with object, equipment	338,080	1,005
Struck by object	167,730	607
Struck against object	85,500	8
Caught in object, equipment, material	54,970	387
Fall to lower level	79,310	664
Fall on same level	167,180	84
Slips, trips	36,150	—
Overexertion	298,130	6
Overexertion in lifting	159,970	—
Repetitive motion	43,790	—
Exposed to harmful substance	51,860	501
Transportation accidents	61,170	2,493
Highway accident	39,070	1,437
Nonhighway accident, except air, rail, water	9,500	340
Pedestrian, nonpassenger struck by vehicle, mobile equipment	9,760	391
Fires, explosions	2,600	159
Assault, violent act	21,470	792
By person	14,560	567
By other	6,910	225
All other	134,940	29

Source: National Safety Council tabulations of Bureau of Labor Statistics data.
Note: Because of rounding and data exclusion of nonclassifiable responses, data may not sum to the totals. Dashes (—) indicate data that do not meet publication guidelines.
[a]Days away from work include those that result in days away from work with or without restricted work activity or job transfer.
[b]Excludes farms with fewer than 11 employees.

[c]Data for mining operators in coal, metal, and nonmetal mining and for employees in railroad transportation are provided to BLS by the Mine Safety and Health Administration, U.S. Department of Labor; and the Federal Railroad Administration, U.S. Department of Transportation. Independent mining contractors are excluded from the coal, metal, and nonmetal mining industries. MSHA and FRA data do not reflect the changes in OSHA record-keeping requirements in 2002.
[d]In the fatalities column, non-Hispanic categories include cases with Hispanic origin not reported.

AGRICULTURE, FORESTRY, FISHING, HUNTING

The Agriculture, Forestry, Fishing and Hunting industry sector includes growing crops, raising animals, harvesting timber, and harvesting fish and other animals from a farm, ranch, or their natural habitats, and agricultural support services.

Employment in Agriculture, Forestry, Fishing, and Hunting totaled 2,141,000 in 2005 of which 1,156,000 were private sector employees.

NUMBER OF NONFATAL OCCUPATIONAL INJURIES AND ILLNESSES INVOLVING DAYS AWAY FROM WORK[a] AND FATAL OCCUPATIONAL INJURIES BY SELECTED WORKER AND CASE CHARACTERISTICS, UNITED STATES, AGRICULTURE, FORESTRY, FISHING, AND HUNTING, 2005

Characteristic	Nonfatal Cases[b]	Fatalities
Total	**18,870**	**715**
Sex		
Men	15,540	680
Women	3,330	35
Age		
Under 16	—	19
16 to 19	880	21
20 to 24	2,440	30
25 to 34	5,250	62
35 to 44	4,440	118
45 to 54	3,880	128
55 to 64	1,570	120
65 and over	290	212
Occupation		
Management, business, and financial	260	355
Professional and related	170	—
Service	550	5
Sales and related	30	—
Office and administrative support	190	—
Farming, fishing, and forestry	13,920	300
Construction and extractive	90	—
Installation, maintenance, and repair	700	5
Production	1,030	—
Transportation and material moving	1,910	43
Military occupations	—	—
Race or ethnic origin[c]		
White, non-Hispanic	5,280	565
Black, non-Hispanic	710	27
Hispanic	10,200	94
Other, multiple, and not reported	2,660	29
Nature of injury, illness		
Sprains, strains	5,390	—
Fractures	2,000	—
Cuts, lacerations, punctures	2,100	15
Bruises, contusions	2,520	—
Heat burns	50	15
Chemical burns	110	—
Amputations	240	—
Carpal tunnel syndrome	60	—
Tendonitis	60	—
Multiple injuries	1,020	193
Soreness, Pain	1,170	—
Back pain	530	—
All other	4,160	485

Characteristic	Nonfatal Cases[b]	Fatalities
Part of body affected		
Head	1,800	146
Eye	880	—
Neck	140	15
Trunk	5,670	164
Back	3,000	—
Shoulder	990	—
Upper extremities	4,280	5
Finger	2,200	—
Hand, except finger	600	—
Wrist	560	—
Lower extremities	4,710	—
Knee	1,520	—
Foot, toe	850	—
Body systems	430	175
Multiple	1,600	204
All other	250	—
Source of injury, illness		
Chemicals, chemical products	500	7
Containers	1,570	9
Furniture, fixtures	300	—
Machinery	1,660	78
Parts and materials	1,690	18
Worker motion or position	2,460	—
Floor, ground surfaces	3,500	28
Handtools	1,050	5
Vehicles	1,810	383
Health care patient	—	—
All other	4,340	183
Event or exposure		
Contact with object, equipment	7,310	219
Struck by object	3,630	153
Struck against object	1,610	—
Caught in object, equipment, material	1,380	65
Fall to lower level	1,690	27
Fall on same level	1,900	—
Slips, trips	460	—
Overexertion	2,310	—
Overexertion in lifting	1,280	—
Repetitive motion	230	—
Exposed to harmful substance	830	51
Transportation accidents	1,080	346
Highway accident	490	92
Nonhighway accident, except air, rail, water	310	162
Pedestrian, nonpassenger struck by vehicle, mobile equipment	220	22
Fires, explosions	20	16
Assault, violent act	850	50
By person	60	6
By other	790	44
All other	2,190	—

Source: National Safety Council tabulations of Bureau of Labor Statistics data.
Note: Because of rounding and data exclusion of nonclassifiable responses, data may not sum to the totals. Dashes (—) indicate data that do not meet publication guidelines.
[a]Days away from work include those that result in days away from work with or without restricted work activity or job transfer.

[b]Excludes farms with fewer than 11 employees.
[c]In the fatalities column, non-Hispanic categories include cases with Hispanic origin not reported.

MINING

The Mining industry sector includes extraction of naturally occurring mineral solids, such as coal and ores; liquid minerals, such as crude petroleum; and gases, such as natural gas. It also includes quarrying, well operations, beneficiating, other preparation customarily performed at the site, and mining support activities.

Mining employment in 2005 amounted to 620,000 workers of which 609,000 were private sector employees.

NUMBER OF NONFATAL OCCUPATIONAL INJURIES AND ILLNESSES INVOLVING DAYS AWAY FROM WORK[a] AND FATAL OCCUPATIONAL INJURIES BY SELECTED WORKER AND CASE CHARACTERISTICS, UNITED STATES, MINING, 2005

Characteristic	Nonfatal Cases[b]	Fatalities
Total	**9,020**	**159**
Sex		
Men	8,790	158
Women	230	—
Age		
Under 16	—	—
16 to 19	180	6
20 to 24	1,040	19
25 to 34	2,490	46
35 to 44	1,920	33
45 to 54	2,310	35
55 to 64	950	13
65 and over	100	7
Occupation		
Management, business, and financial	40	—
Professional and related	70	5
Service	—	—
Sales and related	20	—
Office and administrative support	50	—
Farming, fishing, and forestry	—	—
Construction and extractive	4,900	94
Installation, maintenance, and repair	1,140	13
Production	750	7
Transportation and material moving	2,040	37
Military occupations	—	—
Race or ethnic origin[c]		
White, non-Hispanic	2,220	118
Black, non-Hispanic	90	—
Hispanic	560	29
Other, multiple, and not reported	6,140	8
Nature of injury, illness		
Sprains, strains	3,210	—
Fractures	1,590	—
Cuts, lacerations, punctures	670	—
Bruises, contusions	1,030	—
Heat burns	210	6
Chemical burns	100	—
Amputations	160	—
Carpal tunnel syndrome	40	—
Tendonitis	—	—
Multiple injuries	380	59
Soreness, Pain	320	—
Back pain	70	—
All other	1,310	89

Characteristic	Nonfatal Cases[b]	Fatalities
Part of body affected		
Head	640	31
Eye	280	—
Neck	160	—
Trunk	3,000	28
Back	1,670	—
Shoulder	630	—
Upper extremities	2,070	—
Finger	1,030	—
Hand, except finger	250	—
Wrist	260	—
Lower extremities	2,150	—
Knee	850	—
Foot, toe	360	—
Body systems	100	33
Multiple	880	62
All other	—	—
Source of injury, illness		
Chemicals, chemical products	630	—
Containers	390	—
Furniture, fixtures	—	—
Machinery	1,200	30
Parts and materials	1,600	21
Worker motion or position	430	—
Floor, ground surfaces	1,370	12
Handtools	530	—
Vehicles	850	62
Health care patient	—	—
All other	2,010	26
Event or exposure		
Contact with object, equipment	3,900	53
Struck by object	2,090	28
Struck against object	670	—
Caught in object, equipment, material	1,060	25
Fall to lower level	560	11
Fall on same level	820	—
Slips, trips	140	—
Overexertion	2,130	—
Overexertion in lifting	680	—
Repetitive motion	70	—
Exposed to harmful substance	520	16
Transportation accidents	410	60
Highway accident	260	35
Nonhighway accident, except air, rail, water	80	15
Pedestrian, nonpassenger struck by vehicle, mobile equipment	60	—
Fires, explosions	70	14
Assault, violent act	—	5
By person	—	—
By other	—	—
All other	410	—

Source: National Safety Council tabulations of Bureau of Labor Statistics data.
Note: Because of rounding and data exclusion of nonclassifiable responses, data may not sum to the totals. Dashes (—) indicate data that do not meet publication guidelines.
[a] Days away from work include those that result in days away from work with or without restricted work activity or job transfer.

[b] Data for mining operators in coal, metal, and nonmetal mining are provided to BLS by the Mine Safety and Health Administration, U.S. Department of Labor. Independent mining contractors are excluded from the coal, metal, and nonmetal mining industries. MSHA data do not reflect the changes in OSHA record-keeping requirements in 2002.
[c] In the fatalities column, non-Hispanic categories include cases with Hispanic origin not reported.

CONSTRUCTION

The Construction industry sector includes establishments engaged in construction of buildings, heavy construction other than buildings, and specialty trade contractors such as plumbing, electrical, carpentry, etc.

In 2005, employment in the Construction industry totaled 10,740,000 workers of which 8,895,000 were private sector employees.

NUMBER OF NONFATAL OCCUPATIONAL INJURIES AND ILLNESSES INVOLVING DAYS AWAY FROM WORK[a] AND FATAL OCCUPATIONAL INJURIES BY SELECTED WORKER AND CASE CHARACTERISTICS, UNITED STATES, CONSTRUCTION, 2005

Characteristic	Nonfatal Cases	Fatalities
Total	**157,070**	**1,192**
Sex		
Men	153,750	1,171
Women	3,320	21
Age		
Under 16	—	—
16 to 19	4,820	39
20 to 24	20,580	111
25 to 34	47,320	250
35 to 44	43,180	273
45 to 54	28,120	289
55 to 64	9,230	163
65 and over	1,360	67
Occupation		
Management, business, and financial	1,970	65
Professional and related	520	—
Service	1,250	—
Sales and related	400	—
Office and administrative support	980	5
Farming, fishing, and forestry	—	—
Construction and extractive	126,670	934
Installation, maintenance, and repair	15,080	79
Production	3,720	30
Transportation and material moving	6,310	70
Military occupations	—	—
Race or ethnic origin[b]		
White, non-Hispanic	90,070	758
Black, non-Hispanic	6,160	89
Hispanic	32,770	315
Other, multiple, and not reported	28,090	30
Nature of injury, illness		
Sprains, strains	54,490	—
Fractures	18,090	—
Cuts, lacerations, punctures	24,160	38
Bruises, contusions	11,240	—
Heat burns	1,230	23
Chemical burns	770	—
Amputations	1,260	—
Carpal tunnel syndrome	640	—
Tendonitis	570	—
Multiple injuries	6,690	432
Soreness, Pain	10,290	—
Back pain	3,560	—
All other	27,630	691

Characteristic	Nonfatal Cases	Fatalities
Part of body affected		
Head	12,860	314
Eye	6,390	—
Neck	2,370	24
Trunk	48,240	163
Back	30,190	12
Shoulder	7,980	—
Upper extremities	37,580	—
Finger	15,710	—
Hand, except finger	7,160	—
Wrist	5,120	—
Lower extremities	39,200	6
Knee	12,630	—
Foot, toe	8,590	—
Body systems	1,650	217
Multiple	13,690	463
All other	1,300	—
Source of injury, illness		
Chemicals, chemical products	1,620	35
Containers	6,820	17
Furniture, fixtures	2,850	5
Machinery	9,740	140
Parts and materials	36,700	142
Worker motion or position	20,780	—
Floor, ground surfaces	32,010	383
Handtools	13,270	10
Vehicles	8,360	276
Health care patient	30	—
All other	24,890	183
Event or exposure		
Contact with object, equipment	55,590	244
Struck by object	30,640	130
Struck against object	12,600	—
Caught in object, equipment, material	6,170	111
Fall to lower level	21,750	384
Fall on same level	12,360	—
Slips, trips	4,900	—
Overexertion	28,520	—
Overexertion in lifting	15,720	—
Repetitive motion	2,490	—
Exposed to harmful substance	5,520	164
Transportation accidents	6,190	318
Highway accident	3,600	154
Nonhighway accident, except air, rail, water	980	53
Pedestrian, nonpassenger struck by vehicle, mobile equipment	1,460	97
Fires, explosions	380	40
Assault, violent act	460	31
By person	180	20
By other	280	11
All other	18,910	8

Source: National Safety Council tabulations of Bureau of Labor Statistics data.
Note: Because of rounding and data exclusion of nonclassifiable responses, data may not sum to the totals. Dashes (—) indicate data that do not meet publication guidelines.

[a]Days away from work include those that result in days away from work with or without restricted work activity or job transfer.
[b]In the fatalities column, non-Hispanic categories include cases with Hispanic origin not reported.

MANUFACTURING

The Manufacturing industry sector includes establishments engaged in the mechanical or chemical transformation of materials, substances, or components into new products. It includes durable and nondurable goods such as food, textiles, apparel, lumber, wood products, paper and paper products, printing, chemicals and pharmaceuticals, petroleum and coal products, rubber and plastics products, metals and metal products, machinery, electrical equipment, and transportation equipment.

Manufacturing employment in 2005 was 16,173,000 workers of which 15,839,000 were private sector employees.

NUMBER OF NONFATAL OCCUPATIONAL INJURIES AND ILLNESSES INVOLVING DAYS AWAY FROM WORK[a] AND FATAL OCCUPATIONAL INJURIES BY SELECTED WORKER AND CASE CHARACTERISTICS, UNITED STATES, MANUFACTURING, 2005

Characteristic	Nonfatal Cases	Fatalities
Total	**209,130**	**393**
Sex		
Men	163,220	358
Women	45,740	35
Age		
Under 16	—	—
16 to 19	4,310	10
20 to 24	19,320	28
25 to 34	46,100	52
35 to 44	56,720	90
45 to 54	53,400	108
55 to 64	24,300	72
65 and over	2,680	32
Occupation		
Management, business, and financial	2,070	33
Professional and related	2,600	8
Service	4,090	7
Sales and related	1,270	10
Office and administrative support	7,240	5
Farming, fishing, and forestry	640	—
Construction and extractive	8,020	19
Installation, maintenance, and repair	14,680	51
Production	130,980	160
Transportation and material moving	37,180	94
Military occupations	—	—
Race or ethnic origin[b]		
White, non-Hispanic	108,640	275
Black, non-Hispanic	17,130	42
Hispanic	33,460	60
Other, multiple, and not reported	402,420	16
Nature of injury, illness		
Sprains, strains	74,190	—
Fractures	17,120	5
Cuts, lacerations, punctures	24,970	29
Bruises, contusions	16,700	—
Heat burns	3,500	15
Chemical burns	1,780	—
Amputations	3,750	—
Carpal tunnel syndrome	5,380	—
Tendonitis	1,860	—
Multiple injuries	7,650	114
Soreness, Pain	13,600	—
Back pain	4,830	—
All other	38,640	224

Characteristic	Nonfatal Cases	Fatalities
Part of body affected		
Head	16,000	97
Eye	9,670	—
Neck	2,250	11
Trunk	68,380	73
Back	38,590	9
Shoulder	15,150	—
Upper extremities	68,110	—
Finger	30,750	—
Hand, except finger	10,940	—
Wrist	12,680	—
Lower extremities	37,760	9
Knee	13,380	—
Foot, toe	9,730	—
Body systems	2,510	60
Multiple	12,910	141
All other	1,220	—
Source of injury, illness		
Chemicals, chemical products	4,500	23
Containers	24,310	18
Furniture, fixtures	6,120	—
Machinery	26,880	73
Parts and materials	36,840	58
Worker motion or position	37,440	—
Floor, ground surfaces	24,500	44
Handtools	12,030	—
Vehicles	11,540	118
Health care patient	20	—
All other	24,940	51
Event or exposure		
Contact with object, equipment	76,940	136
Struck by object	31,830	68
Struck against object	16,310	—
Caught in object, equipment, material	21,450	68
Fall to lower level	7,830	42
Fall on same level	18,330	5
Slips, trips	5,350	—
Overexertion	47,930	—
Overexertion in lifting	24,670	—
Repetitive motion	15,240	—
Exposed to harmful substance	10,430	35
Transportation accidents	4,670	109
Highway accident	1,930	51
Nonhighway accident, except air, rail, water	1,130	18
Pedestrian, nonpassenger struck by vehicle, mobile equipment	1,470	20
Fires, explosions	700	26
Assault, violent act	640	36
By person	320	22
By other	320	14
All other	21,070	—

Source: National Safety Council tabulations of Bureau of Labor Statistics data.
Note: Because of rounding and data exclusion of nonclassifiable responses, data may not sum to the totals. Dashes (—) indicate data that do not meet publication guidelines.

[a]Days away from work include those that result in days away from work with or without restricted work activity or job transfer.
[b]In the fatalities column, non-Hispanic categories include cases with Hispanic origin not reported.

WHOLESALE TRADE

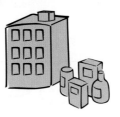

Establishments in Wholesale Trade generally sell merchandise to other businesses. The merchandise includes the outputs of agriculture, mining, manufacturing, and certain information industries, such as publishing.

Wholesale Trade employed 4,570,000 people in 2005 of which 4,354,000 were private sector employees.

NUMBER OF NONFATAL OCCUPATIONAL INJURIES AND ILLNESSES INVOLVING DAYS AWAY FROM WORK[a] AND FATAL OCCUPATIONAL INJURIES BY SELECTED WORKER AND CASE CHARACTERISTICS, UNITED STATES, WHOLESALE TRADE, 2005

Characteristic	Nonfatal Cases	Fatalities
Total	**80,170**	**209**
Sex		
Men	69,180	201
Women	10,990	8
Age		
Under 16	—	—
16 to 19	1,840	—
20 to 24	7,450	8
25 to 34	20,970	39
35 to 44	22,110	39
45 to 54	16,980	63
55 to 64	8,400	40
65 and over	1,960	15
Occupation		
Management, business, and financial	1,670	7
Professional and related	990	—
Service	1,130	—
Sales and related	5,750	45
Office and administrative support	6,310	—
Farming, fishing, and forestry	660	—
Construction and extractive	1,190	7
Installation, maintenance, and repair	9,940	32
Production	8,650	8
Transportation and material moving	43,870	100
Military occupations	—	—
Race or ethnic origin[b]		
White, non-Hispanic	39,490	158
Black, non-Hispanic	5,940	11
Hispanic	12,600	35
Other, multiple, and not reported	22,140	5
Nature of injury, illness		
Sprains, strains	36,090	—
Fractures	6,730	—
Cuts, lacerations, punctures	6,370	7
Bruises, contusions	6,450	—
Heat burns	530	9
Chemical burns	340	—
Amputations	620	—
Carpal tunnel syndrome	930	—
Tendonitis	270	—
Multiple injuries	3,100	78
Soreness, Pain	5,970	—
Back pain	2,420	—
All other	12,770	111

Characteristic	Nonfatal Cases	Fatalities
Part of body affected		
Head	4,520	40
Eye	1,670	—
Neck	1,350	—
Trunk	31,350	36
Back	19,310	—
Shoulder	5,430	—
Upper extremities	15,940	—
Finger	6,210	—
Hand, except finger	2,160	—
Wrist	3,260	—
Lower extremities	19,680	—
Knee	7,540	—
Foot, toe	4,100	—
Body systems	590	39
Multiple	6,390	87
All other	340	—
Source of injury, illness		
Chemicals, chemical products	680	7
Containers	16,400	—
Furniture, fixtures	1,890	5
Machinery	4,890	17
Parts and materials	10,330	13
Worker motion or position	11,410	—
Floor, ground surfaces	12,090	19
Handtools	2,500	—
Vehicles	12,350	125
Health care patient	—	—
All other	7,630	17
Event or exposure		
Contact with object, equipment	21,450	49
Struck by object	10,370	27
Struck against object	5,420	—
Caught in object, equipment, material	4,030	22
Fall to lower level	4,770	16
Fall on same level	8,580	—
Slips, trips	2,580	—
Overexertion	22,930	—
Overexertion in lifting	12,630	—
Repetitive motion	2,290	—
Exposed to harmful substance	1,890	14
Transportation accidents	6,390	106
Highway accident	3,890	91
Nonhighway accident, except air, rail, water	1,290	5
Pedestrian, nonpassenger struck by vehicle, mobile equipment	1,130	8
Fires, explosions	120	9
Assault, violent act	400	12
By person	210	5
By other	190	7
All other	8,780	—

Source: National Safety Council tabulations of Bureau of Labor Statistics data.
Note: Because of rounding and data exclusion of nonclassifiable responses, data may not sum to the totals. Dashes (—) indicate data that do not meet publication guidelines.

[a]Days away from work include those that result in days away from work with or without restricted work activity or job transfer.
[b]In the fatalities column, non-Hispanic categories include cases with Hispanic origin not reported.

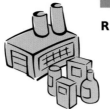

RETAIL TRADE

Establishments in Retail Trade generally sell merchandise in small quantities for personal or household consumption. This sector includes both store and nonstore retailers.

Retail Trade employed 16,733,000 people in 2005 of which 15,678,000 were private sector employees.

NUMBER OF NONFATAL OCCUPATIONAL INJURIES AND ILLNESSES INVOLVING DAYS AWAY FROM WORK[a] AND FATAL OCCUPATIONAL INJURIES BY SELECTED WORKER AND CASE CHARACTERISTICS, UNITED STATES, RETAIL TRADE, 2005

Characteristic	Nonfatal Cases	Fatalities
Total	**175,880**	**400**
Sex		
Men	104,650	344
Women	70,850	56
Age		
Under 16	—	—
16 to 19	11,060	13
20 to 24	23,910	39
25 to 34	38,620	68
35 to 44	39,200	90
45 to 54	35,660	85
55 to 64	18,750	61
65 and over	6,740	44
Occupation		
Management, business, and financial	2,850	7
Professional and related	1,380	—
Service	15,210	13
Sales and related	60,910	214
Office and administrative support	23,720	26
Farming, fishing, and forestry	160	—
Construction and extractive	2,800	—
Installation, maintenance, and repair	19,420	26
Production	8,760	8
Transportation and material moving	40,200	99
Military occupations	—	—
Race or ethnic origin[b]		
White, non-Hispanic	80,640	249
Black, non-Hispanic	10,250	56
Hispanic	13,460	42
Other, multiple, and not reported	71,530	53
Nature of injury, illness		
Sprains, strains	75,690	—
Fractures	12,320	5
Cuts, lacerations, punctures	18,550	181
Bruises, contusions	17,660	—
Heat burns	1,790	—
Chemical burns	1,030	—
Amputations	800	—
Carpal tunnel syndrome	1,920	—
Tendonitis	740	—
Multiple injuries	6,720	79
Soreness, Pain	12,650	—
Back pain	4,300	—
All other	25,990	129

Characteristic	Nonfatal Cases	Fatalities
Part of body affected		
Head	11,710	116
Eye	3,810	—
Neck	2,520	9
Trunk	61,710	108
Back	38,630	14
Shoulder	11,260	—
Upper extremities	40,330	—
Finger	15,680	—
Hand, except finger	6,860	—
Wrist	8,520	—
Lower extremities	40,700	—
Knee	15,480	—
Foot, toe	9,810	—
Body systems	1,830	27
Multiple	15,650	136
All other	1,430	—
Source of injury, illness		
Chemicals, chemical products	2,390	6
Containers	35,040	—
Furniture, fixtures	11,210	—
Machinery	12,030	—
Parts and materials	13,810	20
Worker motion or position	24,970	—
Floor, ground surfaces	34,540	32
Handtools	8,140	25
Vehicles	13,770	131
Health care patient	—	—
All other	19,980	178
Event or exposure		
Contact with object, equipment	51,720	26
Struck by object	28,480	20
Struck against object	13,680	—
Caught in object, equipment, material	6,600	6
Fall to lower level	9,890	18
Fall on same level	26,920	15
Slips, trips	4,550	—
Overexertion	45,820	—
Overexertion in lifting	29,050	—
Repetitive motion	5,340	—
Exposed to harmful substance	4,860	10
Transportation accidents	5,480	121
Highway accident	3,030	87
Nonhighway accident, except air, rail, water	890	6
Pedestrian, nonpassenger struck by vehicle, mobile equipment	1,390	20
Fires, explosions	500	—
Assault, violent act	2,020	202
By person	1,460	184
By other	570	18
All other	18,760	—

Source: National Safety Council tabulations of Bureau of Labor Statistics data.
Note: Because of rounding and data exclusion of nonclassifiable responses, data may not sum to the totals. Dashes (—) indicate data that do not meet publication guidelines

[a]*Days away from work include those that result in days away from work with or without restricted work activity or job transfer.*
[b]*In the fatalities column, non-Hispanic categories include cases with Hispanic origin not reported.*

TRANSPORTATION AND WAREHOUSING

This industry sector includes transportation of cargo and passengers, warehousing and storage of goods, scenic and sightseeing transportation, and support activities related to transportation by rail, highway, air, water, or pipeline.

Employment in the Transportation and Warehousing industry sector totaled 4,989,000 in 2005 of which 4,543,000 were private sector employees.

NUMBER OF NONFATAL OCCUPATIONAL INJURIES AND ILLNESSES INVOLVING DAYS AWAY FROM WORK[a] AND FATAL OCCUPATIONAL INJURIES BY SELECTED WORKER AND CASE CHARACTERISTICS, UNITED STATES, TRANSPORTATION AND WAREHOUSING,[b] 2005

Characteristic	Nonfatal Cases	Fatalities
Total	117,440	885
Sex		
Men	90,400	849
Women	23,140	36
Age		
Under 16	—	—
16 to 19	1,750	—
20 to 24	7,390	33
25 to 34	23,690	147
35 to 44	33,440	202
45 to 54	31,980	245
55 to 64	14,560	190
65 and over	2,390	64
Occupation		
Management, business, and financial	520	6
Professional and related	300	—
Service	6,770	6
Sales and related	440	—
Office and administrative support	13,750	14
Farming, fishing, and forestry	50	—
Construction and extractive	1,020	7
Installation, maintenance, and repair	9,340	23
Production	2,360	—
Transportation and material moving	82,650	825
Military occupations	—	—
Race or ethnic origin[c]		
White, non-Hispanic	35,230	621
Black, non-Hispanic	7,690	137
Hispanic	7,050	89
Other, multiple, and not reported	67,560	38
Nature of injury, illness		
Sprains, strains	57,220	—
Fractures	7,330	—
Cuts, lacerations, punctures	5,030	39
Bruises, contusions	11,680	—
Heat burns	430	39
Chemical burns	330	—
Amputations	240	—
Carpal tunnel syndrome	570	—
Tendonitis	290	—
Multiple injuries	4,980	404
Soreness, Pain	11,720	—
Back pain	4,520	—
All other	17,640	396

Characteristic	Nonfatal Cases	Fatalities
Part of body affected		
Head	7,680	156
Eye	2,910	—
Neck	2,290	21
Trunk	46,520	127
Back	28,570	—
Shoulder	9,960	—
Upper extremities	16,880	—
Finger	4,800	—
Hand, except finger	2,120	—
Wrist	3,670	—
Lower extremities	28,690	10
Knee	10,420	—
Foot, toe	5,800	—
Body systems	1,260	116
Multiple	13,280	450
All other	850	—
Source of injury, illness		
Chemicals, chemical products	970	21
Containers	26,900	13
Furniture, fixtures	2,360	—
Machinery	2,810	15
Parts and materials	8,900	24
Worker motion or position	16,760	—
Floor, ground surfaces	19,680	36
Handtools	1,950	5
Vehicles	24,800	715
Health care patient	120	—
All other	12,180	56
Event or exposure		
Contact with object, equipment	24,540	93
Struck by object	12,160	57
Struck against object	6,550	—
Caught in object, equipment, material	3,410	34
Fall to lower level	8,720	25
Fall on same level	11,520	8
Slips, trips	3,590	—
Overexertion	34,740	—
Overexertion in lifting	17,450	—
Repetitive motion	2,350	—
Exposed to harmful substance	2,570	30
Transportation accidents	13,170	662
Highway accident	8,360	491
Nonhighway accident, except air, rail, water	2,180	14
Pedestrian, nonpassenger struck by vehicle, mobile equipment	1,380	76
Fires, explosions	230	10
Assault, violent act	660	54
By person	400	41
By other	250	13
All other	15,370	—

Source: National Safety Council tabulations of Bureau of Labor Statistics data.
Note: Because of rounding and data exclusion of nonclassifiable responses, data may not sum to the totals. Dashes (—) indicate data that do not meet publication guidelines.
[a]Days away from work include those that result in days away from work with or without restricted work activity or job transfer.

[b]Data for employees in railroad transportation are provided to BLS by the Federal Railroad Administration, U.S. Department of Transportation. FRA data do not reflect the changes in OSHA record-keeping requirements in 2002.
[c]In the fatalities column, non-Hispanic categories include cases with Hispanic origin not reported.

The Utilities sector includes establishments that provide electric power generation, transmission, and distribution; natural gas distribution; steam supply; water treatment and distribution; and sewage collection, treatment, and disposal.

The Utilities sector employed 834,000 people in 2005, all of which were private sector employees.

NUMBER OF NONFATAL OCCUPATIONAL INJURIES AND ILLNESSES INVOLVING DAYS AWAY FROM WORK[a] AND FATAL OCCUPATIONAL INJURIES BY SELECTED WORKER AND CASE CHARACTERISTICS, UNITED STATES, UTILITIES, 2005

Characteristic	Nonfatal Cases	Fatalities
Total	7,230	30
Sex		
Men	6,470	30
Women	760	—
Age		
Under 16	—	—
16 to 19	40	—
20 to 24	310	—
25 to 34	1,130	6
35 to 44	2,050	8
45 to 54	2,450	9
55 to 64	1,080	—
65 and over	60	—
Occupation		
Management, business, and financial	120	—
Professional and related	350	—
Service	160	—
Sales and related	120	—
Office and administrative support	1,170	—
Farming, fishing, and forestry	—	—
Construction and extractive	900	—
Installation, maintenance, and repair	3,240	19
Production	820	5
Transportation and material moving	360	—
Military occupations	—	—
Race or ethnic origin[b]		
White, non-Hispanic	3,370	28
Black, non-Hispanic	270	—
Hispanic	130	—
Other, multiple, and not reported	3,440	—
Nature of injury, illness		
Sprains, strains	3,380	—
Fractures	540	—
Cuts, lacerations, punctures	330	—
Bruises, contusions	490	—
Heat burns	70	—
Chemical burns	40	—
Amputations	—	—
Carpal tunnel syndrome	130	—
Tendonitis	20	—
Multiple injuries	270	6
Soreness, Pain	400	—
Back pain	180	—
All other	1,560	24

Characteristic	Nonfatal Cases	Fatalities
Part of body affected		
Head	360	6
Eye	140	—
Neck	90	—
Trunk	2,690	—
Back	1,520	—
Shoulder	520	—
Upper extremities	1,130	—
Finger	310	—
Hand, except finger	250	—
Wrist	280	—
Lower extremities	1,900	—
Knee	760	—
Foot, toe	230	—
Body systems	170	15
Multiple	850	5
All other	40	—
Source of injury, illness		
Chemicals, chemical products	90	—
Containers	340	—
Furniture, fixtures	50	—
Machinery	330	—
Parts and materials	1,080	8
Worker motion or position	1,690	—
Floor, ground surfaces	1,440	7
Handtools	460	—
Vehicles	580	9
Health care patient	—	—
All other	1,170	—
Event or exposure		
Contact with object, equipment	1,340	—
Struck by object	650	—
Struck against object	350	—
Caught in object, equipment, material	180	—
Fall to lower level	590	6
Fall on same level	850	—
Slips, trips	370	—
Overexertion	1,490	—
Overexertion in lifting	630	—
Repetitive motion	300	—
Exposed to harmful substance	420	11
Transportation accidents	450	10
Highway accident	370	7
Nonhighway accident, except air, rail, water	30	—
Pedestrian, nonpassenger struck by vehicle, mobile equipment	20	—
Fires, explosions	30	—
Assault, violent act	160	—
By person	50	—
By other	110	—
All other	1,220	—

Source: National Safety Council tabulations of Bureau of Labor Statistics data.
Note: Because of rounding and data exclusion of nonclassifiable responses, data may not sum to the totals. Dashes (—) indicate data that do not meet publication guidelines.

[a] Days away from work include those that result in days away from work with or without restricted work activity or job transfer.
[b] In the fatalities column, non-Hispanic categories include cases with Hispanic origin not reported.

INFORMATION

The Information sector includes establishments that (a) produce and distribute information and cultural products, (b) provide the means to transmit or distribute these products as well as data or communications, and (c) process data. Included are both traditional and Internet publishing and broadcasting, motion pictures and sound recordings, telecommunications, Internet service providers, Web search portals, data processing, and information services.

The Information sector employed 3,209,000 people in 2005 of which 3,083,000 were private sector employees.

NUMBER OF NONFATAL OCCUPATIONAL INJURIES AND ILLNESSES INVOLVING DAYS AWAY FROM WORK[a] AND FATAL OCCUPATIONAL INJURIES BY SELECTED WORKER AND CASE CHARACTERISTICS, UNITED STATES, INFORMATION, 2005

Characteristic	Nonfatal Cases	Fatalities
Total	**20,690**	**65**
Sex		
Men	13,780	48
Women	6,910	17
Age		
Under 16	—	—
16 to 19	260	—
20 to 24	1,300	5
25 to 34	4,800	8
35 to 44	5,530	16
45 to 54	5,840	18
55 to 64	2,590	13
65 and over	250	5
Occupation		
Management, business, and financial	1,280	—
Professional and related	1,670	—
Service	890	7
Sales and related	1,320	8
Office and administrative support	4,160	—
Farming, fishing, and forestry	—	—
Construction and extractive	280	—
Installation, maintenance, and repair	7,050	11
Production	1,800	—
Transportation and material moving	2,200	30
Military occupations	—	—
Race or ethnic origin[b]		
White, non-Hispanic	7,320	54
Black, non-Hispanic	1,030	—
Hispanic	1,110	6
Other, multiple, and not reported	11,210	—
Nature of injury, illness		
Sprains, strains	8,160	—
Fractures	1,220	—
Cuts, lacerations, punctures	1,440	7
Bruises, contusions	1,730	—
Heat burns	60	—
Chemical burns	30	—
Amputations	50	—
Carpal tunnel syndrome	580	—
Tendonitis	190	—
Multiple injuries	1,120	28
Soreness, Pain	2,290	—
Back pain	870	—
All other	3,820	28

Characteristic	Nonfatal Cases	Fatalities
Part of body affected		
Head	990	10
Eye	320	—
Neck	390	—
Trunk	6,520	16
Back	4,250	—
Shoulder	1,130	—
Upper extremities	4,260	—
Finger	1,020	—
Hand, except finger	530	—
Wrist	1,290	—
Lower extremities	5,010	—
Knee	1,790	—
Foot, toe	1,140	—
Body systems	590	8
Multiple	2,810	30
All other	120	—
Source of injury, illness		
Chemicals, chemical products	310	—
Containers	1,770	—
Furniture, fixtures	430	—
Machinery	1,070	—
Parts and materials	1,440	—
Worker motion or position	4,430	—
Floor, ground surfaces	5,620	—
Handtools	530	—
Vehicles	2,070	43
Health care patient	—	—
All other	3,020	9
Event or exposure		
Contact with object, equipment	3,880	—
Struck by object	1,440	—
Struck against object	1,590	—
Caught in object, equipment, material	590	—
Fall to lower level	2,030	—
Fall on same level	3,760	—
Slips, trips	720	—
Overexertion	3,430	—
Overexertion in lifting	1,690	—
Repetitive motion	1,430	—
Exposed to harmful substance	930	7
Transportation accidents	1,400	41
Highway accident	1,150	35
Nonhighway accident, except air, rail, water	100	—
Pedestrian, nonpassenger struck by vehicle, mobile equipment	20	—
Fires, explosions	—	—
Assault, violent act	220	9
By person	70	7
By other	150	—
All other	2,870	—

Source: National Safety Council tabulations of Bureau of Labor Statistics data.
Note: Because of rounding and data exclusion of nonclassifiable responses, data may not sum to the totals. Dashes (—) indicate data that do not meet publication guidelines.

[a]*Days away from work include those that result in days away from work with or without restricted work activity or job transfer.*
[b]*In the fatalities column, non-Hispanic categories include cases with Hispanic origin not reported.*

Financial Activities includes the Finance and Insurance sector and the Real Estate and Rental and Leasing sector. Included are banks and other savings institutions; securities and commodities brokers, dealers, exchanges, and services; insurance carriers, brokers, and agents; real estate operators, developers, agents, and brokers; and establishments that rent and lease goods such as automobiles, computers, and household and industrial machinery and equipment.

Financial Activities had 9,975,000 workers in 2005 of which 9,187,000 were private sector employees.

NUMBER OF NONFATAL OCCUPATIONAL INJURIES AND ILLNESSES INVOLVING DAYS AWAY FROM WORKa AND FATAL OCCUPATIONAL INJURIES BY SELECTED WORKER AND CASE CHARACTERISTICS, UNITED STATES, FINANCIAL ACTIVITIES, 2005

Characteristic	Nonfatal Cases	Fatalities
Total	**38,250**	**99**
Sex		
Men	20,630	87
Women	17,620	12
Age		
Under 16	—	—
16 to 19	480	—
20 to 24	3,280	8
25 to 34	8,420	15
35 to 44	6,570	17
45 to 54	9,640	30
55 to 64	5,500	18
65 and over	1,060	10
Occupation		
Management, business, and financial	4,560	27
Professional and related	970	—
Service	8,580	10
Sales and related	3,430	26
Office and administrative support	9,680	9
Farming, fishing, and forestry	—	—
Construction and extractive	1,470	5
Installation, maintenance, and repair	4,550	10
Production	500	—
Transportation and material moving	4,380	12
Military occupations	—	—
Race or ethnic origin[b]		
White, non-Hispanic	16,680	68
Black, non-Hispanic	3,120	13
Hispanic	4,640	15
Other, multiple, and not reported	13,810	—
Nature of injury, illness		
Sprains, strains	13,720	—
Fractures	2,450	—
Cuts, lacerations, punctures	3,490	26
Bruises, contusions	2,730	—
Heat burns	510	—
Chemical burns	450	—
Amputations	150	—
Carpal tunnel syndrome	1,740	—
Tendonitis	120	—
Multiple injuries	1,980	31
Soreness, Pain	3,730	—
Back pain	1,290	—
All other	7,160	37

Characteristic	Nonfatal Cases	Fatalities
Part of body affected		
Head	2,970	31
Eye	1,170	—
Neck	720	—
Trunk	11,000	15
Back	7,280	—
Shoulder	1,500	—
Upper extremities	7,600	—
Finger	2,260	—
Hand, except finger	920	—
Wrist	2,610	—
Lower extremities	8,640	—
Knee	3,360	—
Foot, toe	1,560	—
Body systems	1,720	9
Multiple	5,200	40
All other	390	—
Source of injury, illness		
Chemicals, chemical products	1,070	—
Containers	2,800	—
Furniture, fixtures	2,240	—
Machinery	1,990	—
Parts and materials	2,050	5
Worker motion or position	6,800	—
Floor, ground surfaces	9,400	17
Handtools	1,660	—
Vehicles	3,420	40
Health care patient	120	—
All other	6,690	30
Event or exposure		
Contact with object, equipment	8,190	—
Struck by object	4,540	—
Struck against object	2,100	—
Caught in object, equipment, material	590	—
Fall to lower level	3,290	12
Fall on same level	6,690	5
Slips, trips	1,190	—
Overexertion	6,620	—
Overexertion in lifting	3,810	—
Repetitive motion	2,900	—
Exposed to harmful substance	2,570	5
Transportation accidents	2,130	38
Highway accident	1,580	24
Nonhighway accident, except air, rail, water	310	—
Pedestrian, nonpassenger struck by vehicle, mobile equipment	210	6
Fires, explosions	270	—
Assault, violent act	400	33
By person	270	22
By other	120	11
All other	4,000	—

Source: National Safety Council tabulations of Bureau of Labor Statistics data.
Note: Because of rounding and data exclusion of nonclassifiable responses, data may not sum to the totals. Dashes (—) indicate data that do not meet publication guidelines.

aDays away from work include those that result in days away from work with or without restricted work activity or job transfer.
bIn the fatalities column, non-Hispanic categories include cases with Hispanic origin not reported.

PROFESSIONAL AND BUSINESS SERVICES

The Professional and Business Services sector includes legal, accounting, architectural, engineering, computer, consulting, research, advertising, photographic, translation and interpretation, veterinary, and other professional scientific and technical services. Also included are business management and administrative and support activities and waste management and remediation services.

Professional and Business Services employed 13,981,000 people in 2005 of which 11,923,000 were private sector employees.

NUMBER OF NONFATAL OCCUPATIONAL INJURIES AND ILLNESSES INVOLVING DAYS AWAY FROM WORKᵃ AND FATAL OCCUPATIONAL INJURIES BY SELECTED WORKER AND CASE CHARACTERISTICS, UNITED STATES, PROFESSIONAL AND BUSINESS SERVICES, 2005

Characteristic	Nonfatal Cases	Fatalities
Total	**91,840**	**482**
Sex		
Men	62,450	461
Women	29,390	21
Age		
Under 16	—	—
16 to 19	3,340	16
20 to 24	10,920	38
25 to 34	23,070	108
35 to 44	21,580	120
45 to 54	19,730	113
55 to 64	9,540	55
65 and over	3,160	31
Occupation		
Management, business, and financial	2,830	19
Professional and related	8,870	25
Service	30,940	251
Sales and related	2,280	5
Office and administrative support	9,780	8
Farming, fishing, and forestry	40	6
Construction and extractive	3,330	43
Installation, maintenance, and repair	7,230	16
Production	6,450	18
Transportation and material moving	19,690	91
Military occupations	—	—
Race or ethnic originᵇ		
White, non-Hispanic	43,230	276
Black, non-Hispanic	9,050	60
Hispanic	14,330	133
Other, multiple, and not reported	25,240	13
Nature of injury, illness		
Sprains, strains	34,770	—
Fractures	7,390	—
Cuts, lacerations, punctures	7,870	32
Bruises, contusions	7,480	—
Heat burns	490	—
Chemical burns	260	—
Amputations	510	—
Carpal tunnel syndrome	1,590	—
Tendonitis	470	—
Multiple injuries	3,760	177
Soreness, Pain	8,260	—
Back pain	*1,890*	—
All other	19,010	265

Characteristic	Nonfatal Cases	Fatalities
Part of body affected		
Head	5,640	102
Eye	*2,070*	—
Neck	1,610	9
Trunk	29,270	80
Back	*19,040*	—
Shoulder	*5,060*	—
Upper extremities	19,610	—
Finger	*7,080*	—
Hand, except finger	*3,330*	—
Wrist	*4,220*	—
Lower extremities	21,640	—
Knee	*7,430*	—
Foot, toe	*4,320*	—
Body systems	1,900	102
Multiple	10,450	187
All other	1,720	
Source of injury, illness		
Chemicals, chemical products	1,330	20
Containers	9,840	5
Furniture, fixtures	4,360	—
Machinery	5,270	57
Parts and materials	5,790	27
Worker motion or position	14,740	—
Floor, ground surfaces	19,410	66
Handtools	4,060	15
Vehicles	11,130	192
Health care patient	420	—
All other	15,480	99
Event or exposure		
Contact with object, equipment	22,010	82
Struck by object	*10,110*	*46*
Struck against object	*6,190*	—
Caught in object, equipment, material	*3,000*	*34*
Fall to lower level	6,010	65
Fall on same level	14,390	6
Slips, trips	2,410	—
Overexertion	17,070	—
Overexertion in lifting	*10,210*	—
Repetitive motion	3,470	—
Exposed to harmful substance	3,610	72
Transportation accidents	7,880	203
Highway accident	*5,380*	*101*
Nonhighway accident, except air, rail, water	*1,190*	*28*
Pedestrian, nonpassenger struck by vehicle, mobile equipment	*1,190*	*50*
Fires, explosions	50	7
Assault, violent act	3,290	42
By person	*810*	*26*
By other	*2,470*	*16*
All other	11,670	—

Source: National Safety Council tabulations of Bureau of Labor Statistics data.
Note: Because of rounding and data exclusion of nonclassifiable responses, data may not sum to the totals. Dashes (—) indicate data that do not meet publication guidelines.

ᵃ*Days away from work include those that result in days away from work with or without restricted work activity or job transfer.*
ᵇ*In the fatalities column, non-Hispanic categories include cases with Hispanic origin not reported.*

EDUCATIONAL AND HEALTH SERVICES

Educational services includes instruction and training through schools, colleges, universities, and training centers. Health services includes ambulatory health care facilities, hospitals, nursing and residential care facilities, and social assistance for individuals, families, and communities.

Educational and Health Services employed 18,834,000 people in 2005 of which 17,752,000 were private sector employees.

NUMBER OF NONFATAL OCCUPATIONAL INJURIES AND ILLNESSES INVOLVING DAYS AWAY FROM WORK[a] AND FATAL OCCUPATIONAL INJURIES BY SELECTED WORKER AND CASE CHARACTERISTICS, UNITED STATES, EDUCATIONAL AND HEALTH SERVICES, 2005

Characteristic	Nonfatal Cases	Fatalities
Total	**186,400**	**150**
Sex		
Men	39,080	103
Women	147,290	47
Age		
Under 16	—	—
16 to 19	3,400	—
20 to 24	16,680	9
25 to 34	39,880	26
35 to 44	46,340	27
45 to 54	48,390	41
55 to 64	25,860	36
65 and over	4,350	11
Occupation		
Management, business, and financial	4,930	10
Professional and related	59,600	—
Service	101,280	82
Sales and related	480	—
Office and administrative support	10,930	6
Farming, fishing, and forestry	—	—
Construction and extractive	1,030	—
Installation, maintenance, and repair	3,020	8
Production	2,060	—
Transportation and material moving	3,020	37
Military occupations	—	—
Race or ethnic origin[b]		
White, non-Hispanic	83,920	118
Black, non-Hispanic	29,880	14
Hispanic	12,770	8
Other, multiple, and not reported	59,840	10
Nature of injury, illness		
Sprains, strains	96,970	—
Fractures	9,730	5
Cuts, lacerations, punctures	5,640	17
Bruises, contusions	17,430	—
Heat burns	1,750	—
Chemical burns	500	—
Amputations	70	—
Carpal tunnel syndrome	1,370	—
Tendonitis	650	—
Multiple injuries	7,460	69
Soreness, Pain	20,080	—
Back pain	7,850	—
All other	24,750	56

Characteristic	Nonfatal Cases	Fatalities
Part of body affected		
Head	8,750	24
Eye	2,510	—
Neck	3,620	—
Trunk	78,330	16
Back	55,960	—
Shoulder	12,000	—
Upper extremities	29,060	—
Finger	7,760	—
Hand, except finger	4,150	—
Wrist	7,950	—
Lower extremities	35,730	8
Knee	15,390	—
Foot, toe	5,610	—
Body systems	3,220	24
Multiple	26,380	75
All other	1,320	—
Source of injury, illness		
Chemicals, chemical products	2,460	9
Containers	11,020	—
Furniture, fixtures	9,260	—
Machinery	4,360	—
Parts and materials	2,270	7
Worker motion or position	22,420	—
Floor, ground surfaces	42,200	17
Handtools	2,400	5
Vehicles	10,590	91
Health care patient	53,680	—
All other	25,740	20
Event or exposure		
Contact with object, equipment	24,590	5
Struck by object	12,370	—
Struck against object	7,190	—
Caught in object, equipment, material	3,230	—
Fall to lower level	6,650	—
Fall on same level	36,830	10
Slips, trips	5,400	—
Overexertion	66,660	—
Overexertion in lifting	31,560	—
Repetitive motion	3,760	—
Exposed to harmful substance	7,720	11
Transportation accidents	7,400	90
Highway accident	6,270	38
Nonhighway accident, except air, rail, water	390	—
Pedestrian, nonpassenger struck by vehicle, mobile equipment	420	6
Fires, explosions	130	—
Assault, violent act	10,410	28
By person	9,850	12
By other	560	16
All other	16,850	—

Source: National Safety Council tabulations of Bureau of Labor Statistics data.
Note: Because of rounding and data exclusion of nonclassifiable responses, data may not sum to the totals. Dashes (—) indicate data that do not meet publication guidelines.

[a] Days away from work include those that result in days away from work with or without restricted work activity or job transfer.
[b] In the fatalities column, non-Hispanic categories include cases with Hispanic origin not reported.

LEISURE AND HOSPITALITY

The Leisure sector includes establishments that provide arts, entertainment, and recreation experiences such as theatre, dance, music, and spectator sports, museums, zoos, amusement and theme parks, casinos, golf courses, ski areas, marinas, and fitness and sports centers. The

Hospitality sector includes hotels and other traveler accommodations, food services, and drinking places.

The Leisure and Hospitality sector employed 11,618,000 people in 2005 of which 10,931,000 were private sector employees.

NUMBER OF NONFATAL OCCUPATIONAL INJURIES AND ILLNESSES INVOLVING DAYS AWAY FROM WORK[a] AND FATAL OCCUPATIONAL INJURIES BY SELECTED WORKER AND CASE CHARACTERISTICS, UNITED STATES, LEISURE AND HOSPITALITY, 2005

Characteristic	Nonfatal Cases	Fatalities
Total	93,900	213
Sex		
Men	46,560	176
Women	47,340	37
Age		
Under 16	—	—
16 to 19	8,240	12
20 to 24	15,680	19
25 to 34	22,120	41
35 to 44	18,930	42
45 to 54	16,320	50
55 to 64	9,570	35
65 and over	1,920	14
Occupation		
Management, business, and financial	4,170	28
Professional and related	4,080	—
Service	70,440	127
Sales and related	2,600	6
Office and administrative support	2,040	10
Farming, fishing, and forestry	—	—
Construction and extractive	540	—
Installation, maintenance, and repair	2,940	6
Production	2,120	—
Transportation and material moving	4,900	30
Military occupations	—	—
Race or ethnic origin[b]		
White, non-Hispanic	35,680	124
Black, non-Hispanic	7,650	27
Hispanic	16,760	37
Other, multiple, and not reported	33,800	25
Nature of injury, illness		
Sprains, strains	30,520	—
Fractures	6,890	—
Cuts, lacerations, punctures	14,660	83
Bruises, contusions	8,440	—
Heat burns	6,120	—
Chemical burns	490	—
Amputations	460	—
Carpal tunnel syndrome	970	—
Tendonitis	260	—
Multiple injuries	3,830	42
Soreness, Pain	7,830	—
Back pain	2,330	—
All other	13,420	81

Characteristic	Nonfatal Cases	Fatalities
Part of body affected		
Head	4,770	55
Eye	1,620	—
Neck	640	9
Trunk	27,300	44
Back	17,490	5
Shoulder	4,920	—
Upper extremities	29,920	—
Finger	13,260	—
Hand, except finger	6,200	—
Wrist	4,010	—
Lower extremities	19,630	—
Knee	7,740	—
Foot, toe	3,230	—
Body systems	1,520	28
Multiple	8,200	72
All other	1,920	—
Source of injury, illness		
Chemicals, chemical products	1,440	—
Containers	12,500	—
Furniture, fixtures	4,910	—
Machinery	6,330	9
Parts and materials	3,120	10
Worker motion or position	12,820	—
Floor, ground surfaces	23,550	18
Handtools	6,500	13
Vehicles	5,500	55
Health care patient	—	—
All other	17,230	103
Event or exposure		
Contact with object, equipment	28,010	14
Struck by object	14,580	11
Struck against object	9,490	—
Caught in object, equipment, material	2,260	—
Fall to lower level	4,090	9
Fall on same level	20,430	7
Slips, trips	3,580	—
Overexertion	13,020	—
Overexertion in lifting	7,320	—
Repetitive motion	2,580	—
Exposed to harmful substance	8,740	16
Transportation accidents	3,000	55
Highway accident	1,900	26
Nonhighway accident, except air, rail, water	470	11
Pedestrian, nonpassenger struck by vehicle, mobile equipment	260	10
Fires, explosions	—	6
Assault, violent act	1,140	104
By person	720	89
By other	420	14
All other	9,310	—

Source: National Safety Council tabulations of Bureau of Labor Statistics data.
Note: Because of rounding and data exclusion of nonclassifiable responses, data may not sum to the totals. Dashes (—) indicate data that do not meet publication guidelines.

[a]Days away from work include those that result in days away from work with or without restricted work activity or job transfer.
[b]In the fatalities column, non-Hispanic categories include cases with Hispanic origin not reported.

OTHER SERVICES

The Other Services sector includes repair and maintenance of equipment and machinery and personal and household goods, personal care and laundry services, and religious, grant making, civic, professional, and similar organizations.

The Other Services sector employed 6,990,000 people in 2005 of which 5,946,000 were private sector employees.

NUMBER OF NONFATAL OCCUPATIONAL INJURIES AND ILLNESSES INVOLVING DAYS AWAY FROM WORK[a] AND FATAL OCCUPATIONAL INJURIES BY SELECTED WORKER AND CASE CHARACTERISTICS, UNITED STATES, OTHER SERVICES (EXCEPT PUBLIC ADMINISTRATION), 2005

Characteristic	Nonfatal Cases	Fatalities
Total	**28,790**	**210**
Sex		
Men	19,760	193
Women	8,980	17
Age		
Under 16	—	—
16 to 19	950	—
20 to 24	3,470	10
25 to 34	6,640	38
35 to 44	6,890	44
45 to 54	6,600	56
55 to 64	3,380	38
65 and over	730	21
Occupation		
Management, business, and financial	850	19
Professional and related	1,500	—
Service	5,980	53
Sales and related	960	—
Office and administrative support	1,410	—
Farming, fishing, and forestry	30	—
Construction and extractive	250	—
Installation, maintenance, and repair	9,450	84
Production	3,440	15
Transportation and material moving	4,850	29
Military occupations	—	—
Race or ethnic origin[b]		
White, non-Hispanic	16,010	151
Black, non-Hispanic	2,180	25
Hispanic	3,590	27
Other, multiple, and not reported	7,010	7
Nature of injury, illness		
Sprains, strains	9,710	—
Fractures	2,410	—
Cuts, lacerations, punctures	3,590	47
Bruises, contusions	2,190	—
Heat burns	420	6
Chemical burns	130	—
Amputations	130	—
Carpal tunnel syndrome	550	—
Tendonitis	220	—
Multiple injuries	1,150	62
Soreness, Pain	2,510	—
Back pain	*1,010*	—
All other	5,790	97

Characteristic	Nonfatal Cases	Fatalities
Part of body affected		
Head	2,400	45
Eye	*1,300*	—
Neck	320	—
Trunk	8,340	44
Back	*5,380*	—
Shoulder	*1,270*	—
Upper extremities	7,980	—
Finger	*3,030*	—
Hand, except finger	*1,540*	—
Wrist	*1,800*	—
Lower extremities	6,300	—
Knee	*2,280*	—
Foot, toe	*1,390*	—
Body systems	460	44
Multiple	2,680	73
All other	310	—
Source of injury, illness		
Chemicals, chemical products	460	11
Containers	2,000	—
Furniture, fixtures	790	—
Machinery	1,910	14
Parts and materials	3,070	14
Worker motion or position	4,680	—
Floor, ground surfaces	5,130	20
Handtools	1,890	6
Vehicles	2,870	73
Health care patient	100	—
All other	5,900	68
Event or exposure		
Contact with object, equipment	8,620	36
Struck by object	*4,840*	*27*
Struck against object	*1,740*	—
Caught in object, equipment, material	*1,020*	*7*
Fall to lower level	1,440	18
Fall on same level	3,810	—
Slips, trips	920	—
Overexertion	5,470	—
Overexertion in lifting	*3,250*	—
Repetitive motion	1,340	—
Exposed to harmful substance	1,250	23
Transportation accidents	1,510	55
Highway accident	*880*	*33*
Nonhighway accident, except air, rail, water	*160*	*5*
Pedestrian, nonpassenger struck by vehicle, mobile equipment	*440*	*12*
Fires, explosions	80	11
Assault, violent act	840	61
By person	*160*	*42*
By other	*680*	*19*
All other	3,520	—

Source: National Safety Council tabulations of Bureau of Labor Statistics data.
Note: Because of rounding and data exclusion of nonclassifiable responses, data may not sum to the totals. Dashes (—) indicate data that do not meet publication guidelines.

[a]*Days away from work include those that result in days away from work with or without restricted work activity or job transfer.*
[b]*In the fatalities column, non-Hispanic categories include cases with Hispanic origin not reported.*

GOVERNMENT

Government includes public employees at all levels from federal (civilian and military) to state, county, and municipal.

Government employment totaled 21,629,000 in 2005.

NUMBER OF NONFATAL OCCUPATIONAL INJURIES AND ILLNESSES INVOLVING DAYS AWAY FROM WORKª AND FATAL OCCUPATIONAL INJURIES BY SELECTED WORKER AND CASE CHARACTERISTICS, UNITED STATES, GOVERNMENT, 2005

Characteristic	Nonfatal Cases	Fatalities
Total	(b)	520
Sex		
Men		458
Women		62
Age		
Under 16		—
16 to 19		12
20 to 24		45
25 to 34		110
35 to 44		121
45 to 54		116
55 to 64		76
65 and over		40
Occupation		
Management, business, and financial		23
Professional and related		20
Service		259
Sales and related		—
Office and administrative support		21
Farming, fishing, and forestry		10
Construction and extractive		58
Installation, maintenance, and repair		14
Production		9
Transportation and material moving		52
Military occupations		48
Race or ethnic originc		
White, non-Hispanic		396
Black, non-Hispanic		74
Hispanic		31
Other, multiple, and not reported		19
Nature of injury, illness		
Sprains, strains		—
Fractures		11
Cuts, lacerations, punctures		98
Bruises, contusions		—
Heat burns		7
Chemical burns		—
Amputations		—
Carpal tunnel syndrome		—
Tendonitis		—
Multiple injuries		176
Soreness, Pain		—
Back pain		—
All other		225

Characteristic	Nonfatal Cases	Fatalities
Part of body affected		
Head		133
Eye		—
Neck		15
Trunk		81
Back		5
Shoulder		—
Upper extremities		—
Finger		—
Hand, except finger		—
Wrist		—
Lower extremities		9
Knee		—
Foot, toe		—
Body systems		68
Multiple		211
All other		—
Source of injury, illness		
Chemicals, chemical products		8
Containers		—
Furniture, fixtures		—
Machinery		17
Parts and materials		10
Worker motion or position		—
Floor, ground surfaces		44
Handtools		—
Vehicles		285
Health care patient		—
All other		147
Event or exposure		
Contact with object, equipment		39
Struck by object		31
Struck against object		—
Caught in object, equipment, material		8
Fall to lower level		21
Fall on same level		13
Slips, trips		—
Overexertion		—
Overexertion in lifting		—
Repetitive motion		—
Exposed to harmful substance		35
Transportation accidents		279
Highway accident		172
Nonhighway accident, except air, rail, water		17
Pedestrian, nonpassenger struck by vehicle, mobile equipment		57
Fires, explosions		12
Assault, violent act		118
By person		86
By other		30
All other		—

Source: National Safety Council tabulations of Bureau of Labor Statistics data.
Note: Because of rounding and data exclusion of nonclassifiable responses, data may not sum to the totals. Dashes (—) indicate data that do not meet publication guidelines.
ªDays away from work include those that result in days away from work with or without restricted work activity or job transfer.

bData for government entities not collected in the national BLS Survey of Occupational Injuries and Illnesses.
cIn the fatalities column, non-Hispanic categories include cases with Hispanic origin not reported.

OCCUPATIONAL HEALTH

More than 40,000 new skin diseases or disorders cases in 2006.

Approximately 228,000 occupational illnesses were recognized or diagnosed by private employers in 2006 according to the Bureau of Labor Statistics (BLS), a decrease of 6% from 2005. The overall incidence rate of occupational illness for all workers was 24.6 per 10,000 full-time workers. Of the major industry sectors, manufacturing had the highest overall rate for total cases in 2006, 57.7 per 10,000 full-time workers. Agriculture, forestry, fishing, and hunting had the second highest incidence rate, 41.3, followed by utilities with a rate of 39.7. Workers in agriculture, forestry, fishing, and hunting had the highest illness rates for skin diseases and disorders and for poisoning, while workers in education and health services had the highest rate for respiratory conditions. Workers in manufacturing had the highest rates in the hearing loss and "all other illnesses" categories.

Manufacturing accounted for about 36% of new illness cases in 2006. Skin diseases or disorders were the most common illness with 41,400 new cases, followed by

hearing loss with 24,400, respiratory conditions with 17,700, and poisonings with 3,400. Since the revised recordkeeping guidelines that became effective January 1, 2002, no longer provide categories to separately record cases such as disorders associated with repeated trauma or disorders due to physical agents, these cases are now being captured in the "all other illnesses" category, which accounted for 141,100 or about 62% of all new illness cases in 2006.

The table below shows the number of occupational illnesses and the incidence rate per 10,000 full-time workers as measured by the 2006 BLS survey. To convert these to incidence rates per 100 full-time workers, which are comparable to other published BLS rates, divide the rates in the table by 100. The BLS survey records illnesses only for the year in which they are recognized or diagnosed as work-related. Since only recognized cases are included, the figures underestimate the incidence of occupational illness.

NONFATAL OCCUPATIONAL ILLNESS INCIDENCE RATES AND NUMBER OF ILLNESSES BY TYPE OF ILLNESS AND INDUSTRY SECTOR, 2006

Industry Sector	All Illnesses	Skin Diseases, Disorders	Respiratory Conditions	Poisoning	Hearing Loss	All Other Occupational Illnesses
Incidence Rate per 10,000 Full-Time Workers						
Private Sector [a,b]	**24.6**	**4.5**	**1.9**	**0.4**	**2.6**	**15.2**
Goods Producing [a,b]	42.6	5.8	1.7	0.6	9.1	25.4
Agriculture, forestry, fishing & hunting [a]	41.3	13.5	1.3	1.8	1.7	23.0
Mining [b,c]	11.8	3.6	0.5	(d)	1.4	6.1
Construction	14.9	3.4	1.1	0.8	0.4	9.1
Manufacturing	57.7	6.6	2.1	0.4	14.2	34.4
Service providing	18.8	4.0	2.0	0.3	0.5	11.9
Wholesale trade	10.3	1.9	1.6	0.1	0.5	6.2
Retail trade	13.2	2.7	1.2	0.2	0.1	9.1
Transportation and warehousing	25.7	2.5	1.6	0.3	3.4	17.9
Utilities	39.7	9.1	0.8	0.7	13.7	15.3
Information	14.0	1.8	0.5	0.1	1.4	10.2
Financial activities	10.8	0.9	1.2	0.1	0.1	8.5
Professional and business services	14.7	4.6	1.2	(d)	0.2	7.9
Education and health services	37.4	7.3	5.1	0.2	0.1	24.7
Leisure and hospitality	16.2	5.4	1.5	0.2	0.2	8.9
Other services	10.8	3.4	1.1	0.2	0.2	5.9
Number of Illnesses (in thousands)						
Private Sector [a,b]	**228.0**	**41.4**	**17.7**	**3.4**	**24.4**	**141.1**
Goods producing [a,b]	96.9	13.2	3.8	1.3	20.8	57.7
Agriculture, forestry, fishing & hunting [a]	3.6	1.2	0.1	0.2	0.1	2.0
Mining [b,c]	0.8	0.2	(e)	(d)	0.1	0.4
Construction	10.4	2.4	0.8	0.5	0.3	6.4
Manufacturing	82.1	9.4	2.9	0.6	20.2	48.9
Service providing	131.1	28.1	13.9	2.1	3.6	83.4
Wholesale trade	5.8	1.1	0.9	(e)	0.3	3.5
Retail trade	15.8	3.2	1.4	0.3	0.1	10.8
Transportation and warehousing	10.5	1.0	0.7	0.1	1.4	7.3
Utilities	2.1	0.5	(e)	(e)	0.7	0.8
Information	3.9	0.5	0.1	(e)	0.4	2.8
Financial activities	8.0	0.7	0.9	0.1	(e)	6.3
Professional and business services	19.1	6.0	1.6	(d)	0.3	10.3
Education and health services	49.0	9.6	6.7	0.3	0.1	32.3
Leisure and hospitality	13.8	4.6	1.3	0.2	0.2	7.5
Other services	3.3	1.0	0.3	0.1	0.1	1.8

Source: Bureau of Labor Statistics, U.S. Department of Labor. Components may not add to totals due to rounding.
[a] Private sector includes all industries except government, but excludes farms with less than 11 employees.
[b] Data for mining do not reflect the changes OSHA made to its recordkeeping requirements effective January 1, 2002; therefore, estimates for this industry are not comparable with estimates for other industries.
[c] Mining includes quarrying and oil and gas extraction.
[d] Data do not meet publication guidelines.
[e] Data too small to be displayed.

NATIONAL SAFETY COUNCIL

INJURY FACTS®

Between 1912 and 2006, motor-vehicle deaths per 10,000 registered vehicles were reduced 95%, from 33 to less than 2. In 1912, there were 3,100 fatalities when the number of registered vehicles totaled only 950,000. In 2006, there were 44,700 fatalities, but registrations soared to 252 million.

While mileage data were not available in 1912, the 2006 mileage death rate of 1.49 per 100,000,000 vehicle miles was down 2% from the revised 2005 rate of 1.52, and is the lowest on record. Disabling injuries in motor-vehicle accidents totaled 2,400,000 in 2006, and total motor-vehicle costs were estimated at $258.6 billion. Costs include wage and productivity losses, medical expenses, administrative expenses, motor-vehicle property damage, and employer costs.

Motor-vehicle deaths decreased 2% from 2005 to 2006 and increased 1% from 2004 to 2005. Miles traveled

was up less than 0.5%, the number of registered vehicles increased 2%, and the population increased 1%. As a result, the mileage death rate was down 2%, the registration death rate was down 4%, and the population death rate was down 3% from 2005 to 2006.

Compared with 1996, 2006 motor-vehicle deaths increased by about 2%. However, mileage, registration, and population death rates were all sharply lower in 2006 compared to 1996 (see chart on next page).

The word "accident" may be used in this section as well as the word "crash." When used, "accident" has a specific meaning as defined in the *Manual on Classification of Motor Vehicle Traffic Accidents, ANSI D16.1-2007*. "Crash" is generally used by the National Highway Traffic Safety Administration to mean the same as accident, but it is not formally defined.

Deaths **44,700**
Disabling injuries **2,400,000**
Cost . . . . **$258.6 billion**
Motor-vehicle mileage . . . . **2,995 billion**
Registered vehicles in the United States **251,800,000**
Licensed drivers in the United States **202,700,000**
Death rate per 100,000,000 vehicle miles **1.49**
Death rate per 10,000 registered vehicles **1.77**
Death rate per 100,000 population **14.9**

MOTOR-VEHICLE ACCIDENT OUTCOMES, UNITED STATES, 2006

Severity	Deaths or Injuries	Accidents or Crashes	Drivers (Vehicles) Involved
Fatal (within 1 year)	44,700	40,500	60,600
Disabling injury	2,400,000	1,600,000	2,900,000
Property damage (including unreported) and nondisabling injury		8,800,000	15,000,000
Total		**10,400,000**	**18,000,000**
Fatal (within 30 days)	42,642	38,588	57,695
Injury (disabling and nondisabling)	2,575,000	1,746,000	3,176,000
Police-reported property damage		4,189,000	7,325,000
Total		**5,973,588**	**10,558,000**

Source: National Safety Council estimates (top half) and National Highway Traffic Safety Administration (bottom half).

TRAVEL, DEATHS, AND DEATH RATES, UNITED STATES, 1925–2006

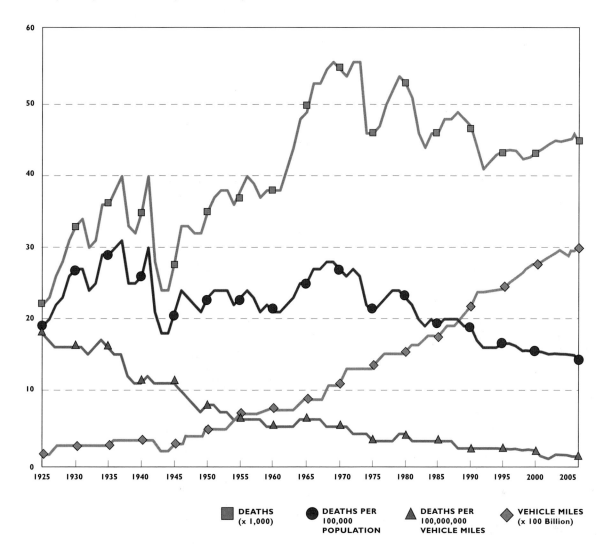

DEATHS DUE TO MOTOR-VEHICLE ACCIDENTS, 2006

TYPE OF EVENT AND AGE OF VICTIM

All Motor-Vehicle Accidents

Includes deaths involving mechanically or electrically powered highway-transport vehicles in motion (except those on rails), both on and off the highway or street.

	Total	Change from 2005	Death Rate[a]
Deaths	44,700	–2%	14.9
Nonfatal injuries	2,400,000		

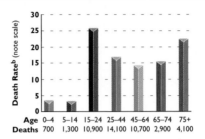

Collision Between Motor Vehicles

Includes deaths from collisions of two or more motor vehicles. Motorized bicycles and scooters, trolley buses, and farm tractors or road machinery traveling on highways are motor vehicles.

	Total	Change from 2005	Death Rate[a]
Deaths	18,500	–5%	6.2
Nonfatal injuries	1,820,000		

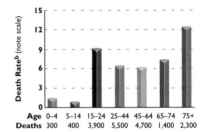

Collision with Fixed Object

Includes deaths from collisions in which the first harmful event is the striking of a fixed object such as a guardrail, abutment, impact attenuator, etc.

	Total	Change from 2005	Death Rate[a]
Deaths	13,400	+1%	4.5
Nonfatal injuries	338,000		

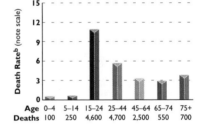

Pedestrian Accidents

Includes all deaths of persons struck by motor vehicles, either on or off a street or highway, regardless of the circumstances of the accident.

	Total	Change from 2005	Death Rate[a]
Deaths	6,100	–2%	2.0
Nonfatal injuries	70,000		

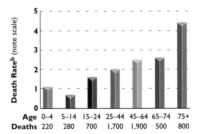

See footnotes on page 89.

Noncollision Accidents

Includes deaths from accidents in which the first injury or damage-producing event was an overturn, jackknife, or other type of noncollision.

	Total	Change from 2005	Death Rate[a]
Deaths	5,300	0%	1.8
Nonfatal injuries	110,000		

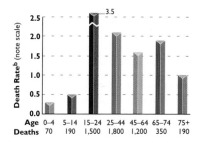

Collision with Pedalcycle

Includes deaths of pedalcyclists and motor-vehicle occupants from collisions between pedalcycles and motor vehicles on streets, highways, private driveways, parking lots, etc.

	Total	Change from 2005	Death Rate[a]
Deaths	1,100	+10%	0.4
Nonfatal injuries	55,000		

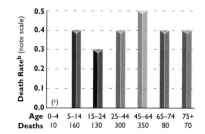

Collision with Railroad Train

Includes deaths from collisions of motor vehicles (moving or stalled) and railroad vehicles at public or private grade crossings. In other types of accidents, classification requires motor vehicle to be in motion.

	Total	Change from 2005	Death Rate[a]
Deaths	200	0%	0.1
Nonfatal injuries	1,000		

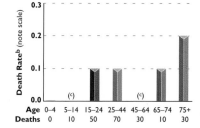

Other Collision

Includes deaths from motor-vehicle collisions not specified in other categories above. Most of the deaths arose out of accidents involving animals or animal-drawn vehicles.

	Total	Change from 2005	Death Rate[a]
Deaths	100	0%	(c)
Nonfatal Injuries	6,000		

Note: Procedures and benchmarks for estimating deaths by type of accident and age were changed in 1990. Estimates for 1987 and later years are not comparable to earlier years. The noncollision and fixed object categories were most affected by the changes.
[a]Deaths per 100,000 population.
[b]Deaths per 100,000 population in each age group.
[c]Death rate was less than 0.05.

Motor-vehicle crashes are the leading cause of death for people between the ages of 2 and 34. Motor-vehicle crashes are also the leading cause of unintentional-injury (accidental) death for persons of each single year of age from 2 to 39, and again for each single year of age from 50 to 72. This is a summary of the most important issues that affect traffic safety.

Occupant protection. Forty-nine states and the District of Columbia have mandatory belt use laws in effect, with the laws in twenty-five of the states and the District of Columbia allowing standard (primary) enforcement. The observed safety belt use rate was 81% in 2006, down slightly from the all-time high of 82% in 2005. The latest observational surveys show motorcycle helmet use has declined by 20 percentage points over 5 years, from 71% in 2000 to 51% in 2006, a statistically significant drop that corresponds to a 70% increase in nonuse.

Alcohol. Although all states and the District of Columbia have 21-year-old minimum drinking age laws and have by law created a threshold making it illegal to drive with a BAC of 0.08 g/dl or higher, traffic fatalities in alcohol-related crashes were essentially unchanged from 2005 to 2006 and rose 3% from 1996-2006. About 41% of all traffic fatalities in 2006 involved an intoxicated or alcohol-impaired driver or nonoccupant and there was an average of one alcohol-related fatality every 30 minutes.

Speeding. Excessive speed was a factor in 31% of all traffic fatalities in 2006 and, similar to alcohol, the number of crashes attributable to speeding has not changed appreciably over the last decade. Nearly half of all speeding-related fatalities in 2005 occurred on roads where the posted speed limit was 55 miles per hour or greater and nearly 90% occurred on roads that were *not* interstate highways. It has been estimated that speeding-related crashes cost the nation over $40 billion annually.

Distracted driving. Inattention to the driving task is a contributing factor in 78% of crashes and 65% of near crashes according to data from observational studies. Driver inattention was categorized as involving secondary task engagement, fatigue, driving-related inattention to the forward roadway (e.g., looking at rearview mirror), and non-specific eye glance. Secondary task distraction was the most common form of inattention, with wireless devices the most frequent

distraction. Talking and listening was the most common wireless device task associated with crashes, near crashes, and incidents. According to the latest observational study, about 5% of drivers were observed using hand-held cell phones, while another 1% was observed using headsets or manipulating hand-held devices.

Motorcycles. Fatalities among motorcycle riders and passengers have increased by 123% between 1996 and 2006, while nonfatal injuries have increased by 60% over the same period. With the number of registered motorcycles increasing by 61% from 1996 through 2005 and miles traveled up only slightly, the death rate per 100 million miles driven has increased by 95%. In contrast to earlier years, almost half of fatally injured riders are now over 40 years of age.

Large trucks. About 12% of traffic fatalities in 2006 resulted from a crash involving a large truck (gross vehicle weight rating greater than 10,000 pounds) and over three-quarters of the deaths were occupants of vehicles other than the large truck. Large trucks were more likely to be involved in a multiple vehicle fatal crash than passenger vehicles—83% vs. 61%, respectively.

Young drivers. Total fatalities in crashes involving drivers 15 to 20 years old numbered 8,177 in 2006, virtually unchanged from 2005. Although the 7,463 15 to 20 year old drivers involved in fatal crashes in 2006 represented a 8% decrease from the 8,074 involved in 1996, driver fatalities among this age group increased by 3% over the same time period. According to the latest 2004 mortality figures, motor-vehicle crashes are the leading cause of death for 15 to 20 year olds. In 2006, 12.9% of all the drivers involved in fatal crashes were between 15 and 20 years old, a figure far out of proportion to this age group's 6.3% of all licensed drivers in 2005.

Pedestrians. There were about 6,100 pedestrian deaths and 70,000 injuries in motor-vehicle accidents in 2006. The majority (about 61%) of pedestrian deaths and injuries occur when pedestrians improperly cross roadways or intersections or dart/run into streets. Pedestrians in age groups beginning with those aged 15 and older are more likely to cross improperly, while those in younger age groups are more likely to dart/run into the roadway.

ESTIMATING MOTOR-VEHICLE CRASH COSTS

There are two methods commonly used to measure the costs of motor-vehicle crashes. One is the *economic cost* framework and the other is the *comprehensive cost* framework.

Economic costs may be used by a community or state to estimate the economic impact of motor-vehicle crashes that occurred within its jurisdiction in a given time period. It is a measure of the productivity lost and expenses incurred because of the crashes. Economic costs, however, should not be used for cost-benefit analysis because they do not reflect what society is willing to pay to prevent a statistical fatality or injury.

There are five economic cost components: (a) wage and productivity losses, which include wages, fringe benefits, household production, and travel delay; (b) medical expenses including emergency service costs; (c) administrative expenses, which include the administrative cost of private and public insurance plus police and legal costs; (d) motor-vehicle damage including the value of damage to property; and (e) uninsured employer costs for crashes involving workers.

The information below shows the average economic costs in 2006 per death (*not* per fatal crash), per injury (*not* per injury crash), and per property damage crash.

ECONOMIC COSTS, 2006

Death	**$1,210,000**
Nonfatal Disabling Injury	**$55,000**
Incapacitating injury[a]	*$62,500*
Nonincapacitating evident injury[a]	*$20,300*
Possible injury[a]	*$11,500*
Property Damage Crash (including minor injuries)	**$8,200**

Comprehensive costs include not only the economic cost components, but also a measure of the value of lost quality of life associated with the deaths and injuries, that is, what society is willing to pay to prevent them. The values of lost quality of life were obtained through empirical studies of what people actually pay to reduce their safety and health risks, such as through the purchase of air bags or smoke detectors.

Comprehensive costs should be used for cost-benefit analysis, but because the lost quality of life represents only a dollar equivalence of intangible qualities, they do not represent real economic losses and should not be used to determine the economic impact of past crashes.

The information below shows the average comprehensive costs in 2006 on a per person basis.

COMPREHENSIVE COSTS, 2006

Death	**$4,000,000**
Incapacitating injury[a]	*$201,100*
Nonincapacitating evident injury[a]	*$51,400*
Possible injury[a]	*$24,400*
No Injury	**$2,200**

Source: National Safety Council estimates (see the Technical Appendix) and Children's Safety Network Economics and Insurance Resource Center, Pacific Institute for Research and Evaluation.

Note: The National Safety Council's cost estimating procedures were extensively revised for the 1993 edition and additional revisions were made for the 2005–2006 edition. The costs are not comparable to those of prior years.

[a]*Manual on Classification of Motor Vehicle Traffic Accidents, ANSI D16.1-2007 (7th ed.). (2007). Itasca, IL: National Safety Council..*

STATE LAWS

All states and the District of Columbia have 21-year-old drinking age and child safety seat laws. Breath alcohol ignition interlock device laws are in effect in 45 states. Mandatory belt use laws are in effect in 49 states plus the District of Columbia, of which 26 states and D.C. are standard enforcement. Graduated licensing is in effect in some form in all states and the District of Columbia.

STATE LAWS

State	Alcohol Laws — Administrative License Revocation[a]	BAC Limit[b]	Zero Tolerance Limit[c] for Minors	Alcohol Ignition Interlock Device[d]	Mandatory Belt Use Law — Enforcement	Seating Positions Covered by Law	Graduated Licensing Laws — Minimum Instructional Permit Period[e]	Minimum Hours of Supervised Driving[f]	Passenger Restrictions	Nighttime Driving Restrictions	Unrestricted License Minimum Age[g]
Alabama	1996	0.08	0.02	no	standard	front	6 mo.	30/–	yes	yes	16 yrs.
Alaska	1983	0.08	0.00	yes	standard	all	6 mo.	none	yes	yes	16 yrs.
Arizona	1992	0.08	0.00	yes	secondary	front	6 mo.	25/5	yes	yes	16 yrs.
Arkansas	1995	0.08	0.02	yes	secondary	front	until 16 yrs.	none	no	no	18 yrs.
California	1989	0.08	0.01	yes[h]	standard	all	6 mo.	50/10	yes	yes	16 yrs.
Colorado	1983	0.08	0.02	yes[h]	secondary	front	12 mo.	50/10	yes	yes	17 yrs.
Connecticut	1990	0.08	0.02	yes[h]	standard	front[i]	6 mo.	none	yes	no	16 yrs., 4 mo.
Delaware	yes	0.08	0.02	yes[h]	standard	all	12 mo.	50/10	yes	yes	17 yrs.
Dist. of Columbia	yes	0.08	0.00	no	standard	all	6 mo.	40+10[j]	yes	yes	18 yrs.
Florida	1990	0.08	0.02	yes[h]	secondary[k]	front	12 mo.	50/10	no	yes	18 yrs.
Georgia	1995	0.08	0.02	yes[h]	standard	front[i]	12 mo.	40/6	yes	yes	18 yrs.
Hawaii	1990	0.08	0.02	no	standard	front[i]	6 mo.	50/10	yes	yes	17 yrs.
Idaho	1994	0.08	0.02	yes	secondary	all	6 mo.	50/10	yes	yes	16 yrs.
Illinois	1986	0.08	0.00	yes[h]	standard	front	9 mo.	50/10	yes	yes	18 yrs.
Indiana	yes	0.08	0.02	yes[h]	standard	all	2 mo.	none	yes	yes	18 yrs.
Iowa	1982	0.08	0.02	yes	standard	front	6 mo.	20/2	no	yes	17 yrs.
Kansas	1988	0.08	0.02	yes[h]	secondary	front	6 mo.	50/10	no	no	16 yrs.
Kentucky	no	0.08	0.02	yes[h]	standard	all	6 mo.	60/10	yes	yes[m]	17 yrs.
Louisiana	1984	0.08	0.02	yes	standard	front[i]	3 mo.	none	yes	yes	17 yrs.
Maine	1984	0.08	0.00	no	standard	all	6 mo.	35/5	yes	yes	16 yrs., 6 mo.
Maryland	1989	0.08[l]	0.02	yes[h]	standard	front[i]	6 mo.	60/10	yes	yes	17 yrs., 9 mo.
Massachusetts	1994	0.08	0.02	yes	secondary	all	6 mo.	40/–	yes	yes	18 yrs.
Michigan	no	0.08	0.02	yes[h]	standard	front[i]	6 mo.	50/10	no	yes	17 yrs.
Minnesota	1976	0.08	0.00	yes	secondary	front[i]	6 mo.	30/10	no	no	17 yrs.
Mississippi	1983	0.08	0.02	yes[h]	standard	front	6 mo.	none	no	yes	16 yrs.
Missouri	1987	0.08	0.02	yes[h]	secondary	front[i]	6 mo.	40/10	yes	yes	18 yrs.
Montana	2007	0.08	0.02	yes	secondary	all	6 mo.	50/10	yes	yes	18 yrs.
Nebraska	1993	0.08	0.02	yes	standard	front[i]	6 mo.	50/10	yes	yes	17 yrs.
Nevada	1983	0.08	0.02	yes[h]	secondary	all	6 mo.	50/10	yes	yes	18 yrs.
New Hampshire	1993	0.08	0.02	yes[h]	(k)	(k)	6 mo.	20/–	no	yes	18 yrs.
New Jersey	no	0.08	0.01	yes[h]	standard	front	12 mo.	none	yes	yes	18 yrs.
New Mexico	1984	0.08	0.02	yes	standard	all	6 mo.	50/10	yes	yes	16 yrs., 6 mo.
New York	1994[n]	0.08[l]	0.02	yes[h]	standard	front[i]	6 mo.	20/–	yes	yes	18 yrs.
North Carolina	1983	0.08	0.00	yes[h]	standard	all	12 mo.	none	yes	yes	16 yrs., 6 mo.
North Dakota	1983	0.08	0.02	yes[h]	secondary	front	6 mo.	none	no	no	16 yrs.
Ohio	1993	0.08	0.02	yes	secondary	front	6 mo.	50/10	no	yes	18 yrs.
Oklahoma	1983	0.08	0.00	yes	standard	front	6 mo.	40/10	yes	yes	18 yrs.
Oregon	1983	0.08	0.00	yes	standard	all	6 mo.	100/–	yes	yes	18 yrs.
Pennsylvania	no	0.08	0.02	yes[h]	secondary	front[i]	6 mo.	50/–	yes	yes	17 yrs., 6 mo.
Rhode Island	no	0.08	0.02	yes[h]	secondary	all	6 mo.	50/10	yes	yes	17 yrs., 6 mo.
South Carolina	1998	0.08	0.02	yes	standard	front[o]	180 days	40/10	yes	yes	17 yrs.
South Dakota	no	0.08	0.02	no	secondary	front	6 mo.	none	no	yes	16 yrs.
Tennessee	no	0.08	0.02	yes	standard	all	6 mo.	50/10	yes	yes	17 yrs.
Texas	1995	0.08	0.00	yes[h]	standard	front[i]	6 mo.	none	yes	yes	18 yrs.
Utah	1983	0.08	0.00	yes	secondary[k]	all	6 mo.	40/10	yes	yes	17 yrs.
Vermont	1969[n]	0.08	0.02	no	secondary	all	12 mo.	40/10	yes	no	16 yrs., 6 mo.
Virginia	1995	0.08	0.02	yes	secondary	front[i]	9 mo.	40/10	yes	yes	18 yrs.
Washington	1998	0.08	0.02	yes	standard	all	6 mo.	50/10	yes	yes	17 yrs.
West Virginia	1981	0.08	0.02	yes	secondary	front[i]	6 mo.	30/–	yes	yes	18 yrs.
Wisconsin	1988	0.08	0.00	yes[h]	secondary	front[o]	12 mo.	30/10	yes	yes	18 yrs.
Wyoming	1973	0.08	0.02	yes	secondary	all	10 days	50/10	yes	yes	17 yrs.

Source: National Safety Council survey of state officials. Laws as of August 2007.
[a] *Year original law became effective, not when grandfather clauses expired.*
[b] *Blood alcohol concentration that constitutes the threshold of legal intoxication.*
[c] *Blood alcohol concentration that constitutes "zero tolerance" threshold for minors (<21 years of age unless otherwise noted).*
[d] *Instruments designed to prevent drivers from starting their cars when breath alcohol content is at or above a set point.*
[e] *Minimum instructional periods often include time spent in driver's education classes.*
[f] *Figures shown as follows: Total hours/Nighttime hours. For example, 25/5 means 25 hours of supervised driving, 5 of which must be at night. Some states (GA, MD, OR, WV) have lower requirements if driver ed is taken.*
[g] *Minimum age to obtain unrestricted license provided driver is crash and violation free. Alcohol restrictions still apply at least until 21.*

[h] *Primarily for repeat offenders.*
[i] *Required for certain ages at all seating positions.*
[j] *40 hours of supervised driving during learner's stage; 10 hours at night during intermediate stage.*
[k] *Standard enforcement law in effect for ages under 18 (FL, NH), under 19 (UT).*
[l] *BAC of 0.07 is prima facia evidence of DUI (MD). BAC of 0.05 –0.07 constitutes driving while ability impaired (NY).*
[m] *During permit period only.*
[n] *Revocation by judicial action (NY) or Department of Motor Vehicles (VT).*
[o] *Belt use required in rear seat if lap/shoulder belt is available.*

Seat belt use was 81% overall in 2006, statistically unchanged from the 82% use rate in 2005 and much higher than the 61% use rate in 1996. These results are from the National Occupant Protection Use Survey conducted annually by the National Highway Traffic Safety Administration.

Belt use was 85% in states with standard (primary) enforcement and 74% in states with secondary enforcement in 2006. The West had the highest use rate among regions (90%) and the Northeast had the lowest (74%).

By vehicle type, belt use was 84% in vans and SUVs, 82% in passenger cars, and 74% in pickup trucks. Belt use was higher in fast traffic (84%) than in slow traffic (79%) and higher in heavy traffic (96%) than in light traffic (81%).

Seat belt use was greater among females (85%) than among males (78%). By age group, use was lowest among those 16–24 years old (76%) and increased with age to 85% among those 70 and older.

Overall, drivers with no passengers were less likely to use seat belts (83%) than those with at least one passenger (87%). On the other hand, drivers aged 16–24, whose overall belt use was 80%, were less likely to wear seat belts when all their passengers were also aged 16–24 (75%) compared to having at least one passenger not in that age group (87%).

Rear-seat belt use was 65% in 2006 compared to 81% among front seat occupants. Rear-seat belt use was higher among occupants aged 8–15 years old (69%) and 70 and older (69%) than among those 16–24 years old (62%) and 25–69 years old (61%). In the 17 states

and D.C. that required seat belt use in all seating positions, rear-seat belt use was 69% compared to 64% in states that required only front seat use.

Child restraint use. Ninety-eight percent of infants were restrained in child safety seats in 2006 as were 89% of children 1–3 years of age and 78% of children 4–7 years old. Most children were observed riding in the rear seat—93% of infants, 94% of children 1–3 years old, and 91% of children 4–7 years old.

Seat belt use by the driver strongly influences the restraint status of child passengers. When the driver was belted, 87% of children were restrained. When the driver was not belted, 58% of children were restrained.

By type of vehicle, child restraint use was highest in vans and SUVs (91%), somewhat lower in pickup trucks (86%), and lowest in passenger cars (78%).

Children from 4 to 7 years old should be restrained in a front-facing safety seat or booster seat depending on the child's height and weight. The National Survey of the Use of Booster Seats (NSUBS) found that, in 2006, 41% were using booster seats, 17% were in child safety seats, 33% were in seat belts, and 9% were unrestrained. Thus, as many as 42% of children in this age group were not properly restrained.

Source: Glassbrenner, D., & Ye, J. (2006). Seat belt use in 2006—overall results. Traffic Safety Facts Research Note, DOT HS 810 677. Washington, DC: National Highway Traffic Safety Administration.
Glassbrenner, D., & Ye, J. (2007). Seat belt use in 2006—demographic results. Traffic Safety Facts Research Note, DOT HS 810 766. Washington, DC: National Highway Traffic Safety Administration.
Glassbrenner, D., & Ye, J. (2007). Rear-seat belt use in 2006. Traffic Safety Facts Research Note, DOT HS 810 765. Washington, DC: National Highway Traffic Safety Administration.
Glassbrenner, D., & Ye, J. (2007). Child restraint use in 2006—overall results. Traffic Safety Facts Research Note, DOT HS 810 737. Washington, DC: National Highway Traffic Safety Administration.
Glassbrenner, D., & Ye, J. (2007). Booster seat use in 2006. Traffic Safety Facts Research Note, DOT HS 810 796. Washington, DC: National Highway Traffic Safety Administration.

SEAT BELT USE, UNITED STATES, 2000–2006

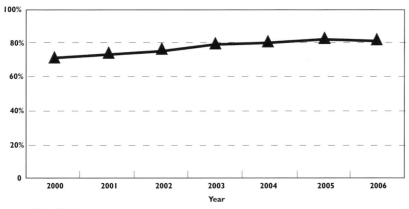

Source: NHTSA, NOPUS.

Safety Belts

- When used, lap/shoulder safety belts reduce the risk of fatal injury to front seat passenger car occupants by 45% and reduce the risk of moderate-to-critical injury by 50%.

- For light truck occupants, safety belts reduce the risk of fatal injury by 60% and moderate-to-critical injury by 65%.

- Forty-nine states and the District of Columbia have mandatory belt use laws in effect, the only exception being New Hampshire. Twenty-three of the states with belt use laws in effect in 2007 specified secondary enforcement (i.e., police officers are permitted to write a citation only after a vehicle is stopped for some other traffic infraction). Twenty-six states and the District of Columbia had laws that allowed primary enforcement, enabling officers to stop vehicles and write citations whenever they observe violations of the belt law.

- Safety belts saved an estimated 15,383 lives in 2006 among passenger vehicle occupants over 4 years old. An *additional* 5,441 lives could have been saved in 2006 if all passenger vehicle occupants over age 4 wore safety belts. From 1975 through 2006, an estimated 226,567 lives were saved by safety belts.

- Safety belts provide the greatest protection against occupant ejection. Among crashes in which a fatality occurred in 2005, only 1% of restrained passenger car occupants were ejected, compared to 31% of unrestrained occupants.

- In 2006, 30,521 occupants of passenger cars, light trucks, vans, and sport utility vehicles (SUVs) were killed in traffic crashes. Of the 28,141 fatalities for which restraint use was known, 15,523 (55%) were restrained and 12,618 (45%) were unrestrained.

PASSENGER VEHICLE OCCUPANT DEATHS BY VEHICLE TYPE AND RESTRAINT USE, UNITED STATES, 2006

Passenger Vehicle Type	Restraint Used Number	Restraint Used Percent	Restraint Not Used Number	Restraint Not Used Percent	Restraint Use Unknown Number	Restraint Use Unknown Percent	Total Number	Total Percent
Passenger Cars	8,325	47%	7,969	45%	1,506	8%	17,800	100%
Pickup Trucks	1,756	29%	3,832	64%	396	7%	5,984	100%
SUVs	1,721	35%	2,865	58%	324	7%	4,910	100%
Vans	810	45%	842	47%	150	8%	1,802	100%
Other Light Trucks	6	24%	15	60%	4	16%	25	100%
Total	12,618	41%	15,523	51%	2,380	8%	30,521	100%

Source: National Center for Statistics and Analysis. (2007). Traffic Safety Facts 2006 Data—Occupant Protection (DOT HS 810 807). Washington, DC: National Highway Traffic Safety Administration.

Air Bags

- Air bags, combined with lap/shoulder belts, offer the best available protection for passenger vehicle occupants. Recent analyses indicate a fatality-reducing effectiveness for air bags of 14% when no safety belt was used and 11% when a safety belt was used in conjunction with air bags.

- Lap/shoulder belts should always be used, even in a vehicle with an air bag. Air bags are a supplemental form of protection and most are designed to deploy only in moderate-to-severe *frontal* crashes.

- Children in rear-facing child seats should not be placed in the front seat of vehicles equipped with passenger-side air bags. The impact of the deploying air bag could result in injury to the child.

- An estimated 2,796 lives were saved by air bags in 2006 and a total of 22,466 lives were saved from 1987 through 2006.

- Beginning September 1997, all new passenger cars were required to have driver and passenger side air bags. In 1998, the same requirement went into effect for light trucks.

Child Restraints

• Child restraints saved an estimated 425 lives in 2006 among children under the age of 5. Of the 425 lives saved, 392 were attributed to the use of child safety seats while 32 lives were spared with the use of adult belts.

• At 100% child safety seat use for children under the age of 5, an estimated 96 *additional* lives could have been saved in 2006.

• All states and the District of Columbia have had child restraint use laws in effect since 1985.

• Research has shown that child safety seats reduce fatal injury in passenger cars by 71% for infants (less than 1 year old), and by 54% for toddlers (1–4 years old). For infants and toddlers in light trucks, the corresponding reductions are 58% and 59%, respectively.

• In 2006, there were 361 occupant fatalities among children less than 4 years of age. Of these fatalities, 109 (32%) were totally unrestrained. Of the 309 fatalities among children 4 to 7 years of age for which restraint use was known, 116 (41%) were unrestrained.

• An estimated 8,325 lives have been saved by child restraints from 1975 through 2006.

ESTIMATED NUMBER OF LIVES SAVED BY RESTRAINT SYSTEMS, 1975–2006

Restraint Type	1975–98	1999	2000	2001	2002	2003	2004	2005	2006
Seat Belts	112,531	11,941	12,882	13,295	14,264	15,095	15,548	15,688	15,383
Child Restraints	4,877	447	479	388	383	447	455	424	425
Air Bags	4,230	1,491	1,716	1,978	2,324	2,519	2,660	2,752	2,796

Source: National Center for Statistics and Analysis. (2007). Traffic Safety Facts 2006 Data—Occupant Protection (DOT HS 810 807). Washington, DC: National Highway Traffic Safety Administration.

Motorcycle Helmets

• Motorcycle helmets are estimated to be 37% effective in preventing fatal injuries to motorcycle riders.

• It is estimated that motorcycle helmets saved the lives of 1,658 motorcyclists in 2006. An *additional* 752 lives could have been saved if all motorcyclists had worn helmets.

• Reported helmet use rates for fatally injured motorcyclists in 2006 were 59% for operators and 45% for passengers, compared with the corresponding rates of 58% and 50%, respectively, in 2005.

• In 2006, 20 states, the District of Columbia, and Puerto Rico required helmet use by all motorcycle operators and passengers. In another 26 states, only persons under a specific age, usually 18, were required to wear helmets. Four states had no laws requiring helmet use.

• Motorcycle helmet use declined from 71% in 2000 to 51% in 2006 according to the National Occupant Protection Use Survey. The drop in use represents a 70% increase in nonuse of helmets.

Source: National Center for Statistics and Analysis. (2007). Traffic Safety Facts 2006 Data—Occupant Protection (DOT HS 810 807); Traffic Safety Facts 2006 Data—Motorcycles (DOT HS 810 806). Washington, DC: National Highway Traffic Safety Administration.

ALCOHOL

According to studies conducted by the National Highway Traffic Safety Administration (NHTSA), about 41% of all traffic fatalities in 2006 involved an intoxicated or alcohol-impaired driver or nonmotorist—an increase of 1% from 2005. The total number of alcohol-related fatalities was 17,602, essentially unchanged from the 17,590 alcohol-related fatalities in 2005. In 2006, 32% of all traffic fatalities occurred in crashes where at least one driver or motorcycle [MC] operator was intoxicated (blood alcohol concentration [BAC] of 0.08 grams per deciliter [g/dl] or greater). A total of 13,470 people were killed in such crashes, a less than 1% decline from the 2005 total of 13,582. The following data summarizes the extent of alcohol involvement in motor-vehicle crashes involving at least one driver or MC operator with BAC of 0.08 g/dl or greater:

- Traffic fatalities in alcohol-related crashes rose by 0.1% from 2005 to 2006 and increased by 3% from 1996 to 2006. (See corresponding chart.) In 1996, alcohol-related fatalities accounted for 41% of all traffic deaths.

- The increase in traffic fatalities in alcohol-related crashes from 2005 to 2006 was due solely to an

increase in the number of high-alcohol crashes, where the driver or MC operator had a BAC of 0.08 g/dl or greater.

- The only increases from 2005 to 2006 in the number of alcohol-related fatalities by age group were seen among the 16- to 20-year-old and 21- to 34-year-old age groups, which increased by about 4% and 1%, respectively. All other age groups showed decreases, ranging from less than –0.5% for those under 16 years of age to –7.1% for those age 65 or greater.

- About 82% of the alcohol-related fatalities in 2006 involved driver/MC operators or their passengers, while the remainder of the deaths occurred to occupants of other vehicles (11.9%), nonoccupants (6.0%), and others (0.2%)

- In 2006, while drivers age 21 to 34 constituted 31% of all drivers involved in fatal crashes, they were over-represented among the drivers/MC operators with BACs of 0.08 g/dl or greater, comprising 43% of such drivers/MC operators involved in fatal crashes. The 35–44 age group was also slightly over-represented, making up 18% of drivers/MC operators in fatal crashes and 21% of those with BACs of 0.08 g/dl or greater.

PERCENT OF ALL TRAFFIC FATALITIES THAT OCCURRED IN ALCOHOL-RELATED CRASHES, 1996–2006

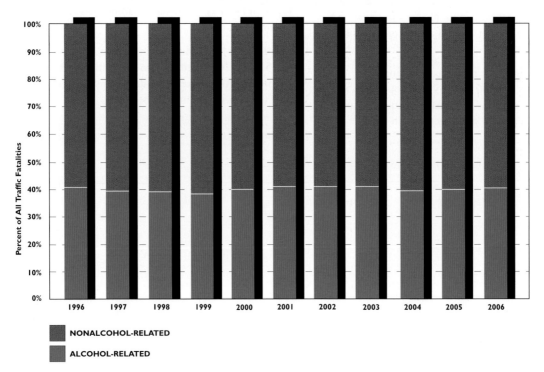

• From 2005 to 2006, the number of drivers/MC operators involved in fatal crashes that had a BAC of 0.08 g/dl or greater increased 6% in both the 16–20 and 65+ age groups, while the 21–34 and 35–44 age groups each showed declines of 1% and the 45–64 age group declined 2%. However, the only change from 2005-2006 in the percentage distribution by age group of drivers/MC operators involved in fatal crashes with BAC 0.08 g/dl or higher was a 10% increase for the 16–20 year old age group.

• Males continue to comprise the majority—81% in 2006—of all drivers involved in fatal crashes with a BAC of 0.08 g/dl or greater. The number of female drivers involved in such crashes increased by 9% (from 1,990 in 2005 to 2,168 in 2006) in spite of an overall 3% drop in the number of female drivers involved in fatal collisions in 2006.

• About 85% of drivers involved in fatal crashes in 2006 with a BAC of 0.08 g/dl or greater were driving passenger cars or light trucks, while a further 11% were motorcycle operators. Nearly 60% of such driver/MC operators were involved in a fatal crash on the weekend and over two-thirds of the crashes were single vehicle crashes.

• All states and the District of Columbia now have 21-year-old minimum drinking age laws. In 2006, all states plus the District of Columbia had by law created a threshold making it illegal to drive with a BAC of 0.08 g/dl or higher.

• The cost of alcohol-related motor-vehicle crashes is estimated by the National Safety Council at $38.6 billion in 2006.

Source: National Center for Statistics and Analysis. (2007). 2006 Traffic Safety Annual Assessment—Alcohol-Related Fatalities. Washington, DC: National Highway Traffic Safety Administration.

DRIVERS INVOLVED IN FATAL CRASHES AND NUMBER WITH BAC ≥ .08 BY AGE GROUP, 2005–2006

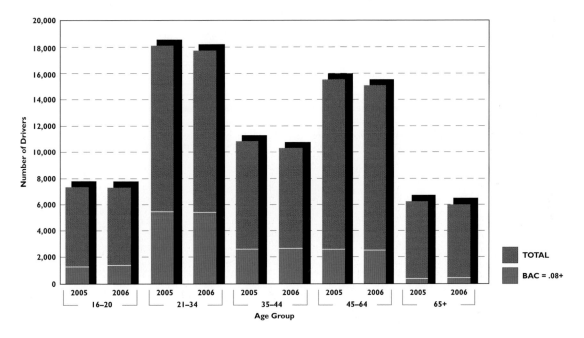

TYPE OF MOTOR-VEHICLE ACCIDENT

Although motor-vehicle deaths occur more often in collisions between motor vehicles than any other type of accident, this type represents only about 41% of the total. Collisions between a motor vehicle and a fixed object were the next most common type, with about 30% of the deaths, followed by pedestrian accidents and noncollisions (rollovers, etc.).

While collisions between motor vehicles accounted for less than half of motor-vehicle fatalities, this accident type represented 76% of injuries, 68% of injury accidents, and 68% of all accidents. Single-vehicle accidents involving collisions with fixed objects, pedestrians, and noncollisions, on the other hand,

accounted for a greater proportion of fatalities and fatal accidents compared to less serious accidents. These three accident types made up 55% of fatalities and 57% of fatal accidents, but 29% or less of injuries, injury accidents, or all accidents.

Of collisions between motor vehicles, angle collisions cause the greatest number of deaths, about 9,600 in 2006 and the greatest number of nonfatal injuries as well as fatal and injury accidents. The table below shows the estimated number of motor-vehicle deaths, injuries, fatal accidents, injury accidents, and all accidents, for various types of accidents.

MOTOR-VEHICLE DEATHS AND INJURIES AND NUMBER OF ACCIDENTS BY TYPE OF ACCIDENT, 2006

Type of Accident	Deaths	Nonfatal Injuries	Fatal Accidents	Injury Accidents	All Accidents
Total	**44,700**	**2,400,000**	**40,500**	**1,600,000**	**10,400,000**
Collision with—					
Pedestrian	6,100	70,000	4,700	55,000	100,000
Other motor vehicle	18,500	1,820,000	15,500	1,090,000	7,110,000
Angle collision	9,600	912,000	8,200	497,000	2,840,000
Head-on collision	4,900	175,000	4,000	66,000	250,000
Rear-end collision	2,700	592,000	2,200	461,000	3,170,000
Sideswipe and other two-vehicle collisions	1,300	141,000	1,100	66,000	850,000
Railroad train	200	1,000	200	1,000	3,000
Pedalcycle	1,100	55,000	800	40,000	82,000
Animal, animal-drawn vehicle	100	6,000	100	6,000	500,000
Fixed object	13,400	338,000	13,300	320,000	2,265,000
Noncollision	**5,300**	**110,000**	**5,100**	**88,000**	**340,000**

Source: National Safety Council estimates, based on data from the National Highway Traffic Safety Administration Fatality Analysis Reporting System and General Estimates System. Procedures for estimating the number of accidents by type were changed for the 1998 edition and are not comparable to estimates in previous editions (See Technical Appendix).

Speeding is one of the major factors contributing to the occurrence of deaths, injuries, and property damage related to motor-vehicle crashes. The role of speeding in crash causation can be described in terms of its effect on the driver, the vehicle, and the road. Excessive-speed driving reduces the amount of time the driver has to react in a dangerous situation to avoid a crash. Speeding increases vehicle stopping distance and also reduces the ability of road safety structures such as guardrails, impact attenuators, crash cushions, median dividers, and concrete barriers to protect vehicle occupants in a crash.

The National Highway Traffic Safety Administration (NHTSA) estimates that speeding-related crashes[a] cost the nation $40.4 billion in 2000, or 18% of the entire cost of motor-vehicle crashes in the United States. These economic losses are equivalent to $110.7 million per day or $4.6 million per hour.

Speeding was a factor in 31% of all traffic fatalities in 2006, killing an average of 37 vehicle occupants per day. The total number of fatal motor-vehicle crashes

attributable to speeding has not changed appreciably over the last decade with over 10,000 occurring every year.

Forty-one percent of all speeding-related fatalities in 2006 occurred on roads where the posted speed limit was 55–65 miles per hour and an additional 7% occurred on roads with the posted speed limit of 65 miles per hour or more. Eighty-seven percent occurred on roads that were *not* interstate highways.

Speed was a factor in 37% of fatal crashes that occurred in construction or maintenance work zones.

Speeding is more common among male drivers than females and among the young compared to older drivers. The highest incidence of speeding in fatal crashes was 39% of males ages 15 to 20. The graph below shows how speeding varies by age and sex.

Source: National Center for Statistics and Analysis. (2007). Traffic Safety Facts 2006 Data—Speeding. Washington, DC: National Highway Traffic Safety Administration. DOT HS 810 814.
[a] A crash is considered speeding-related if the driver was charged with a speeding-related offense or if racing, driving too fast for conditions, or exceeding the posted speed limit was indicated as a contributing factor in the crash.

PERCENT OF DRIVERS IN FATAL CRASHES WHO WERE SPEEDING, 2006

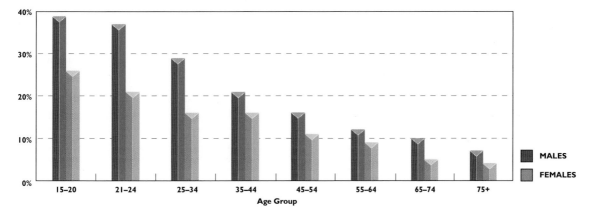

DISTRACTED DRIVING

Inattention to the driving task is a contributing factor in 78% of crashes and 65% of near crashes according to data from the 100-car naturalistic driving study. Driver inattention was categorized four ways: secondary task engagement, fatigue, driving-related inattention to the forward roadway (e.g., looking at rearview mirror), and non-specific eye glance.

Secondary task distraction was the most common of the four forms of inattention. Within this category, wireless devices were the most frequent distraction followed by (in decreasing frequency) passengers, interior distractions, vehicle-related distractions, personal hygiene, dining, external distractions, talking/singing with no passenger apparent, smoking, daydreaming, and others.

Talking and listening was the most common wireless device task associated with crashes, near crashes, and incidents. Dialing hand-held cell phones was also a frequent task associated with near crashes and incidents.

In the 100-car study, the vehicles were instrumented to observe driving behavior, performance, and the driving environment so as to understand pre-crash causal and contributing factors. The cars were driven approximately two million miles over 12 to 13 months by 241 drivers and almost 43,000 hours of data were collected. Data were collected for 69 crashes and 761 near crashes (defined as a conflict situation requiring a rapid, severe evasive maneuver to avoid a crash).

Source: Neale, V.L., Dingus, T.A., Klauer, S.G., Sudweeks, J., & Goodman, M. (no date). An Overview of the 100-car naturalistic study and findings. Retrieved November 9, 2007, from www.nhtsa.dot.gov/portal/nhtsa_static_file_downloader.jsp?file=/staticfiles/DOT/NHTSA/N RD/Multimedia/PDFs/Crash%20Avoidance/2005/100Car_ESV05summary.pdf.

DRIVER CELL PHONE USE

Five percent of drivers were observed using a hand-held cell phone in the 2006 National Occupant Protection Use Survey conducted by the National Highway Traffic Safety Administration. Another 0.6% were using observable headsets and 0.4% were manipulating observable hand-held devices.

Hand-held phone use was highest (8%) among young drivers 16–24 years old and lowest among drivers aged 70 and older (1%). Use was higher among females

(6%) than males (4%). Use also varied by vehicle type—6% for van and SUV drivers, 5% for pickup truck drivers, and 4% for passenger car drivers.

Cell phones were in use by 6% of drivers with no passengers and 2% among drivers with at least one passenger.

Source: Glassbrenner, D., & Ye, T.J. (2007). Driver cell phone use in 2006—overall results. Traffic Safety Facts Research Note. DOT HS 810 790. Washington, DC: National Highway Traffic Safety Administration.

DRIVER HAND-HELD PHONE USE, UNITED STATES, 2000–2006

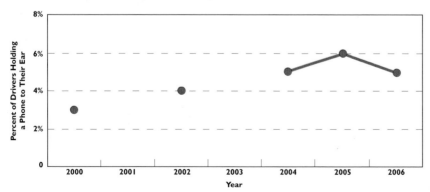

Source: NHTSA, NOPUS.

IMPROPER DRIVING

In most motor-vehicle accidents, factors are present relating to the driver, the vehicle and the road, and it is the interaction of these factors that often sets up the series of events that result in an accident. The table below relates only to the driver, and shows the principal kinds of improper driving in accidents in 2006 as reported by police.

Exceeding the posted speed limit or driving at an unsafe speed was the most common error in fatal accidents. Right-of-way violations predominated in the injury accidents and all accidents categories.

While some drivers were under the influence of alcohol or other drugs, this represents the driver's physical condition—not a driving error. See page 96 for a discussion of alcohol involvement in traffic accidents.

Correcting the improper practices listed below could reduce the number of accidents. This does not mean, however, that road and vehicle conditions can be disregarded.

IMPROPER DRIVING REPORTED IN ACCIDENTS, 2006

Kind of Improper Driving	Fatal Accidents	Injury Accidents	All Accidents
Total	100.0%	100.0%	100.0%
Improper driving	**65.1**	**65.8**	**62.6**
Speed too fast or unsafe	19.6	15.1	12.9
Right of way	11.4	17.3	14.4
Failed to yield	*7.5*	*12.4*	*10.9*
Disregarded signal	*1.9*	*3.0*	*2.1*
Passed stop sign	*2.0*	*1.9*	*1.4*
Drove left of center	7.8	1.9	1.6
Made improper turn	3.8	4.3	4.6
Improper overtaking	1.5	0.7	0.8
Followed too closely	0.9	7.3	9.0
Other improper driving	20.1	19.2	19.3
No improper driving stated	**34.9**	**34.2**	**37.4**

Source: Based on reports from 26 state traffic authorities. Percents may not add to totals due to rounding.

LARGE TRUCKS

In 2006, 4,995 fatalities resulted from a traffic crash involving a large truck and 75% of these deaths were occupants of vehicles other than the large truck. An estimated 106,000 people were injured in large truck crashes in 2006. A large truck is one with gross vehicle weight rating greater than 10,000 pounds.

Large trucks were more likely to be involved in a multiple-vehicle fatal crash than passenger vehicles. In 2005, 83% of large trucks in fatal crashes were in multiple-vehicle crashes compared to 61% of passenger vehicles.

Most large truck fatal crashes occurred in rural areas (61%) and on weekdays (81%) in 2005. Nearly three quarters (74%) of the fatal crashes happened during the daytime on weekdays while on weekends three fifths (60%) occurred at night.

In 2005, only 1% of large truck drivers in fatal crashes were intoxicated.

Source: National Center for Statistics and Analysis. (2007). Motor Vehicle Traffic Crash Fatality Counts and Estimates of People Injured for 2006. DOT HS 810 837. Washington, DC: National Highway Traffic Safety Administration.

National Center for Statistics and Analysis. (2006). Traffic Safety Facts 2005 Data: Large Trucks. DOT HS 810 619. Washington, DC: National Highway Traffic Safety Administration.

FATALITIES IN CRASHES INVOLVING LARGE TRUCKS,
UNITED STATES, 2006

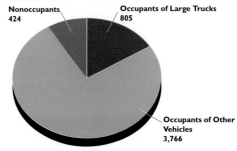

Nonoccupants 424
Occupants of Large Trucks 805
Occupants of Other Vehicles 3,766

MOTORCYCLES

Fatalities among motorcycle riders and passengers have increased 123% between 1996 and 2006. Nonfatal injuries have increased, too, from 55,000 to 88,000 over the same period.

Exposure has also increased. From 1996 through 2005 (the latest year available), the number of registered motorcycles increased 61% from 3.9 million to 6.2 million. Miles traveled is up 9% from 9.9 billion to 10.8 billion. Consequently, the death rate has increased 95% from 21.78 to 42.49 deaths per 100 million miles traveled.

The mileage death rate for motorcyclists was 37 times greater than for passenger cars and light trucks in 2005.

Motorcycles accounted for about 3% of registered vehicles in 2005 and less than one half percent of vehicle miles traveled while accounting for 11% of all traffic fatalities, 13% of occupant fatalities, and 4% of all occupant injuries.

Fatally injured motorcycle riders are older now. In 1996, 45% of fatally injured riders were younger than 30 and 30% of fatally injured riders were 40 years old or older. In 2006, 32% were under 30 and 47% were 40 or older.

In 2006, speeding was a factor in 37% of fatal motorcycle crashes compared to 23% for fatal passenger car crashes. One fourth (25%) of motorcycle operators in fatal crashes had invalid licenses compared to 13% for passenger car drivers.

Twenty seven percent of motorcycle operators involved in fatal crashes were intoxicated (BAC ? .08 g/dL) compared to 23% of passenger car drivers, 24% of light truck drivers, and 1% of large truck drivers.

Motorcycle helmets are estimated to be 37% effective in preventing fatal injuries to operators. NHTSA estimated that helmets saved the lives of 1,658 motorcyclists in 2006 and that an additional 752 lives could have been saved if all motorcyclists wore helmets.

While motorcyclist fatalities have increased in recent years, helmet use had decreased. In 2000, 71% of riders wore helmets. In 2006 the use rate dropped to 51%.

In 2006, 20 states and the District of Columbia had laws requiring helmet use by all motorcycle riders and 26 states required use by riders under 18 or 21 years old. Four states (Colorado, Iowa, Illinois, and New Hampshire) had no helmet use laws.

Source: National Center for Statistics and Analysis. (2007). Traffic Safety Facts 2006 Data: Motorcycles. DOT HS 810 806. Washington, DC: National Highway Traffic Safety Administration.

MOTORCYCLIST DEATHS AND DEATH RATES, UNITED STATES, 1996–2006

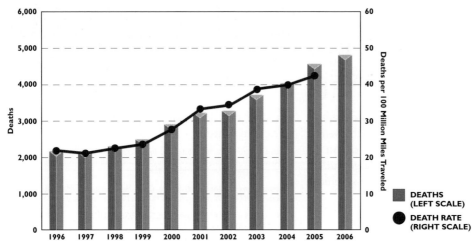

SCHOOL BUS TRANSPORTATION

School bus-related crashes killed 150 persons nationwide in 2006, according to data from the National Highway Traffic Safety Administration.

A school bus-related crash is defined by NHTSA to be any crash in which a vehicle, regardless of body design, used as a school bus is directly or indirectly involved, such as a crash involving school children alighting from a vehicle.

Over the period from 2001–2006, about 72% of the deaths in school bus-related crashes were occupants of vehicles other than the school bus and 18% were pedestrians. About 4% were school bus passengers and 3% were school bus drivers.

Of the 21 pedestrians killed in school bus-related crashes in 2006, 15 were struck by the school bus.

Out of the people injured in school bus-related crashes from 2001 through 2006, about 46% were school bus passengers, 9% were school bus drivers, and another 42% were occupants of other vehicles. The remainder were pedestrians, pedalcyclists, and other or unknown type persons.

Characteristics of school bus transportation

Forty-nine states reported that about 24.1 million public school pupils were transported at public expense and 37 states reported that public funds were used to transport another 0.9 million private school pupils. These data are prepared by *School Bus Fleet* (vol. 53, no. 10) for the 2004–2005 school year with 12 states reporting for prior school years and 4 for 2005–2006. This compares to estimates from the U.S. Department of Education of enrollments in fall 2004 in grades K–12 of about 48.6 million public school pupils and 6.4 million private school pupils nationwide. Fifty states employed a total of 473,044 school buses, and the buses in 41 states traveled about 3.9 billion route miles.

DEATHS AND INJURIES IN SCHOOL BUS–RELATED CRASHES, UNITED STATES, 2001–2006

	2001	2002	2003	2004	2005	2006
Deaths						
Total	141	129	140	133	134	150
School bus driver	6	1	6	3	5	1
School bus passenger	12	2	5	4	5	5
Pedestrian	22	20	27	30	30	21
Pedalcyclist	4	5	2	3	6	2
Occupant of other vehicle	95	100	100	93	87	121
Other or Unknown	2	1	0	0	1	0
Injuries						
Total	13,000	18,000	19,000	17,000	11,000	12,000
School bus driver	1,000	1,000	2,000	1,000	1,000	2,000
School bus passenger	6,000	9,000	9,000	8,000	4,000	5,000
Pedestrian	(a)	1,000	(a)	1,000	(a)	(a)
Pedalcyclist	(a)	(a)	(a)	(a)	(a)	(a)
Occupant of other vehicle	5,000	7,000	8,000	7,000	6,000	5,000
Other or Unknown	(a)	(a)	(a)	(a)	(a)	(a)

Source: National Highway Traffic Safety Administration.
a Less than 500.

AGE OF DRIVER

The table below shows the total number of licensed drivers and drivers involved in accidents by selected ages and age groups. Also shown is the rate of accident involvement on the basis of the number of drivers in each age group. The fatal accident involvement rates per 100,000 drivers in each age group ranged from a low of 22 for drivers 35 to 44 and 65 to 74 years of age to a high of 61 for drivers aged 21. The all accident involvement rates per 100 drivers in each age group ranged from 5 for drivers in the 65–74 and 75 and over age groups to 21 for drivers in the 16, 17, and 18 year old age groups.

On the basis of miles driven by each age group, however, involvement rates (not shown in the table) are highest for young and old drivers. For drivers aged 16 to 19, the fatal involvement rate per 100 million vehicle miles traveled was 9.2 in 1990, about three times the overall rate for all drivers in passenger vehicles, 3.0. The rate for drivers aged 75 and over was 11.5, the highest of all age groups. The same basic "U"-shaped curve is found for injury accident involvement rates.[a]

[a]Massie, D., Campbell, K., & Williams, A. (1995). Traffic accident involvement rates by driver age and gender. Accident Analysis and Prevention, 27 (1), 73–87.

AGE OF DRIVER—TOTAL NUMBER AND NUMBER IN ACCIDENTS, 2006

Age Group	Licensed Drivers		Drivers in ...					
	Number	Percent	Fatal Accidents			All Accidents		
			Number	Percent	Rate[a]	Number	Percent	Rate[b]
Total	202,700,000	100.0%	60,600	100.0%	30	18,000,000	100.0%	9
Under 16	37,000	(c)	300	0.5	(d)	260,000	1.4	(d)
16	1,830,000	0.9	800	1.3	44	380,000	2.1	21
17	2,578,000	1.3	1,300	2.1	50	550,000	3.1	21
18	3,009,000	1.5	1,800	3.0	60	620,000	3.4	21
19	3,265,000	1.6	1,900	3.1	58	610,000	3.4	19
19 and under	10,719,000	5.3	6,100	10.1	57	2,420,000	13.4	23
20	3,340,000	1.6	1,800	3.0	54	570,000	3.2	17
21	3,266,000	1.6	2,000	3.3	61	510,000	2.8	16
22	3,267,000	1.6	1,800	3.0	55	470,000	2.6	14
23	3,394,000	1.7	1,800	3.0	53	470,000	2.6	14
24	3,570,000	1.8	1,600	2.6	45	470,000	2.6	13
20–24	16,837,000	8.3	9,000	14.9	53	2,490,000	13.8	15
25–34	40,776,000	20.1	11,200	18.5	27	3,620,000	20.1	9
35–44	45,587,000	22.5	10,000	16.5	22	3,350,000	18.6	7
45–54	36,699,000	18.1	9,500	15.7	26	3,080,000	17.1	8
55–64	23,322,000	11.5	6,400	10.6	27	1,680,000	9.3	7
65–74	17,277,000	8.5	3,800	6.3	22	800,000	4.4	5
75 and over	11,483,000	5.7	4,600	7.6	40	560,000	3.1	5

Source: National Safety Council estimates. Drivers in accidents based on data from National Highway Traffic Safety Administration's Fatality Analysis Reporting System and General Estimates System. Total licensed drivers from the Federal Highway Administration; age distribution by National Safety Council.
Note: Percents may not add to total due to rounding.
[a] Drivers in fatal accidents per 100,000 licensed drivers in each age group.
[b] Drivers in all accidents per 100 licensed drivers in each age group.
[c] Less than 0.05.
[d] Rates for drivers under age 16 are substantially overstated due to the high proportion of unlicensed drivers involved.

Motor-vehicle crashes are the leading cause of death for young people 15–20 years old. In 2004 (the latest year available), according to a National Safety Council analysis of National Center for Health Statistics mortality data, 6,499 young people died in crashes. More than half of them (56%) were drivers.

In 2006, 7,463 young drivers were involved in fatal crashes and 1.6 million were involved in police-reported crashes of all severities according to National Highway Traffic Safety Administration data. Young drivers represent 6.3% of all licensed drivers but 12.9% of drivers in fatal crashes and 16% of drivers in all crashes.

In 2006, 3,490 young drivers were killed in crashes (see the graph below) and another 272,000 were injured.

Twenty-three percent of young drivers involved in fatal crashes had been drinking. Five percent had a Blood Alcohol Concentration (BAC) between .01 and .07 g/dL and 18% were intoxicated (BAC .08 or greater). Of those who were fatally injured, 25% were intoxicated.

Intoxication rates increase as the age of the driver increases. Among fatally injured drivers age 15, 17% were intoxicated; age 16, 16% were intoxicated; age 17, 19%; age 18, 23%; age 19, 28%; and age 20, 33%.

Speeding is likely to be a factor in fatal crashes involving young drivers. In 2006, 39% of young male drivers and 26% of young female drivers were speeding at the time of the fatal crash. Twenty percent of young drivers in fatal crashes had a previous speeding conviction.

The combination of speeding and alcohol is also a factor. Among drivers under age 21 involved in fatal crashes, 28% of those who were speeding also had a BAC of .08 g/dL or greater, compared to 13% of nonspeeding drivers with a BAC $\geq$ .08 g/dL.

Source: National Center for Statistics and Analysis. (2007). Traffic Safety Facts 2006 Data: Young Drivers. DOT HS 810 817. Traffic Safety Facts 2006 Data: Speeding. DOT HS 810 814. Washington, DC: National Highway Traffic Safety Administration.

FATALITIES IN CRASHES INVOLVING DRIVERS 15–20 YEARS OLD, UNITED STATES, 2006

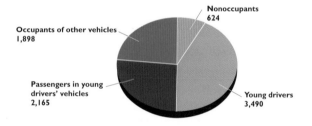

Nonoccupants 624

Occupants of other vehicles 1,898

Passengers in young drivers' vehicles 2,165

Young drivers 3,490

Graduated driver licensing (GDL) is an effective way to reduce the impact of motor-vehicle crashes on the lives of young drivers. GDL is a three-stage licensing system for young beginning drivers consisting of a learner's permit that allows driving only while supervised by a fully licensed driver, an intermediate license that allows unsupervised driving with certain restrictions (usually on young passengers and night time operation), and a full license. Both the learner's permit and intermediate license have minimum age requirements and must be

held for a specified minimum time period. Other requirements and restrictions may apply depending on the state issuing the license.

Summary articles on the science behind GDL and annual updates on GDL research may be found at www.nsc.org/gdlsym and in volume 38, number 2, of the *Journal of Safety Research* (http://www.elsevier.com/wps/find/journaldescription. cws_home/679/description#description).

PEDESTRIANS

In 2006, there were an estimated 6,100 pedestrian deaths and 70,000 injuries in motor-vehicle accidents. About 61% of these deaths and injuries occur when pedestrians improperly cross roadways or intersections or dart/run into streets. Playing, working, standing, etc. in the roadway accounted for over 7% of pedestrian deaths and injuries, while walking with traffic accounted for 4%.

The distribution of pedestrian deaths and injuries by action varies for persons of different ages.

Darting/running into the road was the leading type for the three youngest age groups, varying from 59% for those aged 10 to 14 years to 74% for those aged 0 to 4 years. Improper crossing of the roadway or intersection was the leading type for the 15 to 19, 20 to 24, 25 to 44, 45 to 64, and 65 and over age groups, ranging from 33% for those aged 15 to 19 years to over 45% for those aged 20 to 24 and 65 or older.

DEATHS AND INJURIES OF PEDESTRIANS BY AGE AND ACTION, 2006

| | | Age of Persons Killed or Injured | | | | | | | |
	Total[a]	0–4	5–9	10–14	15–19	20–24	25–44	45–64	65 & Over
All Actions	*100.0%*	*4.8%*	*8.4%*	*12.6%*	*12.3%*	*8.3%*	*25.5%*	*19.5%*	*8.6%*
Totals	**100.0%**	**100.0%**	**100.0%**	**100.0%**	**100.0%**	**100.0%**	**100.0%**	**100.0%**	**100.0%**
Improper crossing of roadway or intersection	32.4%	10.4%	10.3%	14.1%	33.1%	45.5%	36.3%	42.3%	45.7%
Darting or running into roadway	28.8%	74.1%	71.9%	58.8%	29.3%	14.8%	14.3%	14.0%	6.8%
Walking with traffic	3.6%	0.0%	0.0%	1.2%	1.7%	3.2%	6.8%	5.5%	2.4%
Walking against traffic	1.3%	0.0%	0.0%	0.7%	1.4%	1.8%	2.3%	1.5%	0.0%
Playing/working/standing, etc. in roadway	7.6%	5.2%	3.0%	1.8%	4.4%	3.3%	14.5%	7.9%	9.3%
Nonmotorist pushing a vehicle in roadway	0.1%	0.0%	0.0%	0.0%	0.0%	0.0%	0.0%	0.4%	0.0%
Inattentive--talking, eating, etc.	3.6%	0.0%	0.0%	0.0%	8.2%	10.5%	0.6%	0.2%	17.7%
Other action	15.3%	6.9%	1.2%	15.8%	18.9%	13.3%	18.1%	19.7%	11.5%
Not stated	7.3%	3.3%	13.6%	7.6%	3.1%	7.6%	7.3%	8.4%	6.6%

Source: NSC analysis of NHTSA General Estimates System (GES) data.
[a]Total includes "Age Unknown."

PEDESTRIAN DEATHS AND DEATH RATES BY SEX AND AGE GROUP, UNITED STATES, 2004

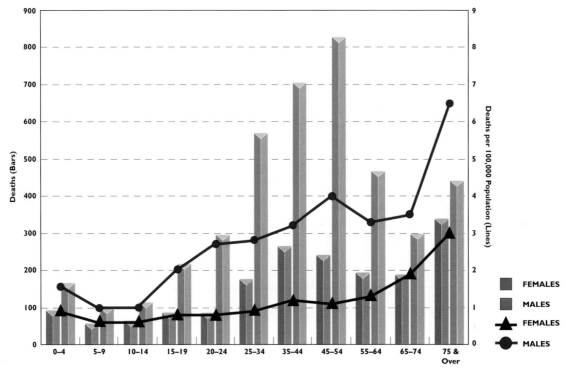

Source: National Safety Council based on National Center for Health Statistics data.

Motor-vehicle deaths in 2006 were at their lowest level in February and increased to their highest level in July. In 2006, the highest monthly mileage death rate of 1.56

deaths per 100,000,000 vehicle miles occurred in July and September. The overall rate for the year was 1.49.

Source: Deaths—National Safety Council estimates. Mileage—Federal Highway Administration, Traffic Volume Trends.

MOTOR-VEHICLE DEATHS AND MILEAGE DEATH RATES BY MONTH, 2006

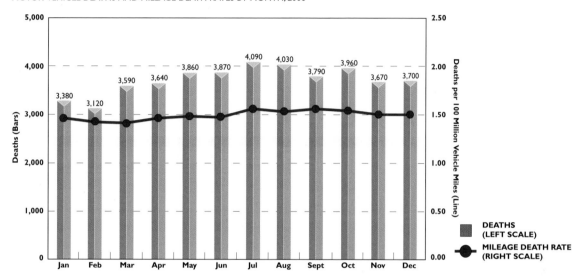

HOLIDAYS

Holidays are traditionally a time of travel for families across the United States and many choose the automobile—with the highest fatality rate of any of the major forms of transportation based on fatalities per passenger mile (see page 134)—as their mode of travel and therefore increase their risk of dying in a motor-vehicle crash. In addition, holidays are often the cause

for celebrations that include the drinking of alcohol, which is a major contributing factor to motor-vehicle crashes. Alcohol-related fatalities in 2005 represented 39% of the total traffic fatalities for the year. The table below shows the number of fatalities for each major holiday period and the percent of those fatalities that were alcohol-related.

MOTOR-VEHICLE DEATHS AND PERCENT ALCOHOL-RELATED DURING HOLIDAY PERIODS, 2001–2006

Year	New Year's Day Deaths[b]	New Year's Day Alcohol-Related[c] %	Memorial Day Deaths[b]	Memorial Day Alcohol-Related[c] %	Independence Day Deaths[b]	Independence Day Alcohol-Related[c] %	Labor Day Deaths[b]	Labor Day Alcohol-Related[c] %	Thanksgiving Deaths[b]	Thanksgiving Alcohol-Related[c] %	Christmas Deaths[b]	Christmas Alcohol-Related[c] %
2001	338 (3)	51	499 (3)	55	173 (1)	62	432 (3)	51	580 (4)	48	575 (4)	48
2002	554 (4)	52	484 (3)	47	662 (4)	48	536 (3)	57	527 (4)	47	114 (1)	54
2003	203 (1)	63	472 (3)	48	500 (3)	55	490 (3)	51	544 (4)	45	488 (4)	46
2004	549 (4)	50	496 (3)	49	502 (3)	49	480 (3)	49	556 (4)	42	370 (3)	49
2005	449 (3)	52	512 (3)	50	565 (3)	53	500 (3)	53	605 (4)	47	383 (3)	50
2006	432 (3)	55	493 (3)	52	629 (4)	49	487 (3)	48	623 (4)	47	379 (3)	51

Source: National Highway Traffic Safety Administration (NHTSA), Fatality Analysis Reporting System and NHTSA, Traffic Safety Facts, 2006 Early Edition.
Note: Dashes indicate data not available.
[a] The length of the holiday period depends on the day of the week on which the holiday falls. Memorial Day and Labor Day are always 3.25 days, Thanksgiving is always 4.25 days, and New Year's, Independence Day, and Christmas are 3.25 days if the holiday falls on Friday through Monday, 4.25 days if on Tuesday or Thursday, and 1.25 days if on Wednesday.
[b] Number in parentheses refers to the number of whole days in the holiday period.
[c] Blood alcohol concentration (BAC) of .01 grams per deciliter (g/dl) or greater. The holiday periods used to calculate the percentages conform to the NHTSA holiday period definitions that add another quarter day to the periods noted in footnote (a).

WORK ZONE DEATHS AND INJURIES

In 2006 there were 1,010 people killed and 37,688 people injured in work zone crashes (see table below). Compared to 2005, work zone fatalities decreased 6% and injuries were almost unchanged. Of the 1,010 people killed in work zones, 769 were in construction zones, 109 were in maintenance zones, 15 were in utility zones, and 117 were in an unknown type of work zone.

Over the 10 years from 1997 through 2006, work zone deaths have ranged from 658 to 1,181 and averaged 983 per year.

Based on a National Safety Council survey in August 2007, 31 states reported having work zone speed laws and 49 states had special penalties for traffic violations in work zones, such as increased or doubled fines. Hawaii and District of Columbia were the only jurisdictions with neither.

PERSONS KILLED AND INJURED IN WORK ZONES, UNITED STATES, 2006

	Total	Vehicle Occupants	Pedestrians	Pedalcyclists	Other Nonmotorists
Killed	1,010	866	126	12	6
Injured	37,688	36,695	653	190	150

Source: National Safety Council analysis of data from National Highway Traffic Safety Administration Fatality Analysis Reporting System (FARS) and General Estimates Systems (GES).

EMERGENCY VEHICLES

CRASHES INVOLVING EMERGENCY VEHICLES, UNITED STATES, 2006

	Ambulance		Fire Truck/Car		Police Car	
	Total	Emergency Use[a]	Total	Emergency Use[a]	Total	Emergency Use[a]
Emergency vehicles in fatal crashes	22	10	18	15	103	34
Emergency vehicles in injury crashes	1,439	755	957	782	8,939	3,784
Emergency vehicles in all crashes	**4,767**	**2,165**	**4,283**	**3,171**	**27,868**	**11,522**
Emergency vehicle drivers killed	2	1	3	2	33	13
Emergency vehicle passengers killed	6	3	1	1	3	2
Other vehicle occupants killed	14	7	13	11	66	23
Nonmotorists killed	3	1	2	2	18	3
Total killed in crashes	**25**	**12**	**19**	**16**	**120**	**41**
Total injured in crashes	**2,416**	**1,552**	**1,416**	**1,185**	**13,676**	**6,765**

Source: National Safety Council analysis of data from National Highway Traffic Safety Administration Fatality Analysis Reporting System (FARS) and General Estimates Systems (GES).
[a]Emergency lights and/or sirens in use.

The National Safety Council and the National Highway Traffic Safety Administration (NHTSA) count motor-vehicle crash deaths using somewhat different criteria. The Council counts total motor-vehicle-related fatalities—both traffic and nontraffic—that occur within one year of the crash. This is consistent with the data compiled from death certificates by the National Center for Health Statistics (NCHS). The Council uses the NCHS death certificate data as the final count of deaths from all causes.

NHTSA counts only traffic fatalities that occur within 30 days of the crash in its Fatality Analysis Reporting System (FARS). This means that the FARS count omits about 800 to 1,000 motor-vehicle-related deaths each year that occur more than 30 days after the crash. Nontraffic fatalities (those that do not occur on public highways; e.g., parking lots, private roads and driveways), which account for 900 to 1,400 deaths annually, are also omitted. By using a 30-day cut off, NHTSA can issue a "final" count about eight months after the reference year.

Because of the time it takes to process 2.4 million death certificates, the NCHS data are not available until about 22 months after the reference year. This means, for example, that this edition of *Injury Facts* includes the 2004 NCHS final counts by cause of death including motor-vehicle crashes and estimates of the totals for 2005 and 2006. For motor-vehicle deaths, these estimates are based on data supplied by traffic authorities in 50 states and the District of Columbia. For other causes of death, the estimates are based on data supplied by state vital statistics authorities. See the Technical Appendix for more information on estimation procedures.

The graph below shows the NCHS death certificate counts of total motor-vehicle deaths through 2004 and the NSC estimates for 2005 and 2006 compared to the NHTSA FARS counts of traffic deaths.

MOTOR-VEHICLE DEATHS: NSC AND NHTSA, 1992–2006

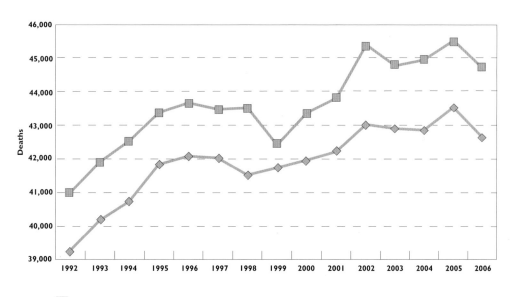

◻ NATIONAL SAFETY COUNCIL

◆ NATIONAL HIGHWAY TRAFFIC SAFETY ADMINISTRATION

MOTOR-VEHICLE DEATHS AND RATES

MOTOR-VEHICLE DEATHS AND RATES, UNITED STATES, 1913–2006

Year	No. of Deaths	Estimated No. of Vehicles (Millions)	Estimated Vehicle Miles (Billions)	Estimated No. of Drivers (Millions)	Death Rates Per 10,000 Motor Vehicles	Per 100,000,000 Vehicle Miles	Per 100,000 Population
1913	4,200	1.3	(a)	2.0	33.38	(a)	4.4
1914	4,700	1.8	(a)	3.0	26.65	(a)	4.8
1915	6,600	2.5	(a)	3.0	26.49	(a)	6.6
1916	8,200	3.6	(a)	5.0	22.66	(a)	8.1
1917	10,200	5.1	(a)	7.0	19.93	(a)	10.0
1918	10,700	6.2	(a)	9.0	17.37	(a)	10.3
1919	11,200	7.6	(a)	12.0	14.78	(a)	10.7
1920	12,500	9.2	(a)	14.0	13.53	(a)	11.7
1921	13,900	10.5	(a)	16.0	13.25	(a)	12.9
1922	15,300	12.3	(a)	19.0	12.47	(a)	13.9
1923	18,400	15.1	85	22.0	12.18	21.65	16.5
1924	19,400	17.6	104	26.0	11.02	18.65	17.1
1925	21,900	20.1	122	30.0	10.89	17.95	19.1
1926	23,400	22.2	141	33.0	10.54	16.59	20.1
1927	25,800	23.3	158	34.0	11.07	16.33	21.8
1928	28,000	24.7	173	37.0	11.34	16.18	23.4
1929	31,200	26.7	197	40.0	11.69	15.84	25.7
1930	32,900	26.7	206	40.0	12.32	15.97	26.7
1931	33,700	26.1	216	39.0	12.91	15.60	27.2
1932	29,500	24.4	200	36.0	12.09	14.75	23.6
1933	31,363	24.2	201	35.0	12.96	15.60	25.0
1934	36,101	25.3	216	37.0	14.27	16.71	28.6
1935	36,369	26.5	229	39.0	13.72	15.88	28.6
1936	38,089	28.5	252	42.0	13.36	15.11	29.7
1937	39,643	30.1	270	44.0	13.19	14.68	30.8
1938	32,582	29.8	271	44.0	10.93	12.02	25.1
1939	32,386	31.0	285	46.0	10.44	11.35	24.7
1940	34,501	32.5	302	48.0	10.63	11.42	26.1
1941	39,969	34.9	334	52.0	11.45	11.98	30.0
1942	28,309	33.0	268	49.0	8.58	10.55	21.1
1943	23,823	30.9	208	46.0	7.71	11.44	17.8
1944	24,282	30.5	213	45.0	7.97	11.42	18.3
1945	28,076	31.0	250	46.0	9.05	11.22	21.2
1946	33,411	34.4	341	50.0	9.72	9.80	23.9
1947	32,697	37.8	371	53.0	8.64	8.82	22.8
1948	32,259	41.1	398	55.0	7.85	8.11	22.1
1949	31,701	44.7	424	59.3	7.09	7.47	21.3
1950	34,763	49.2	458	62.2	7.07	7.59	23.0
1951	36,996	51.9	491	64.4	7.13	7.53	24.1
1952	37,794	53.3	514	66.8	7.10	7.36	24.3
1953	37,956	56.3	544	69.9	6.74	6.97	24.0
1954	35,586	58.6	562	72.2	6.07	6.33	22.1
1955	38,426	62.8	606	74.7	6.12	6.34	23.4
1956	39,628	65.2	631	77.9	6.07	6.28	23.7
1957	38,702	67.6	647	79.6	5.73	5.98	22.7
1958	36,981	68.8	665	81.5	5.37	5.56	21.3
1959	37,910	72.1	700	84.5	5.26	5.41	21.5
1960	38,137	74.5	719	87.4	5.12	5.31	21.2
1961	38,091	76.4	738	88.9	4.98	5.16	20.8
1962	40,804	79.7	767	92.0	5.12	5.32	22.0
1963	43,564	83.5	805	93.7	5.22	5.41	23.1
1964	47,700	87.3	847	95.6	5.46	5.63	25.0
1965	49,163	91.8	888	99.0	5.36	5.54	25.4
1966	53,041	95.9	930	101.0	5.53	5.70	27.1
1967	52,924	98.9	962	103.2	5.35	5.50	26.8
1968	54,862	103.1	1,016	105.4	5.32	5.40	27.5
1969	55,791	107.4	1,071	108.3	5.19	5.21	27.7
1970	54,633	111.2	1,120	111.5	4.92	4.88	26.8
1971	54,381	116.3	1,186	114.4	4.68	4.57	26.3
1972	56,278	122.3	1,268	118.4	4.60	4.43	26.9
1973	55,511	129.8	1,309	121.6	4.28	4.24	26.3
1974	46,402	134.9	1,290	125.6	3.44	3.59	21.8
1975	45,853	137.9	1,330	129.8	3.33	3.45	21.3
1976	47,038	143.5	1,412	133.9	3.28	3.33	21.6

See source and footnotes on page 111.

MOTOR-VEHICLE DEATHS AND RATES, UNITED STATES, 1913–2006, Cont.

Year	No. of Deaths	Estimated No. of Vehicles (Millions)	Estimated Vehicle Miles (Billions)	Estimated No. of Drivers (Millions)	Death Rates Per 10,000 Motor Vehicles	Per 100,000,000 Vehicle Miles	Per 100,000 Population
1977	49,510	148.8	1,477	138.1	3.33	3.35	22.5
1978	52,411	153.6	1,548	140.8	3.41	3.39	23.6
1979	53,524	159.6	1,529	143.3	3.35	3.50	23.8
1980	53,172	161.6	1,521	145.3	3.29	3.50	23.4
1981	51,385	164.1	1,556	147.1	3.13	3.30	22.4
1982	45,779	165.2	1,592	150.3	2.77	2.88	19.8
1983	44,452	169.4	1,657	154.2	2.62	2.68	19.0
1984	46,263	171.8	1,718	155.4	2.69	2.69	19.6
1985	45,901	177.1	1,774	156.9	2.59	2.59	19.3
1986	47,865	181.4	1,835	159.5	2.63	2.60	19.9
1987	48,290	183.9	1,924	161.8	2.63	2.51	19.9
1988	49,078	189.0	2,026	162.9	2.60	2.42	20.1
1989	47,575	191.7	2,107	165.6	2.48	2.26	19.3
1990	46,814	192.9	2,148	167.0	2.43	2.18	18.8
1991	43,536	192.5	2,172	169.0	2.26	2.00	17.3
1992	40,982	194.4	2,240	173.1	2.11	1.83	16.1
1993	41,893	198.0	2,297	173.1	2.12	1.82	16.3
1994	42,524	201.8	2,360	175.4	2.11	1.80	16.3
1995	43,363	205.3	2,423	176.6	2.11	1.79	16.5
1996	43,649	210.4	2,486	179.5	2.07	1.76	16.5
1997	43,458	211.5	2,562	182.7	2.05	1.70	16.2
1998	43,501	215.0	2,632	185.2	2.02	1.65	16.1
1999	42,401	220.5	2,691	187.2	1.92	1.58	15.5
2000	43,354	225.8	2,747	190.6	1.92	1.58	15.8
2001	43,788	235.3	2,797	191.3	1.86	1.57	15.4
2002	45,380	234.6	2,856	194.3	1.93	1.59	15.8
2003	44,757	236.8	2,890	196.2	1.89	1.55	15.4
2004[b]	44,933	243.0	2,965	199.0	1.85	1.52	15.3
2005[b]	45,500	247.4	2,990	200.5	1.84	1.52	15.4
2006[c]	44,700	251.8	2,995	202.7	1.77	1.49	14.9
Changes							
1996 to 2006	+2%	+20%	+20%	+13%	−14%	−15%	−10%
2005 to 2006	−2%	+2%	([d])	+1%	−4%	−2%	−3%

Source: Deaths from National Center for Health Statistics except 1964, 2005, and 2006, which are National Safety Council estimates based on data from the National Highway Traffic Safety Administration's Fatality Analysis Reporting System. See Technical Appendix for comparability. Motor-vehicle registrations, mileage and drivers estimated by Federal Highway Administration except 2006 registrations and drivers which are National Safety Council estimates.
[a]Mileage data inadequate prior to 1923.
[b]Revised.
[c]Preliminary.
[d]Change less than 0.5%.

MOTOR-VEHICLE DEATHS BY TYPE OF ACCIDENT

MOTOR-VEHICLE DEATHS BY TYPE OF ACCIDENT, UNITED STATES, 1913–2006

Year	Total Deaths	Deaths from Collision with —							Deaths from Noncollision Accidents	Nontraffic Deaths[a]
		Pedestrians	Other Motor Vehicles	Railroad Trains	Streetcars	Pedal-cycles	Animal-Drawn Vehicle or Animal	Fixed Objects		
1913	4,200	(b)	(b)	(b)	(b)	(b)	(b)	(b)	(b)	(c)
1914	4,700	(b)	(b)	(b)	(b)	(b)	(b)	(b)	(b)	(c)
1915	6,600	(b)	(b)	(b)	(b)	(b)	(b)	(b)	(b)	(c)
1916	8,200	(b)	(b)	(b)	(b)	(b)	(b)	(b)	(b)	(c)
1917	10,200	(b)	(b)	(b)	(b)	(b)	(b)	(b)	(b)	(c)
1918	10,700	(b)	(b)	(b)	(b)	(b)	(b)	(b)	(b)	(c)
1919	11,200	(b)	(b)	(b)	(b)	(b)	(b)	(b)	(b)	(c)
1920	12,500	(b)	(b)	(b)	(b)	(b)	(b)	(b)	(b)	(c)
1921	13,900	(b)	(b)	(b)	(b)	(b)	(b)	(b)	(b)	(c)
1922	15,300	(b)	(b)	(b)	(b)	(b)	(b)	(b)	(b)	(c)
1923	18,400	(b)	(b)	(b)	(b)	(b)	(b)	(b)	(b)	(c)
1924	19,400	(b)	(b)	1,130	410	(b)	(b)	(b)	(b)	(c)
1925	21,900	(b)	(b)	1,410	560	(b)	(b)	(b)	(b)	(c)
1926	23,400	(b)	(b)	1,730	520	(b)	(b)	(b)	(b)	(c)
1927	25,800	10,820	3,430	1,830	520	(b)	(b)	(b)	(b)	(c)
1928	28,000	11,420	4,310	2,140	570	(b)	(b)	540	8,070	(c)
1929	31,200	12,250	5,400	2,050	530	(b)	(b)	620	9,380	(c)
1930	32,900	12,900	5,880	1,830	480	(b)	(b)	720	9,970	(c)
1931	33,700	13,370	6,820	1,710	440	(b)	(b)	870	9,570	(c)
1932	29,500	11,490	6,070	1,520	320	350	400	800	8,500	(c)
1933	31,363	12,840	6,470	1,437	318	400	310	900	8,680	(c)
1934	36,101	14,480	8,110	1,457	332	500	360	1,040	9,820	(c)
1935	36,369	14,350	8,750	1,587	253	450	250	1,010	9,720	(c)
1936	38,089	15,250	9,500	1,697	269	650	250	1,060	9,410	(c)
1937	39,643	15,500	10,320	1,810	264	700	200	1,160	9,690	(c)
1938	32,582	12,850	8,900	1,490	165	720	170	940	7,350	(c)
1939	32,386	12,400	8,700	1,330	150	710	200	1,000	7,900	(c)
1940	34,501	12,700	10,100	1,707	132	750	210	1,100	7,800	(c)
1941	39,969	13,550	12,500	1,840	118	910	250	1,350	9,450	(c)
1942	28,309	10,650	7,300	1,754	124	650	240	850	6,740	(c)
1943	23,823	9,900	5,300	1,448	171	450	160	700	5,690	(c)
1944	24,282	9,900	5,700	1,663	175	400	140	700	5,600	(c)
1945	28,076	11,000	7,150	1,703	163	500	130	800	6,600	(c)
1946	33,411	11,600	9,400	1,703	174	450	130	950	8,900	(c)
1947	32,697	10,450	9,900	1,736	102	550	150	1,000	8,800	(c)
1948	32,259	9,950	10,200	1,474	83	500	100	1,000	8,950	(c)
1949	31,701	8,800	10,500	1,452	56	550	140	1,100	9,100	838
1950	34,763	9,000	11,650	1,541	89	440	120	1,300	10,600	900
1951	36,996	9,150	13,100	1,573	46	390	100	1,400	11,200	966
1952	37,794	8,900	13,500	1,429	32	430	130	1,450	11,900	970
1953	37,956	8,750	13,400	1,506	26	420	120	1,500	12,200	1,026
1954	35,586	8,000	12,800	1,289	28	380	90	1,500	11,500	1,004
1955	38,426	8,200	14,500	1,490	15	410	90	1,600	12,100	989
1956	39,628	7,900	15,200	1,377	11	440	100	1,600	13,000	888
1957	38,702	7,850	15,400	1,376	13	460	80	1,700	11,800	1,016
1958	36,981	7,650	14,200	1,316	9	450	80	1,650	11,600	929
1959	37,910	7,850	14,900	1,202	6	480	70	1,600	11,800	948
1960	38,137	7,850	14,800	1,368	5	460	80	1,700	11,900	995
1961	38,091	7,650	14,700	1,267	5	490	80	1,700	12,200	1,065
1962	40,804	7,900	16,400	1,245	3	500	90	1,750	12,900	1,029
1963	43,564	8,200	17,600	1,385	10	580	80	1,900	13,800	990
1964	47,700	9,000	19,600	1,580	5	710	100	2,100	14,600	1,123
1965	49,163	8,900	20,800	1,556	5	680	120	2,200	14,900	1,113
1966	53,041	9,400	22,200	1,800	2	740	100	2,500	16,300	1,108
1967	52,924	9,400	22,000	1,620	3	750	100	2,350	16,700	1,165
1968	54,862	9,900	22,400	1,570	4	790	100	2,700	17,400	1,061
1969	55,791	10,100	23,700	1,495	2	800	100	3,900d	15,700d	1,155
1970	54,633	9,900	23,200	1,459	3	780	100	3,800	15,400	1,140
1971	54,381	9,900	23,100	1,378	2	800	100	3,800	15,300	1,015
1972	56,278	10,300	23,900	1,260	2	1,000	100	3,900	15,800	1,064
1973	55,511	10,200	23,600	1,194	2	1,000	100	3,800	15,600	1,164
1974	46,402	8,500	19,700	1,209	1	1,000	100	3,100	12,800	1,088
1975	45,853	8,400	19,550	979	1	1,000	100	3,130	12,700	1,033
1976	47,038	8,600	20,100	1,033	2	1,000	100	3,200	13,000	1,026

See source and footnotes on page 113.

MOTOR-VEHICLE DEATHS BY TYPE OF ACCIDENT, UNITED STATES, 1913–2006, Cont.

Year	Total Deaths	Deaths from Collision with —							Deaths from Noncollision Accidents	Nontraffic Deaths[a]
		Pedestrians	Other Motor Vehicles	Railroad Trains	Streetcars	Pedal-cycles	Animal-Drawn Vehicle or Animal	Fixed Objects		
1977	49,510	9,100	21,200	902	3	1,100	100	3,400	13,700	1,053
1978	52,411	9,600	22,400	986	1	1,200	100	3,600	14,500	1,074
1979	53,524	9,800	23,100	826	1	1,200	100	3,700	14,800	1,271
1980	53,172	9,700	23,000	739	1	1,200	100	3,700	14,700	1,242
1981	51,385	9,400	22,200	668	1	1,200	100	3,600	14,200	1,189
1982	45,779	8,400	19,800	554	1	1,100	100	3,200	12,600	1,066
1983	44,452	8,200	19,200	520	1	1,100	100	3,100	12,200	1,024
1984	46,263	8,500	20,000	630	0	1,100	100	3,200	12,700	1,055
1985	45,901	8,500	19,900	538	2	1,100	100	3,200	12,600	1,079
1986	47,865	8,900	20,800	574	2	1,100	100	3,300	13,100	998
1987	48,290	7,500[e]	20,700	554	1	1,000[e]	100	13,200[e]	5,200[e]	993
1988	49,078	7,700	20,900	638	2	1,000	100	13,400	5,300	1,054
1989	47,575	7,800	20,300	720	2	900	100	12,900	4,900	989
1990	46,814	7,300	19,900	623	2	900	100	13,100	4,900	987
1991	43,536	6,600	18,200	541	1	800	100	12,600	4,700	915
1992	40,982	6,300	17,600	521	2	700	100	11,700	4,100	997
1993	41,893	6,400	18,300	553	3	800	100	11,500	4,200	994
1994	42,524	6,300	18,900	549	1	800	100	11,500	4,400	1,017
1995	43,363	6,400	19,000	514	(c)	800	100	12,100	4,400	1,032
1996	43,649	6,100	19,600	373	(c)	800	100	12,100	4,600	1,127
1997	43,458	5,900	19,900	371	(c)	800	100	12,000	4,400	1,118
1998	43,501	5,900	19,700	309	(c)	700	100	12,200	4,600	1,310
1999	42,401	6,100	18,600	314	1	800	100	11,800	4,700	1,436
2000	43,354	5,900	19,100	321	(c)	800	100	12,300	4,800	1,360
2001	43,788	6,100	18,800	324	3	800	100	12,800	4,900	1,345
2002	45,380	6,100	19,200	283	(c)	800	100	13,600	5,300	1,315
2003	44,757	6,000	19,300	245	(c)	800	100	13,100	5,200	1,417
2004[f]	44,933	6,000	19,600	253	(c)	900	100	13,000	5,100	1,501
2005[f]	45,500	6,200	19,400	200	(c)	1,000	100	13,300	5,300	—
2006[g]	44,700	6,100	18,500	200	(c)	1,100	100	13,400	5,300	—
Changes in Deaths										
1996 to 2006	+2%	0%	−6%	−46%	—	+38%	0%	+11%	+15%	—
2005 to 2006	−2%	−2%	−5%	0%	—	+10%	0%	+1%	0%	—

Source: Total deaths from National Center for Health Statistics except 1964 and 2005–2006, which are National Safety Council estimates based on data from the National Highway Traffic Safety Administration's Fatality Analysis Reporting System. Most totals by type are estimated and may not add to the total deaths. See Technical Appendix for comparability.
[a] See definition, page 191. Nontraffic deaths are included in appropriate accident type totals in table; in 2004, 30% of the nontraffic deaths were pedestrians.
[b] Insufficient data for approximations.
[c] Data not available.
[d] 1969 through 1986 totals are not comparable to previous years.
[e] Procedures and benchmarks for estimating deaths for certain types of accidents were changed for the 1990 edition. Estimates for 1987 and later years are not comparable to earlier years.
[f] Revised.
[f] Preliminary.

MOTOR-VEHICLE DEATHS BY AGE

MOTOR-VEHICLE DEATHS BY AGE, UNITED STATES, 1913–2006

Year	All Ages	Under 5 Years	5–14 Years	15–24 Years	25–44 Years	45–64 Years	65–74 Years	75 & Over[a]
1913	4,200	300	1,100	600	1,100	800	300	
1914	4,700	300	1,200	700	1,200	900	400	
1915	6,600	400	1,500	1,000	1,700	1,400	600	
1916	8,200	600	1,800	1,300	2,100	1,700	700	
1917	10,200	700	2,400	1,400	2,700	2,100	900	
1918	10,700	800	2,700	1,400	2,500	2,300	1,000	
1919	11,200	900	3,000	1,400	2,500	2,100	1,300	
1920	12,500	1,000	3,300	1,700	2,800	2,300	1,400	
1921	13,900	1,100	3,400	1,800	3,300	2,700	1,600	
1922	15,300	1,100	3,500	2,100	3,700	3,100	1,800	
1923	18,400	1,200	3,700	2,800	4,600	3,900	2,200	
1924	19,400	1,400	3,800	2,900	4,700	4,100	2,500	
1925	21,900	1,400	3,900	3,600	5,400	4,800	2,800	
1926	23,400	1,400	3,900	3,900	5,900	5,200	3,100	
1927	25,800	1,600	4,000	4,300	6,600	5,800	3,500	
1928	28,000	1,600	3,800	4,900	7,200	6,600	3,900	
1929	31,200	1,600	3,900	5,700	8,000	7,500	4,500	
1930	32,900	1,500	3,600	6,200	8,700	8,000	4,900	
1931	33,700	1,500	3,600	6,300	9,100	8,200	5,000	
1932	29,500	1,200	2,900	5,100	8,100	7,400	4,800	
1933	31,363	1,274	3,121	5,649	8,730	7,947	4,642	
1934	36,101	1,210	3,182	6,561	10,232	9,530	5,386	
1935	36,369	1,253	2,951	6,755	10,474	9,562	5,374	
1936	38,089	1,324	3,026	7,184	10,807	10,089	5,659	
1937	39,643	1,303	2,991	7,800	10,877	10,475	6,197	
1938	32,582	1,122	2,511	6,016	8,772	8,711	5,450	
1939	32,386	1,192	2,339	6,318	8,917	8,292	5,328	
1940	34,501	1,176	2,584	6,846	9,362	8,882	5,651	
1941	39,969	1,378	2,838	8,414	11,069	9,829	6,441	
1942	28,309	1,069	1,991	5,932	7,747	7,254	4,316	
1943	23,823	1,132	1,959	4,522	6,454	5,996	3,760	
1944	24,282	1,203	2,093	4,561	6,514	5,982	3,929	
1945	28,076	1,290	2,386	5,358	7,578	6,794	4,670	
1946	33,411	1,568	2,508	7,445	8,955	7,532	5,403	
1947	32,697	1,502	2,275	7,251	8,775	7,468	5,426	
1948	32,259	1,635	2,337	7,218	8,702	7,190	3,173	2,004
1949	31,701	1,667	2,158	6,772	8,892	7,073	3,116	2,023
1950	34,763	1,767	2,152	7,600	10,214	7,728	3,264	2,038
1951	36,996	1,875	2,300	7,713	11,253	8,276	3,444	2,135
1952	37,794	1,951	2,295	8,115	11,380	8,463	3,472	2,118
1953	37,956	2,019	2,368	8,169	11,302	8,318	3,508	2,271
1954	35,586	1,864	2,332	7,571	10,521	7,848	3,247	2,203
1955	38,426	1,875	2,406	8,656	11,448	8,372	3,455	2,214
1956	39,628	1,770	2,640	9,169	11,551	8,573	3,657	2,268
1957	38,702	1,785	2,604	8,667	11,230	8,545	3,560	2,311
1958	36,981	1,791	2,710	8,388	10,414	7,922	3,535	2,221
1959	37,910	1,842	2,719	8,969	10,358	8,263	3,487	2,272
1960	38,137	1,953	2,814	9,117	10,189	8,294	3,457	2,313
1961	38,091	1,891	2,802	9,088	10,212	8,267	3,467	2,364
1962	40,804	1,903	3,028	10,157	10,701	8,812	3,696	2,507
1963	43,564	1,991	3,063	11,123	11,356	9,506	3,786	2,739
1964	47,700	2,120	3,430	12,400	12,500	10,200	4,150	2,900
1965	49,163	2,059	3,526	13,395	12,595	10,509	4,077	3,002
1966	53,041	2,182	3,869	15,298	13,282	11,051	4,217	3,142
1967	52,924	2,067	3,845	15,646	12,987	10,902	4,285	3,192
1968	54,862	1,987	4,105	16,543	13,602	11,031	4,261	3,333
1969	55,791	2,077	4,045	17,443	13,868	11,012	4,210	3,136
1970	54,633	1,915	4,159	16,720	13,446	11,099	4,084	3,210
1971	54,381	1,885	4,256	17,103	13,307	10,471	4,108	3,251
1972	56,278	1,896	4,258	17,942	13,758	10,836	4,138	3,450
1973	55,511	1,998	4,124	18,032	14,013	10,216	3,892	3,236
1974	46,402	1,546	3,332	15,905	11,834	8,159	3,071	2,555
1975	45,853	1,576	3,286	15,672	11,969	7,663	3,047	2,640
1976	47,038	1,532	3,175	16,650	12,112	7,770	3,082	2,717

See source and footnotes on page 115.

MOTOR-VEHICLE DEATHS BY AGE, UNITED STATES, 1913–2006, Cont.

Year	All Ages	Under 5 Years	5–14 Years	15–24 Years	25–44 Years	45–64 Years	65–74 Years	75 & Over[a]
1977	49,510	1,472	3,142	18,092	13,031	8,000	3,060	2,713
1978	52,411	1,551	3,130	19,164	14,574	8,048	3,217	2,727
1979	53,524	1,461	2,952	19,369	15,658	8,162	3,171	2,751
1980	53,172	1,426	2,747	19,040	16,133	8,022	2,991	2,813
1981	51,385	1,256	2,575	17,363	16,447	7,818	3,090	2,836
1982	45,779	1,300	2,301	15,324	14,469	6,879	2,825	2,681
1983	44,452	1,233	2,241	14,289	14,323	6,690	2,827	2,849
1984	46,263	1,138	2,263	14,738	15,036	6,954	3,020	3,114
1985	45,901	1,195	2,319	14,277	15,034	6,885	3,014	3,177
1986	47,865	1,188	2,350	15,227	15,844	6,799	3,096	3,361
1987	48,290	1,190	2,397	14,447	16,405	7,021	3,277	3,553
1988	49,078	1,220	2,423	14,406	16,580	7,245	3,429	3,775
1989	47,575	1,221	2,266	12,941	16,571	7,287	3,465	3,824
1990	46,814	1,123	2,059	12,607	16,488	7,282	3,350	3,905
1991	43,536	1,076	2,011	11,664	15,082	6,616	3,193	3,894
1992	40,982	1,020	1,904	10,305	14,071	6,597	3,247	3,838
1993	41,893	1,081	1,963	10,500	14,283	6,711	3,116	4,239
1994	42,524	1,139	2,026	10,660	13,966	7,097	3,385	4,251
1995	43,363	1,004	2,055	10,600	14,618	7,428	3,300	4,358
1996	43,649	1,035	1,980	10,576	14,482	7,749	3,419	4,408
1997	43,458	933	1,967	10,208	14,167	8,134	3,370	4,679
1998	43,501	921	1,868	10,026	14,095	8,416	3,410	4,765
1999	42,401	834	1,771	10,128	13,516	8,342	3,276	4,534
2000	43,354	819	1,772	10,560	13,811	8,867	3,038	4,487
2001	43,788	770	1,686	10,725	14,020	9,029	2,990	4,568
2002	45,380	733	1,614	11,459	14,169	9,701	3,113	4,591
2003	44,757	766	1,642	10,972	13,794	10,032	2,967	4,584
2004[b]	44,933	778	1,653	10,987	13,699	10,369	2,974	4,473
2005[b]	45,500	700	1,500	10,900	14,200	10,600	3,100	4,500
2006[c]	44,700	700	1,300	10,900	14,100	10,700	2,900	4,100
Changes in Deaths								
1996 to 2006	+2%	−32%	−34%	+3%	−3%	+38%	−15%	−7%
2005 to 2006	−2%	0%	−13%	0%	−1%	+1%	−6%	−9%

Source: 1913 to 1932 calculated from National Center for Health Statistics data for registration states; 1933 to 1963, 1965 to 2004 are NCHS totals. All other figures are National Safety Council estimates. See Technical Appendix for comparability.
[a] Includes "age unknown." In 2004 these deaths numbered 26.
[b] Revised.
[c] Preliminary.

MOTOR-VEHICLE DEATH RATES BY AGE

MOTOR-VEHICLE DEATH RATES[a] BY AGE, UNITED STATES, 1913–2006

Year	All Ages	Under 5 Years	5–14 Years	15–24 Years	25–44 Years	45–64 Years	65–74 Years	75 & Over
1913	4.4	2.3	5.5	3.1	3.8	5.3	8.5	
1914	4.8	2.5	5.7	3.5	4.1	6.2	9.3	
1915	6.6	3.5	7.3	5.0	5.6	8.8	13.5	
1916	8.1	4.7	8.6	6.0	7.0	10.7	15.8	
1917	10.0	5.6	10.6	7.4	8.6	12.6	18.6	
1918	10.3	6.9	12.3	7.7	8.3	13.7	21.2	
1919	10.7	7.5	13.9	7.5	8.1	12.4	24.1	
1920	11.7	8.6	14.6	8.7	8.8	13.5	27.0	
1921	12.9	9.0	14.5	9.2	10.2	15.4	31.0	
1922	13.9	9.2	15.0	10.8	11.1	17.2	34.9	
1923	16.5	9.7	15.6	13.4	13.6	21.0	40.5	
1924	17.1	11.1	16.1	14.3	13.7	21.8	43.7	
1925	19.1	11.0	15.6	17.2	15.8	25.0	48.9	
1926	20.1	11.0	15.9	18.6	17.1	26.3	51.4	
1927	21.8	12.8	16.0	20.0	18.8	28.9	56.9	
1928	23.4	12.7	15.5	21.9	20.2	32.4	62.2	
1929	25.7	13.4	15.6	25.6	22.3	35.6	68.6	
1930	26.7	13.0	14.7	27.4	23.9	37.0	72.5	
1931	27.2	13.3	14.5	27.9	24.8	37.4	70.6	
1932	23.6	11.3	12.0	22.6	22.0	32.9	63.6	
1933	25.0	12.0	12.7	24.8	23.4	34.7	63.1	
1934	28.6	11.7	13.0	28.6	27.2	40.7	71.0	
1935	28.6	12.3	12.2	29.2	27.6	39.9	68.9	
1936	29.7	13.2	12.6	30.8	28.2	41.3	70.5	
1937	30.8	13.0	12.7	33.2	28.2	42.0	75.1	
1938	25.1	11.0	10.8	25.4	22.5	34.3	64.1	
1939	24.7	11.2	10.4	26.5	22.6	32.2	60.2	
1940	26.1	11.1	11.5	28.7	23.5	33.9	62.1	
1941	30.0	12.7	12.6	35.7	27.5	37.0	68.6	
1942	21.1	9.5	8.8	25.8	19.2	26.9	44.5	
1943	17.8	9.4	8.6	20.6	16.1	21.9	37.6	
1944	18.3	9.6	9.1	22.5	16.6	21.6	38.2	
1945	21.2	10.0	10.3	27.8	19.7	24.2	44.1	
1946	23.9	11.9	10.8	34.4	21.1	26.4	49.6	
1947	22.8	10.5	9.7	32.8	20.3	25.7	48.2	
1948	22.1	11.0	9.8	32.5	19.8	24.3	39.6	55.4
1949	21.3	10.7	9.0	30.7	19.9	23.4	37.8	53.9
1950	23.0	10.8	8.8	34.5	22.5	25.1	38.8	52.4
1951	24.1	10.9	9.2	36.0	24.7	26.5	39.5	53.0
1952	24.3	11.3	8.7	38.6	24.7	26.7	38.5	50.8
1953	24.0	11.5	8.5	39.1	24.5	25.8	37.7	52.6
1954	22.1	10.4	8.1	36.2	22.6	24.0	33.9	49.0
1955	23.4	10.2	8.0	40.9	24.5	25.2	35.1	47.1
1956	23.7	9.4	8.4	42.9	24.6	25.3	36.2	46.4
1957	22.7	9.2	8.0	39.7	23.9	24.8	34.4	45.5
1958	21.3	9.1	8.1	37.0	22.3	22.6	33.5	42.3
1959	21.5	9.1	7.9	38.2	22.2	23.2	32.3	41.8
1960	21.2	9.6	7.9	37.7	21.7	22.9	31.3	41.1
1961	20.8	9.2	7.6	36.5	21.8	22.5	30.7	40.5
1962	22.0	9.3	8.1	38.4	22.9	23.7	32.2	41.7
1963	23.1	9.8	8.0	40.0	24.3	25.2	32.6	44.3
1964	25.0	10.5	8.8	42.6	26.8	26.6	35.5	45.2
1965	25.4	10.4	8.9	44.2	27.0	27.0	34.6	45.4
1966	27.1	11.4	9.7	48.7	28.5	27.9	35.4	46.2
1967	26.8	11.2	9.5	48.4	27.8	27.1	35.6	45.4
1968	27.5	11.1	10.1	49.8	28.8	27.0	35.1	46.0
1969	27.7	12.0	9.9	50.7	29.1	26.6	34.3	42.0
1970	26.8	11.2	10.2	46.7	27.9	26.4	32.7	42.2
1971	26.3	10.9	10.5	45.7	27.4	24.7	32.4	41.3
1972	26.9	11.1	10.7	47.1	27.4	25.3	32.0	42.6
1973	26.3	11.9	10.5	46.3	27.2	23.6	29.4	39.1
1974	21.8	9.4	8.6	40.0	22.4	18.8	22.6	30.1
1975	21.3	9.8	8.6	38.7	22.1	17.5	21.9	30.1
1976	21.6	9.8	8.4	40.3	21.8	17.6	21.6	30.1

See source and footnotes on page 117.

MOTOR-VEHICLE DEATH RATES[a] BY AGE, UNITED STATES, 1913–2006, Cont.

Year	All Ages	Under 5 Years	5–14 Years	15–24 Years	25–44 Years	45–64 Years	65–74 Years	75 & Over
1977	22.5	9.5	8.5	43.3	22.7	18.1	20.9	29.3
1978	23.6	9.9	8.6	45.4	24.6	18.2	21.5	28.7
1979	23.8	9.1	8.3	45.6	25.6	18.4	20.7	28.1
1980	23.4	8.7	7.9	44.8	25.5	18.0	19.1	28.0
1981	22.4	7.4	7.5	41.1	25.2	17.6	19.4	27.5
1982	19.8	7.5	6.7	36.8	21.5	15.5	17.5	25.2
1983	19.0	7.0	6.6	34.8	20.6	15.0	17.2	26.0
1984	19.6	6.4	6.7	36.4	21.0	15.6	18.2	27.7
1985	19.3	6.7	6.9	35.7	20.5	15.4	17.9	27.5
1986	19.9	6.6	7.0	38.5	21.0	15.2	18.1	28.3
1987	19.9	6.6	7.1	37.1	21.3	15.7	18.8	29.1
1988	20.1	6.7	7.1	37.8	21.2	15.9	19.5	30.2
1989	19.3	6.6	6.5	34.6	20.8	15.9	19.4	29.8
1990	18.8	6.0	5.8	34.2	20.4	15.7	18.5	29.7
1991	17.3	5.6	5.6	32.1	18.3	14.2	17.5	28.9
1992	16.1	5.2	5.2	28.5	17.1	13.6	17.6	27.8
1993	16.3	5.5	5.3	29.1	17.3	13.5	16.7	30.0
1994	16.3	5.8	5.4	29.5	16.8	13.9	18.1	29.4
1995	16.5	5.1	5.4	29.3	17.5	14.2	17.6	29.4
1996	16.5	5.4	5.2	29.2	17.3	14.4	18.3	29.0
1997	16.2	4.9	5.1	27.9	17.0	14.7	18.2	29.9
1998	16.1	4.9	4.8	26.9	16.9	14.7	18.5	29.8
1999	15.5	4.4	4.5	26.8	16.3	14.1	18.0	27.8
2000	15.7	4.3	4.5	27.5	16.8	14.5	16.7	27.0
2001	15.4	4.0	4.1	26.8	16.5	14.0	16.3	26.8
2002	15.8	3.7	3.9	28.2	16.8	14.6	17.0	26.5
2003	15.4	3.9	4.0	26.6	16.4	14.6	16.2	26.0
2004[b]	15.3	3.9	4.1	26.4	16.3	14.7	16.1	25.1
2005[b]	15.3	3.4	3.7	25.9	16.9	14.6	16.8	24.8
2006[c]	14.9	3.4	3.2	25.7	16.8	14.3	15.3	22.4
Changes in Rates								
1996 to 2006	−10%	−37%	−38%	−12%	−3%	−1%	−16%	−23%
2005 to 2006	−3%	0%	−14%	−1%	−1%	−2%	−9%	−10%

Source: 1913 to 1932 calculated from National Center for Health Statistics data for registration states; 1933 to 1963, 1965 to 2004 are NCHS totals. All other figures are National Safety Council estimates. See Technical Appendix for comparability.
[a] Death rates are deaths per 100,000 population in each age group.
[b] Revised.
[c] Preliminary.

NATIONAL SAFETY COUNCIL

INJURY FACTS®

HOME AND COMMUNITY, 2006

The Home and Community venue is the combination of the Home class and the Public class. Home and Community together with the Occupational and Transportation venues make up the totality of unintentional injuries. Home and Community includes all unintentional injuries that are not work related and do not involve motor vehicles on streets and highways.

In 2006, an estimated 72,600 unintentional-injury deaths occurred in the Home and Community venue, or 61% of all unintentional-injury deaths that year. The number of deaths was up about 4% from the revised 2005 total of 70,000. Another 20,200,000 people suffered nonfatal disabling injuries. The death rate per 100,000 population was 24.2, up 3% from the revised 2005 rate.

About 1 out of 15 people experienced an unintentional injury in the Home and Community venue and about 1 out of 4,100 people died from such an injury. About 40% of the deaths and disabling injuries involved workers while they were away from work (off the job).

The graph on the next page shows the five leading causes of unintentional-injury deaths in the Home and Community venue and the broad age groups (children, youths and adults, and the elderly) affected by them. This is one way to prioritize issues in this venue. Below is a graph of the trend in deaths and death rates from 1996 to the present. Similar graphs for the Public and Home classes are on pages 122 and 126.

The National Safety Council adopted the Bureau of Labor Statistics' Census of Fatal Occupational Injuries count for work-related unintentional injuries beginning with 1992 data. Because of the lower Work class total resulting from this change, adjustments had to be made to the Home and Public classes. Long-term historical comparisons for these three classes should be made with caution. Also, beginning with 1999 data, deaths are now classified according to the 10th revision of the *International Classification of Diseases*. Caution should be used in comparing data classified under the 10th revision with prior revisions. See the Technical Appendix for more information about both changes.

Deaths **72,600**
Disabling injuries **20,200,000**
Deaths rate per 100,000 population **24.2**
Costs . . . . **$251.9 billion**

HOME AND COMMUNITY DEATHS AND DEATH RATES, UNITED STATES, 1996–2006

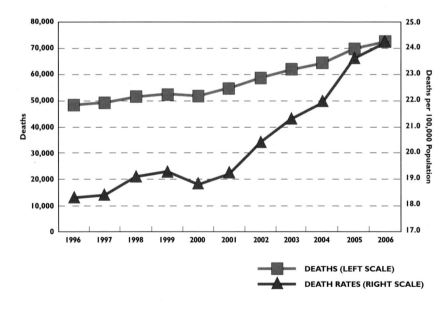

LEADING CAUSES OF UNINTENTIONAL-INJURY DEATHS IN HOME AND COMMUNITY, UNITED STATES, 2006

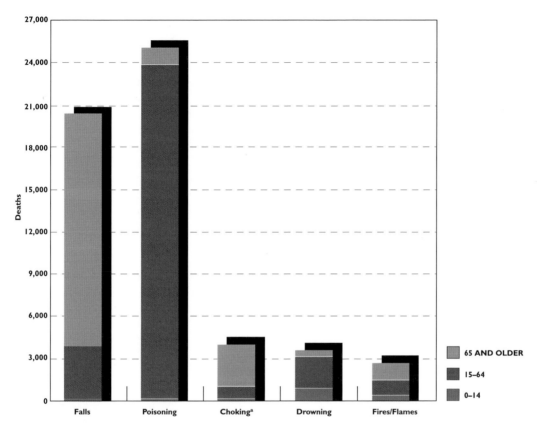

*Inhalation and ingestion of food or other object that obstructs breathing.

CAUSES OF UNINTENTIONAL-INJURY DEATHS IN HOME AND COMMUNITY, UNITED STATES, 2006

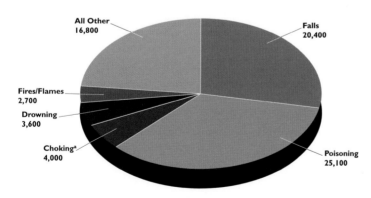

*Inhalation and ingestion of food or other object that obstructs breathing.

PUBLIC, 2006

Between 1912 and 2006, public unintentional-injury deaths per 100,000 population were reduced 65% from 30 to 10.0 (after adjusting for the 1948 change in classification). In 1912, an estimated 28,000 to 30,000 persons died from public nonmotor-vehicle injuries. In 2006, with a population tripled, and travel and recreational activity greatly increased, 30,000 persons died of public unintentional injuries and 10,000,000 suffered disabling injuries. The public class excludes deaths and injuries involving motor vehicles and persons at work or at home.

The number of public unintentional-injury deaths was up 2% from the revised 2005 figure of 29,400. The death rate per 100,000 population increased from 9.9 to 10.0, or 1%.

With an estimated 10,000,000 disabling unintentional injuries occurring in public places and a population of more than 299 million people, on average about one person in 30 experienced such an injury.

The Council adopted the Bureau of Labor Statistics' Census of Fatal Occupational Injuries count for work-related unintentional injuries beginning with 1992 data. This affected long-term historical comparisons for the Work, Home, and Public classes. Beginning with 1999 data, deaths are classified according to the 10th revision of the *International Classification of Diseases*. Caution should be used in comparing current data with data classified under prior revisions. See the Technical Appendix for more information.

Deaths **30,000**
Disabling injuries **10,000,000**
Death rate per 100,000 population **10.0**
Costs . . . . **$101.8 billion**

PUBLIC DEATHS AND DEATH RATES, UNITED STATES, 1996–2006

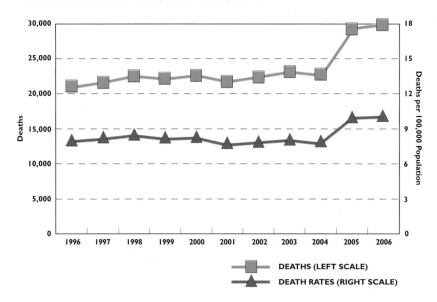

PUBLIC, 2006 (CONT.)

PRINCIPAL TYPES OF PUBLIC UNINTENTIONAL-INJURY DEATHS, UNITED STATES, 1986–2006

Year	Total Public[a]	Falls	Drowning	Poisoning	Suffocation by Ingestion	Fires/ Burns	Firearms	Mechanical Suffocation	Air Transport	Water Transport	Rail Transport[b]
1986	18,700	3,900	3,600	(c)	(c)	500	600	(c)	800	900	400
1987	18,400	4,000	3,200	(c)	(c)	500	600	(c)	900	800	400
1988	18,400	4,100	3,100	(c)	(c)	500	600	(c)	700	800	400
1989	18,200	4,200	3,000	(c)	(c)	500	600	(c)	800	700	400
1990	17,400	4,300	2,800	(c)	(c)	400	500	(c)	700	800	400
1991	17,600	4,500	2,800	(c)	(c)	400	600	(c)	700	700	500
1992	19,000	4,400	2,500	(c)	(c)	200	400	(c)	700	700	600
1993	19,700	4,600	2,800	(c)	(c)	200	400	(c)	600	700	600
1994	19,600	4,700	2,400	(c)	(c)	200	400	(c)	600	600	600
1995	20,100	5,000	2,800	(c)	(c)	200	300	(c)	600	700	500
1996	21,000	5,300	2,500	(c)	(c)	200	300	(c)	700	600	500
1997	21,700	5,600	2,600	(c)	(c)	200	300	(c)	500	600	400
1998	22,600	6,000	2,900	(c)	(c)	200	300	(c)	500	600	500
1999[d]	22,200	4,800	2,600	2,800	2,000	200	300	500	500	600	400
2000	22,700	5,500	2,400	2,900	2,200	(c)	(c)	300	500	500	400
2001	21,800	5,600	2,400	2,700	2,100	(c)	(c)	300	700	500	400
2002	22,500	5,900	2,500	3,600	2,200	(c)	(c)	300	500	500	400
2003	23,200	6,300	2,400	3,400	2,200	(c)	(c)	300	600	500	400
2004[e]	22,700	6,700	2,400	3,400	2,200	(c)	(c)	200	400	500	400
2005[e]	29,400	8,300	2,700	4,700	3,100	(c)	(c)	300	400	500	400
2006[f]	30,000	8,600	2,500	5,100	2,700	(c)	(c)	200	400	600	400

Source: National Safety Council estimates based on data from the National Center for Health Statistics and state vital statistics departments. The Council adopted the Bureau of Labor Statistics' Census of Fatal Occupational Injuries count for work-related unintentional injuries retroactive to 1992 data. Because of the lower Work class total resulting from this change, several thousand unintentional-injury deaths that had been classified by the Council as work-related, had to be reassigned to the Home and Public classes. For this reason long-term historical comparisons for these three classes should be made with caution. See the Technical Appendix for an explanation of the methodological changes.
[a] *Includes some deaths not shown separately.*
[b] *Includes subways and elevateds.*
[c] *Estimates not available.*
[d] *In 1999, a revision was made in the International Classification of Diseases. See the Technical Appendix for comparability with earlier years.*
[e] *Revised.*
[f] *Preliminary.*

PRINCIPAL TYPES OF PUBLIC UNINTENTIONAL-INJURY DEATHS, UNITED STATES, 2006

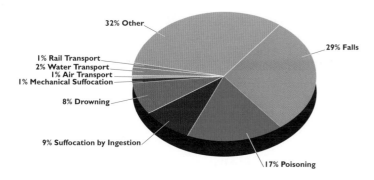

32% Other
29% Falls
1% Rail Transport
2% Water Transport
1% Air Transport
1% Mechanical Suffocation
8% Drowning
9% Suffocation by Ingestion
17% Poisoning

DEATHS DUE TO UNINTENTIONAL PUBLIC INJURIES, 2006

TYPE OF EVENT AND AGE OF VICTIM

All Public

Includes deaths in public places or places used in a public way and not involving motor vehicles. Most sports, recreation, and transportation deaths are included. Excludes deaths in the course of employment.

	Total	Change from 2005	Death Rate[a]
Deaths	30,000	+2%	10.0

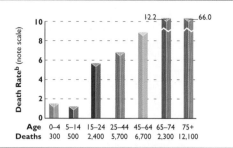

Falls

Includes deaths from falls from one level to another or on the same level in public places. Excludes deaths from falls in moving vehicles.

	Total	Change from 2005	Death Rate[a]
Deaths	8,600	+4%	2.9

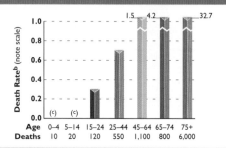

Poisoning

Includes deaths from drugs, medicines, other solid and liquid substances, and gases and vapors. Excludes poisonings from spoiled foods, salmonella, etc., which are classified as disease deaths.

	Total	Change from 2005	Death Rate[a]
Deaths	5,100	+9%	1.7

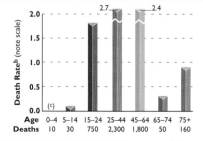

Choking

Includes deaths from unintentional ingestion or inhalation of food or other objects resulting in the obstruction of respiratory passages.

	Total	Change from 2005	Death Rate[a]
Deaths	2,700	−13%	0.9

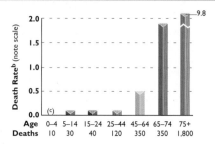

Drowning

Includes drownings of person swimming or playing in water, or falling into water, except on home premises or at work. Excludes drownings involving boats, which are in water transportation.

	Total	Change from 2005	Death Rate[a]
Deaths	2,500	−7%	0.8

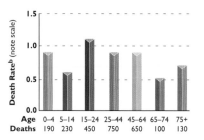

See footnotes on page 125.

TYPE OF EVENT AND AGE OF VICTIM

Water Transport

Includes deaths in water transport accidents from falls, burns, etc., as well as drownings. Excludes crews and persons traveling in the course of employment.

	Total	Change from 2005	Death Rate[a]
Deaths	600	+20%	0.2

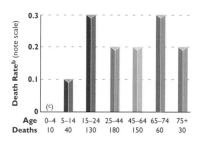

Age	0–4	5–14	15–24	25–44	45–64	65–74	75+
Deaths	10	40	130	180	150	60	30

Air Transport

Includes deaths in private flying, passengers in commercial aviation, and deaths of military personnel in the U.S. Excludes crews and persons traveling in the course of employment.

	Total	Change from 2005	Death Rate[a]
Deaths	400	0%	0.1

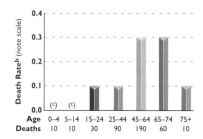

Age	0–4	5–14	15–24	25–44	45–64	65–74	75+
Deaths	10	10	30	90	190	60	10

Railroad

Includes deaths arising from railroad vehicles in motion (except involving motor vehicles), subway and elevated trains, and persons boarding or alighting from standing trains. Excludes crews and persons traveling in the course of employment.

	Total	Change from 2005	Death Rate[a]
Deaths	400	0%	0.1

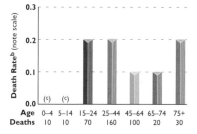

Age	0–4	5–14	15–24	25–44	45–64	65–74	75+
Deaths	10	10	70	160	100	20	30

Mechanical Suffocation

Includes deaths from hanging and strangulation, and suffocation in enclosed or confined spaces, cave-ins, or by bed clothes, plastic bags, or similar materials.

	Total	Change from 2005	Death Rate[a]
Deaths	200	–33%	0.1

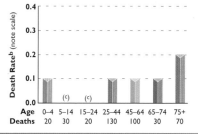

Age	0–4	5–14	15–24	25–44	45–64	65–74	75+
Deaths	20	30	20	130	100	30	70

All Other Public

Most important types included are: excessive natural heat or cold, firearms, fires and flames, and machinery.

	Total	Change from 2005	Death Rate[a]
Deaths	9,500	+6%	3.2

[a]Deaths per 100,000 population.
[b]Deaths per 100,000 population in each age group.
[c]Death rate less than 0.05.

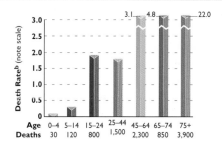

Age	0–4	5–14	15–24	25–44	45–64	65–74	75+
Deaths	30	120	800	1,500	2,300	850	3,900

HOME, 2006

Between 1912 and 2006, unintentional-home-injury deaths per 100,000 population were reduced 43% from 28 to 14.2 (after adjusting for the 1948 classification change). In 1912, when there were 21 million households, an estimated 26,000 to 28,000 persons were killed by unintentional home injuries. In 2006, with more than 112 million households and the population tripled, home deaths numbered 42,600.

The injury total of 10,200,000 means that 1 person in 29 in the United States was disabled one full day or more by unintentional injuries received in the home in 2006. Disabling injuries are more numerous in the home than in the workplace and in motor-vehicle crashes combined.

The National Health Interview Survey indicates that about 15,415,000 episodes of medically-attended home

injuries occurred in 2005 (the latest year available). This means that about 1 person in 19 incurred a home injury requiring medical attention. About 46% of all medically attended injuries occurred at home.

The National Safety Council adopted the Bureau of Labor Statistics' Census of Fatal Occupational Injuries count for work-related unintentional injuries beginning with 1992 data. This affected long-term historical comparisons for the Work, Home, and Public classes. Beginning with 1999 data, deaths are classified according to the 10th revision of the *International Classification of Diseases*. Caution should be used in comparing current data with data classified under prior revisions. See the Technical Appendix for more information.

Deaths **42,600**
Disabling Injuries **10,200,000**
Death rate per 100,000 population **14.2**
Costs . . . . **$150.1 billion**

HOME DEATHS AND DEATH RATES, UNITED STATES, 1996–2006

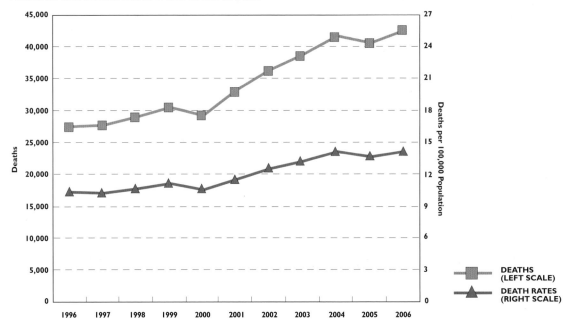

HOME, 2006 (CONT.)

PRINCIPAL TYPES OF HOME UNINTENTIONAL-INJURY DEATHS, UNITED STATES, 1986–2006

Year	Total Home	Falls	Fires/ Burns[a]	Suffocation by Ingestion	Mechanical Suffocation	Drowning	Poisoning	Natural Heat/Cold	Firearms	Other
1986	21,700	6,100	4,000	2,500	600	(b)	4,300	(b)	800	3,400
1987	21,400	6,300	3,900	2,500	600	(b)	4,100	(b)	800	3,200
1988	22,700	6,600	4,100	2,600	600	(b)	4,800	(b)	800	3,200
1989	22,500	6,600	3,900	2,500	600	(b)	5,000	(b)	800	3,100
1990	21,500	6,700	3,400	2,300	600	(b)	4,500	(b)	800	3,200
1991	22,100	6,900	3,400	2,200	700	(b)	5,000	(b)	800	3,100
1992	24,000	7,700	3,700	1,500	700	900	5,200	(b)	1,000	3,300
1993	26,100	7,900	3,700	1,700	700	900	6,500	(b)	1,100	3,600
1994	26,300	8,100	3,700	1,600	800	900	6,800	(b)	900	3,500
1995	27,200	8,400	3,500	1,500	800	900	7,000	(b)	900	4,200
1996	27,500	9,000	3,500	1,500	800	900	7,300	(b)	800	3,700
1997	27,700	9,100	3,200	1,500	800	900	7,800	(b)	700	3,500
1998	29,000	9,500	2,900	1,800	800	1,000	8,400	(b)	600	4,000
1999c	30,500	7,600	3,000	1,900	1,100	900	9,300	700	600	5,400
2000	29,200	7,100	2,700	2,100	1,000	1,000	9,800	400	500	4,600
2001	33,200	8,600	3,000	2,000	1,100	900	11,300	400	600	5,300
2002	36,200	9,700	2,800	1,900	1,100	900	13,900	400	500	5,000
2003	38,600	10,300	2,900	2,100	1,000	800	15,900	400	500	4,700
2004d	41,500	11,300	2,900	2,200	1,200	900	17,500	400	400	4,700
2005d	40,600	11,700	2,400	1,700	1,000	900	18,400	300	500	3,700
2006e	42,600	11,800	2,500	1,300	800	1,100	20,000	300	500	4,300

Source: National Safety Council estimates based on data from National Center for Health Statistics and state vital statistics departments. The Council adopted the Bureau of Labor Statistics' Census of Fatal Occupational Injuries count for work-related unintentional injuries retroactive to 1992 data. Because of the lower Work class total resulting from this change, several thousand unintentional-injury deaths that had been classified by the Council as work-related, had to be reassigned to the Home and Public classes. For this reason long-term historical comparisons for these three classes should be made with caution. See the Technical Appendix for an explanation of the methodological changes.
a Includes deaths resulting from conflagration, regardless of nature of injury.
b Included in Other.
c In 1999, a revision was made in the International Classification of Diseases. See the Technical Appendix for comparability with earlier years.
d Revised.
e Preliminary.

PRINCIPAL TYPES OF HOME UNINTENTIONAL-INJURY DEATHS, UNITED STATES, 2006

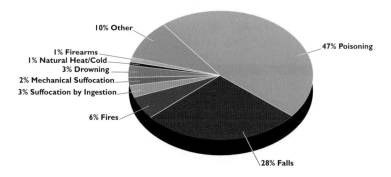

DEATHS DUE TO UNINTENTIONAL HOME INJURIES, 2006

TYPE OF EVENT AND AGE OF VICTIM

All Home

Includes deaths in the home and on home premises to occupants, guests, and trespassers. Also includes hired household workers but excludes other persons working on home premises.

	Total	Change from 2005	Death Rate[a]
Deaths	42,600	+5%	14.2

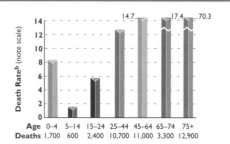

Poisoning

Includes deaths from drugs, medicines, other solid and liquid substances, and gases and vapors. Excludes poisonings from spoiled foods, salmonella, etc., which are classified as disease deaths.

	Total	Change from 2005	Death Rate[a]
Deaths	20,000	+9%	6.7

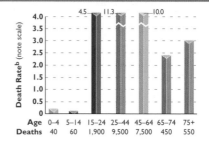

Falls

Includes deaths from falls from one level to another or on the same level in the home or on home premises.

	Total	Change from 2005	Death Rate[a]
Deaths	11,800	+1%	3.9

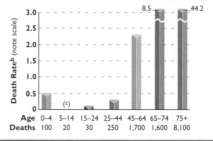

Fires, Flames, and Smoke

Includes deaths from fires, burns, and injuries in conflagrations in the home—such as asphyxiation, falls, and struck by falling objects. Excludes burns from hot objects or liquids.

	Total	Change from 2005	Death Rate[a]
Deaths	2,500	+4%	0.8

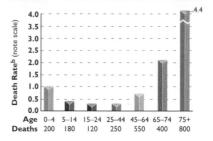

Choking

Includes deaths from unintentional ingestion or inhalation of objects or food resulting in the obstruction of respiratory passages.

	Total	Change from 2005	Death Rate[a]
Deaths	1,300	−24%	0.4

See footnotes on page 137.

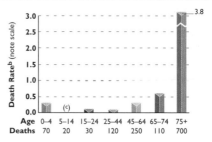

TYPE OF EVENT AND AGE OF VICTIM

Mechanical Suffocation

Includes deaths from smothering by bed clothes, thin plastic materials, etc.; suffocation by cave-ins or confinement in closed spaces; and mechanical strangulation and hanging.

	Total	Change from 2005	Death Rate[a]
Deaths	800	−20%	0.3

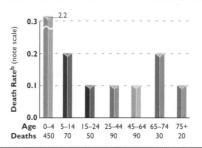

Drowning

Includes drownings of persons in or on home premises—such as in swimming pools and bathtubs. Excludes drowning in floods and other cataclysms.

	Total	Change from 2005	Death Rate[a]
Deaths	1,100	+22%	0.4

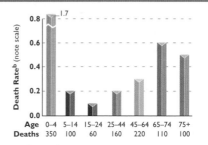

Natural Heat or Cold

Includes deaths resulting from exposure to excessive natural heat and cold (e.g., extreme weather conditions).

	Total	Change from 2005	Death Rate[a]
Deaths	300	0%	0.1

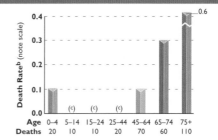

Firearms

Includes firearms injuries in or on home premises—such as while cleaning or playing with guns. Excludes deaths from explosive materials.

	Total	Change from 2005	Death Rate[a]
Deaths	500	0%	0.2

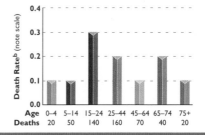

All Other Home

Most important types included are: struck by or against objects, machinery, and electric current.

	Total	Change from 2005	Death Rate[a]
Deaths	4,300	+16%	1.4

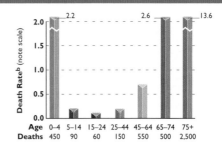

[a] Deaths per 100,000 population.
[b] Deaths per 100,000 population in each age group.
[c] Death rate less than 0.05.

SPORTS AND RECREATION INJURIES

In the U.S. in 2006, basketball injuries resulted in over half a million emergency department visits.

The table below shows estimates of injuries treated in hospital emergency departments and participants associated with various sports and recreational activities. Differences between the two sources in methods, coverage, classification systems, and definitions can affect comparisons among sports. Because this list of sports is not complete, because the frequency and duration of participation is not known, and because the number of participants varies greatly, no inference should be made concerning the relative hazard of these sports or rank with respect to risk of injury. In particular, it is *not* appropriate to calculate injury rates from these data.

SPORTS PARTICIPATION AND INJURIES, UNITED STATES, 2006

Sport or Activity	Participants	Injuries	Percent of Injuries by Age				
			0–4	5–14	15–24	25–64	65 & Over
Archery	6,800,000[a]	3,180	0.0	11.9	26.6	54.2	7.3
Baseball	14,600,000	163,834	2.6	49.2	27.8	19.6	0.8
Softball	12,400,000	111,094	0.3	24.5	32.6	41.8	0.8
Basketball	26,700,000	529,837	0.3	33.5	47.0	19.0	0.2
Bicycle riding[b]	35,600,000	480,299	5.7	44.0	17.4	29.5	3.3
Billiards, pool	31,800,000	4,722	9.0	22.5	17.0	48.3	2.8
Bowling	44,800,000	18,553	9.8	15.3	14.0	51.6	9.3
Boxing	(c)	13,118	0.0	11.8	51.0	37.2	0.0
Cheerleading	3,800,000	25,966	0.1	45.0	52.7	2.3	0.0
Exercise	(c)	197,406[d]	3.4	16.3	20.6	49.9	9.9
Fishing	40,600,000	73,206	2.8	18.5	13.3	56.5	8.9
Football	17,800,000[e,f]	460,210	0.2	47.8	41.9	10.1	0.1
Golf	24,400,000	37,891[g]	4.1	23.0	9.3	42.0	21.6
Gymnastics	(c)	30,523[h]	4.1	67.6	22.0	6.2	0.0
Hockey, street, roller & field	(c)	6,500[i]	0.0	28.1	62.0	9.9	0.0
Horseback riding	(c)	70,915	1.4	21.7	20.5	52.2	4.2
Horseshoe pitching	(c)	1,542	6.0	32.1	10.1	47.2	4.6
Ice hockey	2,600,000	21,825	0.3	37.5	48.8	13.4	0.0
Ice skating	(c)	22,025[j]	0.9	48.3	21.5	28.1	1.2
Martial arts	4,700,000[e]	24,835	0.8	27.2	29.6	42.4	0.0
Mountain biking	8,500,000	10,135	0.9	8.9	25.9	63.0	1.4
Mountain climbing	(c)	3,875	1.5	9.0	43.4	43.7	1.9
Racquetball, squash & paddleball	(c)	6,702	0.2	4.6	18.7	69.5	6.7
Roller skating	(c)	69,989[k]	0.6	59.0	13.3	26.4	0.7
Rugby	(c)	10,589	0.0	4.1	77.2	18.8	0.0
Scuba diving	(c)	1,963	0.0	4.1	6.9	89.0	0.0
Skateboarding	9,700,000	125,713	1.2	50.6	38.8	9.0	0.3
Snowboarding	5,200,000	50,660	0.0	28.2	54.6	17.0	0.1
Snowmobiling	(c)	7,293	0.0	8.7	38.2	49.2	3.9
Soccer	14,000,000	186,544	0.6	43.5	37.3	18.4	0.2
Swimming	56,500,000	178,412[l]	10.3	41.3	18.3	27.3	2.8
Tennis	10,400,000	22,425	0.6	15.4	22.1	48.1	13.8
Track & field	(c)	20,459	0.3	44.7	50.5	4.2	0.3
Volleyball	11,100,000	57,387	0.1	28.0	41.9	28.9	1.0
Water skiing	6,300,000	9,928	0.1	8.4	39.2	52.3	0.0
Weight lifting	32,900,000	73,425	3.1	9.0	39.1	46.8	1.9
Wrestling	(c)	36,943	0.0	35.2	59.6	5.0	0.2

Source: Participants—National Sporting Goods Association; figures include those seven years of age or older who participated more than once per year except for bicycle riding and swimming, which include those who participated six or more times per year. Injuries—Consumer Product Safety Commission; figures include only injuries treated in hospital emergency departments.
a Data for 2005.
b Excludes mountain biking.
c Data not available.
d Includes exercise equipment (407,708 injuries) and exercise activity (149,698 injuries).
e Data for 2004.
f Includes 9,600,000 in touch football and 8,200,000 in tackle football.
g Excludes golf carts (13,411 injuries).
h Excludes trampolines (109,522 injuries).
i Includes field hockey (5,238 injuries) and roller hockey (1,262 injuries). Excludes 29,597 injuries in hockey, unspecified.
j Excludes 11,394 injuries in skating, unspecified.
k Includes roller skating (42,305 injuries) and in-line skating (27,684 injuries).
l Includes injuries associated with swimming, swimming pools, pool slides, diving or diving boards, and swimming pool equipment.

A recent study analyzed data from the National Electronic Injury Surveillance System—All Injury Program (NEISS-AIP) for the period 2001–2005 in an effort to characterize sports- and recreation-related (SR-related) traumatic brain injuries (TBIs) among patients treated in U.S. hospital emergency departments (EDs). The results of the analysis indicated that an estimated 207,830 patients with nonfatal SR-related TBIs were treated in EDs each year during the study period. Overall, TBIs accounted for 5.1% of all SR-related ED visits.

Males accounted for over 70% of SR-related TBI ED visits overall, while the highest rates of visits for both males and females occurred among those aged 10–14 years, followed by those aged 15–19 years. The greatest number of visits were associated with bicycling, football, playground activities, basketball, and riding all-terrain vehicles (ATVs). Activities for which TBI accounted for greater than 7.5% of ED visits for that activity included horseback riding (11.7%), ice skating (10.4%), riding ATVs (8.4%), tobogganing/sledding (8.3%), and bicycling (7.7%). The percentage of patients with SR-related TBIs who were subsequently hospitalized or transferred to another facility for

additional care was over three times higher than the percentage for those with SR-related injuries overall. Activities associated with the greatest proportion of TBI-related ED visits requiring either hospitalization or transfer included riding ATVs, riding mopeds/ minibikes/dirt bikes, bicycling, golfing, and riding scooters.

Young persons aged 5–18 years accounted for an estimated 60% of ED visits for SR-related injuries and 65% of ED visits for SR-related TBIs and should therefore be a key target of prevention measures. The primary components of TBI prevention in SR-related activities include (a) using protective equipment appropriate for the sport or activity—such as a helmet—that fits properly and is worn correctly and consistently, (b) following all appropriate safety policies, and (c) following all the rules of the sport. All of those involved in the SR-related activity, including players, parents, and coaches, should be aware of all the signs and symptoms of TBI and be prepared to take appropriate action when such an injury is suspected.

Source: Centers for Disease Control and Prevention (2007, July 27). Nonfatal Traumatic Brain Injuries from Sports and Recreation Activities—United States, 2001–2005. *Morbidity and Mortality Weekly Report, 56(29), 733–737.*

ESTIMATED ANNUAL RATE OF NONFATAL, SPORTS- AND RECREATION-RELATED TRAUMATIC BRAIN INJURIES TREATED IN EMERGENCY DEPARTMENTS BY AGE GROUP AND SEX, UNITED STATES, 2001–2005

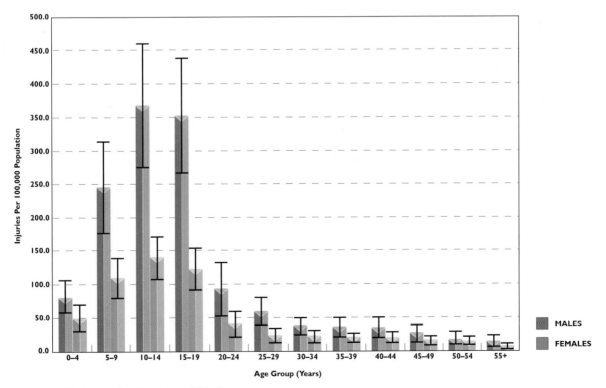

Source: National Electronic Injury Surveillance System—All Injury Program.
Note: Range indicated on bars is the 95% confidence interval of the estimated annual rates.

WEATHER

Temperature extremes caused 46% of weather-related deaths in 2006.

A variety of weather events resulted in 555 deaths in the 50 United States and District of Columbia in 2006. Temperature extremes (almost all due to extreme heat) accounted for 46% of the deaths. Most of these (246 of the 253) occurred in July and August.

Unlike 2005, in which four hurricanes caused more than 1,400 fatalities, there were no hurricane-related deaths in 2006.

The data on weather-related deaths was compiled by the National Climatic Data Center (NCDC), which is part of the National Oceanic and Atmospheric Administration. NCDC data may differ from data based on death certificates that appears elsewhere in *Injury Facts®*.

WEATHER-RELATED DEATHS, UNITED STATES, 2006

Event	Total	Jan	Feb	Mar	Apr	May	Jun	Jul	Aug	Sep	Oct	Nov	Dec
Total	555	25	17	50	51	26	39	157	144	26	4	11	5
Temperature Extremes	253	0	1	0	0	1	5	124	122	0	0	0	0
Flood	76	3	0	12	3	8	22	5	6	10	4	0	3
Tornado	67	1	0	11	38	3	0	0	1	1	0	10	2
Lightning	43	1	0	1	3	3	8	15	8	4	0	0	0
Thunderstorm/High Winds	42	6	6	5	4	6	2	4	1	7	0	1	0
Snow/Ice	28	13	5	8	2	0	0	0	0	0	0	0	0
Ocean/Lake Surf	25	0	0	0	1	5	2	8	5	4	0	0	0
Wild/Forest Fire	15	0	1	13	0	0	0	1	0	0	0	0	0
Fog	3	1	2	0	0	0	0	0	0	0	0	0	0
Dust Storm	2	0	2	0	0	0	0	0	0	0	0	0	0
Precipitation	1	0	0	0	0	0	0	0	1	0	0	0	0
Drought	0	0	0	0	0	0	0	0	0	0	0	0	0
Funnel Cloud/Waterspout	0	0	0	0	0	0	0	0	0	0	0	0	0
Hail	0	0	0	0	0	0	0	0	0	0	0	0	0
Hurricane/Tropical Storm	0	0	0	0	0	0	0	0	0	0	0	0	0

Source: National Safety Council analysis of National Climatic Data Center data.

WEATHER-RELATED FATALITIES BY MONTH, UNITED STATES, 2006

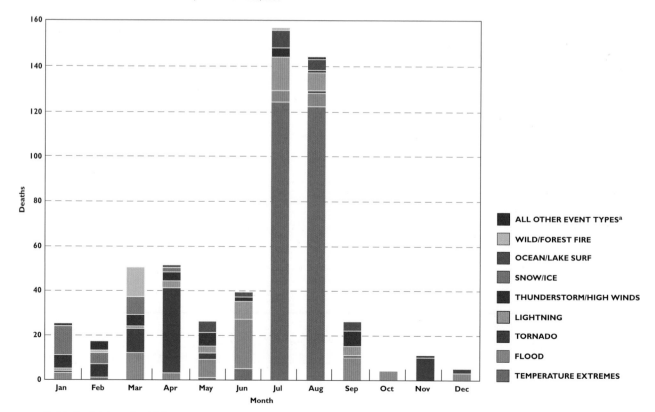

a Includes fog, dust storm and precipitation.

FIREARMS

Unintentional firearms-related deaths down 11% in 2004.

Firearm-related deaths from unintentional, intentional, and undetermined causes totaled 29,625 in 2004, a decrease of 11% from 2003. Suicides accounted for 56.6% of firearms deaths, 39.4% were homicides, and 2.2% were unintentional deaths. Males dominate all categories of firearms deaths and accounted for 86.2% of the total.

The numbers of homicide deaths by firearms decreased in 2004 after increasing for three consecutive years.

Unintentional deaths decreased for the third year, while suicide deaths decreased for the second year.

Hospital emergency department surveillance data indicate an estimated 16,555 nonfatal unintentional firearm-related injuries in 2004. For assault there were an estimated 43,592 nonfatal injuries and 3,352 intentionally self-inflicted nonfatal injuries.

Source: National Safety Council analysis of National Center for Health Statistics mortality data and National Center for Injury Prevention and Control injury surveillance data using WISQARS™ (http://www.cdc.gov/ncipc/wisqars/).

DEATHS INVOLVING FIREARMS BY AGE AND SEX, UNITED STATES, 2004

Type & Sex	All Ages	Under 5 Years	5–14 Years	15–19 Years	20–24 Years	25–44 Years	45–64 Years	65–74 Years	75 & Over
Total Firearms Deaths	**29,625**	**58**	**300**	**2,499**	**4,053**	**11,044**	**7,450**	**1,887**	**2,334**
Male	25,546	31	231	2,206	3,700	9,463	6,127	1,665	2,123
Female	4,079	27	69	293	353	1,581	1,323	222	211
Unintentional	**651**	**15**	**48**	**81**	**92**	**198**	**141**	**40**	**36**
Male	575	11	40	75	86	180	119	33	31
Female	76	4	8	6	6	18	22	7	5
Suicide	**16,756**	**—**	**59**	**787**	**1,318**	**5,155**	**5,677**	**1,631**	**2,129**
Male	14,529	—	50	688	1,202	4,358	4,755	1,475	2,001
Female	2,227	—	9	99	116	797	922	156	128
Homicide	**11,672**	**42**	**184**	**1,582**	**2,555**	**5,430**	**1,533**	**195**	**151**
Male	9,961	20	134	1,399	2,328	4,693	1,171	140	76
Female	1,711	22	50	183	227	737	362	55	75
Legal Intervention	**311**	**0**	**0**	**27**	**52**	**172**	**50**	**5**	**5**
Male	302	0	0	26	52	169	46	4	5
Female	9	0	0	1	0	3	4	1	0
Undetermined[a]	**235**	**1**	**9**	**22**	**36**	**89**	**49**	**16**	**13**
Male	179	0	7	18	32	63	36	13	10
Female	56	1	2	4	4	26	13	3	3

Source: National Safety Council tabulation of National Center for Health Statistics mortality data.
Note: Dashes (—) indicate category not applicable.
[a]Undetermined means the intentionality of the deaths (unintentional, homicide, suicide) was not determined.

FIREARMS DEATHS BY INTENTIONALITY AND YEAR, UNITED STATES, 1995–2004

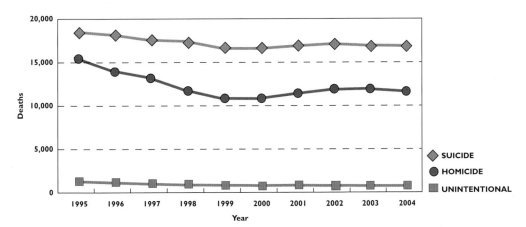

TRANSPORTATION MODE COMPARISONS

Passenger transportation incidents account for three out of ten unintentional-injury deaths. But the risk of death to the passenger, expressed on a per mile basis, varies greatly by transportation mode. Highway travel by personal vehicle presents the greatest risk; air, rail, and bus travel have much lower death rates. The tables below show the latest information on passenger transportation deaths and death rates.

The statistics for automobiles, vans, sport utility vehicles (SUVs), pickups, and other light trucks shown in the tables below represent all passenger vehicle usage, both intercity and local. The bus data also include intercity and local (transit) bus travel. Railroad includes both intercity (Amtrak) and local commuting travel. Scheduled airlines includes both large airlines and commuter airlines, but excludes on-demand air taxis and charter operations. In comparing the four modes, drivers of automobiles (except taxis), vans, SUVs, and pickup trucks are considered passengers. Bus drivers and airline or railroad crews are not considered passengers.

Other comparisons are possible based on passenger-trips, vehicle-miles, or vehicle-trips, but passenger-miles is the most commonly used basis for comparing the safety of various modes of travel.

TRANSPORTATION ACCIDENT DEATH RATES, 2003–2005

| Mode of Transportation | 2005 | | | 2003–2005 Average Death Rate |
	Passenger Deaths	Passenger Miles (billions)	Deaths per 100,000,000 Passenger Miles	
Passenger automobiles[a]	18,547	2,687.0	0.69	0.71
Vans, SUVs, pickup trucks[b]	12,982	1,737.1	0.75	0.76
Buses[c]	44	59.3	0.07	0.06
Transit buses	2	22.0	0.01	0.02
Intercity buses	30	37.3	0.08	0.04
Railroad passenger trains[d]	16	15.8	0.10	0.05
Scheduled airlines[e]	20	583.7	0.003	0.003

Source: Highway passenger deaths—Fatality Analysis Reporting System data. Railroad passenger deaths and miles—Federal Railroad Administration. Airline passenger deaths—National Transportation Safety Board. Airline passenger miles—Bureau of Transportation Statistics. Passenger miles for transit buses—American Public Transit Association. All other figures—National Safety Council estimates.
[a]Includes taxi passengers. Drivers of passenger automobiles are considered passengers.
[b]Includes 2-axle, 4-tire vehicles under 10,000 lbs GVWR other than automobiles.
[c]Figures exclude school buses but include "other" and "unknown" bus types.
[d]Includes Amtrak and commuter rail service.
[e]Includes large airlines and scheduled commuter airlines; excludes charter, cargo, and on-demand service and suicide/sabotage.

PASSENGER DEATHS AND DEATH RATES, UNITED STATES, 1996–2005

| Year | Passenger Automobiles | | Vans, SUVs, Pickup Trucks | | Buses | | Railroad Passenger Trains | | Scheduled Airlines | |
	Deaths	Rate[a]	Deaths	Rate[a]	Deaths	Rate[a]	Deaths	Rate[a]	Deaths	Rate[a]
1996	22,359	0.96	—	—	10	0.02	12	0.09	329	0.08
1997	21,920	0.92	—	—	4	0.01	6	0.05	42	0.01
1998	21,099	0.86	—	—	26	0.05	4	0.03	0	0.00
1999	20,763	0.83	10,666	0.72	39	0.07	14	0.10	17	0.003
2000	20,444	0.80	11,435	0.76	3	0.01	4	0.03	87	0.02
2001	20,221	0.78	11,690	0.76	11	0.02	3	0.02	279	0.06
2002	20,408	0.77	12,186	0.77	36	0.06	7	0.05	0	0.00
2003	19,718	0.74	12,551	0.78	31	0.05	3	0.02	24	0.005
2004	19,183	0.71	12,678	0.75	27	0.05	3	0.02	13	0.002
2005	18,547	0.69	12,982	0.75	44	0.07	16	0.10	20	0.003
10-year average	20,466	0.81	—	—	23	0.04	7	0.05	81	0.02

Source: See table above. Note: Dashes (—) indicate data not available.
[a]Deaths per 100,000,000 passenger miles.

PASSENGER DEATH RATES, UNITED STATES, 2003–2005

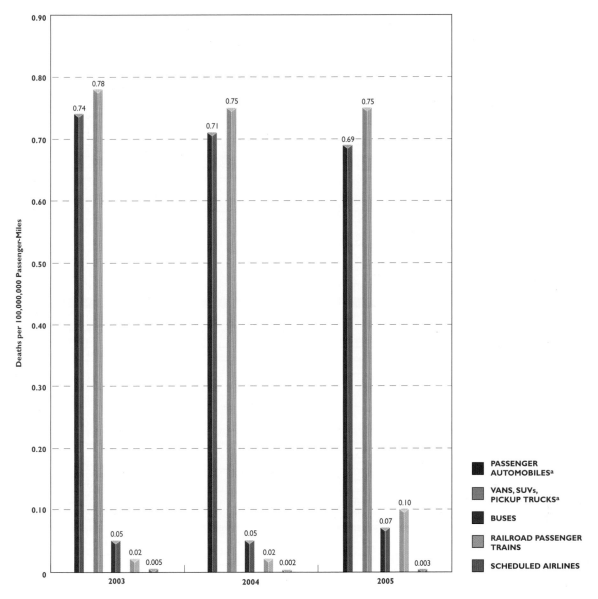

PASSENGER
AUTOMOBILES[a]

VANS, SUVs,
PICKUP TRUCKS[a]

BUSES

RAILROAD PASSENGER
TRAINS

SCHEDULED AIRLINES

[a]Drivers of these vehicles are considered passengers.

AVIATION

In 2006, there were 13 aircraft accidents that resulted in 755 fatalities to passengers according to preliminary full-year data reported by the International Civil Aviation Organization (ICAO). Compared to 2005, the 2006 data show a 24% decline in the number of fatal accidents that is offset by a 6% increase in the number of passenger deaths. The 755 deaths resulted in a preliminary fatality rate of 0.0193 per 100 million passenger-kilometers—just marginally higher than 2005 due to an increase of about 5% in passenger-kilometers.

WORLDWIDE SCHEDULED AIR SERVICE ACCIDENTS, DEATHS, AND DEATH RATES, 1991–2006

Year	Fatal Accidents[a]	Passenger Deaths	Death Rate[b]	Year	Fatal Accidents[a]	Passenger Deaths	Death Rate[b]
1991	29	638	0.03	1999	21	499	0.02
1992	28	1,070	0.06	2000	18	757	0.03
1993	33	864	0.04	2001	13	577	0.02
1994	27	1,170	0.05	2002	13	791	0.025
1995	25	711	0.03	2003	7	466	0.015
1996	24	1,146	0.05	2004	9	203	0.01
1997	25	921	0.04	2005	17	712	0.0191
1998	20	904	0.03	2006[c]	13	755	0.0193

Source: International Civil Aviation Organization. Figures include the USSR up to 1992 and the Commonwealth of Independent States thereafter.
[a]*Involving a passenger fatality and an aircraft with maximum take-off mass >2,250 kg.*
[b]*Passenger deaths per 100 million passenger-kilometers.*
[c]*Preliminary data.*

U.S. CIVIL AVIATION ACCIDENTS, DEATHS, AND DEATH RATES, 2001–2006

	Accidents		Total Deaths[a]	Accident Rates			
				Per 100,000 Flight-Hours		Per Million Aircraft-Miles	
Year	Total	Fatal		Total	Fatal	Total	Fatal
Large Airlines[b]							
2001[c]	41	6	531	0.216	0.012	0.0053	0.0003
2002	35	0	0	0.209	0	0.0051	0
2003	51	2	22	0.302	0.012	0.0073	0.0003
2004	24	1	13	0.132	0.005	0.0032	0.0001
2005	34	3	22	0.182	0.016	0.0043	0.0004
2006	25	2	50	0.132	0.011	0.0031	0.0003
Commuter Airlines[b]							
2001	7	2	13	2.330	0.666	0.1624	0.0464
2002	7	0	0	2.559	0	0.1681	0
2003	2	1	2	0.627	0.313	0.0422	0.0211
2004	4	0	0	1.324	0	0.0855	0
2005	6	0	0	2.034	0	0.1312	0
2006	3	1	2	1.071	0.357	0.0668	0.0223
On-Demand Air Taxis[b]							
2001	72	18	60	2.40	0.60	—	—
2002	60	18	35	2.06	0.62	—	—
2003	73	18	42	2.49	0.61	—	—
2004	66	23	64	2.04	0.71	—	—
2005	66	11	18	1.73	0.29	—	—
2006	54	10	16	1.50	0.28	—	—
General Aviation[b]							
2001[c]	1,727	325	562	6.78	1.27	—	—
2002[c]	1,715	345	581	6.69	1.33	—	—
2003[c]	1,740	352	633	6.68	1.34	—	—
2004[c]	1,619	314	559	6.49	1.26	—	—
2005[c]	1,669	321	563	7.20	1.38	—	—
2006[c]	1,515	303	698	6.64	1.32	—	—

Source: National Transportation Safety Board: 2006 preliminary, 2001–2005 revised; exposure data for rates from Federal Aviation Administration.
Note: Dash (—) indicates data not available.
[a] *Includes passengers, crew members, and others such as persons on the ground.*
[b] *Civil aviation accident statistics collected by the National Transportation Safety Board are classified according to the Federal air regulations under which the flights were made. The classifications are (1) large airlines operating scheduled service under Title 14, Code of Federal Regulations, part 121 (14 CFR 121); (2) commuter carriers operating scheduled service under 14 CFR 135; (3) unscheduled, "on-demand" air taxis under 14 CFR 135; and (4) "general aviation," which includes accidents involving aircraft flown under rules other than 14 CFR 121 and 14 CFR 135. Not shown in the table is nonscheduled air carrier operations under 14 CFR 121 which experienced 6 accidents, but no fatalities in 2006. Since 1997, Large Airlines includes aircraft with 10 or more seats, formerly operated as commuter carriers under 14 CFR 135.*
[c] *Suicide/sabotage/terrorism and stolen/unauthorized cases are included in "accident" and fatality totals but excluded from rates—Large Airlines, 2001 (4 crashes/265 deaths); General Aviation, 2001 (3/1), 2002 (6/5), 2003 (2/1), 2004 (3/0), 2005 (2/1), 2006 (1/1).*

RAILROAD

Railroad deaths totaled 909 in 2006, a 3% increase from the 2005 total of 886, but a 4% decrease from the 1997–2005 average of 946. In 2006, there was a 3% increase in fatalities at highway-rail crossings and a 2% increase in fatalities that occurred in other types of incidents. The latter included 517 deaths, or 96%, to trespassers. Sixteen employees were killed while on duty, a 36% decrease compared to the 2005 death toll and a 38% decrease from the 1997–2005 average of 26. Deaths to passengers on trains totaled 2, thus reaching the lowest level in a decade, down from 16 deaths in 2005 and the nine-year average of 7.

The ratio of railroad-related deaths to nonfatal injuries and illnesses is approximately 1:10. In 2006, railroad accidents resulted in 8,244 cases of nonfatal conditions, compared to 9,421 in 2005 and the 1997–2005 average of 10,721. Twelve percent of the total was attributed to highway-rail crossing incidents, which increased by less than 1% over the 2005 total of 1,023 and by 14% over the 1997–2005 average of 1,196. Of the 5,177 nonfatal occupational injuries and illnesses reported in 2006, less than 2% were attributed to highway-rail crossing incidents.

DEATHS AND NONFATAL CASES IN RAILROAD ACCIDENTS AND INCIDENTS, UNITED STATES, 1997–2006

Year	Total	Highway-Rail Crossing Incident?		Occurring in Other Than Highway-Rail Crossing Incident		Employees On Duty At Highway-Rail Crossing?		Passengers on Trains[a] At Highway-Rail Crossing?	
		Yes	No	Trespassers	Others	Yes	No	Yes	No
Deaths									
1997	1,063	461	602	533	69	0	37	0	6
1998	1,008	431	577	536	41	4	23	2	2
1999	932	402	530	479	51	2	29	11	3
2000	937	425	512	463	49	2	22	0	4
2001	971	421	550	511	39	1	21	0	3
2002	951	357	594	540	54	1	19	0	7
2003	868	334	534	501	33	1	18	1	2
2004	895	372	523	475	48	2	23	0	3
2005	886	358	528	462	66	2	23	0	16
2006	909	369	540	517	23	4	12	0	2
Nonfatal conditions									
1997	11,767	1,540	10,227	516	9,711	111	8,184	43	558
1998	11,459	1,303	10,156	513	9,643	122	8,276	19	516
1999	11,700	1,396	10,304	445	9,859	140	8,482	43	438
2000	11,643	1,219	10,424	414	10,010	100	8,323	10	648
2001	10,985	1,157	9,828	404	9,424	97	7,718	20	726
2002	11,103	999	10,104	395	9,709	110	6,534	26	851
2003	9,247	1,035	8,212	398	7,814	76	6,172	74	649
2004	9,166	1,092	8,074	404	7,670	116	5,899	25	664
2005	9,421	1,023	8,398	413	7,985	112	5,690	32	892
2006	8,244	1,029	7,215	470	6,745	95	5,082	86	594

Source: Federal Railroad Administration.
[a] Passenger cases include all circumstances, including getting on/off standing trains, stumbling aboard trains, assaults, train accidents, crossing incidents, etc.

CASUALTIES AT PUBLIC AND PRIVATE HIGHWAY-RAIL CROSSINGS, UNITED STATES, 1997–2006

Year	Deaths				Nonfatal Conditions			
	Total	Motor-Vehicle Related	Pedestrians	Others	Total	Motor-Vehicle Related	Pedestrians	Others
1997	461	419	38	4	1,540	1,494	33	13
1998	431	369	50	12	1,303	1,257	33	13
1999	402	345	45	12	1,396	1,338	35	23
2000	425	361	51	13	1,219	1,169	34	16
2001	421	345	67	9	1,157	1,110	31	16
2002	357	310	35	12	999	939	29	31
2003	334	281	50	3	1,035	1,000	28	7
2004	372	290	73	9	1,092	1,056	30	6
2005	358	282	58	18	1,023	976	37	10
2006	369	304	54	11	1,029	995	29	5

Source: Federal Railroad Administration.

UNINTENTIONAL POISONINGS

Poisoning deaths up 8% from 2003 to 2004.

Deaths from unintentional poisoning numbered 20,950 in 2004, the latest year for which data are available. The death rate per 100,000 population was 7.1—9.6 for males and 4.7 for females. Total poisoning deaths increased 8% from 19,457 in 2003 and are 2.3 times the 1994 total. See pages 42–45 for long-term trends.

Almost half of the poisoning deaths (47%) were classified in the "narcotics and psychodysleptics (hallucinogens), not elsewhere classified," category, which includes many illegal drugs such as cocaine, heroin, cannabinol, and LSD.

Carbon monoxide poisoning is included in the category of "other gases and vapors." Deaths due to alcohol poisoning numbered 358 in 2004, but alcohol may also be present in combination with other drugs.

Additional information on human poisoning exposure cases may be found on pages 140–141.

UNINTENTIONAL POISONING DEATHS BY TYPE, AGE, AND SEX, UNITED STATES, 2004

Type of Poison	All Ages	0–4 Years	5–14 Years	15–19 Years	20–24 Years	25–44 Years	45–64 Years	65 Years & Over
Both Sexes								
Total Poisoning Deaths	**20,950**	**31**	**55**	**643**	**1,616**	**10,085**	**7,610**	**910**
Deaths per 100,000 population	*7.1*	*0.2*	*0.1*	*3.1*	*7.7*	*12.0*	*10.8*	*2.5*
Nonopioid analgesics, antipyretics and antirheumatics (X40)[a]	212	1	1	2	10	84	81	33
Antiepileptic, sedative-hypnotic, antiparkinsonism and psychotropic drugs, n.e.c. (X41)	1,300	1	1	21	90	650	495	42
Narcotics and psychodysleptics (hallucinogens), n.e.c. (X42)	9,798	7	15	318	829	4,931	3,537	161
Other drugs acting on the autonomic nervous system (X43)	22	2	0	1	1	8	8	2
Other and unspecified drugs, medicaments and biological substances (X44)	8,506	10	12	249	633	4,046	3,096	460
Alcohol (X45)	358	0	2	16	19	155	151	15
Organic solvents and halogenated hydrocarbons and their vapors (X46)	67	0	1	4	6	26	22	8
Other gases and vapors (X47)	562	9	21	25	22	160	179	146
Pesticides (X48)	3	0	0	1	0	0	1	1
Other and unspecified chemical and noxious substances (X49)	122	1	2	6	6	25	40	42
Males								
Total Poisoning Deaths	13,934	18	30	494	1,271	6,849	4,839	433
Deaths per 100,000 population	*9.6*	*0.2*	*0.1*	*4.6*	*11.8*	*16.2*	*14.0*	*2.9*
Nonopioid analgesics, antipyretics and antirheumatics (X40)	80	1	1	0	4	31	33	10
Antiepileptic, sedative-hypnotic, antiparkinsonism and psychotropic drugs, n.e.c. (X41)	787	1	0	9	66	412	286	13
Narcotics and psychodysleptics (hallucinogens), n.e.c. (X42)	7,136	5	11	271	668	3,583	2,504	94
Other drugs acting on the autonomic nervous system (X43)	9	0	0	1	1	5	2	0
Other and unspecified drugs, medicaments and biological substances (X44)	5,102	4	5	175	486	2,524	1,723	185
Alcohol (X45)	277	0	2	11	18	129	105	12
Organic solvents and halogenated hydrocarbons and their vapors (X46)	57	0	1	4	6	22	17	7
Other gases and vapors (X47)	408	7	9	18	16	128	139	91
Pesticides (X48)	2	0	0	1	0	0	0	1
Other and unspecified chemical and noxious substances (X49)	76	0	1	4	6	15	30	20
Females								
Total Poisoning Deaths	7,016	13	25	149	345	3,236	2,771	477
Deaths per 100,000 population	*4.7*	*0.1*	*0.1*	*1.5*	*3.4*	*7.7*	*7.6*	*2.3*
Nonopioid analgesics, antipyretics and antirheumatics (X40)	132	0	0	2	6	53	48	23
Antiepileptic, sedative-hypnotic, antiparkinsonism and psychotropic drugs, n.e.c. (X41)	513	0	1	12	24	238	209	29
Narcotics and psychodysleptics (hallucinogens), n.e.c. (X42)	2,662	2	4	47	161	1,348	1,033	67
Other drugs acting on the autonomic nervous system (X43)	13	2	0	0	0	3	6	2
Other and unspecified drugs, medicaments and biological substances (X44)	3,404	6	7	74	147	1,522	1,373	275
Alcohol (X45)	81	0	0	5	1	26	46	3
Organic solvents and halogenated hydrocarbons and their vapors (X46)	10	0	0	0	0	4	5	1
Other gases and vapors (X47)	154	2	12	7	6	32	40	55
Pesticides (X48)	1	0	0	0	0	0	1	0
Other and unspecified chemical and noxious substances (X49)	46	1	1	2	0	10	10	22

Source: National Safety Council tabulations of National Center for Health Statistics mortality data.
Note: n.e.c. means not elsewhere classified.
[a] Numbers following titles refer to external cause of injury and poisoning classifications in ICD-10.

UNINTENTIONAL POISONING DEATHS, UNITED STATES, 1995–2004

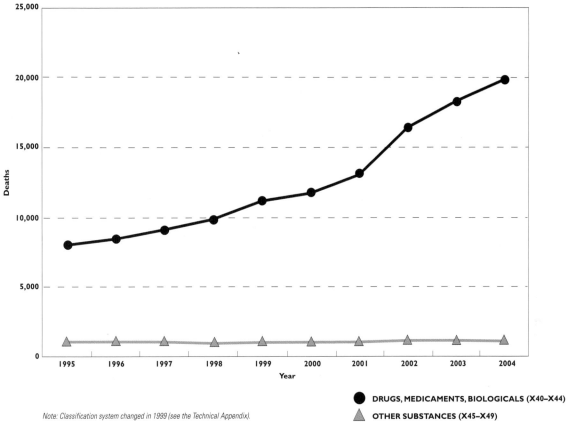

DRUGS, MEDICAMENTS, BIOLOGICALS (X40–X44)

OTHER SUBSTANCES (X45–X49)

Note: Classification system changed in 1999 (see the Technical Appendix).

Unintentional (accidental) poisoning deaths and death rates have more than tripled over the past 20 years. Fatal unintentional poisonings now exceed fall-related deaths and are the second leading cause of accidental deaths after motor-vehicle crashes.

The evidence seems to indicate that the increase in poisoning mortality is primarily among adults (ages 20–64) of both sexes and is mainly attributable to abuse of opioid analgesics.

Trends

• The most rapid growth in the death rate from 1992 through 2005 occurred among the 45–64 year old age group followed by the 25-44 age group and the 15-24 age group.

• The increase in poisoning deaths, particularly those involving drugs, occurred among both males and females.

• Poisoning deaths due to drugs, medicaments, and biologicals tripled from 1992 to 2003 while deaths due to other substances remained constant.

Unintentional Poisoning Involving Adults

• Between 1993 and 2003, the overall increase in the poisoning death rate for the 20-64 age group was 107%.

• The greatest increases in death *rates* occurred among non-Hispanic white females (+320%) followed by non-Hispanic white males (157%).

• The largest *numerical* increases also occurred among non-Hispanic white males and females.

• Drug poisoning deaths among other races and among Hispanics changes relatively little over the decade.

Prescription and Illicit Drugs

• From 1999 to 2004, there is a very strong correlation between prescription drug sales per capita and the unintentional poisoning death rate, indicating that mortality rates are associated with prescription drug use.

• With the exception of PCP, use of many illicit drugs is strongly correlated over time with the number of unintentional poisoning deaths.

• There is a very strong relationship between unintentional drug poisoning death rates and total sales of opioid analgesics. Oxycodone and hydrocodone account for most of the increase in sales of opioid analgesics.

• The most rapid growth in new nonmedical users of drugs has been users of pain relievers.

• The rate of sales of prescription opioid analgesics in states is related to the drug poisoning mortality rate. There is a strong and statistically significant correlation between high drug-poisoning mortality rates and high overall consumption of opioid analgesics in states. The correlation was greatest for oxycodone and methadone.

Drug poisoning death rates by race, sex, and age group are shown in the figure. For blacks, the highest death rates for both males and females are in the 45–54 age group, whereas for whites and other races the death rate is greatest in the 35–44 age group.

DRUG POISONING DEATH RATES, AGES 20–64, UNITED STATES, 2002–2004

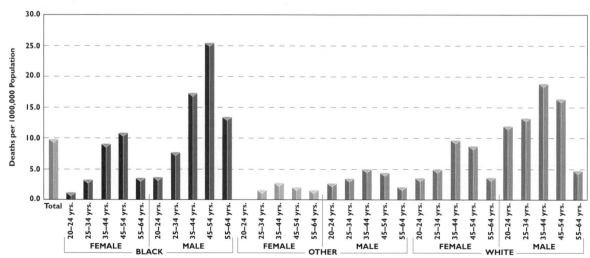

Source: NSC analysis of NCHS mortality data using WONDER.

FATAL VS. NONFATAL
UNINTENTIONAL POISONING

Most people think of poisoning as a childhood issue. That is true for nonfatal poisonings, but not for fatal poisonings as shown on the previous pages. The graphs below show the distribution of fatal and nonfatal poisonings by age groups. The poisoning exposure data are from the American Association of Poison Control Centers and represents the calls received by poison control centers. The fatality data are from death certificates.

It is evident that nonfatal exposures occur predominantly among young children whereas fatal poisoning are overwhelmingly among adults. Other poison control center data show that the types of substances associated with nonfatal childhood poison exposures are primarily those found around the household such as cosmetics and personal care products, cleaning substances, nonprescription analgesics, and topicals. Adult poisoning deaths primarily involve drugs and medicines. This disparity has important consequences for education and prevention efforts.

POISONING EXPOSURES AND DEATHS BY AGE GROUP, UNITED STATES, SELECTED YEARS

POISONING EXPOSURES, 2005   POISONING DEATHS, 2004

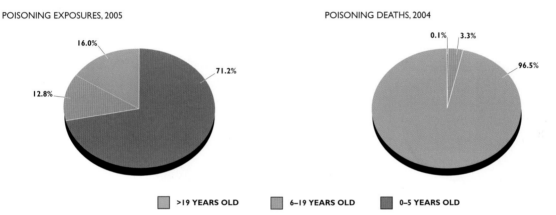

>19 YEARS OLD   6–19 YEARS OLD   0–5 YEARS OLD

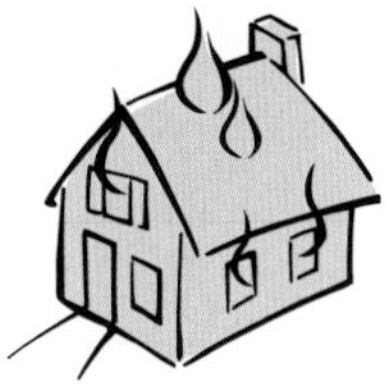

Smoke Alarms

As of 2004, 24 of every 25 (96%) U.S. homes surveyed by telephone had at least one smoke alarm. However, during the period 2000–2004, operating smoke alarms were present in only half of the 375,200 home fires reported annually to U.S. fire departments. Nearly two-thirds of the annual average of 2,970 home fire deaths during this period occurred in homes without working smoke alarms, including 22% in properties in which smoke alarms were present and failed to operate properly and 43% in which no smoke alarms were present at all. Batteries were missing or disconnected in more than half of the home fires where smoke alarms failed to operate properly, and in an additional 20% of cases, smoke alarm failure was due to dead batteries.

An in-home survey showed that in 20% of homes that had at least one smoke alarm installed, not a single one was working. Including homes without smoke alarms and homes with only non-working alarms, a full one-quarter of U.S. households do not have the protection of even one working smoke alarm. Equipping every home with working smoke alarms would decrease home fire deaths by an estimated 30%, thus saving an estimated 890 lives per year.

HOME STRUCTURE FIRES AND DEATHS BY SMOKE ALARM STATUS, 2000–2004 ANNUAL AVERAGES

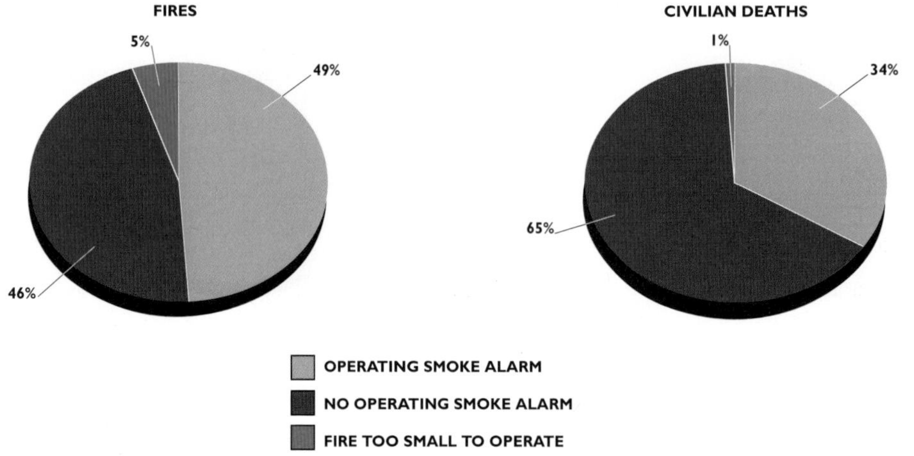

Source: Ahrens, M. (2007, April). U.S. experience with smoke alarms and other fire detection/alarm equipment. *Quincy, MA:* National Fire Protection Association.

Automatic Sprinklers

Based on 2000–2004 data reported to U.S. fire departments, sprinklers operate in 93% of all reported structure fires large enough to activate sprinklers. When they operate, sprinkler systems are effective 97% of the time, resulting in a combined performance reliability of 90%. The fire death rate per 1,000 reported fires in structures where sprinklers are present is lower by at least 57% and the rate of property damage per reported structure fire is lower by 34-68%. Further, 89% of reported structure fires have flame damage confined to the room of origin when sprinklers are present, compared to 57% when no sprinklers are present.

When people die in fires despite the presence of operating sprinkler systems, it is often because they are very close to the fire when it begins, they had some severe vulnerabilities or limitations before the fire began—such as the elderly, or, as in the case when three or more people die, it is because of participation in firefighting activities or more often explosions or flash fires. Although sprinkler systems are now common in hotels and motels and in department stores, the fact that they are still rare in places where most fire deaths occur, such as educational properties, offices, most stores, and especially homes, offers considerable potential for expanded use of sprinklers to reduce the loss of life and property to fire.

Source: Hall, J. R., Jr. (2007, June). U.S. experience with sprinklers and other automatic fire extinguishing equipment. *Quincy, MA: National Fire Protection Association.*

OLDER ADULT FALLS

During 2001–2003, there were an estimated 1,689,000 fall injury episodes annually among noninstitutionalized adults ages 65 and older. The annualized rate of fall injury episodes was 51 per 1,000 population.

The rate of falls increased with age. For persons 65–74, there were 33 fall episodes per 1,000 population. For persons 75–84, the rate was 65 and for persons 85 and older, the rate was 92.

Rates were higher among women than men except for the oldest age group. For males 65–74 the rate was 25 and for females 39. Among those 75–84 the rates were 43 for males and 80 for females. Both males and females 85 and older had a rate of 92 per 1,000.

Fall episode rates were significantly higher for persons who were never married, divorced, separated, or widowed (66 per 1,000) than for married or cohabitating people (40 per 1,000).

Fall injury episodes were more common among people with self-assessed fair or poor health status (78 per

1,000) compared to those with excellent or very good health (36 per 1,000) or good health (46 per 1,000).

Some health conditions are associated with greater risk of falls. Older adults who reported having heart disease, stroke, cancer, diabetes, or vision problems had higher fall rates than people without those conditions. Older adults who had great difficulty walking one-quarter mile, standing for two hours, stooping, or climbing 10 steps without resting had higher fall rates than adults who had some difficulty or less with these tasks.

More than half (57%) of the fall injury episodes resulted from slipping, tripping, or stumbling. Another 27% resulted from loss of balance, dizziness, fainting, or seizure. More than half (55%) of fall episodes occurred on floor or level ground and 16% happened on stairs, steps, or escalators. About 8% of episodes involved curbs and sidewalks, and 8% involved chars, beds, sofas, or other furniture.

Source: Schiller, J.S., Kramarow, E.A., & Dey, A.N. (2007). Fall injury episodes among noninstitutionalized older adults: United States, 2001–2003. Advance Data From Vital and Health Statistics, No. 392. Hyattsville, MD: National Center for Health Statistics.

CONSEQUENCES OF FALL INJURY EPISODES AMONG ADULTS 65 AND OLDER, UNITED STATES, 2001–2003

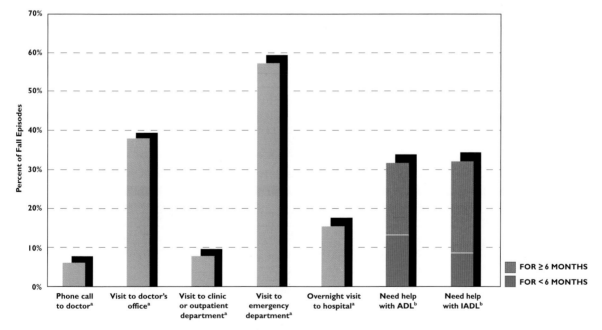

[a]For advice or treatment.
[b]ADL means Activities of Daily Living (bathing, dressing, eating, transfer between bed and chair, ect.). IADL means Instrumental Activities of Daily Living (housework, preparing meals, taking medications, using the telephone, managing money, etc.).

RISKS BY AGE GROUP

The leading risks for unintentional-injury (U-I) vary with age and are different for deaths and for nonfatal injuries. The tables here and on the next page list, for seven age groups, the five leading causes of unintentional-injury death and the five leading causes of hospital emergency department (ED) visits, which is one measure of nonfatal injuries.

For all ages, the five leading causes account for 82.6% of all U-I deaths and 71.0% of U-I ED visits. Only motor-vehicle crashes and falls are common to both lists. Motor-vehicle crashes rank first for U-I deaths and fourth for U-I ED visits. Falls rank third for U-I deaths and first for ED U-I visits.

The five leading causes of U-I deaths account for between 78.1% and 92.2% of such deaths depending

on the age group. The leading causes of unintentional-injury ED visits account for between 66.6% and 88.3% of such hospital visits.

For deaths, motor-vehicle crashes, poisoning, falls, choking, and drowning are most often among the top five with fires, flames, and smoke, and mechanical suffocation sometimes included. For ED visits, falls, struck by or against, overexertion, motor-vehicle occupant injuries, and cut or pierce injuries are most often in the top five. In the younger age groups, bites and stings (except dog bites), foreign body injuries, and pedal cycle injuries sometimes are among the leading risks.

LEADING UNINTENTIONAL INJURY RISKS, ALL AGES, UNITED STATES, 2004

Rank	Unintentional-Injury Deaths			Emergency Department U-I Visits		
	Event	Number	Percent	Event	Number	Percent
—	Total	112,012	100.0	Total	29,654,475	100.0
1	Motor-vehicle crashes	44,933	40.1	Falls	8,058,498	27.2
2	Poisoning	20,950	18.7	Struck by or against	4,430,171	14.9
3	Falls	18,807	16.8	Overexertion	3,279,383	11.1
4	Choking[a]	4,470	4.0	Motor-vehicle occupant	3,000,866	10.1
5	Drowning	3,308	3.0	Cut or pierce	2,285,191	7.7

LEADING UNINTENTIONAL INJURY RISKS, YOUNG CHILDREN (AGES 0–4), UNITED STATES, 2004

Rank	Unintentional-Injury Deaths			Emergency Department U-I Visits		
	Event	Number	Percent	Event	Number	Percent
—	Total	2,693	100.0	Total	2,318,530	100.0
1	Motor-vehicle crashes	778	28.9	Falls	1,014,617	43.8
2	Mechanical suffocation	722	26.8	Struck by or against	398,865	17.2
3	Drowning	492	18.3	Bite or sting (except dog)	157,754	6.8
4	Fires, flames, and smoke	249	9.2	Foreign body	122,850	5.3
5	Choking[a]	128	4.8	Cut or pierce	92,939	4.0

LEADING UNINTENTIONAL INJURY RISKS, CHILDREN AND YOUNG ADOLESCENTS (AGES 5–14), UNITED STATES, 2004

Rank	Unintentional-Injury Deaths			Emergency Department U-I Visits		
	Event	Number	Percent	Event	Number	Percent
—	Total	2,666	100.0	Total	4,375,935	100.0
1	Motor-vehicle crashes	1,653	62.0	Falls	1,345,293	30.7
2	Drowning	269	10.1	Struck by or against	997,876	22.8
3	Fires, flames, and smoke	255	9.6	Overexertion	346,777	7.9
4	Mechanical suffocation	82	3.1	Cut or pierce	270,926	6.2
5	Poisoning	55	2.1	Pedalcyclist	241,954	5.5

LEADING UNINTENTIONAL INJURY RISKS, TEENS AND YOUNG ADULTS (AGES 15–24), UNITED STATES, 2004

Rank	Unintentional-Injury Deaths			Emergency Department U-I Visits		
	Event	Number	Percent	Event	Number	Percent
—	Total	15,449	100.0	Total	6,009,246	100.0
1	Motor-vehicle crashes	10,987	71.1	Struck by or against	980,050	16.3
2	Poisoning	2,259	14.6	Motor-vehicle occupant	914,024	15.2
3	Drowning	574	3.7	Falls	869,363	14.5
4	Falls	241	1.6	Overexertion	739,741	12.3
5	Fires, flames, and smoke	186	1.2	Cut or pierce	498,856	8.3

See footnotes on page 145.

LEADING UNINTENTIONAL INJURY RISKS, ADULTS (AGES 24–44), UNITED STATES, 2004

Rank	Unintentional-Injury Deaths			Emergency Department U-I Visits		
	Event	Number	Percent	Event	Number	Percent
—	Total	29,503	100.0	Total	8,946,613	100.0
1	Motor-vehicle crashes	13,699	46.4	Falls	1,579,224	17.7
2	Poisoning	10,085	34.2	Overexertion	1,318,584	14.7
3	Falls	979	3.3	Struck by or against	1,244,434	13.9
4	Drowning	820	2.8	Motor-vehicle occupant	1,114,009	12.5
5	Fires, flames, and smoke	553	1.9	Cut or pierce	839,051	9.4

LEADING UNINTENTIONAL INJURY RISKS, ADULTS (AGES 45–64), UNITED STATES, 2004

Rank	Unintentional-Injury Deaths			Emergency Department U-I Visits		
	Event	Number	Percent	Event	Number	Percent
—	Total	26,593	100.0	Total	5,034,392	100.0
1	Motor-vehicle crashes	10,369	39.0	Falls	1,398,855	27.8
2	Poisoning	7,610	28.6	Overexertion	624,143	12.4
3	Falls	2,577	9.7	Struck by or against	594,568	11.8
4	Fires, flames, and smoke	902	3.4	Motor-vehicle occupant	561,024	11.1
5	Choking[a]	721	2.7	Cut or pierce	460,993	9.2

LEADING UNINTENTIONAL INJURY RISKS, OLDER ADULTS (AGES 65–74), UNITED STATES, 2004

Rank	Unintentional-Injury Deaths			Emergency Department U-I Visits		
	Event	Number	Percent	Event	Number	Percent
—	Total	8,116	100.0	Total	1,126,713	100.0
1	Motor-vehicle crashes	2,974	36.6	Falls	538,822	47.8
2	Falls	2,255	27.8	Struck by or against	105,124	9.3
3	Choking[a]	538	6.6	Motor-vehicle occupant	104,071	9.2
4	Poisoning	421	5.2	Overexertion	87,394	7.8
5	Fires, flames, and smoke	349	4.3	Cut or pierce	77,342	6.9

LEADING UNINTENTIONAL INJURY RISKS, ELDERLY (AGES 75 AND OLDER), UNITED STATES, 2004

Rank	Unintentional-Injury Deaths			Emergency Department U-I Visits		
	Event	Number	Percent	Event	Number	Percent
—	Total	26,992	100.0	Total	1,839,803	100.0
1	Falls	12,648	46.9	Falls	1,311,827	71.3
2	Motor-vehicle crashes	4,473	16.6	Struck by or against	109,110	5.9
3	Choking[a]	2,724	10.1	Motor-vehicle occupant	81,708	4.4
4	Fires, flames, and smoke	735	2.7	Overexertion	80,002	4.3
5	Poisoning	489	1.8	Cut or pierce	44,820	2.4

Source: National Safety Council analysis of NCHS mortality data and CDC, NCIPC, NEISS-AIP data.
[a] Inhalation and ingestion of food or other object obstructing breathing.

INJURIES ASSOCIATED WITH CONSUMER PRODUCTS

Over 2 million injury-related emergency department visits each year are associated with stairs, steps, floors, and flooring materials

The following list of items found in and around the home was selected from the U.S. Consumer Product Safety Commission's National Electronic Injury Surveillance System (NEISS) for 2006. The NEISS estimates are calculated from a statistically representative sample of hospitals in the United States. Injury totals represent estimates of the number of hospital emergency department-treated cases nationwide associated with various products. However, product involvement may or may not be the cause of the injury.

CONSUMER PRODUCT–RELATED INJURIES TREATED IN HOSPITAL EMERGENCY DEPARTMENTS, 2006
(excluding most sports or sports equipment; see also page 130)

Description	Injuries
Home Workshop Equipment	
Saws (hand or power)	95,317
Hammers	34,829
Drills	21,524
Household Packaging and Containers	
Household containers & packaging	215,537
Bottles and jars	74,148
Bags	38,468
Paper products	25,836
Housewares	
Knives	434,331
Tableware and flatware (excl. knives)	97,531
Drinking glasses	75,803
Cookware, bowls and canisters	31,898
Waste containers, trash baskets, etc.	31,020
Scissors	29,547
Manual cleaning equipment (excl. buckets)	24,260
Other kitchen gadgets	23,433
Home Furnishing, Fixtures, and Accessories	
Beds	526,331
Chairs	317,888
Tables, n.e.c.[a]	317,795
Household cabinets, racks, and shelves	279,322
Bathtubs and showers	241,377
Ladders	186,732
Sofas, couches, davenports, divans, etc.	150,995
Rugs and carpets	127,017
Other furniture[b]	118,473
Toilets	69,574
Misc. decorating items	56,042
Stools	50,370
Benches	30,204
Mirrors or mirror glass	25,451
Sinks	24,232
Electric lighting equipment	20,601
Home Structures and Construction Materials	
Floors or flooring materials	1,191,161
Stairs or steps	1,143,751
Other doors[c]	317,825
Ceilings and walls	308,501
Nails, screws, tacks or bolts	154,217
Porches, balconies, open-side floors	138,605
Windows	130,309
Fences or fence posts	110,011
House repair and construction materials	103,853
Door sills or frames	50,698
Counters or countertops	44,231
Handrails, railings or banisters	43,048
Poles	39,404
Glass doors	28,932

Description	Injuries
General Household Appliances	
Refrigerators	31,878
Ranges or ovens, not specified	29,697
Heating, Cooling, and Ventilating Equipment	
Pipes (excluding smoking pipes)	31,920
Home Communication and Entertainment Equipment	
Televisions	53,824
Sound recording and reproducing equipment	20,600
Personal-Use Items	
Footwear	136,156
Wheelchairs	115,743
Crutches, canes, walkers	85,346
Jewelry	83,897
Daywear	48,131
First aid equipment	44,020
Desk supplies	39,237
Razors and shavers	38,773
Coins	33,871
Other clothing[d]	29,941
Luggage	23,239
Hair grooming equipment and accessories	20,108
Yard and Garden Equipment	
Lawn mowers	78,740
Pruning, trimming and edging equipment	39,888
Chainsaws	28,261
Other unpowered garden tools[e]	26,119
Sports and Recreation Equipment	
Bicycles	490,434
Skateboards	125,713
Trampolines	109,522
Toys, n.e.c.	103,644
Swimming pools	92,239
Minibikes or trailbikes	84,129
Monkey bars or other playground climbing	79,332
Swings or swing sets	55,349
Slides or sliding boards	49,916
Scooters (unpowered)	44,115
Dancing	43,869
Aquariums and other pet supplies	39,592
Other playground equipment[f]	29,837
Gas, air, or spring operated guns	22,517
Miscellaneous Products	
Carts	50,000
Hot water	38,410
Elevators, escalators, moving walks	20,974

Source: U.S. Consumer Product Safety Commission, National Electronic Injury Surveillance System, Product Summary Report, All Products, CY2006.
Note: Products are listed above if the estimate was greater than 20,000 cases.
n.e.c. = not elsewhere classified.
[a] Excludes baby changing and television tables or stands.

[b] Excludes cabinets, racks shelves, desks, bureaus, chests, buffets, etc.
[c] Excludes glass doors and garage doors.
[d] Excludes costumes, masks, daywear, footwear, nightwear, and outerwear.
[e] Includes cultivators, hoes, pitchforks, rakes, shovels, spades, and trowels.
[f] Excludes monkey bars, seesaws, slides, and swings.

PEDALCYCLES

The estimated number of deaths from collisions between pedalcycles and motor vehicles increased from about 750 in 1940 to 1,200 in 1980, then declined to about 1,100 in 2006. Nonfatal disabling injuries were estimated to number 55,000 in 2006.

In 2004, 724 pedalcyclists died in motor-vehicle crashes and 119 in other accidents according to National Center for Health Statistics mortality data. Males accounted for nearly 87% of all pedalcycle deaths, more than six times the female fatalities.

Emergency-room-treated injuries associated with bicycles and bicycle accessories were estimated to total 485,669 in 2005 and 490,434 in 2006, according to

the U.S. Consumer Product Safety Commission (see also page 146).

Thompson, Rivara, and Thompson (1989) estimated that bicycle helmets reduce the risk of all head injuries by up to 85% and reduce the risk of brain injuries by as much as 88%. In 2007, 21 states, the District of Columbia, and at least 149 localities had bicycle helmet-use laws according to the Bicycle Helmet Safety Institute.

National Safety Council estimates and tabulations of National Center for Health Statistics mortality data. Data from Bicycle Helmet Safety Institute retrieved 11/14/07 from www.bhsi.org. Thompson, R.S., Rivara, F.P., & Thompson, D.C. (1989). A case-control study of the effectiveness of bicycle safety helmets. New England Journal of Medicine, 320(21), 1361-1367.

PEDALCYCLE DEATHS AND DEATH RATES BY SEX AND AGE GROUP, UNITED STATES, 2004

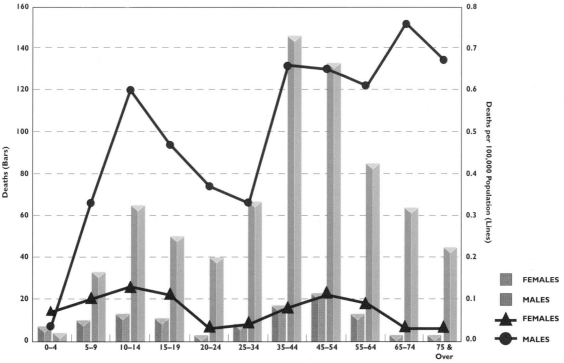

Source: National Safety Council based on National Center for Health Statistics data.

PEDALCYCLE FATALITIES BY MONTH, UNITED STATES, 2004

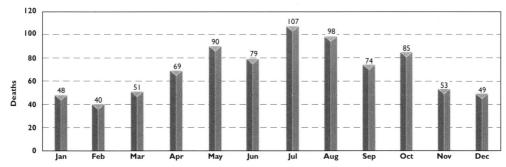

NATIONAL SAFETY COUNCIL

INJURY FACTS®

INTENTIONAL INJURIES

Injuries may be divided into three broad groups—unintentional, intentional, and undetermined intent. Most of *Injury Facts* presents data on unintentional (accidental) injuries. This section presents data on intentional injuries.

Under the World Health Organization's Safe Communities initiative, for which the National Safety Council is the affiliate support center in the United States, injury prevention is not limited to unintentional injuries. Data on intentional injuries are presented here to support Safety Communities and complement the unintentional-injury data shown in other sections of *Injury Facts*.

Intentional injuries may be divided into four subgroups—intentional self-harm (suicide), assault (homicide), legal intervention, and operations of war. The diagram below illustrates the injury groupings and shows the death totals for 2004.

INJURY DEATHS BY INTENT, UNITED STATES, 2004

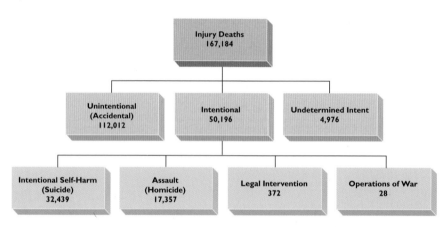

Intentional self-harm includes suicide and attempted suicide by purposely self-inflicted poisoning or injury. The most common methods of intentional self-harm that result in death are firearms; hanging, strangulation, and suffocation; and poisoning.

Assault includes homicide and injuries inflicted by another person with intent to injure or kill (excluding legal intervention and operations of war). The most common means of homicide are firearms; sharp objects; and hanging, strangulation, and suffocation.

Legal intervention includes legal execution. Operations of war include injuries to military personnel and civilians caused by war and civil insurrection. The death must have occurred in the United States. In the vital statistics system, war deaths (and other deaths) occurring outside the United States are counted by the country in which they occurred.

AGE AND SEX

Each of the three broad groups of injuries were among the 15 leading causes of deaths in the United States in 2004. Unintentional injuries ranked 5th, intentional self-harm ranked 11th, and assault ranked 15th.

Intentional self-harm ranked as high as second (after unintentional injuries) for persons aged 14–16 and 28–33 and ranked third for those aged 13, 17–27, and 34. Suicide deaths were highest at age 47 (781). Assault

ranked as high as second (after unintentional injuries) for persons aged 17–27. It ranked third among people aged 1, 2, 4, 9, 15, 16, and 28–31. Homicide deaths were highest at age 24 (671). **For people ages 15–31, accidents, suicide, and homicide are the three leading causes of death.** The graph below shows the number of deaths due to injuries by single year of age from 0 to 99.

INJURY DEATHS BY AGE, UNITED STATES, 2004

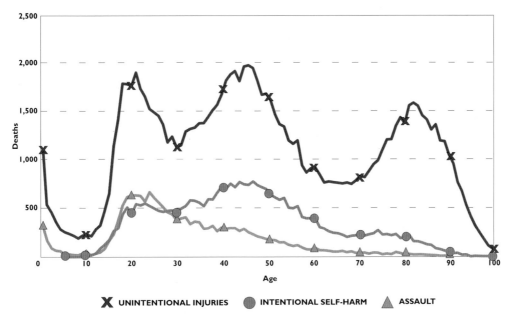

Source: National Safety Council analysis of National Center for Health Statistics mortality data.

Males have higher death rates than females for injuries of all intents. Males also have higher nonfatal injury rates than females for unintentional injuries and assault.

Females, however, have a higher injury rate than males for intentional self-harm.

DEATH AND NONFATAL INJURY RATES BY INTENT AND SEX, UNITED STATES, 2004

Sex	Deaths per 100,000 Population			Nonfatal Injuries per 100,000 Population		
	Unintentional	Homicide	Suicide	Unintentional	Assault	Self-Harm
Both Sexes	38.2	5.9	11.1	9,344	585	145
Males	49.9	9.4	17.7	10,423	713	124
Females	26.8	2.5	4.6	8,294	462	165
Ratio of Male to Female	1.8	3.8	3.8	1.3	1.5	0.8

Source: CDC, NCIPC, WISQARS.

TRENDS

The graph below shows the trends from 1992 to the present in injury deaths and death rates. Unintentional-injury deaths and death rates have increased by 33.4% and 16.6%, respectively. Suicide deaths increased 6.4% but the death rate declined 7.0%. Homicide deaths and death rates decreased 31.0% and 39.7%, respectively, over the 1992–2004 period. Age-adjusted death rates, which remove the effects of the changing age distribution of the population, increased 13.4% for unintentional injuries, decreased 8.5% for suicide, and decreased 37.6% for homicide.

INJURY DEATHS AND DEATH RATES, UNITED STATES, 1992–2004

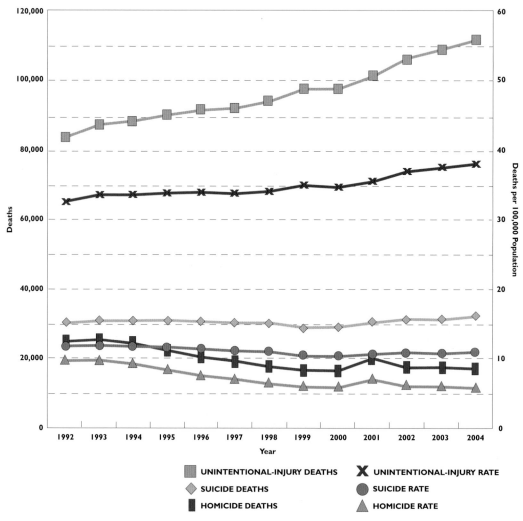

Source: National Safety Council analysis of National Center for Health Statistics mortality data.

Several national surveys provide information on the amount of medical care provided for injuries. The National Electronic Injury Surveillance System All Injuries Program (NEISS-AIP) provides estimates of the number of episodes of injury treated in hospital emergency departments. The most recent estimates (2006) are 27.7 million cases involving unintentional injuries, 1.7 million involving assault, and 0.4 million involving self harm.[a]

The National Hospital Ambulatory Medical Care Survey (NHAMCS) is another survey of emergency department visits with results that are similar to the NEISS-AIP. The latest NHAMCS estimates (2005) are 28.4 unintentional injury visits, 1.7 million assault visits, and 0.4 million self-harm visits.[b]

The NHAMCS also provides estimates of the number of hospital outpatient department visits for injuries. In 2005, about 5.4 million visits were for unintentional injuries and 240,000 were for intentional injuries.[c]

The National Ambulatory Medical Care Survey (NAMCS) gives estimates of the number of physician office visits for injuries. The survey estimated about 40.9 million office visits for unintentional injuries and 1.8 million visits for intentional injuries.[d]

According to the National Hospital Discharge Survey, about 2.0 million people were hospitalized for intentional and unintentional injuries in 2005.[e]

Apart from surveys of medical care utilization for intentional injuries, there are estimates of the general incidence of self-harm and violent behavior within the population. Overall, there is one suicide for every 25 attempts. For youth between 15 and 24, the ratio is one suicide for every 100–200 attempts. And for adults 65 and older there is one suicide for every four attempts.[f]

The National Crime Victimization Survey for 2005 found a total of 23.4 million victimizations (involving either a person or household as the victim) of which 5.4 million were personal crimes and 18.0 million were property crimes. Of the personal crimes, 5.2 million were crimes of violence, which include rape and sexual assault, robbery, assault, and of which 1.7 million involved completed violence and 3.5 million involved attempted or threatened violence.[g]

[a] CDC, NCIPC, WISQARS. Retrieved October 25, 2007, from http://webappa.cdc.gov/sasweb/ncipc/nfirates2001.html.
[b] Nawar, E.W., Niska, R.W., & Xu, J. (2007). National hospital ambulatory medical care survey: 2005 emergency department summary. Advance Data From Vital and Health Statistics, No. 386. Hyattsville, MD: National Center for Health Statistics.
[c] Middleton, K., Hing, E., & Xu, J. (2007). National hospital ambulatory medical care survey: 2005 outpatient department summary. Advance Data From Vital and Health Statistics, No. 389. Hyattsville, MD: National Center for Health Statistics.
[d] Cherry, D.K., Woodwell, D.A., & Rechtsteiner, E.A. (2007). National ambulatory medical care survey: 2005 summary. Advance Data From Vital and Health Statistics, No. 387. Hyattsville, MD: National Center for Health Statistics.
[e] DeFrances, C.J., & Hall, M.J. (2007). 2005 national hospital discharge survey. Advance Data From Vital and Health Statistics, No. 385. Hyattsville, MD: National Center for Health Statistics.
[f] Goldsmith, S.K., Pellmar, T.C., Kleinman, A.M., & Bunney, W.E. (Eds.). (2002). Reducing Suicide: A National Imperative. Washington, DC: National Academy Press.
[g] Bureau of Justice Statistics. (2006). Criminal Victimization in the United States, 2005 Statistical Tables. NCJ 215244. Washington, DC: U.S. Department of Justice.

ASSAULT/HOMICIDE

Assault includes homicide and injuries inflicted by another person with intent to injure or kill (excluding legal intervention and operations of war). The four leading forms of fatal assault injuries account for 84% of the total—firearms (67%), sharp objects (12%), hanging, strangulation, and suffocation (4%), and other maltreatment syndromes (1%) (maltreatment other than neglect and abandonment, and sexual assault by bodily force).

ASSAULT/HOMICIDE DEATHS AND DEATH RATES BY AGE GROUP, UNITED STATES, 2004

	Total	0–4	5–14	15–24	25–44	45–64	65–74	75+
Total	17,357	702	329	5,085	7,479	2,887	446	429
Rate[a]	5.9	3.5	0.8	12.2	8.9	4.1	2.4	2.4
Firearms	11,624	42	184	4,127	5,398	1,530	193	150
Rate[a]	4.0	0.2	0.5	9.9	6.4	2.2	1.0	0.8
Sharp objects	2,079	19	34	484	929	461	77	75
Rate[a]	0.7	0.1	0.1	1.2	1.1	0.7	0.4	0.4
Hanging, strangulation, and suffocation	664	71	27	106	272	127	32	29
Rate[a]	0.2	0.4	0.1	0.3	0.3	0.2	0.2	0.2
Other maltreatment syndromes	174	153	8	1	7	2	0	3
Rate[a]	0.1	0.8	(b)	(b)	(b)	(b)	0.0	(b)
Other means	2,816	417	76	367	873	767	144	172
Rate[a]	1.0	2.1	0.2	0.9	1.0	1.1	0.8	1.0

[a]*Deaths per 100,000 population in each age group.*
[b]*Less than 0.05.*

HOMICIDE DEATH RATES BY AGE GROUP, UNITED STATES, 1992–2004

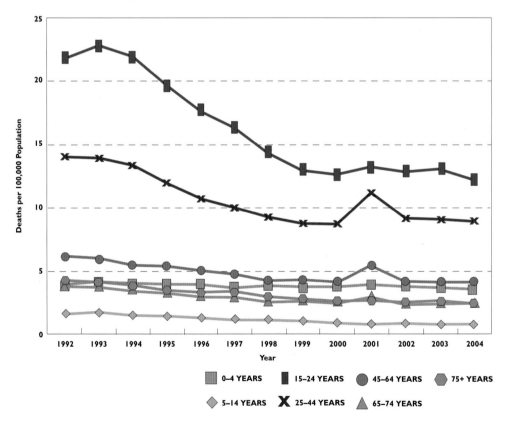

Source: National Safety Council analysis of National Center for Health Statistics mortality data.

INTENTIONAL SELF-HARM/SUICIDE

Intentional self-harm includes suicide and attempted suicide by purposely self-inflicted poisoning or injury. The four leading forms of fatal self-harm injuries account for 92% of the total—firearms (52%), hanging, strangulation, and suffocation (23%), self-poisoning by drugs and medicines (13%), and self-poisoning by other chemicals and noxious substances (5%). It is generally accepted that children under 5 years of age cannot commit suicide.

INTENTIONAL SELF-HARM/SUICIDE DEATHS AND DEATH RATES BY AGE GROUP, UNITED STATES, 2004

	Total	0–4	5–14	15–24	25–44	45–64	65–74	75+
Total	32,439	—	285	4,316	11,712	10,917	2,279	2,930
Rate[a]	11.0	—	0.7	10.4	13.9	15.4	12.3	11.9
Firearms	16,750	—	59	2,104	5,151	5,677	1,631	2,128
Rate[a]	5.7	—	0.1	5.0	6.1	8.0	8.8	11.9
Hanging, strangulation, and suffocation	7,336	—	206	1,516	3,259	1,806	229	320
Rate[a]	2.5	—	0.5	3.6	3.9	2.6	1.2	1.8
Poisoning by drugs and medicines	4,208	—	15	272	1,711	1,876	162	172
Rate[a]	1.4	—	(b)	0.7	2.0	2.7	0.9	1.0
Poisoning by other substances	1,592	—	1	91	652	662	73	114
Rate[a]	0.5	—	(b)	0.2	0.8	0.9	0.4	0.6
Other means	2,553	—	5	333	939	896	184	196
Rate[a]	0.9	—	(b)	0.8	1.1	1.3	1.0	1.1

Note: Dashes (—) indicate not applicable.
[a]*Deaths per 100,000 population in each age group.*
[b]*Less than 0.05.*

SUICIDE DEATH RATES BY AGE GROUP, UNITED STATES, 1992–2004

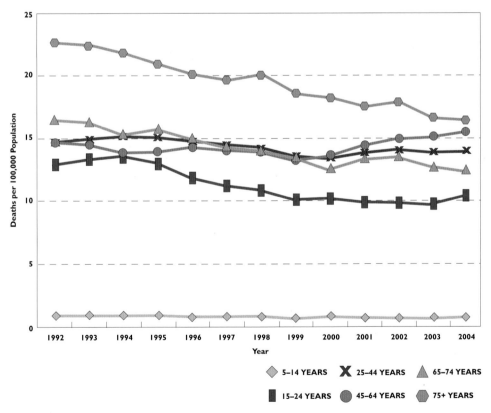

Source: National Safety Council analysis of National Center for Health Statistics mortality data.

NATIONAL SAFETY COUNCIL

INJURY FACTS®

STATE DATA

Motor-vehicle crashes are the leading cause of U-I deaths in 47 states.

This section on state-level data includes data for occupational and motor-vehicle injuries as well as general injury mortality.

Death rates for unintentional injuries (U-I) can vary greatly from one type of injury to the next and from state to state. The graph on the next page shows for each state the death rates (per 100,000 population) for total unintentional-injury deaths and the four leading types of unintentional-injury deaths nationally—motor-vehicle crashes, poisonings, falls, and choking (inhalation or ingestion of food or other object that obstructs breathing).

The map on page 160 shows graphically the overall unintentional-injury death rates by state. Rates by region were lowest in New England and highest in the east south central states.

The charts on pages 161 through 163 show (a) total unintentional-injury deaths and where U-I rank as a cause of death in each state, and (b) the five leading causes of U-I deaths in each state.

Unintentional injuries as a whole are the fifth leading cause of death in the United States and in 23 states. U-I are the third leading cause of death in Alaska, Arizona, Mississippi, New Mexico, and the District of Columbia and the fourth leading cause in 18 states. U-I rank sixth in four states (Maine, Maryland, New Jersey, and New York), and eighth in Massachusetts.

In 2004, motor-vehicle crashes were the leading cause of U-I deaths in 47 states. Falls were the leading cause in Rhode Island and Vermont. The leading cause in the District of Columbia and Washington was poisoning.

The second leading cause of U-I deaths was poisoning in 28 states and falls in 20 states. Motor-vehicle crashes were second in Rhode Island, Vermont, Washington, and the District of Columbia. (Poisoning and falls were tied for second in Hawaii and it is included in both counts.)

The most common third leading causes of U-I deaths were falls in 28 states and the District of Columbia, and poisoning in 16 states. Choking ranked third in three states (Massachusetts, Nebraska, and Rhode Island), fire in Maryland, and drowning in Alaska.

Choking was the fourth leading cause of U-I deaths in 29 states, while the fourth ranking cause was drowning in 13 states, and fires, flames, and smoke in five states and the District of Columbia. Poisoning ranked fourth in Nebraska, and air transport in Alaska and Montana, struck by or against in Vermont, and mechanical suffocation in Nevada (tied with drowning). (Choking and fire were tied in South Carolina and it is included in both counts.)

Fires, burns, and smoke was the fifth leading U-I cause of death in 22 states. Drowning ranked fifth in 13 states, and choking was fifth in 13 states and the District of Columbia. The fifth ranking cause was mechanical suffocation in Minnesota, Nevada (tied with drowning), Rhode Island, and Wyoming, water transport in Alaska, and poisoning in Rhode Island. (Fires and drowning were tied in Massachusetts. Drowning and choking were tied in Montana and Vermont. Ties are included in both counts.)

The table on pages 164 and 165 shows the number of U-I deaths by state for the 15 most common types of injury events. State populations are also shown to facilitate computation of detailed death rates.

The table on page 166 consists of a 4-year state-by-state comparison of unintentional-injury deaths and death rates for 2001 through 2004.

Page 167 shows fatal occupational injuries by state and counts of deaths for some of the principal types of events—transportation accidents, assaults and violent acts, contacts with objects and equipment, falls, exposure to harmful substances or environments, and fires and explosions.

Nonfatal occupational injury and illness incidence rates for most states are shown in the table on page 168 and graphically in the map on page 169. States not shown do not have state occupational safety and health plans.

Pages 170 and 171 show motor-vehicle-related deaths and death rates by state both in tables and maps. The maps show death rates based on population, vehicle miles traveled, and registered vehicles.

UNINTENTIONAL-INJURY DEATH RATES BY STATE, UNITED STATES, 2004

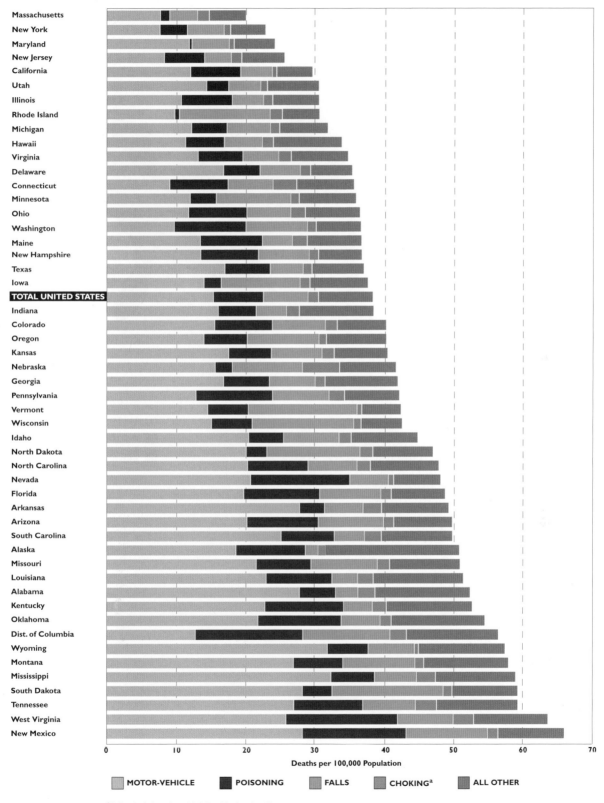

ᵃSuffocation by ingestion or inhalation of food or other object.

UNINTENTIONAL-INJURY DEATH RATES BY STATE

UNINTENTIONAL-INJURY DEATHS PER 100,000 POPULATION BY STATE, 2004

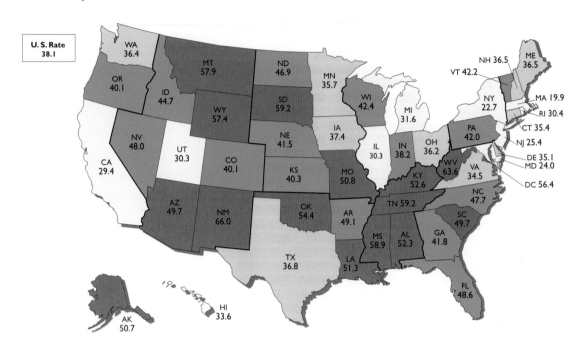

U. S. Rate
38.1

WA 36.4
OR 40.1
MT 57.9
ND 46.9
MN 35.7
NH 36.5
ME 36.5
VT 42.2
ID 44.7
SD 59.2
WI 42.4
NY 22.7
MA 19.9
WY 57.4
IA 37.4
MI 31.6
PA 42.0
RI 30.4
CT 35.4
NV 48.0
UT 30.3
NE 41.5
IL 30.3
IN 38.2
OH 36.2
NJ 25.4
CA 29.4
CO 40.1
KS 40.3
MO 50.8
WV 63.6
VA 34.5
DE 35.1
MD 24.0
DC 56.4
AZ 49.7
NM 66.0
OK 54.4
AR 49.1
TN 59.2
KY 52.6
NC 47.7
MS 58.9
AL 52.3
GA 41.8
SC 49.7
TX 36.8
LA 51.3
FL 48.6
AK 50.7
HI 33.6

REGIONAL RATES

NEW ENGLAND (CT, ME, MA, NH, RI, VT)		28.5
MIDDLE ATLANTIC (NJ, NY, PA)		29.2
EAST NORTH CENTRAL (IL, IN, MI, OH, WI)		34.6
WEST NORTH CENTRAL (IA, KS, MN, MO, NE, ND, SD)		42.8
SOUTH ATLANTIC (DE, DC, FL, GA, MD, NC, SC, VA, WV)		43.4
EAST SOUTH CENTRAL (AL, KY, MS, TN)		55.8
WEST SOUTH CENTRAL (AR, LA, OK, TX)		41.7
MOUNTAIN (AZ, CO, ID, MT, NV, NM, UT, WY)		46.7
PACIFIC (AK, CA, HI, OR, WA)		31.5

Source: National Center for Health Statistics, and U.S. Census Bureau.

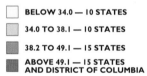

BELOW 34.0 — 10 STATES
34.0 TO 38.1 — 10 STATES
38.2 TO 49.1 — 15 STATES
ABOVE 49.1 — 15 STATES AND DISTRICT OF COLUMBIA

UNINTENTIONAL-INJURY DEATHS BY STATE

The following series of charts is a state-by-state ranking of the five leading causes of deaths due to unintentional injuries (U-I) based on 2004 data. The first line of each section gives the rank of unintentional-injury deaths among all causes of death, the total number of U-I deaths, and the rate of U-I deaths per 100,000 population in the state. The following lines list the five leading types of unintentional-injury deaths in the state along with the number and rate for each type.

TOTAL UNITED STATES

Rank	Cause	Deaths	Rate
5	All U-I	112,012	38.1
1	Motor-vehicle	44,933	15.3
2	Poisoning[a]	20,950	7.1
3	Falls	18,807	6.4
4	Choking[b]	4,470	1.5
5	Drowning[c]	3,308	1.1

ALABAMA

Rank	Cause	Deaths	Rate
4	All U-I	2,363	52.3
1	Motor-vehicle	1,247	27.6
2	Poisoning[a]	235	5.2
3	Falls	147	3.3
4	Choking[b]	112	2.5
5	Fires, flames, smoke	107	2.4

ALASKA

Rank	Cause	Deaths	Rate
3	All U-I	333	50.7
1	Motor-vehicle	122	18.6
2	Poisoning[a]	65	9.9
3	Drowning[c]	34	5.2
4	Air transportation	22	3.3
5	Water transportation	17	2.6

ARIZONA

Rank	Cause	Deaths	Rate
3	All U-I	2,853	49.7
1	Motor-vehicle	1,156	20.1
2	Poisoning[a]	586	10.2
3	Falls	543	9.5
4	Drowning[c]	101	1.8
5	Choking[b]	85	1.5

ARKANSAS

Rank	Cause	Deaths	Rate
5	All U-I	1,350	49.1
1	Motor-vehicle	759	27.6
2	Falls	154	5.6
3	Poisoning[a]	99	3.6
4	Choking[b]	73	2.7
5	Fires, flames, smoke	56	2.0

CALIFORNIA

Rank	Cause	Deaths	Rate
5	All U-I	10,530	29.4
1	Motor-vehicle	4,319	12.1
2	Poisoning[a]	2,551	7.1
3	Falls	1,624	4.5
4	Drowning[c]	380	1.1
5	Fires, flames, smoke	217	0.6

COLORADO

Rank	Cause	Deaths	Rate
4	All U-I	1,843	40.1
1	Motor-vehicle	713	15.5
2	Poisoning[a]	377	8.2
3	Falls	351	7.6
4	Choking[b]	77	1.7
5	Drowning[c]	49	1.1

CONNECTICUT

Rank	Cause	Deaths	Rate
5	All U-I	1,236	35.4
1	Motor-vehicle	317	9.1
2	Poisoning[a]	291	8.3
3	Falls	225	6.4
4	Choking[b]	117	3.3
5	Fires, flames, smoke	31	0.9

DELAWARE

Rank	Cause	Deaths	Rate
5	All U-I	291	35.1
1	Motor-vehicle	139	16.8
2	Falls	48	5.8
3	Poisoning[a]	43	5.2
4	Choking[b]	12	1.4
5	Fires, flames, smoke	9	1.1

DISTRICT OF COLUMBIA

Rank	Cause	Deaths	Rate
3	All U-I	327	56.4
1	Poisoning[a]	89	15.4
2	Motor-vehicle	74	12.8
3	Falls	73	12.6
4	Fires, flames, smoke	20	3.4
5	Choking[b]	14	2.4

FLORIDA

Rank	Cause	Deaths	Rate
5	All U-I	8,442	48.6
1	Motor-vehicle	3,417	19.7
2	Poisoning[a]	1,885	10.9
3	Falls	1,531	8.8
4	Drowning[c]	388	2.2
5	Choking[b]	262	1.5

GEORGIA

Rank	Cause	Deaths	Rate
4	All U-I	3,732	41.8
1	Motor-vehicle	1,497	16.8
2	Poisoning[a]	587	6.6
3	Falls	583	6.5
4	Fires, flames, smoke	154	1.7
5	Choking[b]	131	1.5

HAWAII

Rank	Cause	Deaths	Rate
4	All U-I	423	33.6
1	Motor-vehicle	143	11.4
2	Falls	69	5.5
2	Poisoning[a]	69	5.5
4	Drowning[c]	61	4.8
5	Choking[b]	19	1.5

IDAHO

Rank	Cause	Deaths	Rate
4	All U-I	623	44.7
1	Motor-vehicle	284	20.4
2	Falls	112	8.0
3	Poisoning[a]	69	4.9
4	Drowning[c]	26	1.9
5	Choking[b]	24	1.7

ILLINOIS

Rank	Cause	Deaths	Rate
5	All U-I	3,858	30.3
1	Motor-vehicle	1,362	10.7
2	Poisoning[a]	927	7.3
3	Falls	567	4.5
4	Choking[b]	169	1.3
5	Fires, flames, smoke	123	1.0

INDIANA

Rank	Cause	Deaths	Rate
5	All U-I	2,380	38.2
1	Motor-vehicle	997	16.0
2	Poisoning[a]	335	5.4
3	Falls	269	4.3
4	Choking[b]	115	1.8
5	Fires, flames, smoke	98	1.6

IOWA

Rank	Cause	Deaths	Rate
5	All U-I	1,105	37.4
1	Motor-vehicle	412	13.9
2	Falls	332	11.2
3	Poisoning[a]	73	2.5
4	Choking[b]	43	1.5
5	Fires, flames, smoke	33	1.1

KANSAS

Rank	Cause	Deaths	Rate
5	All U-I	1,103	40.3
1	Motor-vehicle	479	17.5
2	Falls	199	7.3
3	Poisoning[a]	167	6.1
4	Choking[b]	47	1.7
5	Fires, flames, smoke	39	1.4

See footnotes on page 155.

UNINTENTIONAL-INJURY DEATHS
BY STATE (CONT.)

KENTUCKY

Rank	Cause	Deaths	Rate
5	All U-I	2,179	52.6
1	Motor-vehicle	940	22.7
2	Poisoning[a]	466	11.3
3	Falls	174	4.2
4	Choking[b]	84	2.0
5	Fires, flames, smoke	69	1.7

MARYLAND

Rank	Cause	Deaths	Rate
6	All U-I	1,334	24.0
1	Motor-vehicle	660	11.9
2	Falls	300	5.4
3	Fires, flames, smoke	64	1.2
4	Drowning[c]	45	0.8
5	Choking[b]	38	0.7

MINNESOTA

Rank	Cause	Deaths	Rate
5	All U-I	1,817	35.7
1	Motor-vehicle	612	12.0
2	Falls	543	10.7
3	Poisoning[a]	189	3.7
4	Choking[b]	58	1.1
5	Mechanical suffocation	45	0.9

MONTANA

Rank	Cause	Deaths	Rate
4	All U-I	536	57.9
1	Motor-vehicle	248	26.8
2	Falls	97	10.5
3	Poisoning[a]	66	7.1
4	Air transportation	17	1.8
5	Drowning[c]	12	1.3
5	Choking[b]	12	1.3

NEW HAMPSHIRE

Rank	Cause	Deaths	Rate
5	All U-I	474	36.5
1	Motor-vehicle	175	13.5
2	Poisoning[a]	107	8.2
3	Falls	94	7.2
4	Choking[b]	18	1.4
5	Drowning[c]	9	0.7

NEW YORK

Rank	Cause	Deaths	Rate
6	All U-I	4,376	22.7
1	Motor-vehicle	1,478	7.7
2	Falls	1,014	5.3
3	Poisoning[a]	754	3.9
4	Choking[b]	182	0.9
5	Fires, flames, smoke	181	0.9

LOUISIANA

Rank	Cause	Deaths	Rate
4	All U-I	2,306	51.3
1	Motor-vehicle	1,028	22.9
2	Poisoning[a]	423	9.4
3	Falls	166	3.7
4	Choking[b]	104	2.3
5	Fires, flames, smoke	92	2.0

MASSACHUSETTS

Rank	Cause	Deaths	Rate
8	All U-I	1,281	19.9
1	Motor-vehicle	497	7.7
2	Falls	257	4.0
3	Choking[b]	107	1.7
4	Poisoning[a]	85	1.3
5	Drowning[c]	35	0.5
5	Fires, flames, smoke	35	0.5

MISSISSIPPI

Rank	Cause	Deaths	Rate
3	All U-I	1,704	58.9
1	Motor-vehicle	931	32.2
2	Poisoning[a]	183	6.3
3	Falls	176	6.1
4	Fires, flames, smoke	86	3.0
5	Choking[b]	79	2.7

NEBRASKA

Rank	Cause	Deaths	Rate
5	All U-I	725	41.5
1	Motor-vehicle	272	15.6
2	Falls	175	10.0
3	Choking[b]	93	5.3
4	Poisoning[a]	43	2.5
5	Drowning[c]	22	1.3

NEW JERSEY

Rank	Cause	Deaths	Rate
6	All U-I	2,203	25.4
1	Motor-vehicle	716	8.3
2	Poisoning[a]	500	5.8
3	Falls	334	3.8
4	Choking[b]	128	1.5
5	Fires, flames, smoke	69	0.8

NORTH CAROLINA

Rank	Cause	Deaths	Rate
4	All U-I	4,069	47.7
1	Motor-vehicle	1,722	20.2
2	Poisoning[a]	737	8.6
3	Falls	602	7.1
4	Choking[b]	167	2.0
5	Fires, flames, smoke	131	1.5

MAINE

Rank	Cause	Deaths	Rate
6	All U-I	479	36.5
1	Motor-vehicle	177	13.5
2	Poisoning[a]	116	8.8
3	Falls	56	4.3
4	Choking[b]	28	2.1
5	Drowning[c]	18	1.4

MICHIGAN

Rank	Cause	Deaths	Rate
5	All U-I	3,191	31.6
1	Motor-vehicle	1,230	12.2
2	Falls	628	6.2
3	Poisoning[a]	510	5.1
4	Choking[b]	124	1.2
5	Fires, flames, smoke	122	1.2

MISSOURI

Rank	Cause	Deaths	Rate
4	All U-I	2,923	50.8
1	Motor-vehicle	1,234	21.5
2	Falls	552	9.6
3	Poisoning[a]	449	7.8
4	Choking[b]	106	1.8
5	Fires, flames, smoke	98	1.7

NEVADA

Rank	Cause	Deaths	Rate
4	All U-I	1,119	48.0
1	Motor-vehicle	481	20.6
2	Poisoning[a]	331	14.2
3	Falls	132	5.7
4	Drowning[c]	20	0.9
4	Mechanical suffocation	20	0.9

NEW MEXICO

Rank	Cause	Deaths	Rate
3	All U-I	1,254	66.0
1	Motor-vehicle	533	28.0
2	Poisoning[a]	286	15.0
3	Falls	225	11.8
4	Drowning[c]	31	1.6
5	Choking[b]	29	1.5

NORTH DAKOTA

Rank	Cause	Deaths	Rate
5	All U-I	298	46.9
1	Motor-vehicle	127	20.0
2	Falls	85	13.4
3	Poisoning[a]	19	3.0
4	Choking[b]	12	1.9
5	Drowning[c]	9	1.4

See footnotes on page 155.

OHIO

Rank	Cause	Deaths	Rate
5	All U-I	4,152	36.2
1	Motor-vehicle	1,345	11.7
2	Poisoning[a]	957	8.3
3	Falls	717	6.3
4	Choking[b]	236	2.1
5	Fires, flames, smoke	105	0.9

OKLAHOMA

Rank	Cause	Deaths	Rate
5	All U-I	1,918	54.4
1	Motor-vehicle	764	21.7
2	Poisoning[a]	420	11.9
3	Falls	201	5.7
4	Fires, flames, smoke	68	1.9
5	Drowning[c]	62	1.8

OREGON

Rank	Cause	Deaths	Rate
5	All U-I	1,439	40.1
1	Motor-vehicle	501	14.0
2	Falls	267	7.4
3	Poisoning[a]	222	6.2
4	Drowning[c]	61	1.7
5	Choking[b]	40	1.1

PENNSYLVANIA

Rank	Cause	Deaths	Rate
5	All U-I	5,196	42.0
1	Motor-vehicle	1,587	12.8
2	Poisoning[a]	1,354	10.9
3	Falls	1,004	8.1
4	Choking[b]	272	2.2
5	Fires, flames, smoke	173	1.4

RHODE ISLAND

Rank	Cause	Deaths	Rate
5	All U-I	328	30.4
1	Falls	140	13.0
2	Motor-vehicle	106	9.8
3	Choking[b]	19	1.8
4	Drowning[c]	15	1.4
5	Poisoning[a]	6	0.6
5	Mechanical suffocation	6	0.6

SOUTH CAROLINA

Rank	Cause	Deaths	Rate
4	All U-I	2,084	49.7
1	Motor-vehicle	1,048	25.0
2	Poisoning[a]	321	7.7
3	Falls	183	4.4
4	Choking[b]	103	2.5
4	Fires, flames, smoke	75	1.8

SOUTH DAKOTA

Rank	Cause	Deaths	Rate
4	All U-I	456	59.2
1	Motor-vehicle	216	28.0
2	Falls	124	16.1
3	Poisoning[a]	33	4.3
4	Fires, flames, smoke	14	1.8
5	Choking[b]	10	1.3

TENNESSEE

Rank	Cause	Deaths	Rate
4	All U-I	3,486	59.2
1	Motor-vehicle	1,578	26.8
2	Poisoning[a]	585	9.9
3	Falls	454	7.7
4	Choking[b]	179	3.0
5	Fires, flames, smoke	134	2.3

TEXAS

Rank	Cause	Deaths	Rate
4	All U-I	8,289	36.8
1	Motor-vehicle	3,816	16.9
2	Poisoning[a]	1,461	6.5
3	Falls	1,051	4.7
4	Choking[b]	296	1.3
5	Drowning[c]	273	1.2

UTAH

Rank	Cause	Deaths	Rate
4	All U-I	734	30.3
1	Motor-vehicle	347	14.3
2	Falls	112	4.6
3	Poisoning[a]	75	3.1
4	Drowning[c]	26	1.1
5	Choking[b]	22	0.9

VERMONT

Rank	Cause	Deaths	Rate
5	All U-I	262	42.2
1	Falls	97	15.6
2	Motor-vehicle	90	14.5
3	Poisoning[a]	36	5.8
4	Struck by, against	6	1.0
5	Drowning[c]	4	0.6
5	Choking[b]	4	0.6

VIRGINIA

Rank	Cause	Deaths	Rate
5	All U-I	2,578	34.5
1	Motor-vehicle	982	13.1
2	Poisoning[a]	476	6.4
3	Falls	383	5.1
4	Choking[b]	132	1.8
5	Fires, flames, smoke	110	1.5

WASHINGTON

Rank	Cause	Deaths	Rate
5	All U-I	2,257	36.4
1	Poisoning[a]	634	10.2
2	Motor-vehicle	602	9.7
3	Falls	545	8.8
4	Choking[b]	81	1.3
5	Drowning[c]	71	1.1

WEST VIRGINIA

Rank	Cause	Deaths	Rate
4	All U-I	1,152	63.6
1	Motor-vehicle	465	25.7
2	Poisoning[a]	292	16.1
3	Falls	147	8.1
4	Choking[b]	54	3.0
5	Fires, flames, smoke	29	1.6

WISCONSIN

Rank	Cause	Deaths	Rate
4	All U-I	2,331	42.4
1	Motor-vehicle	828	15.1
2	Falls	799	14.5
3	Poisoning[a]	320	5.8
4	Choking[b]	59	1.1
5	Drowning[c]	55	1.0

WYOMING

Rank	Cause	Deaths	Rate
4	All U-I	290	57.4
1	Motor-vehicle	160	31.6
2	Falls	34	6.7
3	Poisoning[a]	30	5.9
4	Drowning[c]	11	2.2
5	Mechanical suffocation	9	1.8

Source: National Safety Council tabulations of National Center for Health Statistics mortality data.
[a] Solid, liquid, gas, and vapor poisoning.
[b] Inhalation or ingestion of food or other objects.
[c] Excludes transport drownings.

UNINTENTIONAL-INJURY DEATHS BY STATE AND EVENT

UNINTENTIONAL-INJURY DEATHS BY STATE AND TYPE OF EVENT, UNITED STATES, 2004

State	Population (000)	Total[a]	Motor-vehicle[b]	Poisoning	Falls	Choking[c]	Drowning[d]	Fires Flames, and Smoke	Mechanical Suffocation
Total U.S.	293,638	112,012	44,933	20,950	18,807	4,470	3,308	3,229	1,421
Alabama	4,517	2,363	1,247	235	147	112	55	107	23
Alaska	657	333	122	65	12	7	34	7	8
Arizona	5,746	2,853	1,156	586	543	85	101	29	23
Arkansas	2,747	1,350	759	99	154	73	44	56	13
California	35,841	10,530	4,319	2,551	1,624	210	380	217	99
Colorado	4,599	1,843	713	377	351	77	49	16	24
Connecticut	3,494	1,236	317	291	225	117	30	31	10
Delaware	829	291	139	43	48	12	7	9	6
Dist. of Columbia	580	327	74	89	73	14	5	20	0
Florida	17,367	8,442	3,417	1,885	1,531	262	388	142	112
Georgia	8,935	3,732	1,497	587	583	131	109	154	45
Hawaii	1,259	423	143	69	69	19	61	6	2
Idaho	1,395	623	284	69	112	24	26	8	15
Illinois	12,714	3,858	1,362	927	567	169	70	123	61
Indiana	6,223	2,380	997	335	269	115	73	98	64
Iowa	2,954	1,105	412	73	332	43	22	33	18
Kansas	2,738	1,103	479	167	199	47	28	39	18
Kentucky	4,140	2,179	940	466	174	84	58	69	39
Louisiana	4,496	2,306	1,028	423	166	104	90	92	49
Maine	1,314	479	177	116	56	28	18	7	3
Maryland	5,553	1,334	660	16	300	38	45	64	17
Massachusetts	6,436	1,281	497	85	257	107	35	35	7
Michigan	10,093	3,191	1,230	510	628	124	74	122	89
Minnesota	5,094	1,817	612	189	543	58	38	28	45
Mississippi	2,893	1,704	931	183	176	79	50	86	6
Missouri	5,753	2,923	1,234	449	552	106	58	98	48
Montana	926	536	248	66	97	12	12	10	6
Nebraska	1,747	725	272	43	175	93	22	15	6
Nevada	2,332	1,119	481	331	132	18	20	15	20
New Hampshire	1,298	474	175	107	94	18	9	8	5
New Jersey	8,676	2,203	716	500	334	128	56	69	19
New Mexico	1,901	1,254	533	286	225	29	31	22	8
New York	19,292	4,376	1,478	754	1,014	182	88	181	30
North Carolina	8,531	4,069	1,722	737	602	167	95	131	54
North Dakota	636	298	127	19	85	12	9	8	2
Ohio	11,461	4,152	1,345	957	717	236	85	105	72
Oklahoma	3,523	1,918	764	420	201	56	62	68	15
Oregon	3,589	1,439	501	222	367	40	61	36	25
Pennsylvania	12,377	5,196	1,587	1,354	1,004	272	76	173	58
Rhode Island	1,079	328	106	6	140	19	15	4	6
South Carolina	4,195	2,084	1,048	321	183	103	70	75	30
South Dakota	770	456	216	33	124	10	7	14	6
Tennessee	5,886	3,486	1,578	585	454	179	101	134	30
Texas	22,518	8,289	3,816	1,461	1,051	296	273	209	69
Utah	2,422	734	347	75	112	22	26	14	10
Vermont	621	262	90	36	97	4	4	1	2
Virginia	7,472	2,578	982	476	383	132	82	110	30
Washington	6,206	2,257	602	634	545	81	71	49	28
West Virginia	1,811	1,152	465	292	147	54	19	29	10
Wisconsin	5,499	2,331	828	320	799	59	55	52	27
Wyoming	506	290	160	30	34	3	11	1	9

See source and footnotes on page 165.

UNINTENTIONAL-INJURY DEATHS BY STATE AND TYPE OF EVENT, UNITED STATES, 2004, Cont.

State	Natural Heat or Cold	Struck By/Against Object	Machinery	Firearms	Electric Current	Water Transport	Air Transport	Rail Transport	All Other Accidents
Total U.S.	902	833	795	649	382	574	679	457	9,623
Alabama	14	26	17	33	13	13	7	7	307
Alaska	8	2	1	0	0	17	22	0	28
Arizona	67	7	7	13	8	11	32	9	176
Arkansas	13	10	9	16	8	6	9	5	76
California	69	70	66	52	35	40	69	71	658
Colorado	22	13	10	5	2	3	24	4	153
Connecticut	8	9	3	2	2	1	5	5	180
Delaware	1	1	1	1	0	0	0	0	23
Dist. of Columbia	5	0	0	3	1	1	0	2	40
Florida	26	49	26	18	30	60	53	26	417
Georgia	14	29	25	24	17	23	28	16	450
Hawaii	0	1	3	0	1	0	7	0	42
Idaho	7	8	11	8	2	9	13	1	26
Illinois	45	19	24	15	10	16	11	29	410
Indiana	18	12	27	13	6	4	5	16	328
Iowa	8	11	24	3	1	5	3	2	115
Kansas	7	6	17	2	3	1	12	2	76
Kentucky	11	25	22	20	6	7	10	6	242
Louisiana	8	17	18	42	8	47	8	12	194
Maine	5	3	0	0	1	5	1	1	58
Maryland	24	9	14	8	2	11	1	10	115
Massachusetts	13	9	6	3	5	9	5	4	204
Michigan	42	11	24	14	11	19	10	4	279
Minnesota	22	15	14	2	3	18	13	5	212
Mississippi	18	22	6	17	7	18	12	11	82
Missouri	16	29	33	16	17	17	35	9	206
Montana	7	4	3	7	1	7	17	3	36
Nebraska	5	5	4	6	5	2	3	3	66
Nevada	6	4	7	6	3	1	15	3	57
New Hampshire	4	6	2	1	2	1	1	0	41
New Jersey	17	14	9	8	3	6	5	14	305
New Mexico	23	7	3	9	1	0	9	11	57
New York	45	34	18	24	18	13	13	31	453
North Carolina	16	36	45	25	16	15	10	23	375
North Dakota	3	6	8	0	1	3	2	1	12
Ohio	31	24	29	19	15	3	10	16	488
Oklahoma	18	16	9	9	10	6	9	5	250
Oregon	11	8	15	10	2	13	12	7	109
Pennsylvania	46	42	32	26	13	6	10	14	483
Rhode Island	2	2	1	0	1	2	1	1	22
South Carolina	14	18	12	18	9	12	25	7	139
South Dakota	5	1	6	6	0	2	1	1	24
Tennessee	13	28	26	40	5	16	15	7	275
Texas	65	66	57	63	45	44	60	26	688
Utah	9	11	3	3	2	3	4	3	90
Vermont	2	6	1	3	0	0	0	0	16
Virginia	25	24	29	15	11	13	14	2	250
Washington	15	25	26	11	6	23	19	13	109
West Virginia	6	12	6	3	9	6	8	5	81
Wisconsin	19	16	32	6	2	15	14	3	84
Wyoming	4	5	4	1	3	1	7	1	16

Source: National Safety Council analysis of National Center for Health Statistics mortality data.
[a] *Deaths are by place of occurrence and exclude nonresident aliens. See also page 160.*
[b] *See page 170 for motor-vehicle deaths by place of residence.*
[c] *Suffocation by inhalation or ingestion of food or object obstructing breathing.*
[d] *Excludes water transport drownings.*

UNINTENTIONAL-INJURY TRENDS BY STATE

Nationwide, from 2001 to 2004, unintentional-injury (U-I) deaths increased 10% over the four years and the death rate increased 7%. By state, the greatest decrease in U-I deaths occurred in Massachusetts (–13%) and the greatest increase occurred in Nevada (+42%). The death rate decreased the most in Wyoming (–13%) and increased the most West Virginia (+31%).

The table below shows the trend in unintentional-injury deaths and death rates by state over the most recent four years for which data are available.

UNINTENTIONAL-INJURY DEATHS BY STATE, UNITED STATES, 2001–2004

State	Deaths[a]				Deaths per 100,000 Population			
	2004[b]	2003	2002	2001	2004[b]	2003	2002	2001
Total U.S.	112,012	109,277	106,742	101,537	38.1	37.6	37.1	35.6
Alabama	2,363	2,194	2,205	2,210	52.3	48.7	49.2	49.5
Alaska	333	340	350	357	50.7	52.4	54.6	56.4
Arizona	2,853	2,812	2,666	2,549	49.7	50.4	49.0	48.1
Arkansas	1,350	1,239	1,273	1,243	49.1	45.4	47.0	46.2
California	10,530	10,348	10,028	8,010	29.4	29.2	28.7	23.2
Colorado	1,843	1,809	1,837	1,798	40.1	39.8	40.8	40.6
Connecticut	1,236	1,111	1,161	1,049	35.4	31.9	33.6	30.6
Delaware	291	310	312	297	35.1	37.9	38.7	37.3
Dist. of Columbia	327	346	283	324	56.4	62.0	50.1	56.6
Florida	8,442	8,081	7,572	7,093	48.6	47.6	45.4	43.4
Georgia	3,732	3,542	3,389	3,449	41.8	40.5	39.7	41.1
Hawaii	423	451	424	388	33.6	36.1	34.3	31.7
Idaho	623	655	586	572	44.7	47.9	43.6	43.3
Illinois	3,858	3,704	3,974	3,825	30.3	29.3	31.6	30.6
Indiana	2,380	2,150	2,099	2,154	38.2	34.7	34.1	35.2
Iowa	1,105	1,143	1,095	1,033	37.4	38.9	37.3	35.2
Kansas	1,103	1,070	1,103	1,095	40.3	39.3	40.7	40.5
Kentucky	2,179	2,228	2,045	1,948	52.6	54.1	50.0	47.9
Louisiana	2,306	2,229	2,102	2,033	51.3	49.6	47.0	45.5
Maine	479	529	509	486	36.5	40.4	39.2	37.8
Maryland	1,334	1,353	1,290	1,248	24.0	24.5	23.7	23.2
Massachusetts	1,281	1,325	1,358	1,465	19.9	20.6	21.2	22.9
Michigan	3,191	3,224	3,212	3,218	31.6	32.0	32.0	32.2
Minnesota	1,817	1,898	1,918	1,805	35.7	37.5	38.2	36.2
Mississippi	1,704	1,624	1,636	1,518	58.9	56.4	57.1	53.1
Missouri	2,923	2,943	2,761	2,584	50.8	51.5	48.6	45.8
Montana	536	535	555	490	57.9	58.3	60.9	54.1
Nebraska	725	703	756	614	41.5	40.4	43.8	35.7
Nevada	1,119	1,028	930	790	48.0	45.9	42.9	37.7
New Hampshire	474	434	402	373	36.5	33.7	31.5	29.6
New Jersey	2,203	2,263	2,466	2,296	25.4	26.2	28.8	27.0
New Mexico	1,254	1,231	1,142	1,065	66.0	65.5	61.6	58.2
New York	4,376	4,518	4,552	4,896	22.7	23.5	23.8	25.7
North Carolina	4,069	3,866	3,705	3,469	47.7	45.9	44.6	42.3
North Dakota	298	290	264	261	46.9	45.8	41.7	41.0
Ohio	4,152	3,654	4,047	3,774	36.2	32.0	35.5	33.1
Oklahoma	1,918	1,693	1,537	1,663	54.4	48.3	44.1	48.0
Oregon	1,439	1,416	1,393	1,328	40.1	39.7	39.5	38.2
Pennsylvania	5,196	5,061	4,749	4,595	42.0	40.9	38.5	37.4
Rhode Island	328	446	292	281	30.4	41.5	27.3	26.5
South Carolina	2,084	1,966	1,979	1,978	49.7	47.4	48.2	48.7
South Dakota	456	431	385	404	59.2	56.4	50.6	53.3
Tennessee	3,486	3,227	2,976	2,999	59.2	55.2	51.4	52.2
Texas	8,289	8,417	8,237	7,920	36.8	38.1	37.9	37.1
Utah	734	751	775	681	30.3	31.6	33.4	29.9
Vermont	262	248	238	226	42.2	40.1	38.6	36.9
Virginia	2,578	2,584	2,463	2,360	34.5	35.0	33.9	32.8
Washington	2,257	2,137	2,161	2,031	36.4	34.9	35.6	33.9
West Virginia	1,152	1,051	989	872	63.6	58.1	54.8	48.4
Wisconsin	2,331	2,372	2,246	2,094	42.4	43.3	41.3	38.7
Wyoming	290	297	315	326	57.4	59.2	63.1	66.0

Source: Deaths are from the National Center for Health Statistics. Rates are National Safety Council estimates based on data from the National Center for Health Statistics and the U.S. Bureau of the Census.
[a] *Deaths for each state are by place of occurrence and exclude nonresident aliens.*
[b] *Latest official figures.*

FATAL OCCUPATIONAL INJURIES BY STATE

In general, the states with the largest number of persons employed have the largest number of work-related fatalities. The four largest states—California, Florida, New York, and Texas—accounted for about 27% of the total fatalities in the United States. Each state's industry mix, geographic features, age of population, and other characteristics of the workforce must be considered when evaluating state fatality profiles.

FATAL OCCUPATIONAL INJURIES BY STATE AND EVENT OR EXPOSURE, UNITED STATES, 2005–2006

State	2005 Total[a]	2006							
		Total[b]	Transpor-tation[c]	Contact with Objects & Equipment	Falls	Assaults & Violent Acts[d]	Exposure to Harmful Substances or Environments	Fires & Explosions	All Other
Total	5,734	5,703	2,413	983	809	754	525	201	18
Alabama	128	100	42	26	14	8	5	5	—
Alaska	29	44	24	8	—	4	5	—	—
Arizona	99	108	53	10	15	18	12	—	—
Arkansas	80	78	47	8	12	5	—	4	—
California	465	448	167	72	87	61	45	12	—
Colorado	125	137	60	23	13	30	7	3	—
Connecticut	46	38	15	6	4	10	—	—	—
Delaware	11	14	13	—	—	—	—	—	—
Dist. of Columbia	12	7	—	—	—	3	—	—	—
Florida	406	355	141	36	63	54	48	11	—
Georgia	200	192	80	31	33	27	15	4	—
Hawaii	15	30	18	6	—	—	—	—	—
Idaho	35	38	24	7	3	—	—	—	—
Illinois	194	207	86	24	32	36	27	—	—
Indiana	157	148	75	26	19	15	7	6	—
Iowa	90	71	38	11	11	3	4	4	—
Kansas	81	85	43	11	12	7	7	5	—
Kentucky	122	147	77	27	13	15	6	9	—
Louisiana	111	118	50	21	12	13	18	4	—
Maine	15	20	12	3	—	—	—	—	—
Maryland	95	105	39	12	21	24	8	—	—
Massachusetts	75	66	16	10	16	10	13	—	—
Michigan	110	155	60	30	21	21	17	4	—
Minnesota	87	78	29	27	9	5	5	—	—
Mississippi	112	96	45	20	9	8	10	—	—
Missouri	185	166	76	21	23	27	17	—	—
Montana	50	45	30	4	4	3	4	—	—
Nebraska	36	57	17	19	7	6	5	3	—
Nevada	57	49	16	7	10	8	8	—	—
New Hampshire	18	13	4	3	—	3	—	—	—
New Jersey	112	88	39	9	13	18	3	6	—
New Mexico	44	59	29	13	9	3	5	—	—
New York	239	233	71	43	46	37	24	12	—
North Carolina	165	167	66	30	25	22	16	8	—
North Dakota	22	31	16	8	5	—	—	—	—
Ohio	168	193	65	54	22	22	22	7	—
Oklahoma	95	91	59	15	8	—	4	3	—
Oregon	65	72	46	13	6	4	—	—	—
Pennsylvania	224	240	89	44	37	40	22	8	—
Rhode Island	6	10	3	—	3	—	—	—	—
South Carolina	132	93	34	9	19	19	10	—	—
South Dakota	31	37	19	10	—	4	—	—	—
Tennessee	139	153	59	29	14	37	9	5	—
Texas	495	486	200	87	60	59	54	23	—
Utah	54	60	30	9	7	6	7	—	—
Vermont	7	14	6	3	—	—	—	—	—
Virginia	186	164	60	38	18	32	15	—	—
Washington	95	87	40	13	19	4	10	—	—
West Virginia	46	79	26	14	7	3	7	22	—
Wisconsin	125	91	33	24	15	11	4	—	—
Wyoming	46	36	23	7	—	—	—	3	—

Source: U.S. Department of Labor, Bureau of Labor Statistics.
Note: Dashes (—) indicate no data or data that do not meet publication criteria.
[a]Data for 2005 revised and total includes one death for which state of occurrence could not be determined.
[b]Data for 2006 preliminary and total includes four deaths for which state of occurrence could not be determined.
[c]Includes highway, nonhighway, air, water, and rail fatalities, and fatalities resulting from being struck by a vehicle.
[d]Includes violence by persons, self-inflicted injury, and attacks by animals.

NONFATAL OCCUPATIONAL INJURY AND ILLNESS INCIDENCE RATES[a] BY STATE, PRIVATE INDUSTRY, 2005

State	Total Recordable Cases	Cases with Days away from Work[b]	Cases with Job Transfer or Restriction	Other Recordable Cases
Private Industry[c]	**4.6**	**1.4**	**1.0**	**2.2**
Alabama	4.6	1.1	1.1	2.4
Alaska	6.2	2.4	0.6	3.2
Arizona	4.8	1.4	1.0	2.4
Arkansas	5.0	1.2	1.1	2.6
California	4.7	1.3	1.4	2.0
Colorado	—	—	—	—
Connecticut	5.0	1.6	1.2	2.2
Delaware	3.7	1.3	0.6	1.8
Dist. of Columbia	2.0	0.7	0.2	1.0
Florida	4.5	1.2	1.2	2.1
Georgia	4.3	1.1	0.9	2.3
Hawaii	4.9	2.7	0.4	1.8
Idaho	—	—	—	—
Illinois	4.1	1.3	1.0	1.8
Indiana	5.8	1.3	1.5	2.9
Iowa	6.5	1.5	1.6	3.4
Kansas	5.3	1.2	1.2	2.9
Kentucky	6.2	1.8	1.3	3.0
Louisiana	3.1	1.0	0.5	1.6
Maine	7.2	1.7	2.2	3.3
Maryland	4.2	1.5	0.6	2.0
Massachusetts	4.2	1.7	0.6	1.9
Michigan	5.3	1.2	1.4	2.6
Minnesota	5.0	1.3	1.2	2.6
Mississippi	—	—	—	—
Missouri	5.4	1.2	1.4	2.8
Montana	6.6	2.2	0.8	3.7
Nebraska	5.0	1.4	1.0	2.6
Nevada	5.7	1.5	1.4	2.8
New Hampshire	—	—	—	—
New Jersey	3.8	1.4	0.6	1.8
New Mexico	4.4	1.4	0.8	2.2
New York	3.2	1.5	0.2	1.5
North Carolina	4.0	1.1	1.0	1.9
North Dakota	—	—	—	—
Ohio	—	—	—	—
Oklahoma	4.6	1.4	1.2	2.1
Oregon	5.4	1.7	1.2	2.5
Pennsylvania	—	—	—	—
Rhode Island	5.5	2.1	0.7	2.6
South Carolina	3.6	1.1	0.9	1.7
South Dakota	—	—	—	—
Tennessee	4.8	1.2	1.3	2.3
Texas	3.6	1.0	1.0	1.6
Utah	5.6	1.2	1.4	3.0
Vermont	6.2	1.9	0.9	3.4
Virginia	4.0	1.3	0.7	2.0
Washington	6.1	2.0	0.9	3.2
West Virginia	5.5	2.7	0.4	2.5
Wisconsin	5.8	1.7	1.3	2.8
Wyoming	5.8	2.3	0.6	2.9

Source: Bureau of Labor Statistics, U.S. Department of Labor.
Note: Because of rounding, components may not add to totals. Dashes (—) indicate data not available.
[a]*Incidence rates represent the number of injuries and illnesses per 100 full-time workers using 200,000 hours as the equivalent.*
[b]*Days-away-from-work cases include those that result in days away from work with or without job transfer or restriction.*
[c]*Data cover all 50 states.*

NONFATAL OCCUPATIONAL INCIDENCE RATES BY STATE (CONT.)

NONFATAL OCCUPATIONAL INJURY AND ILLNESS INCIDENCE RATES BY STATE, PRIVATE INDUSTRY, 2005

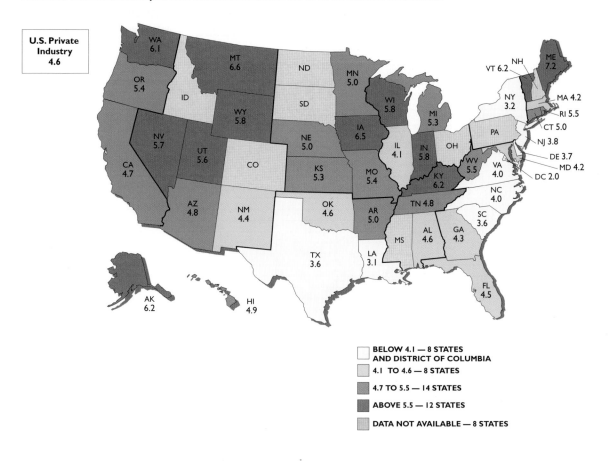

U.S. Private Industry 4.6

WA 6.1
MT 6.6
ND
MN 5.0
OR 5.4
ID
WY 5.8
SD
WI 5.8
MI 5.3
NV 5.7
UT 5.6
CO
NE 5.0
IA 6.5
IL 4.1
IN 5.8
OH
CA 4.7
KS 5.3
MO 5.4
KY 6.2
WV 5.5
AZ 4.8
NM 4.4
OK 4.6
AR 5.0
TN 4.8
NC 4.0
TX 3.6
LA 3.1
MS
AL 4.6
GA 4.3
SC 3.6
AK 6.2
HI 4.9
FL 4.5

VT 6.2
NH
ME 7.2
NY 3.2
MA 4.2
RI 5.5
CT 5.0
PA
NJ 3.8
DE 3.7
MD 4.2
VA 4.0
DC 2.0

BELOW 4.1 — 8 STATES AND DISTRICT OF COLUMBIA

4.1 TO 4.6 — 8 STATES

4.7 TO 5.5 — 14 STATES

ABOVE 5.5 — 12 STATES

DATA NOT AVAILABLE — 8 STATES

STATE DATA

MOTOR-VEHICLE DEATHS BY STATE

MOTOR-VEHICLE DEATHS BY STATE, UNITED STATES, 2003–2006

State	Motor-Vehicle Traffic Deaths (Place of Accident)				Total Motor-Vehicle Deaths[a] (Place of Residence)			
	Number		Mileage Rate[b]		Number		Population Rate[b]	
	2006	2005	2006	2005	2004[c]	2003	2004	2003
Total U.S.[a]	44,700	45,500	1.5	1.5	44,933	44,757	15.3	15.4
Alabama	1,208	1,144	2.0	1.9	1,259	1,069	27.9	23.7
Alaska	74	72	1.5	1.4	119	119	18.1	18.3
Arizona	1,289	1,179	2.2	2.0	1,125	1,097	19.6	19.7
Arkansas	665	654	2.1	2.0	779	720	28.4	26.4
California	4,197	4,304	1.3	1.3	4,417	4,465	12.3	12.6
Colorado	535	606	1.1	1.3	700	707	15.2	15.5
Connecticut	325	292	1.0	0.9	336	283	9.6	8.1
Delaware	147	133	1.5	1.4	141	131	17.0	16.0
Dist. of Columbia	41	49	1.1	1.3	46	64	7.9	11.5
Florida	3,382	3,558	1.7	1.8	3,294	3,248	19.0	19.1
Georgia	1,703	1,740	1.5	1.5	1,497	1,432	16.8	16.4
Hawaii	161	140	1.6	1.4	142	142	11.3	11.4
Idaho	267	275	1.8	1.8	249	283	17.9	20.7
Illinois	1,254	1,365	1.2	1.3	1,513	1,510	11.9	11.9
Indiana	899	938	1.2	1.3	1,006	948	16.2	15.3
Iowa	439	450	1.4	1.4	418	458	14.2	15.6
Kansas	468	428	1.6	1.4	500	494	18.3	18.1
Kentucky	913	985	1.9	2.1	992	940	24.0	22.8
Louisiana	992	963	2.2	2.1	1,022	961	22.7	21.4
Maine	185	169	1.2	1.1	180	201	13.7	15.4
Maryland	651	614	1.2	1.1	671	709	12.1	12.9
Massachusetts	430	439	0.8	0.8	532	529	8.3	8.2
Michigan	1,084	1,129	1.0	1.1	1,307	1,390	12.9	13.8
Minnesota	494	561	0.9	1.0	652	703	12.8	13.9
Mississippi	911	931	2.2	2.2	915	898	31.6	31.2
Missouri	1,096	1,239	1.6	1.8	1,111	1,225	19.3	21.4
Montana	263	251	2.4	2.3	241	258	26.0	28.1
Nebraska	269	276	1.4	1.4	282	307	16.1	17.7
Nevada	432	427	2.1	2.1	422	371	18.1	16.5
New Hampshire	127	164	0.9	1.2	165	130	12.7	10.1
New Jersey	770	701	1.0	0.9	771	786	8.9	9.1
New Mexico	471	488	2.0	2.0	480	435	25.3	23.1
New York	1,435	1,428	1.0	1.0	1,586	1,573	8.2	8.2
North Carolina	1,559	1,534	1.5	1.5	1,691	1,662	19.8	19.7
North Dakota	111	121	1.5	1.6	117	121	18.4	19.1
Ohio	1,238	1,321	1.1	1.2	1,383	1,348	12.1	11.8
Oklahoma	765	800	1.6	1.7	765	721	21.7	20.6
Oregon	477	487	1.3	1.4	501	543	14.0	15.2
Pennsylvania	1,525	1,616	1.4	1.5	1,595	1,652	12.9	13.4
Rhode Island	81	87	1.0	1.0	99	103	9.2	9.6
South Carolina	1,045	1,094	2.1	2.2	1,034	946	24.7	22.8
South Dakota	191	185	2.3	2.2	189	210	24.5	27.5
Tennessee	1,287	1,270	1.8	1.8	1,386	1,308	23.5	22.4
Texas	3,467	3,439	1.5	1.5	3,864	4,022	17.2	18.2
Utah	287	282	1.1	1.1	321	307	13.3	12.9
Vermont	87	73	1.1	0.9	83	74	13.4	12.0
Virginia	961	942	1.2	1.2	1,016	1,009	13.6	13.7
Washington	630	649	1.1	1.2	669	719	10.8	11.7
West Virginia	410	373	2.0	1.8	414	402	22.9	22.2
Wisconsin	712	801	1.2	1.3	815	888	14.8	16.2
Wyoming	195	170	2.1	1.9	121	136	23.9	27.1

Source: Motor-Vehicle Traffic Deaths are provisional counts from state traffic authorities; Total Motor-Vehicle Deaths are from the National Center for Health Statistics (see also page 164).
[a]*Includes both traffic and nontraffic motor-vehicle deaths. See definitions of motor-vehicle traffic and nontraffic accidents on page 191.*
[b]*The mileage death rate is deaths per 100,000,000 vehicle miles; the population death rate is deaths per 100,000 population. Death rates are National Safety Council estimates.*
[c]*Latest year available. See Technical Appendix for comparability.*

MILEAGE DEATH RATES, 2006
MOTOR-VEHICLE TRAFFIC DEATHS PER 100,000,000 VEHICLE MILES

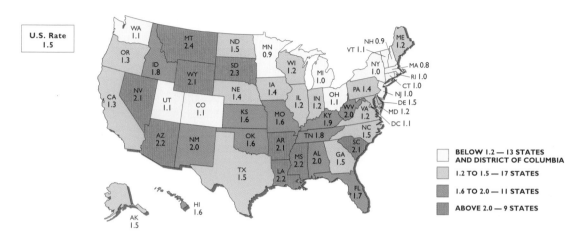

U.S. Rate
1.5

BELOW 1.2 — 13 STATES AND DISTRICT OF COLUMBIA

1.2 TO 1.5 — 17 STATES

1.6 TO 2.0 — 11 STATES

ABOVE 2.0 — 9 STATES

REGISTRATION DEATH RATES, 2006
MOTOR-VEHICLE TRAFFIC DEATHS PER 10,000 MOTOR VEHICLES

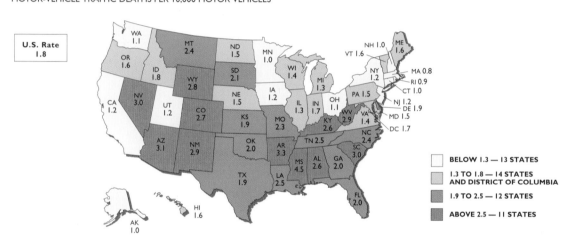

U.S. Rate
1.8

BELOW 1.3 — 13 STATES

1.3 TO 1.8 — 14 STATES AND DISTRICT OF COLUMBIA

1.9 TO 2.5 — 12 STATES

ABOVE 2.5 — 11 STATES

POPULATION DEATH RATES, 2006
MOTOR-VEHICLE TRAFFIC DEATHS PER 100,000 POPULATION

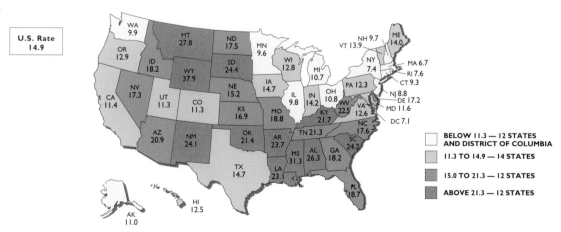

U.S. Rate
14.9

BELOW 11.3 — 12 STATES AND DISTRICT OF COLUMBIA

11.3 TO 14.9 — 14 STATES

15.0 TO 21.3 — 12 STATES

ABOVE 21.3 — 12 STATES

Source: Rates estimated by National Safety Council based on data from state traffic authorities, National Center for Health Statistics, Federal Highway Administration, and the U.S. Census Bureau.

NATIONAL SAFETY COUNCIL

INJURY FACTS®

INTERNATIONAL UNINTENTIONAL-INJURY DEATHS AND DEATH RATES

The term "Accidents and Adverse Effects" used in the International Classification of Diseases system (ICD) refers to all causes of unintentional injury deaths, including transportation accidents, unintentional poisonings, falls, fires, burns, natural and environmental factors, drowning, suffocation, medical and surgical complications and misadventures, and other causes such as those involving machinery, firearms, or electric current. The data presented in the table below are identified by codes V01–X59, Y85–Y86 of the tenth ICD revision (except where noted).

The tables on pages 174 through 177 show the number of injury deaths and the unadjusted death rates for 53 countries for which mortality data and population estimates were obtained.

UNINTENTIONAL INJURY DEATHS AND DEATH RATES BY AGE GROUP, LATEST YEAR AVAILABLE

Country	Year	Deaths		Deaths per 100,000 Population[a]						
		Total	% Male	All Ages	0 to 4	5 to 14	15 to 24	25 to 44	45 to 64	65+
Argentina	2004	10,283	71.2	26.3	20.3	8.5	22.3	23.4	31.4	64.9
Australia	2003	4,956	63.3	24.9	9.9	3.9	23.5	21.1	17.3	79.4
Austria	2005	2,729	61.4	33.1	5.0	3.2	22.6	16.4	24.9	114.0
Belarus[b]	2003	16,513	78.6	167.2	32.9	12.7	80.3	198.1	282.0	188.3
Brazil	2004	57,565	79.9	31.3	15.7	10.4	32.0	34.1	38.5	79.9
Canada	2003	9,047	60.3	28.1	6.2	4.3	22.9	18.6	20.4	103.9
Chile	2004	4,790	77.8	30.3	10.1	6.8	20.5	29.7	40.2	102.3
Colombia	2004	11,034	78.8	26.0	20.0	9.5	26.8	26.0	31.9	84.2
Costa Rica	2004	1,149	74.9	29.0	9.6	7.3	23.1	26.0	34.1	164.3
Croatia	2005	1,896	64.7	42.7	8.7	4.6	29.1	26.0	36.1	126.1
Cuba	2005	4,609	58.7	40.7	10.0	8.2	17.5	21.3	26.3	231.6
Czech Republic	2005	4,270	63.0	41.7	7.8	5.3	25.9	25.8	40.6	130.1
Dominican Republic	2004	1,570	79.6	17.5	5.7	4.6	19.1	24.6	21.6	41.1
Ecuador	2005	4,965	77.7	37.2	21.8	12.5	30.0	41.7	56.2	132.6
El Salvador	2005	2,323	79.3	34.6	11.8	10.2	27.6	42.9	56.1	138.3
Estonia	2005	1,109	76.3	82.4	25.8	11.5	46.2	76.4	137.1	104.9
Finland	2005	3,094	68.4	59.0	6.3	4.8	17.5	31.2	79.0	160.0
France	2004	24,233	54.8	40.0	6.4	2.9	22.7	18.5	25.1	152.6
Germany	2004	18,617	56.7	22.6	4.7	2.3	18.0	11.6	15.2	69.3
Hong Kong, China	2004	825	70.4	12.0	0.8	1.0	5.6	8.6	12.1	42.7
Hungary	2005	5,061	63.8	50.2	6.7	4.1	21.9	29.4	53.0	151.5
Israel	2003	1,274	66.2	19.0	7.0	3.6	15.8	15.7	15.1	81.3
Japan	2004	39,544	61.7	31.3	7.5	3.0	11.2	9.8	21.5	105.8
Kazakhstan[b]	2004	22,128	79.0	147.4	46.9	24.2	105.0	209.8	229.5	192.9
Kyrgyzstan	2005	2,347	75.9	45.9	44.3	9.8	21.5	63.6	93.5	75.4
Latvia	2005	2,227	74.6	96.8	26.6	12.8	43.3	92.9	163.6	123.1
Lithuania	2004	3,071	77.2	89.4	26.0	8.2	43.0	88.0	154.1	127.5
Luxembourg	2005	147	60.5	32.1	10.9	3.5	28.3	25.5	26.7	93.2
Mexico	2005	34,960	76.0	32.9	25.2	8.7	29.3	33.2	43.1	121.1
Netherlands	2004	3,352	53.1	20.6	4.2	2.8	11.6	8.5	11.5	94.1
New Zealand	2003	1,190	62.8	30.1	13.4	6.4	34.2	22.6	25.1	95.2
Nicaragua	2005	1,184	81.1	21.7	10.6	7.2	22.8	25.8	31.0	105.8
Norway	2004	1,980	58.8	43.1	6.9	4.8	27.8	31.0	30.1	151.9
Panama	2004	825	79.5	26.7	22.0	9.1	23.8	27.3	32.5	84.8
Paraguay	2004	1,380	70.4	22.3	11.3	9.3	25.8	28.0	32.1	47.8
Poland	2005	15,844	72.3	41.5	7.9	5.9	25.8	34.0	53.9	96.3
Portugal	2003	3,927	70.1	37.5	9.0	7.5	31.5	28.8	32.9	92.0
Puerto Rico	2003	1,045	80.5	26.9	5.5	3.8	27.6	33.8	29.6	48.4
Republic of Korea	2004	15,954	70.4	32.9	13.9	6.7	13.9	20.7	44.9	144.8
Romania	2004	9,768	75.9	45.1	34.1	13.3	25.0	38.4	64.4	76.2
Russian Federation[b]	2005	315,915	78.0	220.7	38.3	24.2	128.7	269.9	329.9	243.5
Slovakia	2005	2,085	77.6	38.7	11.5	4.7	20.9	31.6	63.4	73.3
Slovenia	2005	746	63.5	37.1	6.8	4.7	25.3	22.9	31.8	113.5
South Africa	2004	10,753	66.7	24.2	24.3	8.6	15.9	30.9	29.1	72.7
Spain	2004	12,278	69.0	28.8	5.9	4.0	24.5	23.1	22.9	71.9
Sweden	2004	3,484	58.3	38.7	8.6	9.2	18.3	17.7	29.5	130.5
Switzerland[b]	2004	3,541	60.6	47.9	5.7	3.4	29.9	27.1	43.0	155.0
Ukraine[b]	2005	69,954	78.8	149.1	36.3	18.4	72.6	170.9	248.5	145.8
United Kingdom	2004	13,167	55.4	22.0	3.9	2.3	15.1	13.4	13.9	77.0
United States of America	2004	112,012	64.3	38.1	13.4	6.5	37.0	35.1	37.6	96.7
Uruguay	2004	1,101	69.1	32.3	29.1	9.0	23.5	22.6	33.8	91.2
Uzbekistan	2005	6,342	75.5	24.2	36.6	11.2	13.7	31.7	34.5	41.2
Venezuela	2004	8,428	76.8	33.8	25.4	12.1	33.9	40.5	41.1	90.5

Source: National Safety Council tabulations of World Health Organization data.
[a]*Population estimates based on data from the World Health Organization and the U.S. Census Bureau (International Data Base)*
[b]*Data include deaths due to all external causes, including self-harm and assault.*

The International Classification of Diseases system (ICD) identifies motor-vehicle traffic accidents by codes V02–V04, V09, V12–V14, V19–V79, V86–V89 of the tenth ICD revision. A motor vehicle is a mechanically or electrically powered device used in the transportation of persons or property on a land highway. A motor-vehicle traffic accident involves a motor vehicle in transport (i.e., in motion or on a roadway) on a public highway.

MOTOR-VEHICLE DEATHS AND DEATH RATES BY AGE GROUP, LATEST YEAR AVAILABLE

Country	Year	Deaths		Deaths per 100,000 Population[a]						
		Total	% Male	All Ages	0 to 4	5 to 14	15 to 24	25 to 44	45 to 64	65+
Argentina	2004	3,114	77.1	8.0	2.3	2.6	9.0	9.2	11.3	10.3
Australia	2003	1,617	72.7	8.1	3.8	2.4	15.7	8.4	6.3	11.0
Austria	2005	413	77.2	5.0	0.8	0.5	10.5	5.0	4.4	6.1
Belarus[b]	2003	2,241	76.1	22.7	2.4	3.7	23.7	28.2	28.3	23.4
Brazil	2004	25,281	82.2	13.7	2.6	3.0	18.3	17.8	16.4	18.0
Canada	2003	2,866	70.0	8.9	1.8	2.5	16.5	9.1	7.9	12.0
Chile	2004	1,174	81.0	7.4	1.6	1.8	6.7	9.5	11.2	10.2
Colombia	2004	5,085	79.4	12.0	3.1	3.6	13.7	14.5	15.2	33.1
Costa Rica	2004	514	82.9	13.0	2.7	3.2	13.6	15.9	18.9	31.7
Croatia	2005	495	79.2	11.1	3.9	1.6	18.1	12.8	9.4	14.0
Cuba	2005	1,158	78.8	10.2	2.3	3.2	9.8	11.6	11.9	16.9
Czech Republic	2005	809	73.5	7.9	1.1	3.0	11.9	8.5	7.4	9.8
Dominican Republic	2004	1,192	81.3	13.3	1.7	2.9	16.4	19.9	16.2	26.7
Ecuador	2005	745	78.9	5.6	1.5	1.0	6.1	7.8	8.7	12.1
El Salvador	2005	1,461	81.6	21.8	4.0	5.9	15.9	29.2	40.9	78.9
Estonia	2005	177	75.7	13.1	4.6	7.2	15.2	16.2	14.3	10.7
Finland	2005	384	76.0	7.3	2.1	2.7	9.5	7.4	6.6	12.0
France	2004	5,151	74.7	8.5	1.5	1.6	17.3	9.9	6.7	9.8
Germany	2004	4,865	72.6	5.9	1.2	1.2	13.1	5.9	4.7	6.7
Hong Kong, China	2004	172	67.4	2.5	0.0	0.3	1.9	1.7	2.7	7.9
Hungary	2005	1,275	75.6	12.6	2.1	2.4	14.2	14.6	14.4	15.0
Israel	2003	321	77.6	4.8	1.5	1.0	7.9	6.6	5.2	4.2
Japan	2004	9,697	69.1	7.7	2.0	1.4	8.0	4.7	6.9	17.1
Kazakhstan[b]	2004	3,042	76.3	20.3	5.4	7.2	19.0	30.5	23.2	20.6
Kyrgyzstan	2005	534	74.2	10.4	1.8	2.5	6.4	18.0	15.7	20.1
Latvia	2005	449	72.2	19.5	2.0	5.1	24.2	24.1	21.7	17.5
Lithuania	2004	737	78.3	21.5	3.2	2.5	27.9	25.1	25.2	23.8
Luxembourg	2005	46	58.7	10.1	3.6	3.5	18.9	12.7	8.0	9.2
Mexico	2005	10,689	78.3	10.1	3.2	2.7	13.0	12.9	12.9	17.7
Netherlands	2004	783	70.9	4.8	0.8	1.4	9.4	4.2	3.6	9.2
New Zealand	2003	504	68.5	12.8	4.3	3.4	24.3	13.5	11.9	15.5
Nicaragua	2005	439	82.2	8.0	2.7	2.3	8.5	11.7	12.7	24.4
Norway	2004	296	72.3	6.4	1.7	1.1	13.4	6.2	4.7	10.9
Panama	2004	392	83.9	12.7	1.5	2.2	15.5	16.4	17.5	28.3
Paraguay	2004	415	78.3	6.7	0.9	1.5	9.4	9.4	11.1	12.8
Poland	2005	4,984	77.5	13.1	2.0	3.0	16.2	14.2	14.2	17.5
Portugal	2003	1,724	79.5	16.5	3.4	3.6	24.5	17.8	15.5	21.3
Puerto Rico	2003	500	78.2	12.9	1.5	2.2	19.5	15.0	14.1	18.2
Republic of Korea	2004	8,012	72.9	16.5	5.9	3.1	9.9	12.0	24.2	57.5
Romania	2004	2,299	76.0	10.6	2.6	4.8	8.8	10.8	12.8	15.6
Russian Federation[b]	2005	40,165	73.1	28.1	4.1	6.8	32.0	35.4	28.8	30.6
Slovakia	2005	625	76.6	11.6	2.3	2.4	12.7	12.5	14.5	14.5
Slovenia	2005	258	73.6	12.8	5.6	3.1	18.1	15.5	10.8	14.9
South Africa	2004	5,153	72.8	11.6	3.9	5.3	9.5	18.4	14.4	15.6
Spain	2004	4,990	77.0	11.7	1.7	2.4	17.9	12.5	10.7	15.1
Sweden	2004	461	74.8	5.1	1.0	0.7	9.0	4.9	4.1	8.7
Switzerland[b]	2004	513	78.2	6.9	1.4	1.5	12.5	6.0	6.4	11.2
Ukraine[b]	2005	9,893	76.2	21.1	3.8	5.1	24.2	26.3	23.7	19.6
United Kingdom	2004	3,315	75.1	5.5	0.9	1.3	10.8	6.6	4.0	6.8
United States of America	2004	44,933	68.6	15.3	3.9	4.1	26.3	16.3	14.7	20.5
Uruguay	2004	347	76.7	10.2	0.4	3.1	11.1	9.5	15.5	16.8
Uzbekistan	2005	2,247	79.2	8.6	3.2	3.8	5.1	13.3	13.7	18.3
Venezuela	2004	3,508	79.7	14.1	3.4	4.1	15.7	19.8	19.2	28.1

Source: National Safety Council tabulations of World Health Organization data.
[a] Population estimates based on data from the World Health Organization and the U.S. Census Bureau (International Data Base).
[b] Data include deaths due to all transportation-related causes, ICD–10 codes V01–V99.

"Accidental falls" are identified by codes W00–W19 in the tenth revision of the International Classification of Diseases system.

FALL-RELATED DEATHS AND DEATH RATES BY AGE GROUP, LATEST YEAR AVAILABLE

Country	Year	Deaths		Deaths per 100,000 Population[a]						
		Total	% Male	All Ages	0 to 4	5 to 14	15 to 24	25 to 44	45 to 64	65+
Argentina	2004	295	69.2	0.8	0.2	0.2	0.4	0.4	0.7	3.5
Australia	2003	717	53.8	3.6	0.2	0.1	1.0	1.0	1.6	21.6
Austria	2005	1,166	49.8	14.2	0.0	0.3	1.6	2.0	7.6	70.1
Belarus	2003	1,181	77.1	12.0	2.2	1.0	3.5	12.3	20.8	18.9
Brazil	2004	6,617	69.7	3.6	0.8	0.5	0.9	2.3	5.0	29.3
Canada	2003	1,978	51.8	6.1	0.1	0.0	0.8	0.9	2.8	39.1
Chile	2004	720	55.8	4.6	0.5	0.2	0.6	1.8	3.7	39.8
Colombia	2004	1,109	78.7	2.6	1.0	0.5	1.2	1.8	4.2	19.6
Costa Rica	2004	79	89.9	2.0	0.3	0.1	1.0	1.5	4.1	11.5
Croatia	2005	747	47.0	16.8	0.5	0.4	0.9	1.7	8.8	82.2
Cuba	2005	1,754	44.9	15.5	0.9	0.1	1.1	1.5	4.7	135.4
Czech Republic	2005	1,474	43.7	14.4	0.8	0.0	0.4	2.3	6.0	84.6
Dominican Republic	2004	30	53.3	0.3	0.2	0.0	0.0	0.0	0.5	4.4
Ecuador	2005	501	79.4	3.7	2.3	0.6	2.3	3.7	6.4	19.4
El Salvador	2005	299	71.2	4.5	1.0	0.6	1.3	3.0	7.1	44.5
Estonia	2005	127	65.4	9.4	0.0	0.0	2.9	5.7	14.0	23.7
Finland	2005	1,239	56.3	23.6	0.4	0.0	0.9	2.3	18.9	110.3
France	2004	5,354	48.2	8.8	0.6	0.1	0.5	1.4	4.5	44.2
Germany	2004	7,913	43.4	9.6	0.5	0.2	0.4	1.1	4.2	44.3
Hong Kong, China	2004	118	62.7	1.7	0.0	0.3	0.3	0.6	1.2	9.4
Hungary	2005	2,102	49.2	20.8	0.0	0.2	0.4	2.7	14.1	103.0
Israel	2003	100	70.0	1.5	0.3	0.1	0.7	0.7	1.1	9.4
Japan	2004	6,412	60.1	5.1	0.5	0.1	0.6	1.0	3.3	19.3
Kazakhstan	2004	479	77.5	3.2	2.2	0.7	2.0	4.6	4.4	4.4
Kyrgyzstan	2005	117	80.3	2.3	3.0	1.2	0.7	2.7	4.6	3.5
Latvia	2005	253	69.2	11.0	1.0	0.4	2.5	6.6	15.6	28.4
Lithuania	2004	434	77.2	12.6	1.9	0.0	1.3	8.2	23.3	30.1
Luxembourg	2005	44	65.9	9.6	0.0	0.0	0.0	5.0	11.6	36.7
Mexico	2005	2,333	78.5	2.2	1.1	0.3	0.8	1.5	3.9	14.8
Netherlands	2004	1,103	46.1	6.8	0.4	0.3	0.3	0.9	3.0	40.4
New Zealand	2003	337	46.6	8.5	0.4	0.3	1.8	0.8	2.9	63.1
Nicaragua	2005	84	76.2	1.5	0.5	0.2	0.8	1.3	3.3	18.4
Norway	2004	783	44.6	17.1	0.0	0.0	1.3	1.1	4.1	105.9
Panama	2004	76	68.4	2.5	0.9	0.6	0.5	1.5	2.7	20.8
Paraguay	2004	33	75.8	0.5	0.6	0.3	0.4	0.3	1.5	0.7
Poland	2005	3,648	51.4	9.6	0.3	0.2	1.1	2.7	7.6	50.2
Portugal	2003	858	52.1	8.2	0.5	0.5	0.7	1.7	5.1	37.2
Puerto Rico	2003	138	73.9	3.6	0.0	0.2	0.2	2.2	4.5	16.0
Republic of Korea	2004	3,358	61.3	6.9	2.0	0.5	0.6	2.8	8.3	46.4
Romania	2004	1,497	79.3	6.9	1.7	0.5	1.4	4.7	12.0	15.5
Russian Federation	2005	12,885	75.3	9.0	1.8	0.8	3.7	8.7	13.6	16.6
Slovakia	2005	472	74.2	8.8	0.8	0.3	1.2	3.6	14.3	32.2
Slovenia	2005	321	52.0	16.0	0.0	0.0	1.5	2.1	9.9	80.8
South Africa	2004	119	64.7	0.3	0.0	0.1	0.1	0.3	0.4	1.6
Spain	2004	1,668	58.0	3.9	0.6	0.3	0.9	1.4	2.8	15.7
Sweden	2004	746	55.4	8.3	0.0	0.0	0.5	0.6	4.2	40.6
Switzerland	2004	1,137	44.6	15.4	0.8	0.1	2.3	1.7	4.3	85.3
Ukraine	2005	3,368	79.7	7.2	1.2	0.5	2.8	6.2	12.2	11.4
United Kingdom	2004	3,763	47.3	6.3	0.2	0.1	0.4	1.1	3.9	31.0
United States of America	2004	18,807	52.4	6.4	0.3	0.1	0.6	1.2	3.6	41.1
Uruguay	2004	38	73.7	1.1	0.0	0.2	0.2	0.8	1.5	3.8
Uzbekistan	2005	444	79.1	1.7	1.9	1.1	1.2	1.9	2.4	3.3
Venezuela	2004	698	63.9	2.8	1.0	0.3	0.9	1.6	3.3	31.1

Source: National Safety Council tabulations of World Health Organization data.
[a] Population estimates based on data from the World Health Organization and the U.S. Census Bureau (International Data Base).

INTERNATIONAL DROWNING DEATHS AND DEATH RATES

The World Health Organization has identified unintentional drowning as a major, but often unrecognized, public health problem. The global mortality rate is estimated at 6.8 cases per 100,000 population, which makes drowning the second leading cause of injury-related death worldwide, following motor-vehicle crashes.[a]

The International Classification of Diseases system (ICD) identifies drowning by codes W65–W74, which include cases of unintentional drowning and submersion while in or following a fall in a bathtub, swimming pool, or natural body of water. Other specified and unspecified cases of drowning and submersion are also included.

[a]van Beeck, E.F., Branche, C.M., Szpilman, D., Modell, J.H., & Bierens, J.J. (2005). A new definition of drowning: towards documentation and prevention of a global public health problem. *Bulletin of the World Health Organization. 83(11): 853-856.*

UNINTENTIONAL DROWNING DEATHS AND DEATH RATES BY AGE GROUP, LATEST YEAR AVAILABLE

Country	Year	Deaths		Deaths per 100,000 Population[a]						
		Total	% Male	All Ages	0 to 4	5 to 14	15 to 24	25 to 44	45 to 64	65+
Argentina	2004	567	80.2	1.4	3.7	1.3	1.6	1.0	1.2	1.1
Australia	2003	192	75.0	1.0	2.2	0.3	1.0	0.9	1.0	1.3
Austria	2005	88	71.6	1.1	1.3	0.3	0.6	0.7	1.4	2.0
Belarus	2003	1,047	80.8	10.6	4.2	3.6	8.6	14.8	12.1	9.9
Brazil	2004	6,431	85.9	3.5	3.3	3.0	4.7	3.5	2.9	3.2
Canada	2003	266	80.5	0.8	0.9	0.6	0.9	0.8	0.7	1.2
Chile	2004	513	88.3	3.2	2.8	1.2	3.8	3.6	3.4	5.4
Colombia	2004	1,115	82.6	2.6	5.0	2.3	3.8	1.8	1.7	2.8
Costa Rica	2004	117	86.3	3.0	2.9	2.3	3.9	2.4	4.5	0.9
Croatia	2005	79	83.5	1.8	0.0	2.0	1.5	1.0	1.8	3.6
Cuba	2005	263	90.5	2.3	1.7	2.6	2.4	2.4	1.9	2.8
Czech Republic	2005	202	74.8	2.0	0.6	0.8	1.8	1.5	2.7	3.0
Dominican Republic	2004	29	58.6	0.3	0.4	0.2	0.2	0.3	0.5	0.6
Ecuador	2005	376	82.4	2.8	3.9	1.7	3.1	2.7	2.6	5.6
El Salvador	2005	310	84.8	4.6	1.8	2.3	6.7	6.6	4.4	4.7
Estonia	2005	59	84.7	4.4	4.6	0.7	3.8	4.9	6.2	3.6
Finland	2005	144	87.5	2.7	2.5	0.8	0.9	2.0	4.5	3.8
France	2004	981	71.9	1.6	1.5	0.3	0.8	1.2	2.0	3.6
Germany	2004	401	71.8	0.5	0.9	0.2	0.3	0.4	0.5	0.9
Hong Kong, China	2004	45	80.0	0.7	0.0	0.3	0.6	0.4	1.0	1.5
Hungary	2005	192	81.8	1.9	1.3	0.7	1.5	2.0	2.5	2.1
Israel	2003	35	74.3	0.5	0.4	0.2	1.0	0.6	0.4	0.6
Japan	2004	5,584	55.6	4.4	1.3	0.7	0.9	0.9	2.9	16.1
Kazakhstan	2004	1,255	82.9	8.4	9.4	5.6	7.1	11.0	8.6	5.6
Kyrgyzstan	2005	258	73.3	5.0	12.6	2.5	3.2	5.5	5.7	4.6
Latvia	2005	250	79.2	10.9	6.9	5.1	6.4	12.8	15.6	9.1
Lithuania	2004	307	82.1	8.9	8.9	2.0	5.3	10.3	11.9	11.2
Luxembourg	2005	2	50.0	0.4	3.6	0.0	0.0	0.0	0.0	1.5
Mexico	2005	2,198	83.8	2.1	3.1	1.3	2.6	1.8	1.9	3.1
Netherlands	2004	96	74.0	0.6	1.5	0.4	0.4	0.2	0.8	1.1
New Zealand	2003	60	80.0	1.5	3.6	0.8	2.0	1.4	1.1	1.7
Nicaragua	2005	196	87.2	3.6	1.2	2.1	5.3	4.1	4.1	6.5
Norway	2004	82	76.8	1.8	1.4	0.3	1.8	1.7	2.0	3.1
Panama	2004	126	85.7	4.1	6.7	2.9	3.2	4.0	3.6	7.5
Paraguay	2004	99	78.8	1.6	1.7	1.0	2.3	1.5	1.8	1.6
Poland	2005	1,011	82.1	2.6	1.8	1.3	2.3	2.4	3.8	2.7
Portugal	2003	167	74.9	1.6	1.3	0.8	1.6	1.3	1.7	2.6
Puerto Rico	2003	46	91.3	1.2	0.7	0.7	2.0	0.8	1.4	1.5
Republic of Korea	2004	964	78.9	2.0	1.3	2.2	1.9	1.4	2.1	4.4
Romania	2004	1,050	76.5	4.8	4.2	3.3	4.0	3.8	6.7	6.1
Russian Federation	2005	14,419	83.6	10.1	4.2	5.9	8.0	12.6	12.5	8.1
Slovakia	2005	138	80.4	2.6	3.1	0.8	1.8	2.1	4.4	2.4
Slovenia	2005	17	76.5	0.8	1.1	0.0	0.0	0.2	1.6	1.9
South Africa	2004	74	74.3	0.2	0.7	0.3	0.1	0.0	0.1	0.1
Spain	2004	572	83.0	1.3	1.2	0.4	1.3	1.1	1.3	2.5
Sweden	2004	98	81.6	1.1	0.6	0.2	0.6	0.5	1.8	2.2
Switzerland	2004	48	68.8	0.6	1.1	0.5	0.5	0.5	0.4	1.5
Ukraine	2005	4,182	84.5	8.9	4.3	5.7	6.8	10.9	11.7	6.5
United Kingdom	2004	201	80.6	0.3	0.4	0.1	0.3	0.4	0.4	0.5
United States of America	2004	3,308	78.4	1.1	2.5	0.7	1.4	1.0	1.0	1.2
Uruguay	2004	71	83.1	2.1	2.3	1.7	3.3	1.6	1.9	2.5
Uzbekistan	2005	1,042	67.5	4.0	15.5	3.3	1.7	2.9	2.7	3.2
Venezuela	2004	598	83.3	2.4	3.4	2.1	3.8	2.1	1.4	1.3

Source: National Safety Council tabulations of World Health Organization data.
[a]Population estimates based on data from the World Health Organization and the U.S. Census Bureau (International Data Base).

OCCUPATIONAL DEATHS

Counts and rates of fatal work-related injuries are shown on this page and the next. Comparisons between countries should be made with caution and take into account the differences in sources, coverage, and kinds of cases included.

OCCUPATIONAL DEATHS BY COUNTRY, 2002–2006

Country	Deaths					Source of Data	Maximum Period[a]	Coverage		
	2002	2003	2004	2005	2006			Worker Types[b]	% of Total Employment[c]	Activities Excluded
Injuries Only — Compensated Cases										
France	686	661	626	—	—	IR	varies	E	75	P
Injuries Only — Reported Cases										
Austria	130	103	132	124	—	IR	none	E, SE	71	none
Azerbaijan	59	52	72	54	81	LR	—	E	—	none
Belarus	228	214	248	235	228	C	same year	E	—	none
Czech Republic	206	199	185	163	152	AR	none	E, SE	95	AF, Pol
Hungary	163	133	160	125	123	LR	90 days	E, SE	98	none
Japan	1,658	1,628	1,620	1,514	1,472	LR	—	E	—	none
Latvia	56	41	61	56	53	S	none	E	—	none
Moldova, Rep. of	41	43	38	49	38	C	none	E	52	none
Norway	39	49	38	48	31	LR	none	E	100	none
Poland	515	515	490	468	493	LR	6 months	E, SE	76	Agr
Puerto Rico	38	29	55	51	—	C	none	E, SE	97	—
Singapore	64	55	51	44	62	LR	none	E	33	none
Slovakia	87	94	79	76	95	C	none	IE	98	none
Spain	805	722	695	662	687	IR	—	—	—	—
Sweden	60	56	57	67	—	IR	none	E, SE	97	none
Taiwan, China	507	401	366	382	—	LR	—	—	—	—
Ukraine	1,227	1,128	1,068	989	972	LR	4 months	E	71	AF
United Kingdom	191	174	179	173	—	LR	1 year	E, SE	92	SF, AT
United States	5,534	5,575	5,764	5,734	—	C	none	E, SE	100	none
Injuries and Commuting Accidents — Compensated Cases										
Croatia	44	47	38	62	76	IR	immediate	E, SE	84	none
Germany	1,071	1,029	949	863	—	IR	none	E, SE	100	none
Italy	934	976	930	918	938	IR	none	I	76	none
Injuries and Commuting Accidents — Reported Cases										
Hong Kong, China	210	171	187	187	—	LR	none	E	77	none
Kyrgyzstan	37	26	41	24	22	LR	none	E	33	none
Lithuania	83	118	94	118	108	LR	none	E, SE	64	AF
Romania	442	423	432	529	353	LR	same year	E, SE	61	AF, P
Russian Federation	3,920	3,540	3,290	3,090	2,881	S	none	E	5	Low
Slovenia	32	40	21	21	32	LR	1 month	I	85	none
Injuries and Diseases — Compensated Cases										
Australia[d]	200	187	159	—	—	IR	3 years	E	83	AF
Canada	934	963	928	1,097	—	IR	none	E, SE	85	AF
Finland	37	43	44	51	—	IR	1 year	E	85	none
Malta	4	12	12	6	8	IR	—	E, SE	—	none
Switzerland	53	46	67	45	—	IR	same year	IE	88	none
Injuries and Diseases — Reported Cases										
Iceland	0	4	2	3	6	AR	none	E	—	none
Sri Lanka	36	42	42	52	84	LR	1 year	E	35	M, E, TSC, C
Turkey	878	811	843	1,096	1,601	IR	—	IE	25	none
Injuries, Diseases, and Commuting Accidents — Compensated Cases										
Costa Rica	60	55	50	60	—	IR	none	I	56	none
Estonia	35	31	34	24	28	IR	1 year	I	100	AF, Pol
Israel	91	88	88	82	84	IR	same year	E, SE	100	none
South Korea[e]	1,271	1,408	1,417	1,288	1,238	IR	—	I	45	none
Syrian Arab Republic	383	174	205	612	—	LR	—	I	46	none
Thailand	650	787	861	1,444	—	IR	—	I	16	none
Injuries, Diseases, and Commuting Accidents — Reported Cases										
Bahrain	14	21	13	29	25	IR	none	E, SE	100	none
Bulgaria	115	114	130	130	—	AR	—	E, SE	35	none
Jordan	49	70	52	63	87	IR	none	E	—	AF
Mexico	1,361	1,427	1,364	1,367	1,328	IR	none	IE	32	none
New Zealand	81	84	82	91	84	IR	1 year	E, SE	100	none

Source: International Labour Office. (2006). Yearly Data of Total and Economically Active Population, Employment, Unemployment, Hours of Work, Wages, Labour Cost, Consumer Price Indices, Occupational Injuries, Strikes and Lockouts: 1969–2005. Data available at http://laborsta.ilo.org
Note: Dash (—) indicates data not available.
[a]*Maximum period between accident and death for death to be counted.*
[b]*Types of workers included in the data.*
[c]*Workers covered by the statistics as a percentage of total employment; latest year available.*
[d]*Excluding Victoria and Australian Capital Territory.*
[e]*Establishments with 10 or more workers.*

Source of Data	Worker Types	Economic Activities		
AR = Administrative reports	E = Employees	AF = Armed forces	D = Domestic services	PA = Public administration
C = Census	I = Insured persons	Agr = Agriculture	E = Electricity, gas, and water	Pol = Police
IR = Insurance records	IE = Insured employees	ASO = Air, sea, offshore accidents	Low = Activities with low rates of injuries	SF = Sea fishing
LR = Labor inspectorate records	SE = Self-employed	AT = Air transport	M = Manufacturing	TSC = Transport, storage, and communications
S = Survey		C = Construction	P = Public sector	

OCCUPATIONAL DEATH RATES

The International Labour Organization (ILO) estimates that approximately 270 million work-related injuries occur worldwide every year. The annual death toll is approaching 350,000 worldwide and is expected to increase even further in the foreseeable future.

Source: International Labour Organization. (2004). Global Estimates of Fatalities Caused by Work Related Diseases and Occupational Accidents, 2002. [http://www.ilo.org/public/english/protection/safework/accidis/globest_2002/dis_world.htm, accessed 8/23/07].

OCCUPATIONAL DEATH RATES BY COUNTRY, 2002–2006

Country	Coverage[a]	2002	2003	2004	2005	2006
Deaths per 100,000 Employed Persons						
Injuries Only						
Azerbaijan	RC	6	6	8	6	8
Belarus	RC	5.9	5.6	6.4	6.1	5.8
Hungary	RC	4.21	3.39	4.1	3.2	3.13
Moldova, Rep. of	RC	5.3	5.6	4.9	6.4	4.7
Norway	RC	1.7	2.1	1.7	2.1	1.3
Poland	RC	4.9	4.9	4.7	4.4	4.6
Sweden	RC	1.4	1.3	1.4	1.6	—
Ukraine	RC	10	9.4	8.9	8.4	8.3
United Kingdom	RC	0.74	0.7	0.7	0.6	—
United States	RC	4	4	4	4	—
Injuries and Commuting Accidents						
Croatia	CC	3.31	3.4	2.7	4.3	5
Germany	CC	2.92	2.83	2.57	2.38	—
Hong Kong, China	RC	8.6	7.2	7.7	7.5	—
Lithuania	RC	8.1	11.3	9	10.9	9.6
Kyrgyzstan	RC	7	5	8	5	5
Romania	RC	7	7	7	9	6
Russian Federation	RC	13.8	13.1	12.9	12.4	11.8
Injuries and Diseases						
Australia	CC	2.5	2.3	1.9	—	—
Canada	CC	6.1	6.1	5.8	6.8	—
Finland	CC	1.8	2.1	2.1	2.4	—
Malta	CC	2.82	8.2	8.1	4	5.2
Injuries, Diseases, and Commuting Accidents						
Israel	CC	3.83	3.6	3.3	3	3
Bahrain	RC	7.5	10	5	10	8
Deaths per 100,000 Workers Insured						
Injuries Only						
France	CC	3.8	3.7	3.5	—	—
Austria	RC	4.74	3.86	5	4.6	—
Czech Republic	RC	4.6	4.5	4.2	3.7	3.4
Slovakia	RC	4.29	4.66	3.91	3.72	4.6
Spain	RC	6.06	5.27	4.89	4.5	4.4
Taiwan, China	RC	6.5	5	4.4	4.5	—
Injuries and Commuting Accidents						
Italy	CC	5	5	5	5	—
Slovenia	RC	4	5.1	2.6	2.6	3.8
Injuries and Diseases						
Switzerland	CC	1.5	1.3	1.9	1.3	—
Turkey	RC	16.8	14.4	13.6	15.8	20.5
Injuries, Diseases, and Commuting Accidents						
Costa Rica	CC	7.5	7	6.1	6.4	—
Estonia	CC	5.98	5.22	5.71	3.95	4.3
Thailand	CC	9.94	11.19	11.66	18.7	—
Bulgaria	RC	6	5.2	6	5.8	—
Mexico	RC	11	12	11	11	10
Deaths per 1,000,000 Hours Worked						
Injuries Only						
Japan	RC	0.01	0.01	0.01	0.01	—
Injuries and Diseases						
Sri Lanka	RC	0.008	0.01	0.007	0.009	0.0135
Injuries, Diseases, and Commuting Accidents						
Jordan	RC	0.052	0.062	0.039	0.025	0.055
South Korea	CC	0.05	0.06	0.06	0.05	0.05

See source and limitations of data on page 170.
Note: Dash (—) indicates data not available.
[a]Includes reported cases (RC) and compensated cases (CC) of occupational fatalities.

NATIONAL SAFETY COUNCIL

INJURY FACTS®

This appendix gives a brief explanation of some of the sources and methods used by the National Safety Council (NSC) Statistics Department in preparing the estimates of deaths, injuries, and costs presented in this book. Because many of the estimates depend on death certificate data provided by the states or the National Center for Health Statistics (NCHS), it begins with a brief introduction to the certification and classification of deaths.

Certification and classification. The medical certification of death involves entering information on the death certificate about the disease or condition directly leading to death, antecedent causes, and other significant conditions. The death certificate is then registered with the appropriate authority and a code is assigned for the underlying cause of death. The underlying cause is defined as "(a) the disease or injury which initiated the train of morbid events leading directly to death, or (b) the circumstances of the accident or violence which produced the fatal injury" (World Health Organization [WHO], 1992). Deaths are classified and coded on the basis of a WHO standard, the *International Statistical Classification of Diseases and Related Health Problems*, commonly known as the International Classification of Diseases or ICD (WHO, 1992). For deaths due to injury and poisoning, the ICD provides a system of "external cause" codes to which the underlying cause of death is assigned. (See pages 18–19 of *Injury Facts*® for a condensed list of external cause codes.)

Comparability across ICD revisions. The ICD is revised periodically and these revisions can affect comparability from year to year. The sixth revision (1948) substantially expanded the list of external causes and provided for classifying the place of occurrence. Changes in the classification procedures for the sixth revision as well as the seventh (1958) and eighth (1968) revisions classified as diseases some deaths previously classified as injuries. The eighth revision also expanded and reorganized some external cause sections. The ninth revision (1979), provided more detail on the agency involved, the victim's activity, and the place of occurrence. The tenth revision, which was adopted in the United States effective with 1999 data, completely revised the transportation-related categories. Specific external cause categories affected by the revisions are noted in the historical tables.

The table at the end of this appendix (page 186) shows the ICD-9 codes, the ICD-10 codes, and a comparability ratio for each of the principal causes of unintentional-injury death. The comparability ratio represents the net effect of the new revision on statistics for the cause of death. The comparability ratio was obtained by classifying a sample of death certificates under both ICD-9 and ICD-10 and then dividing the number of deaths for a selected cause classified under ICD-10 by the number classified to the most nearly comparable ICD-9 cause. A comparability ratio of 1.00 indicates no net change due to the new classification scheme. A ratio less than 1.00 indicates fewer deaths assigned to a cause under ICD-10 than under ICD-9. A ratio greater than 1.00 indicates an increase in assignment of deaths to a cause under ICD-10 compared to ICD-9.

The broad category of "accidents" or "unintentional injuries" under ICD-9 included complications and misadventures of surgical and medical care (E870–E879) and adverse effects of drugs in therapeutic use (E930–E949). These categories are not included in "accidents" or "unintentional injuries" under ICD-10. In 1998, deaths in these two categories numbered 3,228 and 276, respectively.

Under ICD-9, the code range for falls (E880–E888) included a code for "fracture, cause unspecified" (E887). A similar code does not appear in ICD-10 (W00–W19), which probably accounts for the low comparability ratio (0.8409). In 1998, deaths in code E887 numbered 3,679.

Beginning with 1970 data, tabulations published by NCHS no longer include deaths of nonresident aliens. In 2004, there were 916 such accidental deaths, of which 344 were motor-vehicle related.

Fatality estimates. The Council uses four classes and three venues to categorize unintentional injuries. The four classes are Motor Vehicle, Work, Home, and Public. Each class represents an environment and an intervention route for injury prevention through a responsible authority such as a police department, an employer, a home owner, or public health department. The three venues are Transportation, Work, and Home & Community.

Motor vehicle. The Motor-Vehicle class can be identified by the underlying cause of death (see the table on page 186).

Work. The National Safety Council adopted the Bureau of Labor Statistics' Census of Fatal Occupational Injuries (CFOI) figure, beginning with the 1992 data year, as the authoritative count of unintentional work-related deaths. The CFOI system is described in detail in Toscano and Windau (1994).

The 2-Way Split. After subtracting the Motor-Vehicle and Work figures from the unintentional-injury total (ICD-10 codes V01–X59, Y85–Y86), the remainder belong to the Home and Public classes. The Home class can be identified by the "place of occurrence" subclassification (code .0) used with most nontransport deaths; the Public class is the remainder. Missing "place of occurrence" information, however, prevents the direct determination of the Home and Public class totals. Because of this, the Council allocates nonmotor-vehicle, nonwork deaths into the Home and Public classes based on the external cause, age group, and cases with specified "place of occurrence." This procedure, known as the 2-Way Split, uses the most recent death certificate data available from the NCHS and the CFOI data for the same calendar year. For each cause-code group and age group combination, the Motor-Vehicle and Work deaths are subtracted and the remainder, including those with "place of occurrence" unspecified, are allocated to Home and Public in the same proportion as those with "place of occurrence" specified.

The table on page 186 shows the ICD-10 cause-codes and CFOI event codes for the most common causes of unintentional-injury death. The CFOI event codes (BLS, 1992) do not match exactly with ICD cause codes, so there is some error in the allocation of deaths among the classes.

State reporting system. The Council operates a reporting system through which participating states send tabulations of unintentional-injury death data by age group, class, and type of event or industry. This is known as the Injury Mortality Tabulation reporting system. These data are used to make current year estimates based on the most recent 2-Way Split and CFOI data.

Linking up to current year. The benchmark data published by NCHS are usually two years old and the CFOI data are usually one year old. The link-relative technique is used to make current year estimates from these data using the state vital statistics data. This method assumes that the change in deaths from one year to the next in states reporting for both years reflects the change in deaths for the entire nation. The ratio is calculated and multiplied times the benchmark figure resulting in an estimate for the next year. It may be necessary to repeat the process, depending on the reference year of the benchmark. For example, the 2004 NCHS and CFOI data were used this year for a 2-Way Split and state data were used to make estimates for 2005 and 2006 Home and Public classes using the link-relative technique. CFOI data for 2005 and 2006 were also available so it was not necessary to make Work estimates.

Revisions of prior years. When the figures for a given year are published by NCHS, the 2-Way Split based on those figures and the CFOI become the final estimate of unintentional-injury deaths by class, age group, and type of event or industry. Subsequent years are revised by repeating the link-relative process described above. For example, in the current edition of *Injury Facts*®, the 2004 NCHS and CFOI data were used to produce final estimates using the 2-Way Split, the 2005 estimates were revised using more complete state data and 2005 CFOI figures, and the new 2006 estimates were made with the state data available in the late summer of 2007 together with 2006 CFOI data.

Nonfatal injury estimates. The Council uses the concept of "disabling injury" to define the kinds of injuries included in its estimates. See page 23 for the definition of disabling injury and the National Health Interview Survey (NHIS) injury definitions.

Injury to death ratios. There is no national injury surveillance system that provides disabling injury estimates on a current basis. The National Health Interview Survey, a household survey conducted by the NCHS (see page 23), produces national estimates using its own definition of injury (Schiller, Adams, & Coriaty Nelson, 2005). For this reason, the Council uses injury-to-death ratios to estimate nonfatal disabling injuries for the current year. Complete documentation of the procedure, effective with the 1993 edition, may be found in Landes, Ginsburg, Hoskin, and Miller (1990).

The resulting estimates are not direct measures of nonfatal injuries and should not be compared with prior years.

Population sources. All population figures used in computing rates are estimates taken from various reports published by the Bureau of the Census, U.S. Department of Commerce, on their Internet web site (www.census.gov). *Resident* population is used for computing rates.

Costs (pp. 4–7). The procedures for estimating the economic losses due to fatal and nonfatal unintentional injuries were extensively revised for the 1993 edition of *Accident Facts®*. New components were added, new benchmarks adopted, and a new discount rate assumed. All of these changes resulted in significantly higher cost estimates. For this reason, it must be re-emphasized that the cost estimates should not be compared to those in earlier editions of the book.

The Council's general philosophy underlying its cost estimates is that the figures represent income not received or expenses incurred because of fatal and nonfatal unintentional injuries. Stated this way, the Council's cost estimates are a measure of the economic impact of unintentional injuries and may be compared to other economic measures such as gross domestic product, per capita income, or personal consumption expenditures. (See page 91 and "lost quality of life" [p. 185] for a discussion of injury costs for cost-benefit analysis.)

The general approach followed was to identify a benchmark unit cost for each component, adjust the benchmark to the current year using an appropriate inflator, estimate the number of cases to which the component applied, and compute the product. Where possible, benchmarks were obtained for each class: Motor Vehicle, Work, Home, and Public.

Wage and productivity losses include the value of wages, fringe benefits, and household production for all classes, and travel delay for the Motor Vehicle class.

For fatalities, the present value of after-tax wages, fringe benefits, and household production was computed using the human capital method. The procedure incorporates data on life expectancy from the NCHS life tables, employment likelihood from the Bureau of Labor Statistics household survey, and mean earnings from the Bureau of the Census money income survey. The discount rate used was 4%, reduced from 6% used in earlier years. The present value obtained is highly sensitive to the discount rate; the lower the rate, the greater the present value.

For permanent partial disabilities, an average of 17% of earning power is lost (Berkowitz & Burton, 1987). The incidence of permanent disabilities, adjusted to remove intentional injuries, was computed from data on hospitalized cases from the National Hospital Discharge Survey (NHDS) and nonhospitalized cases from the National Health Interview Survey and National Council on Compensation Insurance data on probabilities of disability by nature of injury and part of body injured.

For temporary disabilities, an average daily wage, fringe benefit, and household production loss was calculated and this was multiplied by the number of days of restricted activity from the NHIS.

Travel delay costs were obtained from the Council's estimates of the number of fatal, injury, and property damage crashes and an average delay cost per crash from Miller et al. (1991).

Medical expenses, including ambulance and helicopter transport costs, were estimated for fatalities, hospitalized cases, and nonhospitalized cases in each class.

The incidence of hospitalized cases was derived from the NHDS data adjusted to eliminate intentional injuries. Average length of stay was benchmarked from Miller, Pindus, Douglass, and Rossman (1993b) and adjusted to estimate lifetime length of stay. The cost per hospital day was benchmarked to the National Medical Expenditure Survey (NMES).

Nonhospitalized cases were estimated by taking the difference between total NHIS injuries and hospitalized cases. Average cost per case was based on NMES data adjusted for inflation and lifetime costs.

Medical cost of fatalities was benchmarked to data from the National Council on Compensation Insurance

(1989) to which was added the cost of a premature funeral and coroner costs (Miller et al., 1991).

Cost per ambulance transport was benchmarked to NMES data and cost per helicopter transport was benchmarked to data in Miller et al. (1993a). The number of cases transported was based on data from Rice and MacKenzie (1989) and the National Electronic Injury Surveillance System.

Administrative expenses include the administrative cost of private and public insurance, which represents the cost of having insurance, and police and legal costs.

The administrative cost of motor-vehicle insurance was the difference between premiums earned (adjusted to remove fire, theft, and casualty premiums) and pure losses incurred, based on data from A. M. Best. Workers' compensation insurance administration was based on A. M. Best data for private carriers and regression estimates using Social Security Administration data for state funds and the self-insured. Administrative costs of public insurance (mainly Medicaid and Medicare) amount to about 4% of the medical expenses paid by public insurance, which were determined from Rice and MacKenzie (1989) and Hensler et al. (1991).

Average police costs for motor-vehicle crashes were taken from Miller et al. (1991) and multiplied by the Council's estimates of the number of fatal, injury and property damage crashes.

Legal expenses include court costs, and plaintiff's and defendant's time and expenses. Hensler et al. (1991) provided data on the proportion of injured persons who hire a lawyer, file a claim, and get compensation. Kakalik and Pace (1986) provided data on costs per case.

Fire losses were based on data published by the National Fire Protection Association in the *NFPA Journal*. The allocation into the classes was based on the property use for structure fires and other NFPA data for nonstructure fires.

Motor-vehicle damage costs were benchmarked to Blincoe and Faigin (1992) and multiplied by the Council's estimates of crash incidence.

Employer costs for work injuries is an estimate of the productivity costs incurred by employers. It assumes each fatality or permanent injury resulted in 4 person-months of disruption, serious injuries 1 person-month, and minor to moderate injuries 2 person-days. All injuries to nonworkers were assumed to involve 2 days of worker productivity loss. Average hourly earnings for supervisors and nonsupervisory workers were computed and then multiplied by the incidence and hours lost per case. Property damage and production delays (except motor-vehicle related) are not included in the estimates but can be substantial.

Lost quality of life is the difference between the value of a statistical fatality or statistical injury and the value of after-tax wages, fringe benefits, and household production. Because this does not represent real income not received or expenses incurred, it is not included in the total economic cost figure. If included, the resulting *comprehensive costs* can be used in cost-benefit analysis because the total costs then represent the maximum amount society should spend to prevent a statistical death or injury.

Work deaths and injuries (p. 48). The method for estimating total work-related deaths and injuries is discussed above. The breakdown of deaths by industry division for the current year is obtained from the CFOI and state Injury Mortality Tabulation figures using the link-relative technique (also discussed above).

The estimate of nonfatal disabling injuries by industry division is made by multiplying the estimate of employment for each industry division by the BLS estimate of the incidence rate of cases involving days away from work for each division (e.g., BLS, 2007) and then adjusting the results so that they add to the work-injury total previously established. The "private sector" average incidence rate is used for the government division, which is not covered in the BLS survey.

Employment. The employment estimates for 1992 to the present were changed for the 1998 edition. Estimates for these years in prior editions are not comparable. The total employment figure used by the Council represents the number of persons in the civilian labor force, aged 16 and older, who were wage or salary workers, self-employed, or unpaid family workers, plus active duty military personnel resident in the U.S. The total employment estimate is a combination of three figures—total civilian employment from the Current Population Survey (CPS) as published in *Employment and Earnings*, plus the difference between total resident population and total civilian population, which represents active duty military personnel.

Employment by industry is obtained from an unpublished Bureau of Labor Statistics table titled "Employed and experience unemployed persons by detailed industry and class of worker, Annual Average [year] (based on CPS)."

Time lost (p. 51) is the product of the number of cases and the average time lost per case. Deaths average

150 workdays lost in the current year and 5,850 in future years; permanent disabilities involve 75 and 565 days lost in current and future years, respectively; temporary disabilities involve 17 days lost in the current year only. Off-the-job injuries to workers are assumed to result in similar lost time.

Off-the-job (p. 52) deaths and injuries are estimated by assuming that employed persons incur injuries at the same rate as the entire population.

Motor-Vehicle (pp. 86–117). Estimates of miles traveled, registered vehicles and licensed drivers are published by the Federal Highway Administration in *Highway Statistics* and *Traffic Volume Trends*.

SELECTED UNINTENTIONAL-INJURY CODE GROUPINGS

Manner of Injury	ICD-9 Codes[a]	ICD-10 Codes[b]	Comparability Ratio[c]	OI & ICM[d] Event Codes
Unintentional Injuries	E800–E869, E880–E929[e]	V01–X59, Y85–Y86	1.0305 (1.0278–1.0333)[f]	00–60, 63–9999
Railway accident	E800–E807	V05, V15, V80.6, V81(.2–.9)	n/a	44
Motor-vehicle accident	E810–E825	V02–V04, V09.0, V09.2, V12–V14, V19.0–V19.2, V19.4–V19.6, V20–V79, V80.3–V80.5, V81.0–V81.1, V82.0–V82.1, V83–V86, V87.0–V87.8, V88.0–V88.8, V89.0, V89.2	0.9754 (0.9742–0.9766)	41, 42, 43 with source = 82, 83
Water transport accident	E830–E838	V90–V94	n/a	45
Air transport accident	E840–E845	V95–V97	n/a	46
Poisoning by solids and liquids	E850–58, E860–66	X40–X49	n/a	344
Poisoning by gases and vapors	E867–E869			341
Falls	E880–E888	W00–W19	0.8409 (0.8313–0.8505)	1
Fires and burns	E890–E899	X00–X09	0.9743 (0.9568–0.9918)	51
Drowning	E910	W65–W74	0.9965 (0.9716–1.0213)	381
Suffocation by ingestion or inhalation	E911–E912	W78–W80	n/a	382
Mechanical suffocation	E913	W75–W77, W81–W84	n/a	383, 384, 389
Firearms	E922	W32–W34	1.0579 (1.0331–1.0828)	0220, 0222, 0229 with source = 911[g]

Source: National Safety Council.
Note: n/a means comparability ratio not calculated or does not meet standards of reliability or precision.
[a]WHO (1977).
[b]WHO (1992).
[c]Hoyert, Arias, Smith, et al. (2001). Table III.

[d]BLS (1992).
[e]The National Safety Council has used E800–E949 for unintentional injuries. The code group in the table omits complications and misadventures of surgical and medical care (E870–E879) and adverse effects of drugs in therapeutic use (E930–E949).
[f]Figures in parentheses are the 95% confidence interval for the comparability ratio.
[g]Struck by flying object where the source of injury was a bullet.

Berkowitz, M., & Burton, J.F., Jr. (1987). *Permanent Disability Benefits in Workers' Compensation*. Kalamazoo, MI: W.E. Upjohn Institute for Employment Research.

Blincoe, L.J., & Faigin, B.M. (1992). *Economic Cost of Motor Vehicle Crashes*, 1990. Springfield, VA: National Technical Information Service.

Bureau of Labor Statistics [BLS]. (1992). *Occupational Injury & Illness Classification Manual*. Itasca, IL: National Safety Council.

Bureau of Labor Statistics [BLS]. (2007, October 16). *Workplace Injuries and Illnesses in 2006*. Press release USDL-07-1562.

Hensler, D.R., Marquis, M.S., Abrahamse, A.F., Berry, S.H., Ebener, P.A., Lewis, E.D., Lind, E.A., MacCoun, R.J., Manning, W.G., Rogowski, J.A., & Vaiana, M.E. (1991). *Compensation for Accidental Injuries in the United States*. Santa Monica, CA: The RAND Corporation.

Hoyert, D.L., Arias, E., Smith, B.L., Murphy, S.L., & Kochanek, K.D. (2001). Deaths: final data for 1999. *National Vital Statistics Reports, 49*(8).

Kakalik, J.S., & Pace, N. (1986). *Costs and Compensation Paid in Tort Litigation*. R-3391-ICJ. Santa Monica, CA: The RAND Corporation.

Landes, S.R., Ginsburg, K.M., Hoskin, A.F., & Miller, T.A. (1990). *Estimating Nonfatal Injuries*. Itasca, IL: Statistics Department, National Safety Council.

Miller, T., Viner, J., Rossman, S., Pindus, N., Gellert, W., Douglass, J., Dillingham, A., & Blomquist, G. (1991). *The Costs of Highway Crashes*. Springfield, VA: National Technical Information Service.

Miller, T.R., Brigham, P.A., Cohen, M.A., Douglass, J.B., Galbraith, M.S., Lestina, D.C., Nelkin, V.S., Pindus, N.M., & Smith-Regojo, P. (1993a). Estimating the costs to society of cigarette fire injuries. *Report to Congress in Response to the Fire Safe Cigarette Act of 1990*. Washington, DC: U.S. Consumer Product Safety Commission.

Miller, T.R., Pindus, N.M., Douglass, J.B., & Rossman, S.B. (1993b). *Nonfatal Injury Incidence, Costs, and Consequences: A Data Book*. Washington, DC: The Urban Institute Press.

Rice, D.P., & MacKenzie, E.J. (1989). *Cost of Injury in the United States: A Report to Congress*. Atlanta, GA: Centers for Disease Control and Prevention.

Schiller, J.S., Adams, P.F., & Coriaty Nelson Z. (2005). Summary health statistics for the U.S. population: National health interview survey, 2003. *Vital and Health Statistics, Series 10, No. 224*. Hyattsville, MD: National Center for Health Statistics.

Toscano, G., & Windau, J. (1994). The changing character of fatal work injuries. *Monthly Labor Review, 117*(10), 17–28.

World Health Organization. (1977). *Manual of the International Statistical Classification of Diseases, Injuries, and Causes of Death*. Geneva, Switzerland: Author.

World Health Organization. (1992). *International Statistical Classification of Diseases and Related Health Problems—Tenth Revision*. Geneva, Switzerland: Author.

The following organizations may be useful for obtaining more current data or more detailed information on various subjects in *Injury Facts*®.

American Association of Poison Control Centers
3201 New Mexico Avenue, Suite 330
Washington, DC 20016
(202) 362-7217
www.aapcc.org
info@aapcc.org

Bureau of Labor Statistics
U.S. Department of Labor
2 Massachusetts Avenue, NE
Washington, DC 20212
(202) 691-5200
www.bls.gov
blsdata_staff@bls.gov

Bureau of the Census
U.S. Department of Commerce
Public Information Office
Washington, DC 20233-0001
(800) 321-1995
www.census.gov

Bureau of Justice Statistics
810 7th Street, NW
Washington, DC 20531
(202) 307-0765
www.ojp.usdoj.gov/bjs
askbjs@usdoj.gov

Bureau of Transportation Statistics
U.S. Department of Transportation
400 7th Street, SW, Room 3430
Washington, DC 20590
(800) 853-1351
www.bts.gov
answers@bts.gov

Centers for Disease Control and Prevention
1600 Clifton Road
Atlanta, GA 30333
(800) 311-3435
www.cdc.gov

Chemical Safety Board
2175 K Street, NW, Suite 400
Washington, DC 20037
(202) 261-7600
www.chemsafety.gov
info@csb.gov

Eno Transportation Foundation
1634 I Street, NW, Suite 500
Washington, DC 20006
(202) 879-4700
www.enotrans.com

Environmental Protection Agency, U.S.
1200 Pennsylvania Avenue, NW
Washington, DC 20460
(202) 272-0167
www.epa.gov

European Agency for Safety and Health at Work
Gran Via, 33
E-48009 Bilbao, Spain
Phone: +34 944-794-360
Fax: +34 944-794-383
http://europe.osha.eu.int
information@osha.eu.int

Federal Aviation Administration
U.S. Department of Transportation
National Aviation Safety Data Analysis Center
800 Independence Avenue, SW
Washington, DC 20591
(866) 835-5322
www.faa.gov

Federal Bureau of Investigation
935 Pennsylvania Avenue, NW
Washington, DC 20535-0001
(202) 324-3000
www.fbi.gov

Federal Highway Administration
U.S. Department of Transportation
400 7th Street, SW
Washington, DC 20590
(202) 366-0660
www.fhwa.dot.gov
execsecretariat.fhwa@fhwa.dot.gov

Federal Motor Carrier Safety Administration
U.S. Department of Transportation
400 7th Street, SW
Washington, DC 20590
(800) 832-5660
www.fmcsa.dot.gov

Federal Railroad Administration
U.S. Department of Transportation
1120 Vermont Avenue, NW
Washington, DC 20590
(202) 493-6000
www.fra.dot.gov

Federal Transit Administration
400 7th Street, SW
Washington, DC 20590
www.fta.dot.gov

FedStats
Gateway to official statistical information available to the public from more than 100 federal agencies.
www.fedstats.gov

FirstGov
Gateway to federal, state, local, tribal, and international government websites.
www.firstgov.gov

Insurance Information Institute
110 William Street
New York, NY 10038
(212) 346-5500
www.iii.org

Insurance Institute for Highway Safety
1005 N. Glebe Road, Suite 800
Arlington, VA 22201
(703) 247-1500
www.highwaysafety.org

International Hunter Education Association
P.O. Box 490
Wellington, CO 80549-0490
(970) 568-7954
www.ihea.com
info@ihea.com

International Labour Office
4, rue des Morillons
CH-1211 Geneva 22
Switzerland
Phone: +41-22-799-6111
Fax: +41-22-798-8685
www.ilo.org
ilo@ilo.org

Mine Safety and Health Administration
1100 Wilson Boulevard, 21st Floor
Arlington, VA 22209-3939
(202) 693-9400
www.msha.gov

Motorcycle Safety Foundation
2 Jenner Street, Suite 150
Irvine, CA 92718-3812
(714) 727-3227
www.msf-usa.org

National Academy of Social Insurance
1776 Massachusetts Avenue, NW, Suite 615
Washington, DC 20036-1904
(202) 452-8097
www.nasi.org
nasi@nasi.org

National Center for Education Statistics
U.S. Department of Education
1990 K Street, NW
Washington, DC 20006
(202) 502-7300
http://nces.ed.gov

National Center for Health Statistics
3311 Toledo Road, Room 2217
Hyattsville, MD 20782
(301) 458-4000
www.cdc.gov/nchs

National Center for Injury Prevention and Control
Office Of Communication Resources, Mail Stop K65
4770 Buford Highway, NE
Atlanta, GA 30341-3724
(770) 488-1506
www.cdc.gov/ncipc
ohcinfo@cdc.gov

National Clearinghouse for Alcohol and Drug Information
P.O. Box 2345
Rockville, MD 20847-2345
(301) 468-2600 or (800) 729-6686
www.health.org

National Climatic Data Center
151 Patton Avenue
Asheville, NC 28801-5001
(828) 271-4800
www.ncdc.noaa.gov/oa/ncdc.html
ncdc.info@noaa.gov

National Collegiate Athletic Association
700 W. Washington Street
P.O. Box 6222
Indianapolis, IN 46206-6222
(317) 917-6222
www.ncaa.org

National Council on Compensation Insurance
901 Peninsula Corporate Circle
Boca Raton, FL 33487
(800) NCCI-123 (800-622-4123)
www.ncci.com

National Fire Protection Association
P.O. Box 9101
Batterymarch Park
Quincy, MA 02269-0910
(617) 770-3000 or (800) 344-3555
www.nfpa.org
osds@nfpa.org

National Highway Traffic Safety Administration
U.S. Department of Transportation
400 7th Street, SW
Washington, DC 20590
(888) 327-4236
www.nhtsa.dot.gov
    National Center for Statistics and Analysis (NPO-121)
    (202) 366-4198 or (800) 934-8517
    NCSAweb@nhtsa.dot.gov

National Institute for Occupational Safety and Health
Clearinghouse for Occupational Safety and Health
    Information
4676 Columbia Parkway
Cincinnati, OH 45226
(800) 356-4674
www.cdc.gov/niosh
eidtechinfo@cdc.gov

National Spinal Cord Injury Association
6701 Democracy Boulevard, Suite 300-9
Bethesda, MD 20817
(301) 214-4006
www.spinalcord.org
info@spinalcord.org

National Sporting Goods Association
1601 Feehanville Drive, Suite 300
Mt. Prospect, IL 60056
(800) 815-5422
www.nsga.org
info@nsga.org

National Transportation Safety Board
490 L'Enfant Plaza East, SW
Washington, DC 20594
(202) 314-6000
www.ntsb.gov

Occupational Safety and Health Administration
U.S. Department of Labor
Office of Statistics
200 Constitution Avenue, NW
Washington, DC 20210
(800) 321-OSHA (6742)
www.osha.gov

Prevent Blindness America
211 W. Wacker Dr., Suite 1700
Chicago, IL 60606
(800) 331-2020
www.preventblindness.org
info@preventblindness.org

Transportation Research Board
500 5th Street, NW
Washington, DC 20001
(202) 334-2934
www.nas.edu/trb

U.S. Coast Guard
2100 2nd Street, SW
Washington, DC 20593-0001
(800) 368-5647
www.uscgboating.org
uscginfoline@gcrm.com

U.S. Consumer Product Safety Commission
National Injury Information Clearinghouse
Washington, DC 20207-0001
(301) 504-7921
www.cpsc.gov
clearinghouse@cpsc.gov

World Health Organization
20, avenue Appia
CH-1211 Geneva 27
Switzerland
Phone: +41-22-791-2111
Fax: +41-22-791-3111
www.who.int
info@who.int

Accident is that occurrence in a sequence of events that produces unintended injury, death, or property damage. *Accident* refers to the event, not the result of the event (see *Unintentional injury*).

Death from accident is a death that occurs within one year of the accident.

Disabling injury is an injury causing death, permanent disability, or any degree of temporary total disability beyond the day of the injury.

Fatal accident is an accident that results in one or more deaths within one year.

Home is a dwelling and its premises within the property lines including single-family dwellings and apartment houses, duplex dwellings, boarding and rooming houses, and seasonal cottages. Excluded from *home* are barracks, dormitories, and resident institutions.

Incidence rate, as defined by OSHA, is the number of occupational injuries and/or illnesses or lost workdays per 100 full-time employees (see formula on page 61).

Injury is physical harm or damage to the body resulting from an exchange, usually acute, of mechanical, chemical, thermal, or other environmental energy that exceeds the body's tolerance.

Motor vehicle is any mechanically or electrically powered device not operated on rails, upon which or by which any person or property may be transported upon a land highway. The load on a motor vehicle or trailer attached to it is considered part of the vehicle. Tractors and motorized machinery are included while self-propelled in transit or used for transportation. *Nonmotor vehicle* is any road vehicle other than a motor vehicle, such as a bicycle or animal-drawn vehicle, except a coaster wagon, child's sled, child's tricycle, child's carriage, and similar means of transportation; persons using these latter means of transportation are considered pedestrians.

Motor-vehicle accident is an unstabilized situation that includes at least one harmful event (injury or property damage) involving a motor vehicle in transport (in motion, in readiness for motion, or on a roadway but not parked in a designated parking area) that does not result from discharge of a firearm or explosive device and does not directly result from a cataclysm. [See Committee on Motor Vehicle Traffic Accident Classification (1997), *Manual on Classification of Motor Vehicle Traffic Accidents*, ANSI D16.1-1996, Itasca, IL: National Safety Council.]

Motor-vehicle traffic accident is a motor-vehicle accident that occurs on a trafficway — a way or place, any part of which is open to the use of the public for the purposes of vehicular traffic. *Motor-vehicle nontraffic accident* is any motor-vehicle accident that occurs entirely in any place other than a trafficway.

Nonfatal injury accident is an accident in which at least one person is injured and no injury results in death.

Occupational illness is any abnormal condition or disorder other than one resulting from an occupational injury caused by exposure to environmental factors associated with employment. It includes acute and chronic illnesses or diseases that may be caused by inhalation, absorption, ingestion, or direct contact (see also page 61).

Occupational injury is any injury such as a cut, fracture, sprain, amputation, etc., which results from a work accident or from a single instantaneous exposure in the work environment (see also page 61).

Pedalcycle is a vehicle propelled by human power and operated solely by pedals; excludes mopeds.

Pedestrian is any person involved in a motor-vehicle accident who is not in or upon a motor vehicle or nonmotor vehicle. Includes persons injured while using a coaster wagon, child's tricycle, roller skates, etc. Excludes persons boarding, alighting, jumping, or falling from a motor vehicle in transport who are considered occupants of the vehicle.

Permanent disability (or permanent impairment) includes any degree of permanent nonfatal injury. It includes any injury that results in the loss or complete loss of use of any part of the body or in any permanent impairment of functions of the body or a part thereof.

Property damage accident is an accident that results in property damage but in which no person is injured.

Public accident is any accident other than motor-vehicle that occurs in the public use of any premises. Includes deaths in recreation (swimming, hunting, etc.), in transportation except motor-vehicle, public buildings, etc., and from widespread natural disasters even though some may have happened on home premises. Excludes accidents to persons in the course of gainful employment.

Source of injury is the principal object such as tool, machine, or equipment involved in the accident and is usually the object inflicting injury or property damage. Also called *agency* or *agent.*

Temporary total disability is an injury that does not result in death or permanent disability but that renders the injured person unable to perform regular duties or activities on one or more full calendar days after the day of the injury.

Total cases include all work-related deaths and illnesses and those work-related injuries that result in loss of consciousness, restriction of work or motion, or transfer to another job, or require medical treatment other than first aid.

Unintentional injury is the preferred term for accidental injury in the public health community. It refers to the *result* of an accident.

Work hours are the total number of hours worked by all employees. They are usually compiled for various levels, such as an establishment, a company, or an industry. A work hour is the equivalent of one employee working one hour.

Work injuries (including occupational illnesses) are those that arise out of and in the course of gainful employment regardless of where the accident or exposure occurs. Excluded are work injuries to private household workers and injuries occurring in connection with farm chores that are classified as home injuries.

Workers are all persons gainfully employed, including owners, managers, other paid employees, the self-employed, and unpaid family workers but excluding private household workers.

Work/Motor-vehicle duplication includes *work injuries* that occur in *motor-vehicle accidents* (see *Work injuries* and *Motor-vehicle accident*).

INDEX (CONT.)